Economics in a
Business Context

THOMAS ROTHERHAM
COLLEGE
LIBRARY

Business in Context Series

Editors

David Needle
Head of Undergraduate Studies
East London Business School
University of East London

Professor Eugene McKenna
Chartered Psychologist and
Emeritus Professor
University of East London

Accounting in a Business Context (2nd Edition)
Aidan Berry and Robin Jarvis
ISBN 0 412 58740 8, 400 pages

Behaviour in a Business Context
Richard Turton
ISBN 0 412 37530 3, 400 pages

Business in Context (2nd Edition)
David Needle
ISBN 0 412 4840 2, 352 pages

Economics in a Business Context (2nd Edition)
Alan Neale and Colin Haslam
ISBN 0 412 58760 2, 336 pages

Law in a Business Context
Bill Cole, Peter Shears and Jillinda Tiley
ISBN 0 412 37520 6, 256 pages

Quantitative Techniques in a Business Context
Roger Slater and Peter Ascroft
ISBN 0 412 37570 2, 416 pages

Economics in a Business Context

Second edition

Alan Neale and Colin Haslam
University of East London
Business School
Dagenham
Essex, UK

INTERNATIONAL THOMSON BUSINESS PRESS
I T P An International Thomson Publishing Company

London • Bonn • Boston • Johannesburg • Madrid • Melbourne • Mexico City • New York • Paris
Singapore • Tokyo • Toronto • Albany, NY • Belmont, CA • Cincinnati, OH • Detroit, MI

Economics in a Business Context

First published by Chapman and Hall, 2-6 Boundary Row, London SE1 8HN

 I(**T**)**P** A division of International Thomson Publishing Inc.
The ITP logo is a trademark under licence

British Library Cataloguing-in-Publication Data
A catalogue record for this book is available from the British Library

First edition 1989
Reprinted 1989,1991, 1992
Second edition 1994

Reprinted 1996 by International Thomson Publishing Ltd.

Typeset by Best-set Typesetter Ltd., Hong Kong
Printed in China

ISBN 0-412-58760-2

International Thomson Business Press
Berkshire House
168–173 High Holborn
London WC1V 7AA
UK

International Thomson Business Press
20 Park Plaza
13th Floor
Boston MA 02116
USA

http://www.thomson.com/itbp.html

Contents

Case studies   ix
Series foreword   xi
Preface to the first edition   xv
Preface to the second edition   xix
Acknowledgements   xxi

1   Markets, marketing and cost recovery   1
    Introduction   1
    Consumer demand   2
    Pricing for profit maximization   5
    Product market development   13
    Market composition   19
    Options for increasing sales   23
    Conclusion   33
    Further reading   33
    Exercises   34
    References   35

2   The organization of production for cost reduction and cost
    recovery   36
    Introduction   36
    Traditional economic theory of production and costs 36
    New technology and capital investment   43
    Economies of scale   44
    Productive reorganization for cost reduction and cost
    recovery   52
    The importance of labour costs   62
    Conclusion   65
    Further reading   65
    Exercises   66
    References   66

3   Financial calculations and business enterprise   67
    Introduction   67

The separation of ownership and control   67
Accounting calculations and decision-making   72
The accounting calculation of cost and price   81
The relationship between costs, volume and profit   84
Capital investment decision-making   88
Strategic and operational financial calculation   99
Conclusion   101
Further reading   102
Exercises   102
References   104

4 **Performance evaluation**   105
Introduction   105
Evaluating market performance   106
Evaluating productive performance   111
Evaluating financial performance   115
Shareholder calculations   121
Conclusion   123
Further reading   123
Exercises   124
References   127

5 **Management practice and the limits of management** 128
Introduction   128
What do managers do?   129
Structure before strategy?   134
The Americanization of management   137
From Americanization to Japanization   140
The limits to management   145
Conclusion   147
Further reading   148
Exercises   149
References   149

6 **The labour market environment**   151
Introduction   151
Employment   152
Labour costs   157
Skills   164
Industrial relations   169
Labour market flexibility v. Social Europe   171
Conclusion   174
Further reading   174
Exercises   175
References   175

7 **The financial environment**   177
Introduction   177
The organization of business finance   178
Bank lending   182

	Capital market finance	190
	State finance	199
	Finance for small businesses	200
	Conclusion	200
	Further reading	201
	Exercises	201
	References	202

8 The international environment   204

	Introduction	204
	International trade	205
	Exchange rates	210
	Balance of payments accounts	214
	UK trade performance	216
	International capital movements	220
	International capital flows and the UK balance of payments	225
	European Union	227
	Conclusion	228
	Further reading	228
	Exercises	228
	References	229

9 The natural environment   230

	Introduction	230
	The neo-classical approach to the natural environment	231
	Steady state economics	235
	Types of environmental control	238
	Environmental auditing	245
	Project appraisal	245
	Business responses	249
	Conclusion	252
	Further reading	253
	Exercises	253
	References	254

10 Government economic policies   255

	Introduction	255
	Keynesian theory	256
	Demand management policies	264
	The balance of payments constraint and inflation	266
	Monetarist theory	268
	Monetarist policies	271
	The limitations of macro-economic policy	276
	Industrial policies in the UK	278
	Industrial policies in other countries	283
	Conclusion	285
	Further reading	285
	Exercises	286
	References	287

Statistical appendix   289

Index   307

Case studies

Sinclair computers	4
Tesco	18
Fragmentation in the UK small car market segment	20
Toyota and the exchange rate	31
Hanson Trust – growth through acquisition	32
Economies of scale and the case of British Steel	48
Ford at Highland Park 1909–16	56
Labour costs in motor vehicle manufacturing	64
Budgets and cost control at ABZ	75
Nissan Motor Corporation: divisional income statement	78
Ford UK	87
Net present value and the case of British Steel	94
Eurotunnel – the financial projection	100
Ford's methods – an illustration of factory management	131
Divisionalization at General Motors	135
Whatever happened to IBM?	141
The Japanese car industry – lean producers?	143
Differences in car assembler productivity – a case of now you see it, now you don't	146
A national minimum wage	161
Labour productivity in metal working	167
Working for Toyota	170
Hoover	173
GEC and British Leyland	197
ICI and Hanson	199
UK trade in motor vehicles	217
Integrated circuits	224
Global warming	235
Car exhaust emission control	240
Control of carbon dioxide emissions	242
The energy efficiency of domestic electrical appliances	243
Costing nuclear power	247
3M	250
The housing market and the UK macro-economy	259

Series foreword

This book is part of the 'Business in Context' series. The books in this series are written by lecturers, all with several years' experience of teaching on undergraduate business studies programmes. When the series first appeared in 1989, the original rationale was to place the various disciplines found in the business studies curriculum firmly in a business context. This is still our aim. Business studies attracted a growing band of students throughout the 1980s, a popularity that has been maintained in the 1990s. If anything, that appeal has broadened, and business studies, as well as being a specialism in its own right, is now taken with a range of other subjects, particularly as universities move towards modular degree structures. We feel that the books in this series provide an important focus for the student seeking some meaning in the range of subjects currently offered under the umbrella of business studies.

With the exception of the text, *Business in Context*, which takes the series title as its theme, all the original texts in our series took the approach of a particular discipline traditionally associated with business studies and taught widely on business studies and related programmes. These first books in our series examined business from the perspectives of economics, behavioural science, law, mathematics and accounting. The popularity of the series across a range of courses has meant that the second editions of many of the original texts are about to be published and there are plans to extend the series by examining information technology, operations management, human resource management and marketing.

Whereas in traditional texts it is the subject itself that is the focus, our texts make business the focus. All the texts are based upon the same specific model of business illustrated below. We have called our model 'Business in Context', and the text of the same name is an expansion and explanation of that model.

The model comprises four distinct levels. At the core are found the activities which make up what we know as business, including innovation, operations and production, purchasing, marketing, personnel and finance and accounting. We see these activities operating

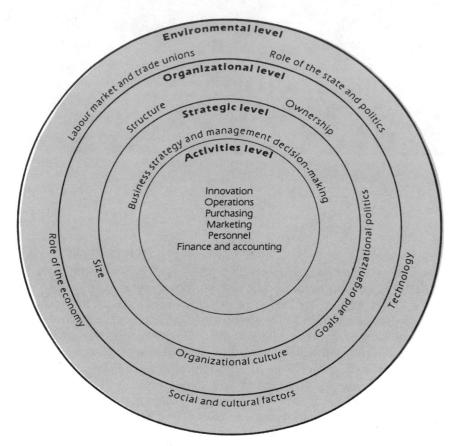

Figure 0.1 Business in context model.

irrespective of the type of business involved; they are found in both the manufacturing and service industry, as well as in the public and private sectors. The second level of our model is concerned with strategy and management decision-making. It is here that decisions are made which influence the direction of the business activities at our core. The third level of our model is concerned with organizational factors within which business activities and management decisions take place. The organizational issues we examine are structure, size, goals and organizational politics, patterns of ownership, and organizational culture. Clear links can be forged between this and other levels of our model, especially between structure and strategy, goals and management decision-making, and how all aspects both contribute to and are influenced by the organizational culture. The fourth level concerns itself with the environment in which businesses operate. The issues here involve social and cultural factors, the role of the state and politics, the role of the economy, and issues relating to both technology and labour. An important feature of this fourth level of our model is that such elements not only operate as opportunities and constraints for business, but also that they are shaped by the three other levels of our model.

This brief description of the 'Business in Context' model illustrates the key features of our series. We see business as dynamic. It is constantly being shaped by and in turn is shaping those managerial, organizational, and environmental contexts within which it operates. Influences go backwards and forwards across the various levels. Moreover, the aspects identified within each level are in constant interaction with one another. Thus the role of the economy cannot be understood without reference to the role of the state; size and structure are inextricably linked; innovation is inseparable from issues of operations, marketing and finance. Understanding how this model works is what business studies is all about, and forms the basis for our series.

In proposing this model we are proposing a framework for analysis and we hope that it will encourage readers to add to and refine the model, and so broaden our understanding of business. Each writer in this series has been encouraged to present a personal interpretation of the model. In this way we hope to build up a more complete picture of business.

Our series therefore aims for a more integrated and realistic approach to business than has hitherto been the case. The issues are complex, but the authors' treatment of them is not. Each book in this series is built around the 'Business in Context' model, and each displays a number of common features that mark out this series. Firstly, we aim to present our ideas in a way that students will find easy to understand and we relate those ideas wherever possible to real business situations. Secondly, we hope to stimulate further study, both by referencing our material and by pointing students towards further reading at the end of each chapter. Thirdly, we use the notion of 'key concepts' to highlight the most significant aspects of the subject presented in each chapter. Fourthly, we use case studies to illustrate our material and stimulate further discussion. Fifthly, we present at the end of each chapter a series of questions, exercises, and discussion topics. To sum up, we feel it most important that each book will stimulate thought and further study and assist the student in developing powers of analysis, a critical awareness, and ultimately a point of view about business issues.

We have already indicated that the series has been devised with the undergraduate business studies student uppermost in our minds. We also maintain that these books are of value wherever there is a need to understand business issues and may therefore be used across a range of different courses including some BTEC Higher programmes and some postgraduate and professional courses.

David Needle and Eugene McKenna

Preface to the first edition

Students and managers of business enterprise who have encountered traditional economics courses often find it difficult to relate and apply what they have learnt to the realities of modern business. This is not surprising, since the traditional approach to economics (sometimes called neo-classical) makes a number of simplifying assumptions which limit its usefulness as a tool for business calculation and strategy. In this book we develop an alternative approach, in which relevant and available information and knowledge are applied to real problems associated with the allocation of resources and management of these resources.

The neo-classical approach takes as its basic framework the phenomenon of market exchange, under conditions of perfect knowledge and information. It focusses attention on market prices as instruments which determine the resources needed to satisfy demand at a given price. Within this framework, it is assumed that:

- market forces bring about an equilibrium where prices equate quantity demanded with quantity supplied; and
- firms respond immediately to changes in equilibrium price by continually re-allocating, in an optimal sense, the resources at their command, in the single-minded pursuit of maximum profitability.

The comments of Fritz Machlup, a leading neo-classical economist, reveal the abstract nature of the approach. Writing in the *American Economic Review* (March, 1967) he said that the model of the firm

> is not . . . designed to serve to explain and predict the behaviour of real firms: instead, it is designed to explain and predict changes in observed prices . . . as effects of particular changes in conditions . . . In this causal connection the firm is only a theoretical link, a mental construct helping to explain how one gets from the cause to the effect.

While market exchange is an important feature of modern industrial life it is not the only one. Modern large firms dominate output and employment in the UK economy. These organizations are bureaucratic, and resources are allocated within them not by market exchange but by administrative procedure. For example, where a firm sub-contracts certain activities such as the supply of components to other firms, the price and product characteristics of these components will be the subject of negotiation, and are only indirectly influenced by market forces. Even final consumer demand is not straightforwardly determined by price alone, but by other so-called non-price factors such as quality, delivery, reliability and after-sales service etc.

The neo-classical framework for understanding firms' economic behaviour could be useful where we could also invoke, in practice, the very strict assumptions governing the model of perfect competition. However where production is dominated by large firms, and products are differentiated across and within market segments, neo-classical theory is less than illuminating. To understand how enterprise resources are allocated in a way which leads to some form of market advantage we need to ask a number of simple questions, to which the answers are often complex.

- How are resources allocated within firms?
- To what extent does the allocation of resources effectively meet the requirements of the market and meet with the firms' initial objectives?
- How are relationships between the firm and its suppliers and distributors structured?
- Why do some firms succeed and others fail, and what lessons can be drawn from this process of comparison?

In this text we will refer to the traditional neo-classical approach, identifying its uses and its limitations as an explanatory tool for business and resource management, although market exchange will not be our central focus. We shall, in contrast, be much more concerned about the calculations that business enterprises make with regard to market opportunities/threats, productive organization of labour and capital, and the financial outcome of the relation that exists between the market and productive performance of the organization. Our approach is an economic one, in that it does focus on how resources are allocated and managed both on a day-to-day and strategic basis. However, maximum efficiency in the management of resources is perhaps an impossible dream. In fact such an outcome could only be achieved under conditions of perfect knowledge, to which any approximation would require the application of massive resources dedicated both to gathering information and organizing the enterprise.

Our work in this text is an attempt to explore the nature of problems faced by the firm across the productive, market and financial boundaries of business organization. The operational and strategic relations we are considering cannot be represented in a unitary or stable way, because they are subject to constant change and controversy. The fact that we have suggested a model of business strategy does not mean that relations between different objectives will remain fixed over the planning time horizon. New objectives will need to be formed as and when new external or internal business conditions arise. Enterprise calculations must be set in a dynamic framework when the relations between different forms of enterprise calculation are rarely supportive and often contradictory.

We have been guided in our approach by the general model of the Business in Context series, of which this book is but one. However, we have adapted this to our own specific needs within the text. Our focus is on the nature and conditions under which enterprise, operational and strategic decisions are made. We consider the forms of calculation made by firms under three headings – the productive, market and financial. We are, however, not just concerned with these enterprise calculations in isolation, but with how they interact to produce either harmonious or contradictory relations. As a result the enterprise needs to pay attention to the changing nature and structure of the market, assessing how best to use available or potential labour and capital resources to meet market requirements, and considering the financial resource implications and possible financial outcomes of the firm's decisions.

In the first four chapters of this text we take a look at the economic calculations made within functional boundaries of the firm – marketing, production, personnel and finance. However, in each chapter we also illustrate, with the use of relevant case study material, how particular enterprise calculations can be privileged possibly at the expense of others. We use this material to encourage the student to consider positively the interrelationship between such things as for example, a decision to invest in new technology which requires either the re-training of labour so that it can be properly utilized, or its introduction in a balanced way into the production process so that it does not compromise the level of production and market share of the firm.

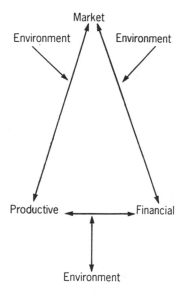

Figure 0.2 The decision-making context of the firm.

Finally we recognize that we cannot isolate the enterprise from an environmental context in which various institutional actors play a vital role in shaping and changing the environment for business. Even where the firm has successfully achieved a relation of balance between the productive, market and financial aspects of resource management, the firm's decisions will be affected by the constraints which are set by the banks, the stock exchange, the government etc. The conditioning role of these institutions in relation to enterprise performance is explored in the latter chapters of this text.

We have included at the end of each chapter a number of exercises. Some of these exercises take the form of data collection and analysis. This is to encourage you to develop those particular skills, and to find out for yourselves how the competitive environment of business is changing. We also make more frequent reference to recent research than is usual in introductory textbooks. This is not to convey a spurious academic 'respectability' for our approach, but to encourage you to check out the sources for yourselves, and to arrive at your own judgements.

Firms in the UK have not been doing particularly well in recent years, and they face the prospect of an increasingly competitive environment in the 1990s. We hope that students will be able to use this text and its case study material to obtain a positive insight into the problems of managing resources around the objective of securing competitive advantage in a changing environment.

PEL, Dagenham, November 1988

Preface to the second edition

Readers who are familiar with the first edition of this text will notice a few similarities, but many differences. Two of the chapters in this edition – those on performance evaluation and on management practice – are new, while the remaining eight chapters have been extensively rewritten and updated. A few of the original case studies have survived with only minor modification, but most are completely fresh (even though, to develop a historical perspective, some of these relate to an earlier epoch).

We make no apology for the fact that so much has changed since the first edition. In the first place, we have taken the opportunity to improve the presentation, structuring the material in such a way as to give more encouragement to readers to develop their own analytical skills. Secondly, we have altered the content to reflect some of the major changes which have taken place in the world economy over the past five years. Thirdly, and most importantly, our own understanding of business problems has developed over this same period, as our research programme has extended to address issues such as market maturity, cost recovery, lean production, Japanese management accounting, financial engineering, Japanese foreign direct investment, hollowing out, labour costs, minimum wages, and energy efficiency.

Traditional economics texts, with their abstract models of business, present an essentially static discourse, and their authors can get away with repeating the same material about supply and demand, or competition and monopoly, in successive editions. Our aim, in contrast, has been to analyse the real-life problems facing actual businesses, and to evaluate the effectiveness and limitations of different management attempts to solve them. Our positions must, necessarily, develop over time, so that each edition of the text can only be a snapshot representation of one stage in an ongoing process of change.

We are mindful of the fact that, by the time many of the students who read this edition embark on their careers, both the business world and our understanding of it will have changed significantly. We see little point in presenting them with 'eternal verities' which will bear little relationship to their work experience. Instead, our hope is that they will be encouraged by the method of enquiry proposed here to use that experience as a basis for *developing* their understanding. The learning curve does not end here!

UEL, Dagenham, January 1994

Acknowledgements

We would like to thank Angela, Rosemary and Paul for their support over the past year. Without this, the book could not have been written. In addition, we would like to acknowledge the roles of Karel Williams, reader at Manchester University, and Professor John Williams, of Aberystwyth University, in developing some of the ideas in this text, and the contributions of our colleagues at the University of East London, Andy Adcroft and Sukhdev Johal, to the new work presented in this second edition.

Markets, marketing and cost recovery

1

In this chapter we explore various characteristics of the markets in which firms sell products, and how these develop over time. The main focus is on firms' need to recover the costs they have incurred in developing and supplying their products, and on the difficulties in achieving this under conditions of market maturity. A number of alternative cost recovery strategies are discussed.

Introduction

Marketing specialists emphasize the need for organizations to develop a 'marketing mix' for their products or services which is consistent with the requirements of their customers. In this chapter, we explore the relationship between the most important elements of that mix – price, product, and promotion – within different organisational and environmental contexts. From the point of view of the firm, however, a more fundamental issue is not so much the extent of satisfaction of consumer demand, but whether or not the firm's costs of production can be recovered from market sales of its products or services.

We start this chapter with a consideration of the traditional neo-classical theory of the firm, which focusses on price as the most significant variable affecting the behaviour of consumers and producers. We suggest that this understanding of competitive markets has limited applicability, as it is based on unrealistic assumptions about the nature of consumer and firm behaviour in the modern industrial world. The chapter goes on to argue that the fundamental objective of any business is to secure a recovery of costs incurred within the business by maintaining sales volume outside of the firm.

Attention is concentrated, therefore, on different types of market conditions, and how these facilitate or limit the possibilities for management of achieving cost recovery.

Consumer demand

The neo-classical analysis of demand for a product divides the influences on quantity demanded (sales) into two categories.

- The product's own price.
- The conditions of demand (a catch-all concept which includes all the influences on demand other than the product's own price – e.g. income, taste, advertising, the prices of substitute or complementary products).

If the conditions of demand remain constant, there will usually be an inverse relationship between a product's own price and sales. This reflects its price elasticity of demand (Key Concept 1.1). One of the main uses of the elasticity concept is to estimate the effect of price changes on revenues. If demand is elastic (i.e. the price elasticity of demand is greater than 1), a rise in price will lead to a fall in total revenue, while a fall in price will lead to a rise in total revenue. If demand is inelastic (i.e. the price elasticity of demand is less than 1), the opposite will be the case. Only if the price elasticity of demand is exactly equal to 1 will a price change have no effect on total revenue.

KEY CONCEPT 1.1
Elasticity

The term elasticity is used in economics to describe the relationship between a proportionate change in one variable and a proportionate change in a related variable.

The term price elasticity of demand describes the sensitivity of quantity demanded to changes in the product's own price, according to the formula

$$\frac{\text{percentage change in quantity demanded}}{\text{percentage change in price}}$$

Thus, if a 10% drop in price leads to a 20% increase in quantity demanded, assuming the conditions of demand remain constant, then the price elasticity of demand is two. (Strictly, it is minus two, but it has become conventional for economists to ignore the negative sign of price elasticity.)

Other elasticity concepts that are often referred to include the following.

1 Income elasticity of demand, with the formula

$$\frac{\text{percentage change in quantity demanded}}{\text{percentage change in income}}$$

2 Elasticity of supply, with the formula

$$\frac{\text{percentage change in quantity supplied}}{\text{percentage change in price}}$$

3 Cross elasticity of demand (between two different products) with the formula

$$\frac{\text{percentage change in quantity demanded of one product}}{\text{percentage change in price of another product.}}$$

Much empirical work has been done in quantifying the price elasticities of demand of different products, particularly in the agricultural sector. In measuring demand relationships it is important to separate out the influence of a change in price from a change in the conditions of demand, or from a change in supply. This involves the use of sophisticated statistical techniques, and is much easier to do with homogeneous products like potatoes than with differentiated products like cars, where it is hard to separate out the effects of price changes from those of product changes. In particular, we have in mind all the non-price characteristics of a product (design, quality, reliability, etc.) which affect the purchaser's decision to consume a particular product. These factors have made it difficult for firms to use traditional concepts of demand elasticity as a guide for price and output decisions.

The model of consumer behaviour on which neo-classical demand theory is based implies that consumers are perfectly informed about the price and quality characteristics of the products on offer, and are constantly altering their expenditure patterns in response to price changes, so as to maximize their total 'utility' (satisfaction). This model is unrealistic, as the range of products on offer in modern markets is immense, and no consumer has the knowledge or inclination to acquire the information which would be needed to make choices in this way. In addition, the model is misleading, as it encourages firms to focus on price as the most important variable influencing demand, instead of factors such as quality, design, reliability, delivery, and after-sales service, which, as we have said, may be more significant in practice.

More sophisticated economic analysis of consumer demand, based on the work of the behavioural economist Peter Earl (1983, 1986), suggests that the choices made by consumers take a different form from that suggested by neo-classical theory. In particular:

- Consumers have priority rankings of wants, some of which need to be satisfied before others can be explored. It follows that the main determinant of long-term changes in the structure of demand is not the pattern of relative prices, but the level of incomes.
- As their incomes rise, consumers are able to purchase new types of products, of which they have no personal experience. To make their choice more manageable, they will typically set a target price range, and confine their exploration to alternatives within that range.
- Within their chosen budget ranges, consumers will judge product alternatives across a range of characteristics. In purchasing an automatic washing machine, for example, a consumer might set a target price range of under £400, and want a fast spin speed, an economy programme facility, good reliability and after-sales service, and delivery within two weeks. If, say, there were three machines which shared these characteristics then the final choice might be made on the basis of what the machine looked like, or price (see Key Concept 1.2).

- When making the transition from one stage of their life cycle to another, or one income bracket to another, consumers often have to make choices for which they have no direct personal experience, yet which they want to be appropriate to their new lifestyle. Here choices will often be guided more by the choices of others than anything else, and products will be chosen to complement each other.

KEY CONCEPT 1.2 *Characteristic filtering*	Modern consumer durables incorporate bundles of different characteristics, which different consumers will evaluate differently. Some car purchasers, for example, will value performance and style higher than reliability and safety, while others will be more concerned about fuel economy and resistance to rust. Characteristic filtering models suggest that, for most consumers, excellent performance in one characteristic does not compensate for poor performance in another. Rather, potential consumers will want to perceive minimum standards being satisfied, in relation to a number of characteristics that are important to them, before they will consider a purchase.

The marketing implications of Earl's approach are clear. Firms would be better advised to research consumer perceptions than to attempt detailed estimation of price/quantity relationships. In particular, they need to discover consumers' target price ranges, and their preferred product characteristics, developing products and promotion strategies in line with their findings. Price-cutting may be useful in re-defining products to appeal to groups who would otherwise have rejected them as too expensive, but in most instances it would be better to price products near the top of the relevant price range, and build in extra features as standard to boost the potential number of consumers they appeal to. Good all-round performance will usually produce more sales than excellent performance in one attribute with poor performance in others, as Sinclair discovered to its cost in the low cost business computer market (Case Study 1.1).

CASE STUDY 1.1 *Sinclair computers*	The Sinclair ZX 80 was the product which in 1980 launched the UK home computer market. By using only the cheapest components, and providing only limited memory, Sinclair was able to sell the ZX 80 by mail order for less than £100, drastically undercutting the existing competition. Over the next three years Sinclair introduced two new models (the ZX 81 and the Spectrum), set up retail sales through High Street outlets like W.H. Smith, and cut prices still further (in 1983, the ZX 81 was selling for less than £40). The Spectrum's colour graphics spawned a range of software based on simulations of arcade games, ensuring a buoyant market among male teenagers (and their parents, convinced that acquisition of a home computer would help their child's education). By 1983, Sinclair were selling 500 000 home computers per year in the UK, a market share of over 50%. Design limitations and poor reliability made the ZX range and the Spectrum unsuitable for serious computer applications, however, and in 1984 Sinclair introduced a new product, the QL, which they hoped would move them up market into the field of business applications. The QL, like earlier Sinclair computers, was designed to a price target, and it sold for

less than £400 (including business software). It incorporated a number of design innovations, including a Microdrive system which attempted to combine the rapid data storage and retrieval of a disc drive with the low cost of cassette storage. The new Microdrives created as many problems as they solved, however, and Sinclair's decision to stick with a keyboard design based on a touch-sensitive membrane made it totally unsuitable for sustained use as a word processor.

If the design of the QL was a disappointment, its marketing was a disaster. The QL was 'launched' before there was even a working prototype, and mail order adverts got customers to part with their money months before supplies were forthcoming. Whether the premature launch was an attempt to upstage the arrival of the Apple Macintosh, or to boost cash flow in advance of a possible share flotation, is a matter of speculation. What is certain is that customer confidence in Sinclair products evaporated, and the QL flopped. Within 18 months of the launch, Sinclair had to halve the price of the QL, while Amstrad successfully opened up the bottom end of the business/professional market with the PCW8256, a reliable product based on tried-and-tested technology which included a monitor and printer in its low price of £399 plus VAT.

In 1985 and 1986, Sinclair's financial position was precarious. Its misguided attempt to break into the business computer market, and the competitive threat from Amstrad, coincided with its founder's failure to interest the public in purchasing electric tricycles (the C5). Salvation eventually came in the form of a deal with arch rivals Amstrad, who agreed to purchase all rights to Sinclair computer products, leaving Sir Clive Sinclair himself free to pursue new developments without the stigma of liquidation.

Further reading
Adamson and Kennedy (1986).

Firms can influence consumer perceptions of their products, and thus demand, through their advertising, though this will be less relevant for firms whose products are already highly valued (Marks and Spencer, or the Body Shop, for example), or for firms whose customers are highly knowledgeable (capital equipment producers, for example), than for other firms. For adverts to be effective, however, they must be designed with a clear understanding of what existing perceptions are. It is no use, for example, emphasizing the maximum speed of a family car if its potential consumers are more interested in fuel economy and reliability. Where consumers feel anxious that an inappropriate purchase may undermine their self-image, adverts can be designed to allay that anxiety. Amstrad, for example, has successfully stressed the advantages of its hi-fi, home computer, and TV/video systems for consumers who do not know how to make up their own systems from separate components. As Earl concludes (1983), 'If firms cannot succeed in moulding consumer thoughts to favour their products, they must discover the structures of the moulds that they should make their products fit.'

Pricing for profit maximization

In the traditional, neo-classical theory of the firm, all firms, irrespective of the different ways they are organized and the different environments in which they operate, are assumed to have a single aim – to maximize their profits in the short run. They do this in two ways.

- Expanding their output up to the point where marginal cost is equal to marginal revenue (see Key Concepts 1.3 and 1.4)
- Setting as high a price as the market will bear.

KEY CONCEPT 1.3
Average and marginal revenue

The total revenue received for a product in a given time period is its price, or average revenue, multiplied by the number of units sold, while marginal revenue is the contribution to total revenue which is made by the last unit sold. If a firm can increase sales of a product without changing its price, then average revenue and marginal revenue will be the same. If it can only increase its sales by dropping its price, however, then marginal revenue will be below average revenue, as the additional revenue earned from the last unit has to be weighed against the revenue which is lost by having to sell the existing output at a lower price. This is illustrated in the hypothetical example below.

Annual sales	Average revenue (price per unit, £)	Total revenue (per year, £)	Marginal revenue* (£)
			52
2 000	52	104 000	
			44
4 000	48	192 000	
			36
6 000	44	264 000	
			28
8 000	40	320 000	
			20
10 000	36	360 000	
			12
12 000	32	384 000	

*Where demand estimates are available for only a limited number of possible prices, as in the above example, marginal revenue is calculated by dividing the increase in total revenue by the increase in sales, and plotting the result midway along the output range, as in the diagram.

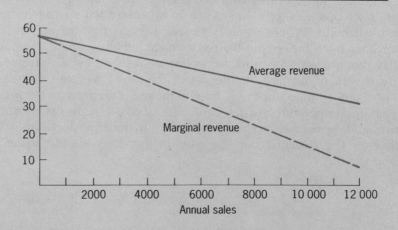

In the short run, some costs are fixed, and some are variable (we leave discussion of the long run, when all costs are variable, to Chapter 2). Average fixed costs (AFC) fall as output is increased. Average variable costs (AVC) often remain constant over a substantial range of output. They may, however, rise when output falls below a critical level, if, for example, labour can no longer be organized as effectively. Average variable costs will certainly rise as output reaches the limits determined by the full capacity of the fixed factors. Average total costs (ATC, equal to AFC plus AVC) therefore fall, and then rise as output is increased.

Marginal cost (MC) is the increase in total cost (TC) when output is increased by one unit. Marginal cost will be equal to average variable cost where this is constant. Where average variable cost is falling, however, marginal cost will be below it, while where average variable cost is rising, marginal cost will be above it. Marginal cost is equal to average total cost where average total cost is at a minimum.

This is illustrated in a hypothetical example below, where a plant has a design capacity of 10 000 units per year, where fixed costs are £100 000 per year, and where normal variable costs are £20 per unit.

Annual output	AFC(£)	AVC(£)	ATC(£)	TC(£)	MC(£)
					75
2 000	50	25	75	150 000	
					19
4 000	25	22	47	188 000	
					16
6 000	16.67	20	36.67	220 000	
					20
8 000	12.50	20	32.50	260 000	
					20
10 000	10	20	30	300 000	
					50
12 000	8.33	25	33.33	400 000	

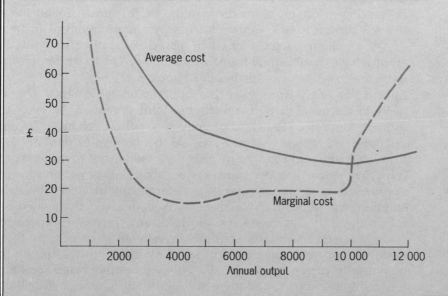

In the long run, as demand and cost conditions change, firms will move out of markets in which they can no longer operate profitably, and into those markets where the prospects of profits seem greatest. In markets where large numbers of firms compete with each other, the long-run tendency is for prices to equal average costs (including within those costs 'normal profit', that element of accounting profit which is necessary for the firm to remain in business). In markets where competition is less intense, long-run prices will be higher than average costs, and firms will be able to make 'monopoly profits'.

The formal neo-classical analysis of profit maximization is complex. It abstracts from all differences in the organizational context of business, and focusses exclusively on a single aspect of the environmental context, the extent of competition. As a result, its predictions are at a high level of generality, and theoretical elegance is achieved at the expense of a low level of realism. Three of its assumptions are particularly questionable.

- Objectives. The suggestion that all private sector firms aim to maximize short-run profits is an oversimplification. Short-run profit is certainly an important objective, but it is not the only one. Business firms, like any organizations, are complex, and different groups within them have different interests. Key decisions in large corporations, for example, are taken by professional managers. These are not traditional entrepreneurs, but salaried employees who may be more interested in the growth of their firms (and their prestige) than in short-run profits. Even in small firms, objectives such as providing jobs for family members may be more important than making the maximum possible profit. In addition, most firms, whatever their size, give priority to their long-term survival. This may encourage the firm to initiate investments which have a depressing effect on short-run profits, or to remain in business despite current losses. Certainly, firms are more involved in processes of change over time than neo-classical theory, with its emphasis on static equilibrium, would allow. This is an important issue which we explore further in Chapter 3.
- Information. Few firms have the information which they would need to calculate their marginal costs and revenues, or even to estimate the price elasticities of demand for their products. It can, of course, be argued that neo-classical theory aims to predict how firms will adjust to changes in costs or demand, not to understand how they reach their decisions. As we shall see, however, lack of appropriate information makes a determinate profit-maximizing solution impossible in oligopolistic markets (markets dominated by a few firms). It also makes it difficult for any firms in competition with each other to make 'sensible' investment decisions, as they each have to make independent decisions about future capacity in response to current price signals. Where investment decisions are taken simultaneously, and there is a significant time-lag before they bring about changes in output, capacity may be expanded too

much in response to an increase in demand, and contracted too much in response to a decrease in demand. It is not surprising, therefore, that unregulated 'perfect' markets, like many world commodity markets, are often characterized by wild swings in prices, rather than the smooth adjustment to equilibrium depicted in traditional textbooks.

- Uncertainty. The neo-classical world is a certain one, in which events never take firms by surprise. Managers have little to do except read correctly the price signals which their markets give them, and time is suspended while they respond to these signals and adjust to a new equilibrium position. In the real world, however, future demand and costs are surrounded with uncertainty and surprise, making optimum achievement of objectives impossible. Firms typically respond to this situation by making do with satisfactory rather than maximum achievement of objectives, or by suppressing competition to reduce the uncertainty (merging with a rival, for example). In addition, they may seek to incorporate flexibility into their planning. Flexibility costs money, and thus depresses short-run profits, but this may be a price worth paying if it enables a firm to respond quicker than its rivals to an unexpected change in market conditions.

Oligopoly

Profit maximization is particularly problematic in the context of oligopolistic market conditions. Under conditions of oligopoly, a few large firms dominate a market, and are able to make monopoly profits as they are protected by barriers to the entry of new firms. Oligopoly is the most common market structure in manufacturing, and is becoming increasingly prevalent in the service sector as well. Problems of information and uncertainty abound in this market structure, and it is extremely difficult for a firm to assess the effect on revenue of changing its price, as this depends on how its rivals will react. Because of this, it is impossible for an oligopolist to predict what its profit-maximizing price will be.

If, for example, a firm considers raising its prices, it does not know whether its rivals will keep their prices at the old level or raise theirs as well. If its rivals all raise their prices, each firm is likely to suffer only a small reduction in sales, and to raise its revenues (assuming the price elasticity of demand for the product is low). If only one firm raises its prices, however, it is likely to suffer a big drop in sales, and a fall in its revenue, as consumers switch to the close substitutes provided by its rivals.

When, on the other hand, a firm is considering cutting its prices, it does not know whether its rivals will drop their prices as well, or keep them at the old price. If its rivals remain at the old price, then the firm is likely to gain in sales, at its rivals' expense, and increase its revenues. Yet if all the firms drop their prices, their gain in sales is likely to be small, and revenues may fall. Even more seriously, the drop in prices

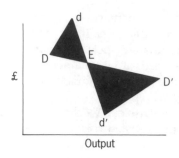

Figure 1.1 Equilibrium of an oligopolist.

may initiate a price cutting war, with potentially disastrous consequences for all firms in the industry.

The oligopolist's dilemma is illustrated in Figure 1.1. dEd' represents the imagined demand curve for a firm's products if all its rivals match any price changes it makes (the shape of this demand curve is the same as that of the industry demand curve), and DED' represents the demand curve for its products assuming its rivals' prices remain unchanged. E represents the existing price and output position of the firm, while the shaded area represents all the possible consequences for sales of a change in this price. As you can see, if a firm is uncertain about how its rivals are going to react to a change in price, it cannot predict the likely effect on sales, and therefore on revenue.

There are three broad possibilities for the price behaviour of an oligopolist within a neo-classical framework – collusion, price wars, or non-price competition.

- Collusion. It is possible for firms to agree to fix their prices and market shares. This has the effect of moving firms up the demand curve dEd', and enabling them to boost their profits by charging higher prices. Such price fixing agreements were common in British manufacturing industry before 1956, but since the Restrictive Practices Court was established in that year, only a few such agreements have been allowed. (This aspect of competition policy is discussed further in Chapter 10.) It is possible for similar results to occur if one or two firms in an oligopolistic market are accepted as price leaders, with other firms following their price changes. The suggestion in neo-classical theory is that price leaders will set prices so as to maximize the joint profits of the industry, as if it were a monopoly, but the danger here is that prices would be set too high, attracting new entrants.
- Price Wars. An oligopolistic firm will usually avoid straightforward price-cutting as a strategy to improve revenues, as it knows its rivals will respond by cutting their prices as well, hitting everyone's profits. It may, however, consider aggressive price cuts if it wants to expand its market share and it considers that a price war will drive one or more rivals out of business, or if it is suffering from

cash-flow problems and needs a short-term injection of funds to survive.

- Price rigidity. Ironically, one of the bravest attempts to resolve the oligopolist's dilemma from within a basically neo-classical framework came from a Marxist economist, Paul Sweezy (1939). Sweezy argued that an oligopolistic firm will normally have pessimistic assessments of how its rivals will react to a price change. In other words, it will predict that if it raises its prices, its rivals will maintain theirs, but that if it drops its prices, its rivals will also drop theirs. In Figure 1.1, DEd' would be the firm's imagined average revenue curve, with a pronounced kink at the existing price, which is indeterminate. If DE is price elastic, while Ed' is price inelastic, then the firm will lose revenue both if it raises its prices or if it drops them. The result, Sweezy suggests, is price rigidity, based on an extreme unwillingness to risk possible negative consequences for revenue of any change in price. Competition between oligopolies then becomes non-price competition, focussing on product changes and expenditure on sales promotion.

Consumer sovereignty

Oligopolistic market conditions also pose problems for the neo-classical assumption that consumers in a market economy are sovereign (see Key Concept 1.5). The most prominent critic of the marketing policies of large corporations is J.K. Galbraith, in his books *The Affluent Society* (1958), *The New Industrial State* (1967), and *Economics and the Public Purpose* (1973). Galbraith suggests that the corporate economy is a planned economy, able to justify huge expenditures on modern capital-intensive technology only through doing everything in its power to suppress the uncertainty of market competition, including creating and managing demand for its products. In his view, the 'accepted sequence', where consumers determine what is produced, has been replaced by a 'revised sequence', where producers determine what is consumed.

KEY CONCEPT 1.5
Consumer sovereignty

In a market economy, neo-classical economics suggests, consumers are sovereign. The implication is that the pursuit of profits by firms guarantees consumer satisfaction, and that consumer wants are ultimately the sole determinant of what firms produce. This can be seen most clearly in the analysis of perfect competition, where, it is assumed, knowledgeable consumers choose between the identical products of a large number of suppliers. Here, it is suggested, the market rewards firms who satisfy consumer demands with short-run profits and long-run survival, and punishes those who do not by driving them out of business. In the long run, supply changes in response to shifts in consumer demand.

Even in the idealized world of perfect competition, we cannot accept the idea that market forces guarantee consumer sovereignty, without considerable qualification. In the first place, the market will supply only those demands that are backed by ability to pay, giving the wants of the rich priority over those of the poor. Secondly, not all consumers want identical products, and some might be prepared to pay a higher price for product differentiation (see Key Concept 1.2). Thirdly, perfectly competitive firms must make investment decisions in isolation from each other, so that adjustment to long-run 'equilibrium' is often far from smooth, with firms oscillating between over-supply and under-supply of the market.

In the real world of oligopolistic competition, where large firms spend considerable sums of money promoting sales of their differentiated products, and consumers make choices on the basis of incomplete information, the notion of consumer sovereignty is particularly difficult to sustain.

Needless to say, marketing practitioners see things differently. T. Levitt, in his classic article *Marketing Myopia* (1960), accuses Galbraith of confusing marketing with selling. Selling, suggests Levitt, focusses on the seller's need to turn products into cash, while marketing concentrates on ensuring that products satisfy the needs of the customer. Indeed, many marketing practitioners see their activities as extending consumer sovereignty, through researching what customers want, ensuring that product design incorporates the research findings, and providing consumers with information about the product.

Is Galbraith right in suggesting that the marketing departments of large firms manipulate consumer demand, or is the marketing profession correct in protesting that all it is doing is providing more effective methods for firms to seek out and meet consumer wants?

It is difficult to go all the way with Galbraith in asserting the power of producers to determine consumer demand for their products. In certain industries it may be the retailer who calls the shots – Marks and Spencer in the UK clothing industry is a classic example. (Interestingly, Galbraith himself analyses the 'countervailing power' of retailers in *The Affluent Society*, though this emphasis disappears in his later works.) More significantly, Galbraith's analysis gives insufficient weight to the combined impact of recession and intensified international competition, in weakening the power of individual corporations to dominate their environment. As many large firms in the US and the UK have discovered to their cost, expertise in promotion and packaging may have little effect in maintaining sales against the negative impact of mass unemployment on consumer expenditure, or against the tendency for consumers to prefer the more innovative products of Japanese firms.

If we recognize limits to the power of individual large firms to manipulate consumers, we cannot accept the claims of some marketing practitioners that this power does not exist. Marketing has a dual function – to ensure that the firm makes products which conform more closely to what consumers are prepared to buy, and to make consumers more favourably inclined to the firm's products. In each case, its main aim is to reduce the level of uncertainty surrounding the firm's revenue function. A marketing orientation may encourage firms to make products which are more in tune with what consumers are prepared to buy (though, as Levitt pointed out in 1975, obsessive segmentation of markets may price products beyond customers' ability to pay). Assessing consumers' willingness to buy is not the same as responding to their demands, however, particularly where they are not in a position to make informed choices.

The promotional aspect of marketing is the hardest to square with consumer sovereignty. It may be possible to argue, as Littlechild has done (1986), that advertising and other promotional activities can perform a positive function for consumers by attracting their attention to products of which they would not otherwise be aware. Yet it is difficult to deny the fact that much advertising works by taking advantage of consumers' lack of information – exaggerating the advantages of products (and neglecting to mention the disadvantages), and emphasizing (in some cases creating) anxieties which, it is suggested, consuming the advertised product will remove. On occasion, advertising promotes products which actually harm the consumer, and in such situations combined action by political authorities and consumer pressure groups may be needed before firms modify their policies.

Product market development

In this section we will demonstrate that there is an inherent contradiction between price reduction and cost recovery, which is ignored in traditional economic theory, where the firm is assumed to operate in a market where unlimited volume growth is possible so long as price continually falls. In reality, firms face market conditions where there are definite limits to the level of demand for a particular product or service. These limits to demand are established by a number of factors, such as consumers' disposable income, the availability of credit, the size of the employed workforce, or the nature of the product replacement cycle.

For companies, product market growth provides the financial resources for further development of existing product types and also investment funds for new product development. The Sony company of Japan is a good example of both these dimensions to product development. Sony was the first company to exploit the use of the transistor in small portable radios. This company successfully expanded volume sales of the transistor radio through price reduction and then applied financial resources into further development of the product. Subsequently, funds were applied to the development of new products like colour televisions, Walkmans, and, more recently, camcorders.

There is no doubt that over the last 50 years the level of consumer demand for a whole range of products and services has been increasing. Price reductions for many consumer durables have made their purchase more accessible to lower-income households, and in the developed economies a high proportion of households now own a car, television, fridge, and washing machine.

For many such products, demand is reaching saturation level, and volume growth rates in retail sales are slowing. We can classify products into two categories: fast-growing new products, and slower-growing established products. Product market maturity is an important point to establish, because, as we shall see later in this chapter, mature market conditions set structural limits on firms' ability to recover costs and sustain growth in net output or value added (see Key Concept 1.6).

KEY CONCEPT 1.6
Value added

The value added by an organization is its sales revenue less its purchases. Value added represents the costs which are incurred by the firm (and the rewards received) in transforming the raw materials and components it has purchased into a finished state ready for sale.

It is normally difficult to identify value added in a company's report and accounts, as purchases are not usually disclosed. Value added can be calculated from items in the accounts, however, by adding labour costs (including social charges) to profits pre-tax and depreciation charges.

Value added = Sales minus purchases
Or
Value added = Wages and salaries + social charges
+ depreciation
+ profit pre-tax and interest.

Value added represents the revenue that is recovered by the firm after paying suppliers of raw materials, components and bought-in services. The resulting value added fund is then distributed as labour costs, depreciation and profits.

Further reading
Cox (1979).

Markets for consumer durables

One way of assessing product market conditions is to compare data over time on unit retail sales for a range of new and established consumer products. Table 1.1 summarizes the retail sales of washing machines, colour televisions and video recorders for the major European markets – France, Italy, Germany and the UK. These four national markets account for 75–80% of total EC sales of these products and so explain to a considerable extent the development of the European product market.

It can be seen that retail sales of the new product – the video recorder – showed rapid growth in the main European markets in the 1980s. In the eight years from 1977 to 1985, the volume of retail sales increased sixty-fold to over 4 million units. However, in the next seven years, from 1985 to 1992, output only doubled. This exemplifies a general condition in which the volume sales of a new product at first expand at a rapid rate, but then increase at a much slower rate. Figure 1.2 represents this pattern of growth for video recorders graphically, using the index numbers from the last column of Table 1.1. The graph takes

Table 1.1 Retail volume sales of washing machines, colour televisions and video recorders in the four major EC markets (France, Italy, Germany and the UK)

Year	Volume sales (million units)			Index of sales (1992 = 100)		
	Washing machines	Colour televisions	Video recorders	Washing machines	Colour televisions	Video recorders
1977	6.028	6.900	0.069	90.46	46.89	0.01
1978	6.672	7.675	0.148	100.12	52.16	0.02
1979	6.429	7.909	0.688	96.47	53.75	0.08
1980	6.291	8.461	0.983	94.40	57.50	0.11
1981	6.016	9.288	4.160	90.28	63.12	0.46
1982	6.145	10.115	4.217	92.21	68.74	0.46
1983	6.275	9.450	4.274	94.16	64.22	0.47
1984	6.290	10.044	3.692	94.39	68.26	0.41
1985	6.350	10.720	4.111	95.29	72.85	0.45
1986	6.720	12.090	5.247	100.84	82.16	0.58
1987	6.910	12.500	6.380	103.69	84.95	0.70
1988	7.010	14.150	7.380	105.19	96.16	0.81
1989	7.040	15.200	8.040	105.64	103.30	0.88
1990	6.772	15.651	9.530	101.62	106.36	1.05
1991	7.604	15.866	8.733	114.11	107.82	0.96
1992	6.664	14.715	9.105	100.00	100.00	1.00

the form of a curve which at first increases at an increasing rate, but then flattens off.

In the case of washing machines, market volumes have remained more or less static during the past two decades, indicating that this is a mature product. Looking at the retail sales for washing machines in Table 1.1, it can be seen that in some years, sales were 10–15% above the 1992 level, and in some years 5–10% below that level, but that in general the index remained fairly static. In a mature market such as this, most households already own the product, so new demand is predominantly replacement demand. In the UK, for example, 90% of households own a washing machine, and they are replaced every eight years on average (see Key Concept 1.7).

When a product market reaches a state of maturity, demand is predominantly determined by consumers replacing their existing product because it is beyond repair or is no longer satisfactory. The extent of the replacement cycle will vary according to factors such as the rate at which the product deteriorates (because of frequency of use, for example) and the costs of repair or replacement relative to household income.

KEY CONCEPT 1.7
Replacement demand and market cyclicality

Electric kettles, for example, will be replaced more frequently than washing machines, because they wear out quicker and cost less to replace.

A cyclical market is generally a mature market in which volume fluctuates around a steady level of demand. If consumers decide to postpone their replacement purchases, this will result in a fall in retail sales, creating a cyclical pattern to sales. The UK car market is a good example of a cyclical market. Here sales fell by 30% in volume terms in the 1989–92 recession, predominantly because both private individuals and company fleet car buyers were postponing their purchases.

The market for colour televisions is more mature than that for video recorders, but less mature than that for washing machines. Referring again to Table 1.1, it can be seen that demand for colour television sets was almost three times greater in 1992 than in 1976. This product's sales growth has not yet slowed down to a mature replacement rate, but its market, as with those for washing machines and video recorders, is subject to conditions of cyclicality in which volume sales fall when replacement or new purchases are postponed.

It is clear from the above three cases that firms cannot rely on unlimited growth in the markets for their products. Instead, they must appreciate that volume growth for a particular product will inevitably slow down as the market approaches saturation levels. Market satura-

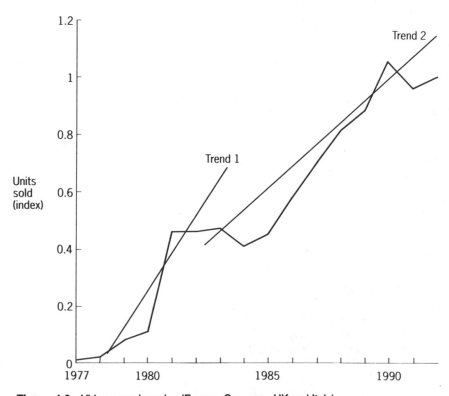

Figure 1.2   Video recorder sales (France, Germany, UK and Italy).

Table 1.2 Growth index and price per unit index for TV and video recorder sales in the UK market

Year	Colour TV unit sales	Market sales (£m.)	Volume index (1992 = 1.00)	Price per unit index (1992 = 100)	Video recorder unit sales	Market sales (£m.)	Volume index (1992 = 1.00)	Price per unit index (1992 = 100)
1983	3.320	1004	0.99	97.24	2.180	990	0.98	151.38
1984	3.250	951	0.97	94.09	1.411	540	0.64	127.57
1985	3.670	956	1.09	83.76	1.660	700	0.75	140.56
1986	3.840	982	1.14	82.23	1.950	800	0.88	136.75
1987	4.000	1200	1.19	96.46	2.150	750	0.97	116.28
1988	4.300	1205	1.28	90.11	2.200	800	0.99	121.21
1989	4.100	1120	1.22	87.84	2.100	765	0.95	121.43
1990	3.450	1065	1.03	99.26	2.140	710	0.97	110.59
1991	3.975	1030	1.18	83.32	2.051	680	0.93	110.52
1992	3.360	1045	1.00	100.00	2.215	665	1.00	100.00

Source: Euromonitor *European Marketing Data and Statistics*, various years.

tion, which is generally reached when 60 to 80% of households own a product, signals that retail sales are constrained by factors such as the replacement cycle or the rate of household formation.

It is often possible for firms to win increased sales by lowering the price per unit, but in product markets where growth is slowing, this may be at the expense of sales revenue and value added. This is shown in Table 1.2, which gives information on volume growth and unit price for colour televisions and video recorders in the UK.

In the case of colour TVs, although there was a short-term rise in volume sales in the UK market during the economic recovery of the mid-1980s, there was little change over the decade 1983–92, during which period price per unit also remained fairly constant. For a firm like Sony, the problem is the lack of any nominal increase in retail sales revenue throughout the period 1983 to 1992 – in nominal terms the market remained around £1 billion, while in real terms (after taking account of inflation) the sales revenue will have fallen.

Although video recorders were introduced more recently than colour TVs, market maturity was again achieved relatively quickly. Sales of video recorders, like those of colour TVs, remained roughly constant throughout the decade 1983–92. More problematic for firms selling video recorders in the UK market is that the retail sales price per unit fell by 51% during this period. The result was a drop of a third in the nominal value of retail sales, from roughly £1 billion to £665 million. In the UK market for video recorders, as with many other European product markets, a number of problems have emerged. First, volume growth rates are slowing as these markets reach maturity, and cyclical

Table 1.3 Market volume for video cameras in Japan

Year	Market volume (million units)	Market value (million yen)
1987	1.2	145 900
1988	1.3	158 000
1989	1.6	161 200
1990	1.85	192 400
1991	1.79	204 000
1992	1.75	210 500

Source: Euromonitor *Consumer Japan.*

fluctuations appear as consumers vary the replacement cycle. Second, in order to defend market share it may be necessary to cut prices, even when sales are stagnant, thus reducing the sales revenue generated in the market.

Many product markets in the major national economies are now saturated, and even new innovative products such as compact disc players rapidly reach a mature replacement cycle of demand. Even in Japan, as Table 1.3 shows, market sales for video cameras stabilized at around 1.8 million units in the period 1990 to 1992.

It is clear that in the main national economies, most product markets are maturing, making it more difficult for firms to sustain sales revenue growth. Firms selling in saturated markets, and at the same time reducing costs to lower prices, are caught in a vicious circle – selling the same volume at lower unit prices results in a lowering of sales revenue. As we shall see in Chapter 3, the financial result of this situation will be a reduction in the real value added generated by the firm.

Supermarkets

Food retailing in the past few years has been characterized by the growing dominance of a few supermarket chains like Tesco and Sainsbury's. In order to expand sales revenue, these supermarket chains have been shifting from smaller to larger outlets. In the case of Tesco, for example, the average size of a retail outlet was 11 250 square feet in 1980, but this doubled over the next decade, so that in 1990 the average store size was 23 900 square feet. The effect of these changes on Tesco's market performance is analysed in Case Study 1.2.

CASE STUDY 1.2
Tesco

The table below takes from Tesco plc's annual report and accounts the weekly sales per square foot in nominal terms, and converts these nominal figures into a real value by deflating by the retail price index (see Key Concept 4.1). These figures suggest that real sales per square foot increased by almost a third between 1980 and 1990, while total floorspace increased by almost a half.

Weekly sales in real terms per square foot of retail space

Year	Weekly sales per sq. ft (£)	Retail price index all items	Real weekly sales per sq ft	Total store size (000 sq ft)	Index of store size (1980 = 100)
1980	5.10	1.00	5.10	6210	100
1981	5.57	1.12	4.97	6840	110.1
1982	5.75	1.21	4.75	7203	116.0
1983	6.32	1.27	4.98	7425	119.6
1984	7.10	1.33	5.34	7362	118.6
1985	8.26	1.42	5.82	7415	119.4
1986	9.14	1.46	6.26	7502	120.8
1987	10.23	1.52	6.73	6997	112.7
1988	11.00	1.60	6.88	8220	132.4
1989	11.51	1.72	6.69	8542	137.6
1990	12.69	1.89	6.71	9071	146.1

It can be seen that from 1987 onwards there was no real volume increase in retail sales per square foot, even though during this period Tesco increased their total store size by 30%. This suggests that by 1990 Tesco was in a situation where they could only increase their sales by increasing the amount of retail space available, either by expanding the size of each outlet or by increasing the number of outlets. Their ability to continue expanding will, however, be limited by the capacity of consumers to increase their expenditure in line with the physical increase in retail space.

Market composition

In addition to addressing the problems posed by the development of market maturity, firms also need to consider changes in the composition of their product markets. To understand market composition of a product market, analysis is needed of the range of products (segments) on offer, and the nature of the competition within each product segment (fragmentation).

In an immature product market we might expect the composition of the market for a particular product to be relatively simple. That is, the product range would be relatively narrow, and the competition between producers relatively limited, in terms of numbers in a particular product market. However, as a product market develops over time the market a firm will have to face will become more complex in terms of its composition, for two reasons: firstly in terms of the model range of products or product variants (what we shall term product *segments*), and secondly in terms of increased competition within each product segment from an increased number of competitors both at home and from overseas in the form of imports to the home market (a process we shall term *fragmentation*).

A good example which illustrates the changing nature and composition of a product market is that of the UK small car market (see Case Study 1.3).

It is not easy or possible to prescribe one 'package' of price and non-price characteristics that will see a producer through a changing market environment. This would indeed be contrary to what we have developed so far, i.e. that there is no one way of marketing toasters because during different stages in the product's life cycle there will of necessity have to be a 'flexible' marketing strategy which adjusts price and non-price factors intelligently to meet changing product market structure and composition. In fact we could conceive of a variety of strategies that depend on the maturity and development of the product market the enterprise is in.

For simplicity we have outlined below four possible product market structures/scenarios which would require different price/non-price responses by the firm in order to preserve or maintain market share.

CASE STUDY 1.3
Fragmentation in the UK small car market segment

The table below shows the effect of increased fragmentation in the UK car segment for small cars on the Rover car company (formerly British Leyland). It can be seen that in the 1960s and early 1970s British Leyland dominated the small car segment with the Mini. This model took a 7–9% share of total UK car registrations in the decade 1965–75.

Sales in the UK small car class

	1965	1970	1975	1980	1985	1991
Ford Fiesta	–	–	–	91 661 (6.0)	124 143 (6.5)	117 181 (7.4)
Austin Mini	104 477 (9.0)	80 740 (7.2)	84 688 (6.9)	61 129 (4.0)		
Austin Metro	–	–	–	–	118 817 (6.2)	60 361 (3.8)
Vauxhall Nova	–	–	–	–	61 358 (3.2)	44 751 (2.8)
Peugeot 205		–	–	–	30 842 (1.5)	46 615 (2.9)
Nissan Micra		–	–	–	28 181 (1.4)	32 571 (2.0)

Note: Figures in ( ) are percentage of total UK car registrations.

In the 1980s the small car segment was increasingly occupied by the products of other UK manufactureers – the Ford Fiesta and the Vauxhall Nova. The effect of first the entrance of UK domestic producers and then penetration by an increasing number of importers was to reduce the volume sales that Rover could obtain from the sale of their new small car, the Metro. By 1991, Metro sales were down to 60 000 units, compared with Mini sales of 104 000 units in 1965.

Fragmentation is a process whereby each product segment in the market is subject to increased competition. Whereas imports took just 20% of the UK new car market in 1970, they now take over 50%. As the level of imports increased to take market share in each of the product segments, the Rover company was left with a smaller share of the overall UK car market. Full line direct competition in the small car market segment has increasingly fragmented the share taken by Rover, and it can no longer take 10% of the UK car market by offering one model in this market segment.

Further reading
Williams *et al.* (1987).

Possible product market structures and composition

Scenario A

Here your firm has a strong market share, in an environment where there is little or no import penetration. In addition there is a narrow product range on offer and only a few firms are in competition so that there is little fragmentation of the product segments available.

At this stage the product market is relatively immature. That is, consumers have had little experience in using these products and non-price factors such as durability and reliability have not yet surfaced in the purchase decision. Given also that the purchase decision is limited to a few models, the tendency would be to decide on price grounds predominantly. Decisions to buy at a higher or lower price would depend on the level of expenditure incurred as a percentage of total income.

Few market segments for product – dominated by home market producers

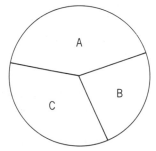

Domestic manufacturers dominate their home market

Figure 1.3 Market segmentation for Scenario A.

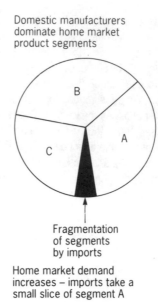

Domestic manufacturers
dominate home market
product segments

Fragmentation
of segments
by imports

Home market demand
increases – imports take a
small slice of segment A

Figure 1.4 Market segmentation for Scenario B.

Scenario B

Here again your firm is one of a number of domestic producers which dominate the market, but there is now an increasing level of import penetration. Your firm may well still have a narrow product range but fragmentation in a particular segment is increasing.

At this stage what might have been a relatively large product market segment is becoming increasingly fragmented by imports or increased domestic competition. Increased competition may well come in the form of increased or similar reliability/durability etc. as the existing products but the price of these may well be lower. It may well be that the prices of the products that are being sold are all roughly equivalent but that the newer products have improved non-price characteristics.

A classic example is that of British motor bikes, which in the early 1970s could not successfully compete with the Japanese in the smaller bike segments of the UK market. The Japanese product was found by users to be easier to maintain, having fewer oil leaks and a convenient electric start (Boston Consulting Group, 1975).

Scenario C

Here domestic producers, including your own firm, are losing market dominance to imports (even though the market may be expanding) and we now have a much wider product range and the possibility that the number of product market segments is also increasing while some of the older-established segments in which your firm has a presence become more fragmented.

At this stage it may well be that domestic manufacturers are 'lagging' in terms of product development and the sort of innovation needed to

Market for product matures
with increased segmentation

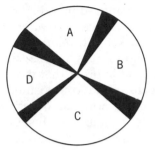

Within each segment importers
now take a share of sales but
their position is still not
dominant in terms of overall
product market sales

Figure 1.5 Market segmentation for Scenario C.

establish a position in new product segments. The objective at this
stage would be either to invest in new product lines and innovate
products for these new segments, or to make improvements to non-
price characteristics of the product mix the firm already has, and try to
defend old product market segments while paying attention to new
product market development.

Scenario D

In this case domestic producers suffer from very high import penetration in which the market is becoming saturated across and within
market segments. As we shall see, if the firm is facing such a market˙

Imports now take a dominant
share of most product segments

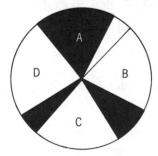

Domestic producers retreat
to market segment niches in
segments B, C and D but still
dominate segment A. Overall,
imports dominate home
market sales

Figure 1.6 Market segmentation for Scenario D.

it is likely that this will affect the full utilization of equipment and depress profits. At this stage the product market strategy becomes one of retreat, which can be managed in a disorderly or orderly way.

With these simple scenarios we have attempted to show that at each stage of the product market's development the firm must make the most effective use of the resources made available to it. Market strategy must be operationally fluid in order that it can react to the dynamics of changing market structure and composition. In essence this text is concerned with examining how, in differing market circumstances, the enterprise needs to organize its resources (finance, labour and capital) around the objective of maintaining or achieving 'competitive advantage' in the particular market targeted by the firm.

Options for increasing sales

As we can see from Case Study 1.3, the UK car market has become much more competitive in terms of the fragmentation within market segments. The position that now exists is what might be termed full line competition, where every producer needs to offer a full range of vehicles in their domestic market to gain the volumes of sales they require to maintain the value added of the business.

We have seen that it is becoming increasingly difficult for firms to sustain sales revenue growth, because product markets in the main national economies are tending to mature. In addition, individual firms face problems of product market segmentation and fragmentation, which further hamper their ability to maintain their value added performance. In this section, we consider the possibilities and limitations associated with different options open to a firm to maintain and/or increase sales volume and revenues.

Shorter overlapping product life cycles

In recent years, it has been argued that in order to survive, firms must pay more attention to their product life cycles, and that more frequent model replacement can help to sustain sales revenue. The product life cycle is a concept much referred to by marketing practitioners. It suggests that products, like people, have limited lives which pass through distinct stages – development, growth, maturity, and decline.

A great many products require updating and redesign to maintain their appeal to the consumer. The objective therefore is to ensure that the last product variant or model type is successful in generating increased sales revenue, because it is from the last model that the funds for its replacement will be generated. It is quite possible for a business to flounder because the last product failed to deliver the required sales revenue. As we have seen in Case Study 1.1, Sinclair was initially successful in introducing new home computer products on the UK market, but subsequent market failure brought about a financial downfall.

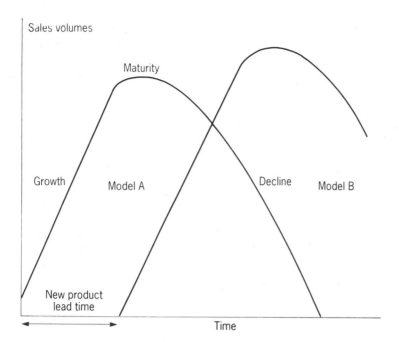

Figure 1.7   Overlapping product life cycle.

Figure 1.7 illustrates the concept of an overlapping product life cycle, where a firm reduces the development lead time for new products and also introduces new variants of existing products before they enter the decline phase of their own life cycles.

The general objective of overlapping product life cycles is to ensure that the company maintains and preferably increases its market share. If the firm can reduce product development lead time and also introduce new product before the downturn in the previous models' sales volume, it will be at an advantage relative to another firm which either takes longer to develop and introduce new model replacements, or which launches new product variants when the previous model range is in the decline phase of the life cycle.

The use of powerful computer technology by firms now allows manufacturers to design products with the use of computer aided design (CAD) software. In areas of product design the use of computer technology can drastically cut the lead time from product conception to construction of prototypes and then final versions of the new product. CAD eliminates the use of traditional engineering and drafting jobs and may also allow the designer to incorporate changes in structural properties, and to make rapid design adjustments. According to Freeman and Jones (1986)

> The designer can analyse for stress, check for compliance with codes, and test for linkages with other modules in a complex system in a matter of seconds. He can modify the design and test out the effects in a variety of ways, without the need for whole sets of new drawings. CAD already facilitates a much closer integration between design, production planning and orders for tooling.

Strategically this technology can allow the firm to react to changing market needs more rapidly by shortening the lead time from design to final manufacture. For industries that operate in rapidly changing markets (hi-fi, TVs, VCRs etc.) the potential of such equipment is obvious. The benefit of new CAD technology is that it can if properly utilized cut the turnaround time from old to new product lines significantly. However, it is of no use designing and redesigning products if this design flexibility is not matched with manufacturing flexibility. In addition, for some products design and development costs are very high and as such the product life cycle has to be, for financial necessity, longer.

Under intense competition in a mature product market, opportunities to increase sales may result more from the failings of competitors than from what your own firm is doing. If a competitor is, for example, late in offering up new product to the consumer, this will release market space, especially if that competitor's product is now on the downside of its product life cycle.

New technology and product mix flexibility

Against the background of the complex market of the 1990s, new technology can offer the manufacturer or service enterprise a number of advantages, which in essence allow the firm to 'match' the now more competitive structure of the market place with the output produced by the firm. Goldhar and Jelinek (1983) describe the possibilities of new technology as 'economies of scope' rather than economies of scale. That is, it is necessary for the firm to produce a variety of output in volume, not standard output in volume. However, this is not to argue that economies of scale are dead because in many circumstances, such as the manufacture of standard components or products where market demand is sufficient, economies of scale still operate.

However, with new computer technologies utilizing computer aided design (CAD), and computer aided manufacturing (CAM), it is becoming possible for the firm to manufacture in volume a variety of output for the now more complex market structure. Where computer aided design and manufacture are integrated then we have what is termed computer integrated manufacture (CIM). The future, it is argued, now lies with automation and not inflexible giantism of the old-fashioned kind. Here the firm can alter its product mix more rapidly than in the past and so adjust to the needs of the market in a more 'flexible' way. An enterprise that is successful with new technology can, it is argued, now maintain throughput by changing the output mix to the requirements of the market without suffering the penalties of underutilized 'dedicated' equipment at low volume. This idea is illustrated with a simple example below.

Production process　　　　　*Market share 10%*

Dedicated technology　　　　Product A 1000 units

Flexible technology Two product types A 500 units

B 500 units

With old dedicated technology the firm can obtain a market share of 10% selling 1000 units. However, consider a situation where the market place becomes more competitive such that with dedicated equipment and a standard product the firm will steadily lose market share and incur increased unit costs of production. With flexible technology it is possible to produce, say, two products A and B, so that where demand for say A falls below 500 units it may well be possible to produce more of product B to compensate and still maintain throughput.

Flexible manufacturing systems (FMS)

According to Shah (1987),

Flexible Manufacturing Systems (FMS) are being implemented at a fast rate in Japan. The driving force behind this development is the priority given to improving productivity rates in a production and market environment characterized by rising costs, decreasing product life spans, increasing numbers of product variants and the resulting shift from rigid production lines to adaptable, computer controlled set ups.

A flexible manufacturing system is one which uses computer software and hardware to establish a production system that can react quickly to the changing requirements of the market place. Such a system uses advanced manufacturing systems that can automatically transfer and process materials for use in final products. Such a system is said to be more flexible than a mass production environment in which standardized products are made on dedicated inflexible equipment.

KEY CONCEPT 1.8
Flexible manufacturing system

Flexible manufacturing		Mass production
Low use ⟵	Dedicated equipment ⟶	High use
High level ⟵	Product differentiation ⟶	Low level
Short run ⟵	Length of production run for product ⟶	Long runs

What then is the difference between a computer aided manufacturing system (CAM) and a flexible manufacturing system? and what are some of the perceived benefits for the firm when it invests in FMS technologies?

It is clear that the difference between CAM and FMS is related to the *extent* of automation and the *diversity* of the parts/products that can be produced. A computer aided manufacturing system might well consist of a number of machines producing one or more parts where manufacturing operations are controlled by a computer, but the raw material drawn from stores is transferred from one machine to another using manual handling. However, an FMS is defined as essentially one in

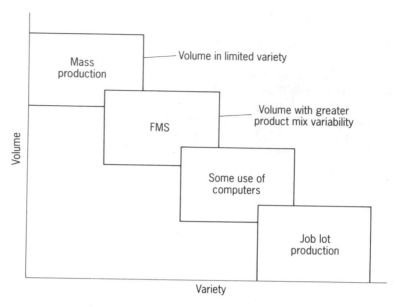

Figure 1.8   The position of FMS. *Source: ECE Recent Trends in Flexible Manufacturing.*

which materials are handled and processed automatically. Thus an FMS is defined as:

> An integrated, computer controlled complex of automated material hand-ling devices and numerically controlled (NC) machine tools that can simultaneously process medium sized volumes of a variety of part types.

We could also use this definition for 'flexible' services and use auto-matic cash dispenser machines as an example. Here a variety of cash dispensing amounts can be obtained as well as a variety of services, where the cash taken out is automatically debited against the account with minimal or no manual operations in between.

It is 'flexibility' that is the main characteristic of FMS. In this sense, flexibility is thought of as the ease with which adjustments to the firm's product mix, to meet changes in demand, take place. Strategically, therefore the most important perceived benefit of FMS technology is that it can deliver variety in volume. FMS, then, it is argued, sits somewhere between traditional mass production of a very few pro-ducts/variants and manufacturing systems of a conventional nature that undertake 'job lot' production. The position of FMS is illustrated in Figure 1.8.

Exports and globalization

Over the last ten to 15 years it has become progressively more difficult for UK manufacturers to maintain sales growth on their home market. Two processes are at work, as we have noted earlier in this chapter: increasing maturity in product markets, resulting in cyclicality of demand, and fragmentation of the domestic market by imports.

Table 1.4 Exports to the EC as percentage of total UK merchandise exports

Year	Exports to the EC (£m.)	Total UK exports (£m.)	EC exports as % of total exports
1979	18 084	40 471	44.68
1980	21 467	47 149	45.53
1981	21 941	50 381	43.55
1982	24 269	55 314	43.87
1983	27 955	60 590	46.14
1984	32 961	70 373	46.84
1985	37 899	78 263	48.43
1986	34 725	72 782	47.71
1987	38 880	79 758	48.75
1988	40 678	82 071	49.56
1989	47 025	93 799	50.13
1990	54 193	103 691	52.26
1991	58 684	104 816	55.99
1992	60 512	108 298	55.88

Source: UK Overseas Trade Statistics.

In response to deteriorating home market conditions, individual firms have a number of options for increasing export sales into overseas markets. The general trend has been to increase direct exports to the EC. As Table 1.4 shows, the share of exports to the EC in total exports from the UK rose from 45% to 56% between 1979 and 1991. The ability to expand exports in the face of difficult home market conditions is, however, an option which is more open to manufacturers than to the service sector.

In general terms, UK firms have not taken full advantage of European markets, and many UK firms still predominantly supply the home market. National car manufacturers generally account for a large percentage of overall export trade and the surpluses and deficits generated in particular national economies. In the UK, the car industry's trade deficit has at times accounted for up to 40% of the overall manufacturing trade deficit, whereas in Japan it accounts for nearly 40% of Japan's trade surplus. Table 1.5 confirms that UK car manufacturers are not exporting a high percentage of their domestic output to European markets (see also Case Study 8.1).

The information in Table 1.5 shows the different patterns of direct exports by destination. American manufacturers have traditionally not directly exported to Europe because, in an earlier period, they established overseas manufacturing operations here, Ford starting

Table 1.5 National car production and exports, 1990

Producing country	National production (000 units)	Exports to:		
		Western Europe	Japan	N. America
Germany	4661	2064	132	290
France	3295	1646	14	2
Italy	1875	698	5	8
UK	1296	345	19	30
Spain	1679	1113	0	0
USA	6077	49	39	–
Japan	9948	1483	–	2154

Source: Society of Motor Manufacturers and Traders, *World Automotive Statistics Yearbook.*

before the war with investment in the UK at Trafford Park and then Dagenham. Spain has been a more recent recipient of foreign direct investment in car manufacturing facilities, and now re-exports 66% of its production. French and German firms directly export 50% and 44% of production, mostly to proximate markets in Western Europe. UK and Italian manufacturers, in contrast, tend to concentrate on their domestic markets.

Direct exports can maintain a company's sales turnover growth when the domestic market starts to mature and growth slackens. Companies which cannot sell the necessary volume on their home market will seek to directly export overseas or to set up transplant manufacture and distribution operations in other major markets (mostly in Europe, North America, and Japan). Each of these options exposes the company to risks associated with the nature and conditions of the export market and the exchange rate obtained on repatriation of funds from the host country in which sales are made.

It is well known that European and American product markets are cyclical and prone to recession. In 1990 to 1992, the US and European markets moved into recession at more or less the same time, damaging the volume sales of both domestic producers and importers. Many Japanese companies, such as Sony, Hitachi, and Nippon Electric, are highly exposed to the cyclical conditions of the US and European markets, as well as facing recession in their home market in 1993. Japanese firms have also come under pressure from exchange rate appreciation, which means that dollars earned in America from direct exports are converted to fewer yen on the return. This point is illustrated for Toyota in Case Study 1.4.

Toyota is the market leader in the Japanese car market, supplying up to 40% of vehicles sold in this market each year, yet even Toyota has had to find extra volume through direct exports to America and Europe.

CASE STUDY 1.4
Toyota and the exchange rate

Toyota vehicle sales

	1992	%	1991	%
Total overseas sales	2 180 742	100	2 095 233	100
N. America	1 130 653	52	1 120 409	54
Europe	433 079	20	442 781	21
East Asia	220 103	10	206 592	10
Middle East	177 226	8	116 712	6
Others	219 681	10	208 739	9

In 1992, Toyota sold a total of 4 511 833 units – of which a quarter were exports to North America, and another quarter exports to other overseas markets. If we assume that 25 per cent of total sales revenue was generated in the North American markets, this would have amounted to 1 127 958 million yen. We can express these yen sales in millions of dollars using the 1992 yen dollar exchange rate:

1992 sales revenue from N. America
  in m. yen: 1 127 958
Sales revenue in million dollars: 9 023   (125 yen to dollar)
Sales revenue in m. yen at 1982 exchange rate: 2 120 405   (235 yen to dollar)

Toyota's sales revenue from its 1992 exports to North America calculated at the 1982 exchange rate would have been worth 2 120 405 million yen – double what was earned on the North American exports ten years later. For further discussion of changes in exchange rates and their effects on business, you should see Chapter 8. This chapter also includes an extended assessment of foreign direct investment.

In addition to the policy of increasing direct exports to compensate for a loss of home market sales, a firm can also purchase another company's market sales either in the domestic market or overseas. As we shall see in Chapter 7, many UK firms are able to exploit the conditions of the UK stock market to take over another firm operating in related or unrelated markets. A takeover offers the possibility of substituting a rapid trajectory of inorganic growth for a slow trajectory of organic growth. In addition to the purchase of other UK firms, it is also possible, where institutional stock market conditions permit, to purchase a firm in an overseas market. Institutional conditions in North America permit the transfer of ownership through share exchange, and many UK firms have taken advantage of these permissive institutional conditions to boost their overseas presence.

In general terms, merger and takeover activity operates as a substitute for expanding the existing businesses. A classic example of an organization which has purchased inorganic growth in sales is Hanson Trust.

This is a business which has expanded its sales volume through extensive takeover activity in the UK and USA. The company has achieved spectacular real growth in sales (after adjusting for inflation) in both the UK and US markets during the last ten years (see Case Study 1.5).

CASE STUDY 1.5
Hanson trust: growth through acquisition

Hanson Trust is classed as a conglomerate firm, and comprises a diverse set of operations ranging from coal and bricks to gold and Jacuzzis. Hanson Trust is a company which has traditionally achieved growth through the acquisition of other companies. This process of growth through acquisition can be termed 'inorganic' growth. Hanson Trust has described its philosophy as follows: 'The group should invest in low technology basic industries providing essential goods and services to proven markets, with definable future prospects' (Annual Report and Accounts, 1986). Others have described Hanson's *modus operandi* as 'financial engineering' and 'the bundling and unbundling of assets'.

There is no doubt that Hanson's growth in real sales has been spectacular, as the table below illustrates.

Year	Sales nominal £ m.	Retail price index (1982 = 1.00)	Real sales revenue index (1982 = 1.00)
1982	1148	1.000	1.000
1983	1484	1.0463	1.236
1984	2382	1.0981	1.890
1985	2674	1.1646	2.000
1986	4312	1.2945	2.902
1987	6682	1.2546	4.639
1988	7396	1.3157	4.897
1989	6998	1.4188	4.297
1990	7153	1.5530	4.012
1991	7691	1.6444	4.074
1992	8798	1.7050	4.495

Hanson Trust's rate of growth in real sales has been well above that achieved in general by UK firms engaged in manufacturing. Over the period 1982 to 1992, Hanson's real sales grew by a factor of 4.5. We can see, however, that real sales reached a plateau in the late 1980s, falling by almost 10% over the four years from 1988 to 1992.

Even though Hanson has purchased a number of very large companies since 1987 (Kaiser Cement, Cons Gold, Peabody, Cavenham and Beazer) these companies have been subject to recessionary conditions in both the UK and the USA. In 1992, Hanson Trust employed 72% of its workforce and made 52% of its sales revenue overseas (particularly in the USA).

Although Hanson has managed substantial growth in real sales, the companies it holds are, like any others, vulnerable to the national market conditions in which they operate. This is particularly so when a large proportion of Hanson Trust sales are concentrated in the basic energy, construction, and aggregates businesses.

Further reading
Adcroft *et al.* (1991)
See also Case Study 7.2, on Hanson and ICI.

Conclusion

In this chapter we have reviewed the neo-classical analysis of market demand, and its suggestion that price reductions inevitably bring about increased sales. What we have observed is that consumers often make choices on the basis of non-price factors, and that reductions of cost and price cannot sustain infinite and indefinite growth in a company's sales revenue. As product markets mature, they reach a point where replacement demand is the norm, and the possibility of postponing replacement purchases creates pronounced cyclical fluctuations in demand, setting clear limits to growth in retail sales volume.

Despite the phenomenon of maturing product markets, many individual firms are still struggling to take cost and price out of the product, in the hope that they can stay one step ahead of the next firm in the cost recovery race. We have considered how a number of internal calculations, such as reduced development lead time, overlapping product life cycles, and new technology might promote cost recovery by the firm, and allow it to deliver variety in volume, so meeting the requirements of a more fragmented market.

In order to escape the limits of a particular home market it is always open to the firm to increase exports, but within the developed European markets this is becoming an increasingly difficult task. Direct exports may provide some benefit to a firm facing domestic market problems, but there are risks attached to this policy – either the exchange rate can work against the firm (as in the case of Japanese exporters, when repatriated funds are depreciated by the exchange rate), or the firm escapes the limits of the domestic market only to find that the overseas market is subject to the same conditions of maturity and cyclicality.

Finally the firm can abandon organic growth policies and substitute inorganic growth, in which it decides it is easier to purchase another company's sales revenue and cash flow than to generate this from an existing portfolio of products. As we saw with Hanson Trust, this too may reach certain limits and cannot be a permanent solution to the fundamental struggle which every business has to face – that of incurring costs against an uncertain level of market demand and associated problems of cost recovery.

Further reading

The first nine chapters of the second edition of Andrew Dunnett's *Understanding the Market* (Longman, 1992) give a good introduction to neo-classical market analysis, while Peter Earl's *Lifestyle Economics* (Wheatsheaf, 1986) provides an incisive and at times entertaining critique.

For an application of the analysis of market conditions to the car industry, see Chapters 5, 6, and 10 of *Cars: Analysis, History and Cases*, by Karel Williams, Colin Haslam, John Williams, and Sukhdev Johal (Berghahn, 1994).

On the benefits of flexible manufacturing systems in relation to market conditions, see C. Kim, Issues on manufacturing flexibility, *Integrated Manufacturing Systems*, vol. 2, no. 2, 1992.

Exercises

1 The following data, from Euromonitor statistics, shows the total volume retail sales for Colour Televisions on the UK home market, and, from 1983, the total value of retail sales.

Year	Colour TVs sold (000 units)	Value of colour TVs sold (£ m.)
1976	923	
1977	1667	
1978	1650	
1979	1805	
1980	1947	
1981	2250	
1982	2600	
1983	3320	1004
1984	3250	951
1985	3670	956
1986	3840	982
1987	4000	1200
1988	4300	1205
1989	4100	1120
1990	3450	1065
1991	3975	1030
1992	3360	1045

(i) Calculate the retail sales price per television from 1983 to 1992 in nominal and real terms per unit (use the retail price index from Key Concept 4.1 in Chapter 4).
Did the total real value of sales increase or decrease during the period 1983 to 1992?

(ii) Graph the volume sales index for colour TVs sold in the UK market, using 1976 as the base year, and comment on the nature of the TV market.

(iii) What would be the general effects of the market conditions you have considered under (i) and (ii) for TV manufacturers?

2 What do you understand by the terms 'organic' and 'inorganic' growth policies?
   Illustrate your answer with case material from this chapter.

3 What do you understand by the term 'globalization'?
   What are the main costs and benefits associated with a globalization of sales policy?

4 What do you understand by the terms 'market fragmentation' and 'market segmentation'?
   To what extent can new technology enable a firm to produce variety in volume?

5 What are the major implications for a firm's value added and profits when the product market it faces is mature and replacement demand is such that the market is also cyclical?

References

Adamson, I. and Kennedy, R. (1986) *Sinclair and the 'Sunrise' Technology,* Penguin, Harmondsworth.

Adcroft, A., Cutler, T., Haslam, C., Williams, J. and Williams, K. (1991) Hanson & ICI: the consequences of financial engineering *University of East London Occasional Papers,* no. 2.

Boston Consulting Group (1975) Strategy Alternatives for the British Motorcycle Industry, HC Paper 532, HMSO, London.

Cox, B. (1979) *Value Added,* Heinemann, London.

Doyle, P. *et al.* (1986) Japanese marketing strategies in the UK. *Journal of International Business Studies.*

Earl, P. (1983) *The Economic Imagination,* Wheatsheaf Books, Brighton.

Earl, P. (1986) *Lifestyle Economics,* Wheatsheaf Books, Brighton.

European Commission for Europe (1986) *Recent Trends in Flexible Manufacturing,* UN, New York.

Freeman, C. and Jones, D. (1986) *Technical Trends and Employment in Engineering and Vehicles,* Gower, Aldershot.

Galbraith, J.K. (1958) *The Affluent Society,* Penguin, Harmondsworth.

Galbraith, J.K. (1967) *The New Industrial State,* Penguin, Harmondsworth.

Galbraith, J.K. (1973) *Economics and the Public Purpose,* Penguin, Harmondsworth.

Goldhar, J. and Jelinck, M. (1983) Plan for economies of scope. *Harvard Business Review,* Nov./Dec. pp. 141–8.

Levitt, T. (1960) Marketing myopia. *Harvard Business Review,* July–August.

Levitt, T. (1975) Retrospective commentary. *Harvard Business Review,* Sept.– Oct.

Littlechild, S.C. (1986) *The Fallacy of the Mixed Economy,* 2nd edn, Institute of Economic Affairs, London.

Shah, R. (1987) Manufacturing operations. In *Manufacturing Systems.* (ed. V. Bignell), Blackwell, Oxford.

Sweezy, P. (1939) Demand under conditions of oligopoly. *Journal of Political Economy.*

Williams, K. *et al.* (1987) *The Breakdown of Austin Rover,* Berg, Leamington Spa.

2 The organization of production for cost reduction and cost recovery

In this chapter, we challenge the traditional economic assumption that volume growth in the market will automatically deliver reductions in unit costs. We see that, in practice, improvements in product design, production flow, and quality control offer more opportunities to reduce production costs, but a number of physical and institutional factors are identified which limit the extent to which business management can fully exploit these opportunities.

Introduction

Over the past 50 years, the rate at which established products and production technologies have become obsolete has increased dramatically. When a competitor introduces a product which embodies new attributes at lower costs, then your firm must decide, if it wishes to remain in business, to follow the competitor's lead. Whether your firm is leading or following the market, it is imperative that you continually adjust not only your product range but also the way your production is organized.

In neo-classical economic theory, production is analysed in terms of the production function – the relationship between resource input and output. This chapter starts with a review of the traditional economic approach, and goes on to suggest that what is lacking is the all-important detail on what goes on within the 'black box' of the firm. Then we consider some of the techniques an organization can employ to manage productive resources in order to achieve cost reduction and promote cost recovery.

Traditional economic theory of production and costs

In traditional micro-economic theory the 'production function' describes the physical relation between output and factor inputs (land, labour, capital and materials). That is, in any production process one or all of the above factors of production will be combined in order to convert raw materials into a finished saleable product (see Key Concept 2.1).

In economics the production function is a mathematical statement of the relationship between the output of the business and factor inputs required to produce that output. Where

$$Q = f(K,L,L,M)$$

In production terms various combinations of factors of production are required (capital, land, labour and materials) to produce different product types. Factors of production are transformed in the production process into a final end product.

KEY CONCEPT 2.1
The production function

Inputs → Production transformation process → Final output

At this stage no costs have been attached to the factors of production used in the production process, although in practice we would attach costs to each of the inputs used in the production process. We are here only concerned with the physical unit inputs of land, labour, capital and materials. In addition to just using a physical measure of the factor inputs of the production process, we are also assuming that the production process we are using combines the factors of production in physically the most efficient way possible. At this point we are only concerned with the 'technical efficiency' of production and not 'economic efficiency', because in the latter case we would need to take the price or cost of factors of production into account. With this distinction in mind we can consider the following two production processes X and Y, both of which use the following labour and capital physical inputs.

Table 2.1 Inputs to processes X and Y

Process	X (units)	Y (units)
Labour input	100	75
Capital input	50	75

In this example both processes would be considered to be equally technically efficient, because both processes use the same number of labour and capital inputs namely 150 units to produce the same output. If process X were, in fact, to use say 120 units of labour and 50 units of capital then the 'rational' business would choose to operate process Y and not X because in physical input terms (with a given state of technology) process X now uses more resources than that of Y to produce the same output.

In practice managers make decisions about which production process is the most efficient in terms of the costs of production (physical inputs times unit costs). The decision about which production process is the more efficient becomes an 'economic' rather than 'technical' one. Using the above example we could allocate the following unit costs to capital and labour.

	£
Unit capital cost	4.00
Unit labour cost	1.00

The costs of producing a given output from process X and process Y now become as shown below.

Table 2.2 Costs of processes X and Y

Process	£ X	£ Y
Labour input × unit costs	100	75
Capital input × unit costs	200	300
Total labour and capital cost	300	375

In economic terms the decision as to which is the most efficient production process becomes complicated when we introduce factor costs into the calculation. It would now appear that Process X is the most economically efficient process because it produces a given output at lower cost than does process Y. Going back to our initial example we can see that the physical combinations of each factor of production differed between processes. If we then introduce differing factor unit costs it is likely that one process (in this case X) will be more economic because it uses relatively more of the cheaper factor input, which in this case is labour. It must also be said that the above is an oversimplification because it considers only a single process stage within the overall production process of a particular firm, and that in practice different firms will have a variety of variable and fixed inputs, because they are either of a different size or they are in a different type of business activity.

In the short run (see Key Concept 2.2) it is possible for a firm to vary labour input but not capital because to change machinery and equipment is by its nature a difficult and time-consuming process. If in the above example managers of process X have to use an extra 20 units more labour in order to produce its given output level, this process is now technically inefficient because it takes 170 units of capital and

Table 2.3 Total costs of processes X and Y

Process	£ X	£ Y
Labour	120	75
Capital	200	300
Total Costs	320	375

labour (50 + 120) to produce the same given output as process Y which is still using 150 units of labour and capital (75 + 75). However, in economic terms, taking into account the unit cost of labour and capital process X is still the more economic of the two by £55.

We have seen that with a given technology the decision about which production process to adopt is made more complicated when we introduce factor costs into the equation. For process Y it was the high unit costs of capital relative to labour coupled with the high physical input of capital relative to process X that were the cause of 'economic inefficiency'. In the long term it may well be possible for the firm to reduce capital input into process Y in order to become economic relative to process X.

So far we have made the assumption that the level of output from a production process remains fixed at a given level. However, over a period of time the output from a production process will vary and so the combinations of factors of production will also adjust to meet changes in the level of output. We could conceive of the following relationship between factor inputs (labour and capital) and output. That is as output from a production process doubles or halves so factor inputs have to double or halve.

In any production process the costs of production are split between those that can vary in the short run, namely variable costs and those that are fixed in the short run.

A firm may wish to increase the level of production output in the short run, but there are a number of constraints on this decision. Extra capacity will be needed which requires either additional plant or equipment. Increasing capacity in the short run would be difficult where capital equipment has to be produced and plant constructed.

In the short run capital is said to be fixed in relation to output. However, it may be possible for the firm to increase output by increasing the labour intensiveness of the production system and increasing out-sourcing from firms that can supply on relatively short notice those components that the firm requires. Paying more in wages and salaries through taking on more employees or by paying more for overtime working would increase variable labour costs. Similarly, an increase in the use of subcontractors would also increase the level of variable bought-in materials and purchases of the organization. Both these actions may be possible in the short run and both would require an increase in variable costs.

KEY CONCEPT 2.2
The concept of the long and short run

Fixed Costs   = Land and capital costs
Variable Costs = Materials and labour

In the long run it will be possible for the firm to add more capital in the form of plant and equipment and land for the construction of new facilities, so that in the long run capital and land are variable factor inputs or costs.

KEY CONCEPT 2.3
Capital and labour productivity

Different firms may be able to obtain productivity levels that are at variance to those of similar competitors using similar technologies. Productivity is a concept that is used to demonstrate statistically how output behaves relative to factor inputs, notably labour and capital.

Productivity differentials arise either because firms are able to improve market share relative to their competitors, who, at the same time utilize similar levels of capital and labour input, or where the firm relative to competitors uses less labour and capital input to produce a similar output level.

In practice we can use a number of ratios to calculate the productivity of labour and capital.

Labour productivity
Labour input can be measured simply in terms of the number of employees at a given process or firm level. Output can be measured in terms of a physical or financial value (usually net output/value added or gross output)

(i)   Output per person employed   Total output/Total number of employees
(ii) Output per person hour   Total output/total hours worked

Capital productivity
Capital inputs are normally measured in terms of gross capital stock, as represented in the annual accounts of the business (i.e. fixed assets, plant and equipment, fixtures tooling etc. less disposals of assets but excluding depreciation).

Capital productivity is usually taken to mean Net Output/Capital stock, where net output is defined as *either*:

(1)   Sales
       − Bought in materials and services
                    or
(2)   Labour costs (wages and salaries etc.)
       + Depreciation
       + Tax and dividends
       + Retained profit.

Sometimes, however, Gross Output/Capital stock is used as the measure of capital productivity, where Gross Output is

        Sales
+/− Stock adjustments made during the year.

Total factor productivity
This measures the total contribution to productivity made by all the factors of production and is essentially an average productivity measure.

$$\text{Total factor productivity} = \frac{\text{Total output}}{\text{Inputs of all factors of production}}$$

Although productivity ratios can be a static ratio it makes much more sense to use productivity ratios in either a relative or dynamic framework. That is comparing one firm with another in similar activities or analysing changes in the firm's productivity performance over a number of years.

Table 2.4 Relationship of inputs to outputs

Output	50 units	100 units	200 units
Factor inputs			
Labour	5 units	10 units	20 units
Capital	20 units	40 units	80 units

Over the output range 50 to 200 units the productivity of labour (output/labour) and the productivity of capital (output/capital) remain constant at ten units of output per unit of labour and 2.5 units of output per unit of capital. That is, in the above example, as output increases or decreases capital and labour inputs adjust so as to maintain a constant pari passu relationship with output, i.e. 'constant returns to scale'. It is also possible to conceive of an example where output from a particular production process increases at a faster rate than the increase in factor inputs, i.e. 'increasing returns to scale'.

Table 2.5 Effect of increasing return to scale

Output	50 units	100 units	200 units
Factor inputs			
Labour	5 units	8 units	12 units
Capital	20 units	30 units	35 units
Output per unit of labour	10 units	12.5 units	16.6 units
Output per unit of capital	2.5 units	3.3 units	5.7 units

In theory increasing returns to scale are often used to represent a situation in which it is possible to increase output to a greater extent than the required increase in labour and capital input. Increasing returns to scale are often associated with methods of 'mass production' such as those applied in the steel industry or motor vehicles industry.

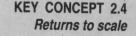

KEY CONCEPT 2.4
Returns to scale

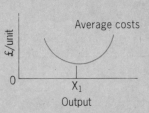

Figure 2.1 The average total cost curve.

In the short run we show the average total cost curve to have a 'U' shape. In order to produce a particular level of output the firm needs to invest in both capital and labour resources. Over the output range OX_1 the firm will be able to reduce average costs of production because increasing returns to scale are said to be obtained. That is, as output expands average fixed costs fall. In addition, labour inputs expand but at a slower rate than output. A doubling of output is met with a less than twofold increase in the use of labour inputs.

Around the point X_1 we could conceive that constant returns are achieved when output increases are just matched with the same proportionate increase in labour inputs. Beyond this point output increases are met with an even greater proportionate increase in the use of labour, possibly because the firm has reached the capacity limits of the capital investment made and therefore needs to increase the payments to labour.

We can use the case of steel production in blast furnaces to illustrate the concept of increasing returns to scale. It is argued that the level of investment required to build a blast furnace is related to the surface area of the furnace. However, where you then decide to double the surface area (that is the capital input), the volume of the furnace (or output) will increase by a factor of three. This relation is founded on the engineering rule which relates the surface area of a cylinder to the volume of that cylinder. We can illustrate this with a simple example in which the capital input doubles but output increases threefold.

Table 2.6 Economies of scale in steelmaking

	Capital input	Output
Small blast furnace	100	100
Large blast furnace	200	300

In the above example, if the market expands sufficiently, it would be rational for a firm to construct a larger blast furnace because in physical capital input-output terms, the larger furnace would be more efficient. That is output obtained per unit of capital input would increase from 1 unit to 1.5 units (100/100 and 300/200).

So far we have considered that with a given technology, decisions concerning the combinations of factor inputs to produce a particular level of output is complicated by the relative cost of each unit of capital and labour used in the production process. In addition, in the short run it is assumed in economic literature that we cannot easily change capital input in the production process (in the short run it is regarded as a fixed factor).

New technology and capital investment

It is clear that organizations exist and function in an environment which is subject to continuous technical change, and in such an environment it is open to a firm to plan and adjust its production processes as certain techniques become obsolete. In the early 1970s the British Steel Corporation wished to change from the old open hearth technology to the basic oxygen system (BOS) of steel production. The new technology of injecting oxygen into the furnace made it possible to increase the speed at which iron could be converted to steel. In the open hearth furnace it would take several hours to convert a tonne of iron to steel but in the new basic oxygen furnace this conversion time was cut down to 30 to 40 minutes. The introduction of the new BOS furnace would allow steelmakers to increase dramatically output from a furnace of similar volume to that of the open hearth system, because it would convert iron to steel at a faster rate. The introduction of this new technology would allow the steel industry to increase the amount of steel produced per unit of labour and capital.

Economies of scale refers to those factors which allow the organization to produce a large volume of output at lower average cost relative to the production of a small volume of output. Where the costs of labour and capital resources are constant a tenfold increase in output would lead to a less than tenfold increase in factor input.

KEY CONCEPT 2.5
Economies of scale

Qty.	Labour costs £	Capital costs £	Unit costs £
10	10	20	3
100	50	100	1.50

At particular points in time (the economist would call this the long run) it is open to a firm to change the technology or production process techniques being used and take on board any changes that have taken place in production process technology. At this stage it is open to a firm to evaluate the future benefits that will arise from a change in technology either at a process stage level or at an overall plant or strategic level. In both cases, of course, it is crucial that the cost/benefit calculations of a particular investment in new technology reflect realistic expectations about future costs and revenues.

If, for example, a firm incorrectly estimates the benefits to be gained from the introduction of a new process stage, this may not seriously damage profitability. However, where the investment in new technology is of strategic importance and requires a substantial commitment of resources, it is essential that the business can obtain the fullest benefits from the investment. Failure at a strategic level may well compromise the financial future of the organization and lead to a fundamental misallocation of resources.

One of the more interesting economic calculations made by many managers and academics to support the rationality of large-scale strategic investment in new technology is that related to 'economies of scale'. In economic texts the theory of economies of scale expresses a relation between output over a given period and unit total costs of producing that output. That is, where output expands it is expected that unit costs of production tend to fall. In the next section we will examine the assumptions that are used to support this economic relation between output and unit costs and introduce a case study that illustrates some of the problems that can practically operate to frustrate obtaining any benefits from investments in economies of scale.

Economies of scale

In the long run it is open to the firm to plan the introduction of new technology which either replaces old process technology within existing facilities or establishes the need for an entirely new 'greenfield site'. The extent and level to which such new investments will be carried out very much depends on the capacity levels the firm requires to meet expected market demand.

At this stage let us assume that there are three plant sizes available to the firm (small, medium, large) and that these plants have the following output and cost profiles.

Table 2.7 Economies of scale with increasing capacity

Output p.a.	1			2	3
	Labour input	Wage rate p.a. £	Total labour cost £m	Capital cost £m	Average total cost per unit £
Small plant					
1000 units	100	10 000	1.0	5.0	6000
Medium plant					
10 000 units	500	10 000	5.0	25.0	3000
Large plant					
100 000 units	1000	10 000	10.00	150.0	1600

From this table it is apparent that as we increase the size of the plant capacity from 1000 units to 100 000 units, we see that the average total cost per unit of production falls from £6000 to £1600. This average total unit cost of production is found by adding the total capital and labour costs together and dividing through by output from each plant. Why does the total average unit cost of production fall when output increases? The answer lies with the relationship between output and labour and capital factor inputs.

$$\text{Total costs} = \text{Fixed (Capital)} + \text{Variable (Labour)}$$

$$\text{Average total costs} = \frac{\text{Fixed} + \text{Variable costs}}{\text{Quantity}}$$

From the small to medium plant output increases by a factor of ten, while the total of labour and capital only increases by a factor of five in each case. That is, as output increases it is not necessary to increase the level of labour used to the same extent, because at higher levels of output the possibilities for the introduction of increased automation reduce the need for labour. With capital investment the same conditions operate in that capital investment need not double in order to double output (see the previous example on the blast furnace).

The relationship between average total unit costs of production and increases in output can be represented in the diagram shown below in Figure 2.2. In this diagram we illustrate how average total unit costs are expected to fall as output increases from a small to a large plant.

If we now assume that we have constructed the medium-sized plant with an average total unit cost of £3000 we are now, in the short run, stuck with this plant size. If output from the medium plant falls below

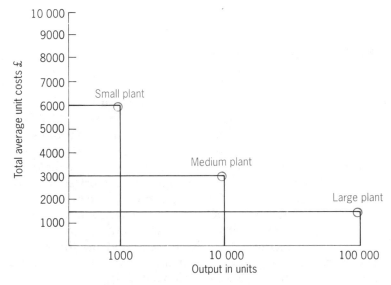

Figure 2.2 The relationship between costs and output.

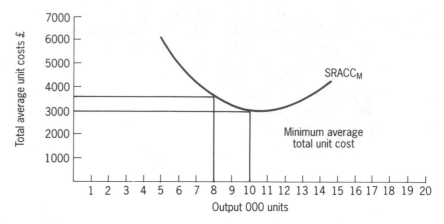

Figure 2.3 The short-run average cost curve.

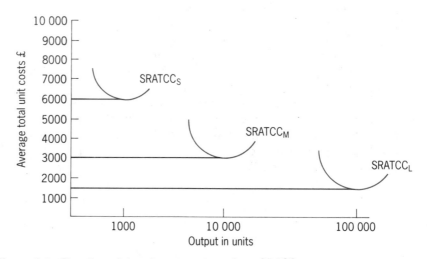

Figure 2.4 The effect of changing returns to scale on SRACCs.

10 000 units to say 8000 units then we move up and to the left on what is termed the Short-run average cost curve (in Figure 2.3 SRACCm) to where average total unit cost is £3750 (£30 million/8000 units). If we produce more than 10 000 units we are operating above the most efficient capacity of this plant (i.e. minimum point on the SRACC). We may well have to pay overtime or sub-contract out work so that average total unit costs start to increase for every extra unit we produce. It is for these reasons we show the SRACC to be 'U' shaped around the point of minimum average total unit cost for each plant.

In the diagram in Figure 2.4 we have illustrated the three short-run average cost curves, the shapes of which are determined by increasing and decreasing returns to scale (Key Concept 2.4).

However, in order to construct a long-run average cost curve

(LRACC)/planning curve/economies of scale curve we have to make a number of very abstract assumptions, for example that over a given output range, there are, at the planning stage, an infinite number of plant sizes open to a firm. The long-run average cost curve is therefore a locus of points which describes the lowest cost of production when all factors of production vary. This is in contrast to the short-run average cost curve which illustrates the lowest cost of producing a range of output when one or more factors of production is fixed (capital and land for example). The long-run average total cost curve is assumed to be a continuous curve, as shown in the diagram below (Figure 2.5) and it is constructed by connecting the set of short-run average cost curves tangentially. We can see at the point * that both the

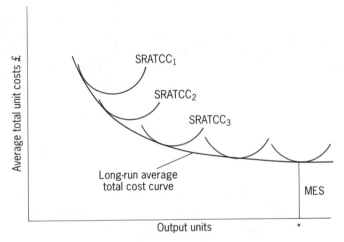

Figure 2.5 Long-run average total cost curve or economies of scale curve.

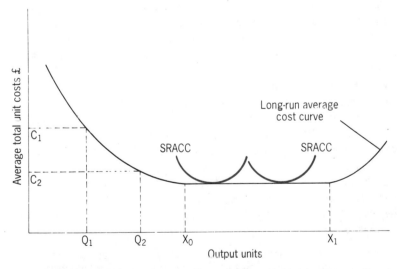

Figure 2.6 Long-run average cost curve illustrating constant total average unit cost range.

SRACC minimum point and the LRACC are tangential; we call this point the minimum efficient scale (MES).

Generally the LRACC is shown to have the following characteristic shape. That is as output and plant size expand so average total unit costs fall up to a point at which unit average total costs reach a minimum termed the point of minimum efficient scale (MES). Beyond this point the curve is shown to have a flat portion illustrating that over certain ranges of output long-run average unit costs remain constant (X_0 to X_1) and are equivalent to the SRACC minimum average unit cost. Long-run average costs are shown to turn up eventually where the sheer scale of operations becomes too complex and unmanageable.

For a firm wishing to plan for an expansion in the level of output with a new technology or given technology, the above economies of scale curve presents the decision-maker or planner with a powerful argument for increasing the scale of operations. That is, mass production from large-scale facilities will present your firm with a long-run average unit cost advantage if you expand output to say Q2 in Figure 2.6 when your competitors produce at Q1 or below. It is this calculation of cost advantage through economies of scale which played a very important role in the British Steel Corporation's plans to expand production capacity from its basic oxygen steel-making facilities in the 1970s as you can see from the case study of British Steel.

CASE STUDY 2.1
Economies of scale and the case of British steel

In the late 1960s the management of British Steel visited Japanese steel producers who had by this time invested successfully in large 'giant' integrated steel-making systems with production capacities in excess of 10 million tonnes. At this time such plants were three to four times larger than those constructed in the UK.

After nationalization in 1967 the industry had access to the sort of funds necessary to bring the UK steel industry up to the standard of the Japanese systems. In 1972 the British Steel Corporation (BSC) had completed its corporate plan. This projected an increase in the level of production and demand for steel from 25 million tonnes to 36 million tonnes by 1983. This investment strategy involved the commitment of £3000 million over a ten-year period at the rate of £300 million per annum. In addition, and crucially, the BSC's corporate plan involved the development and construction of new large integrated steel facilities. The BSC's plan then involved the construction of new large-scale integrated steel facilities in order to obtain the benefits of economies of scale. Port Talbot in Wales would eventually have an ultimate capacity of 6 million tonnes while a new 'greenfield site' at Teesside would have an ultimate capacity of over 11 million tonnes.

The management of BSC were convinced that economies of scale were available to those who were prepared to take the risk of investing in large-scale facilities and that the subsequent benefits, in terms of lower average unit costs of production, were too lucrative to resist.

> Japan is the most efficient producer in the world. There should be no doubt in anyone's mind that their large-scale plant, operating to a standard which we hope to achieve, is the most economic way of producing steel in bulk and at lowest cost (*Accounting for British Steel* p. 92).

At the time management were also supported by academic economists such as A. Cockerill (1974), whose evidence on reductions in unit average costs suggested that the construction of steel facilities up to 10 million tonnes capacity would reveal lower average unit costs. His evidence on unit steel production costs is reproduced in the table and graph below.

Further reading
Bryer, R. and Brignall, T. (1982).
Williams, K. *et al.* (1986).

Table 2.8 Index of unit average costs of production in steel plant

Plant size 000 tonnes	250	1000	2000	5000	10 000
Index of unit:					
Material cost	100	84	81	80	79
Operating costs	100	67	61	60	60
Capital charges	100	68	52	41	40
Total average costs	100	80	75	73	72

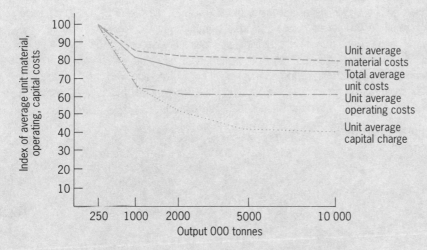

Figure 2.7 Total average cost index for steel manufacture at the British Steel Corporation.

So far the discussion has been related to the 'static' framework of costs and output under the long-run average cost curve. However, implicit in the model and framework of the long-run average cost curve is a dynamic relation between costs and output. It is the case that technical economies of scale are traditionally assumed to result from the introduction of highly specialized production processes, and the classic example of such a mass production system has been the Ford Model T. Nowadays, the development costs of a new car are very large

– between £1 billion and £1.5 billion, and new high fixed cost equipment is also required for its manufacture. All this investment requires a car manufacturer to obtain, over a period of time, long, large production runs to spread capital and operating costs over large volumes of output. If this cannot be achieved then the firm will face a large cost penalty per unit produced.

For a number of reasons the logic of economies of scale is problematic. Firstly we have implicitly assumed that as output expands from the process stage or plant we have installed this will, in the long run, lead to a reduction in unit average costs of production. At the now lower cost and price level, demand for the product will expand to either fill the facilities you have constructed or necessitate the construction of new facilities. However, the most alarming effect of massive 'lumpy' investment against an uncertain market is that in periods of slow market growth for the product being produced, the investment will be in overcapacity until and unless growth in the market operates to utilize fully process investment and plant constructed. A misreading of the nature of the market place can have serious consequences for those who hope to benefit from economies of scale.

KEY CONCEPT 2.6
Lumpy investments in new capacity

When firms invest in new technology they invest in new capacity (in the diagram Q_1 to Q_2) against a projected growth in market sales Gm. If growth continues at Gm then there will be excess capacity constructed (the area of triangle ABC) until time period T_2 when the investment is fully utilized. If output growth is below Gm at Go then the time period over which underutilization takes place is extended, to T_3, whilst a faster than expected growth rate will result in full utilization of the investment at a much earlier time period than expected. Investments are lumpy and when made against an uncertain market growth rate can result in extended periods of underutilization when market demand fails to materialize in the levels expected.

Further reading
Scherer, F.M. (1975).

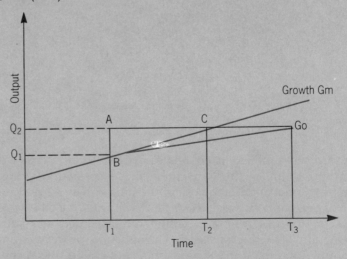

Figure 2.8 Underutilization periods.

Overoptimism and other judgemental errors that frequently may escape serious penalty in times of prosperity may turn out to be catastrophically costly in a period of economic stagnation.

Ohmae, 1982

It is clearly very important to consider the nature and composition of the market place before launching an investment project, and more particularly an investment strategy which commits large amounts of the firm's resources. In the case of British Steel, McKinsey Management Consultants were drafted in to assess the BSC's future market sales potential. They concluded that the firm would need to be producing at most 23 million tonnes of steel by 1983. It was against this background of market uncertainty that the BSC went ahead with a major strategic investment programme.

Secondly, as we have seen, the investment in larger facilities is designed to move the firm down the long-run average cost curve. This as we have seen is typically shown as a smooth curve, in which adjustments down the curve to new ever-larger plant are shown as being unproblematic. However, 'unless the slate is wiped clean and production begins anew on a greenfield site, the enterprise must operate a collection of old and new plants and processes' (Williams *et al.*, 1986).

The general presupposition underlying the traditional economic theory of production costs is that volume growth in the market will automatically deliver unit cost reduction. We have seen, both in this chapter and the previous chapter, that growth in product markets can rarely be sustained at a constant rate over time. In the case of British Steel, a misplaced conviction that demand would continue to grow at its previous rate clearly contributed to its failure to capture economies of scale. Even when global demand for a product is expanding, it can be dangerous to assume that output for particular nationally based firms will increase. In the case of motor vehicles, Table 2.9 shows that

Table 2.9 World production of motor vehicles and production in the USA, Japan and UK

Year	US output (units)	Japanese output (units)	UK output (units)	World output (units)
1950	8 005 859	31 597	783 672	10 529 565
1955	9 204 049	68 932	1 237 068	13 221 695
1960	7 901 502	481 551	1 810 700	16 382 932
1965	11 118 020	1 875 614	2 177 261	24 567 935
1970	8 266 718	5 289 157	2 098 498	29 707 707
1975	8 991 091	6 941 591	1 648 399	33 322 385
1980	8 010 374	11 042 884	1 312 914	38 837 519
1985	11 671 475	12 271 083	1 313 946	44 690 081
1990	9 780 211	13 486 796	1 565 957	46 814 060
1991	8 805 522	13 245 432	1 454 041	44 515 523

Source: Society of Motor Manufacturers and Traders.

although world production increased from 10.5 million units in 1950 to 43.9 million units in 1990, some countries' producers fared better than others. US producers, for example, have maintained volume production slightly above their 1950 levels, while UK producers have been losing volume since the 1960s. Japanese producers, in contrast, dramatically increased their production volumes up to 1990.

Productive reorganization for cost reduction and cost recovery

Even if product markets are growing rapidly and a firm is increasing its volume production, it may still not be able to capture the full positive impact of this volume growth on cost reduction and cost recovery. These twin objectives require that the firm pay careful attention to the internal (re)organization of its resources, so that there is a close inter-relationship between productive organization and the product or service market.

To explore how the resources of the firm can be applied to both reduce internal costs of manufacture and at the same time contribute to cost recovery, we will consider three factors: the design and development of new and existing products, the conditions which promote flow of process and fabricated manufactured goods, and finally the contribution of improved quality control.

Design and development

Many economic and managerial texts pay little attention to the design and development stage of a product's life cycle. This is surprising, given that organizations commit large amounts of labour time and capital equipment to the improvement of existing product ranges or the creation of entirely new products.

The opportunity for cost reduction at the design and development stage comes from a number of sources, starting with the design and development process itself, which is often extremely expensive. In the car industry, for example, it is estimated that the design and development of a new model can cost between £1 billion and £1.5 billion. It is therefore important to reduce any waste in the lead time between the design concept and full manufacture, to achieve a quicker recovery of design and development costs.

It is possible for the design and development process to be organized in such a way that each department or function separately undertakes input into the design and development process, and that each phase of the development cycle starts only after the previous phase has been completed. This is time-consuming, however, and design teams can be set up in such a way that work on different phases is carried out concurrently (see Key Concept 2.7).

Linear process
Here the stages of the design and development process are completed as discrete operations before the next stage of the product's development starts.

KEY CONCEPT 2.7
Linear and simultaneous design processes

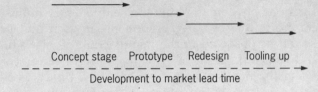

Concept stage   Prototype   Redesign   Tooling up

Development to market lead time

Simultaneous process
Here the stages of the design and development cycle of the product overlap. Where multi-function teams are put together on a development project it is possible to start the next stage before the previous stage has been fully completed.

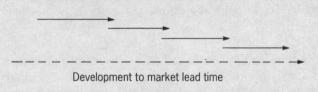

Development to market lead time

According to Marco Iansiti, system-focussed companies form a core multi-function team of scientists, managers and engineers at an early stage in the design and development process. The result is that 'System-focussed companies achieve the best product improvements in the shortest time and at the lowest costs' (Iansiti, 1993). Although the simultaneous approach can shorten design and development lead times, it requires the application of more initial costs in a shorter period of time. As we shall see in Chapter 4, this may not be possible when the existing portfolio of products does not generate sufficient value added to recover its costs.

It is often the case that most of a product's cost is determined by its design. This means that if your firm wants to take cost out of its products, the main opportunity to do this is at the design and development stage. 'According to General Motors executives 70 per cent of the cost of manufacturing truck transmissions is determined at the design stage. A study at Rolls-Royce reveals that design determines 80 per cent of the final production costs of 2000 components' (Whitney, 1989). The importance of design and its contribution to cutting manufacturing costs is particularly recognized in Japan. According to executives at Sony electrical, some 80 per cent of *kaizen* (cost improvement) takes place in the design and development stage (company interview, 1990).

The design and development process can contribute towards taking the cost out of a product in three main ways. First, changes can be made to the type of materials used in the fabrication of a product. This is determined by the extent to which the weight of the product is reduced without compromising the tolerances and stresses the product will have to withstand. Reducing the weight of a product will result in lower material costs per unit of output. In addition it may be possible to substitute a cheaper material for a more expensive one – plastic instead of metal, for example.

Second, it may be possible to refine the componentry in the product, so that there are fewer separate components in each unit produced. This process can be observed in the manufacture of televisions, video recorders and camcorders, all of which now have fewer component parts. Reducing the number of components in a product results in a double saving – cutting both in-house manufacturing costs and the value of components purchased from outside suppliers. Fumio Kodama notes that:

> Carbon fibre is the main material used in 20 per cent of the structural components in the Airbus A320 model. Not only does the material have significantly greater strength than comparable alloys but it can also be manufactured in one piece, eliminating the need for complex and costly assembly. For instance the number of parts in Airbus's tail wing has dropped from 600 to 335.
>
> *Kodama, 1992*

Third, where a new design reduces the number of components, fewer process stages are required, and less labour and machinery is required to produce the article. The design and development process can also reduce production costs by designing out labour and equipment costs. At Digital, for example, K. Nicols illustrates the financial savings available by improved manufacturability:

> Integrating product and manufacturing process design decisions at an early stage of the development cycle is now common practice within the company. Many benefits have resulted through lower part counts, simpler product bill of materials with lower levels, shorter assembly times, simpler production control, less inventory, and less operations and materials costs.
>
> *Nicols, 1992*

The following results were achieved from design for manufacturability for a computer mouse:

Part count reduction (%)	50
Assembly time reduction (%)	65
Reduced assembly operations (%)	33
Part cost savings (%)	40

Finally, design and development can improve flow conditions by influencing process sequence, and by reducing defect rates.

Improved flow

In any manufacturing activity, materials flow through the organization, but at various points in the production process labour costs and depreciation charges stick to the product. Many service activities are similar – in banking, for example, financial information flows through the business, and at various points labour time is used to input or remove the information to complete different transaction cycles. Interruptions to flow, in any business, are a significant source of increased cost.

Improvements in flow are difficult to manage, because they require constant attention to detail. Some of the problems of achieving balanced flow in a process-based industry are illustrated by returning to the case of British Steel.

Firms rarely have production processes that are characterized as having a single product or single process stage. In practice firms operate a collection of processes and produce a range of different products. As a result balancing these systems requires the firm to pay attention to process cycle times, and the complex scheduling of production flows. Firms use complex statistical tools as a means for sequencing and optimizing production flows so that the best use of capacity can be made.

Failure to carry out these calculations can result in bottlenecks where the best equipment is run at the rate of the slowest because imbalances between and across process stages are not corrected for.

KEY CONCEPT 2.8
Plant and process optimization

Investments in new steel-making technology had to be set against older technology such as ironmaking which provided the raw material for the steel furnaces, and the finishing facilities, which roll and shape the finished steel. It is clear that in any overall production process technological change is, more often than not, uneven in its effects and it is necessary to 'match' the output of the new production stage with the old production stage. It is of no use investing in new technology which cannot be fully used because the previous stage was not of a sufficient capacity to balance up the process throughput. In this case the most efficient stage of the production process is constrained by the least efficient stage.

We could, for example, envisage a production process with three stages using different technologies.

Table 2.10 Three-stage production process

	Stage 1	Stage 2	Stage 3
Minimum efficient scale (units)	2000 →	10000 →	5000 → Finished output

At each stage we have different minimum efficient scales (points at which the most efficient or lowest level of unit costs is reached). In the example below the production process balanced would simply consist of five machines at stage one, one at stage two and two at stage three.

$$(5) - - - - - - - - - - (1) - - - - - - - - - (2)$$

Some reserve capacity is assumed to exist at each stage in case of breakdown or demand variation. However, if we assume that a new machine is introduced at stage two which can produce 15 000 units with a minimum efficient scale which significantly reduces unit costs at this stage, we would also need to increase the number of machines at stage one and three if there has been no corresponding improvement in the technology at these other stages. It may well be that there are space constraints which prevent you from putting an extra two or three machines at stage one. Whatever else, the decision to invest in new technology has had 'network' effects throughout the production process, and these other constraints need to be considered.

At the BSC this problem emerged at Scunthorpe where the basic oxygen steel facilities could produce more steel than could be processed by the finishing plant. (R. Pryke, 1981, p. 186.)

Investment in new technology cannot be considered in isolation from the market place or in isolation from other parts of the production process. Investment, if it is to be strategically beneficial, must be incorporated into existing vintages of technology in a balanced and not disruptive way. If a new investment results in imbalance and bottlenecks in the process, this may well cancel out any cost advantages revealed by the introduction of new technology at a particular stage of the process. It may be necessary to increase buffer stocks in order to compensate for imbalances introduced across process stages. Equipment may have to be run at or above its designed capacity to balance up the system with increased problems of breakdown and increased unproductive time. The firm will be constrained by the lowest capacity of the production system.

British Steel's failure to improve flow conditions operating in the firm

---

CASE STUDY 2.2
Ford at Highland Park 1909–16

From 1909 to 1916 Henry Ford produced the Model T at the Highland Park plant in Detroit. As the table below shows, during this period Ford managed to reduce the price of the Model T from 850 dollars to 360 dollars.

Price, costs and labour hours for the Model T

Year	Price per unit ($)	Payroll costs per unit ($)	Material costs per unit ($)	Cars shipped	Labour hours per unit
1909	850	64	590	13 941	357
1910	950	100	544	20 739	400
1911	780	65	348	53 800	222
1912	690	65	407	82 500	250
1913	600	61	319	199 100	216
1914	550	65	371	240 700	127
1915	440	64	255	368 599	123
1916	360	70	262	585 400	134

The conventional explanation of this heroic price and cost reduction is based on the traditional economies of scale theory. Ford, it is suggested, produced a standard product on dedicated equipment using de-skilled workers to obtain the benefits of economies of scale.

There is no doubt that Ford's achievement was volume-driven, but the actual implementation of cost reduction has, within this scenario, always been obscure. How, in practice, did Ford reduce the cost of manufacturing the Model T between 1909 and 1916? Three issues are particularly significant: product design, flow manufacture, and the recomposition of labour tasks.

Product design

The Model T was not, as is often claimed, a totally standardized product. During its life electric lamps replaced gas, electric start replaced manual, and inflated tyres replaced solid rubber. There was a consistent effort to search for design improvements that would combine robustness with light weight, a consideration which was to be of crucial importance when the weight of 500 000 Model Ts would have to be moved around the factory by 1916.

Flow manufacture

More importantly, the Ford operations at Highland Park were struggling to satisfy huge increases in market demand for the car, and throughout the period 1909 to 1916, Ford and his engineers continually sought to improve plant layout in order to improve the flow and throughput capabilities. Machines were laid out in order of use, but layout was subject to continuous adjustment and change. The engine block at first travelled 4000 feet, but by 1914 it was travelling just 334 feet. Machines were secured to wooden floors so that they could easily be uprooted to change layout. Improved flow enabled Ford to make more of the car in-house, saving materials costs, at no extra labour cost per unit. Whereas in 1909 Ford bought in 70% of materials from outside suppliers, this proportion was down to 50% by 1916.

Recomposition of labour

The effect of changing the layout meant that labour tasks had to be completely reviewed all of the time. When machines were placed closer together, it was possible to introduce simple materials transfer devices rather than use indirect labour to do the task. The net result was a reduction in labour hours per unit produced, from 356 to 134. The effect on production costs was limited, because hourly wages rose as hours were taken out – labour costs per unit remained at 65–70 dollars per unit throughout the period.

Further reading

Williams *et al.* (1992, 1993);
Ohno (1988).

resulted in a restriction of output, and as a result higher costs per tonne of steel manufactured. In contrast, the experience of the Ford Model T illustrates the cost reduction possibilities that become available to a firm if it can effectively improve flow. As Case Study 2.2 shows, Ford's management of the Highland Park plant during the period 1909 to 1916 achieved substantial flow improvements, which contributed significantly to cost reduction.

Improvements in flow were an important means by which Ford was able to take costs out of the Model T. Cost reductions were passed on to the consumer in lower prices, creating a win-win situation in the US car market of this time. Falling prices, coupled with improved non-price durability characteristics, made the Model T the best selling car in the US during this period. As the market expanded, this created the pressure to improve flow conditions in the factory so that Ford could produce the Model T both more cheaply and in greater volume. This illustrates a general point that, although improved flow creates opportunities for cost reduction and volume increases, these opportunities can only be realized in an expanding market – material forced to flow against adverse market conditions will result in poor cost recovery.

Cost reduction at Ford Highland Park was, as we have seen, achieved principally by bringing work in a straight line past workers standing at work stations where labour time is spent adding cost to the product. An alternative method of enhancing flow conditions is to move labour with the materials/components, along a U-shaped line. The differences between the two conditions of flow are shown in Key Concept 2.9. This illustrates how the reorganization of both layout and work tasks can affect unit labour costs.

KEY CONCEPT 2.9
Conditions of flow

The concept of linear flow can be represented in the diagram below in which materials flow past the worker standing at the machine. When Ford brought the machines closer together, the gaps between machines could be connected with a slide or roller which sent the component from one machine to the next. The effect was to reduce the indirect labour employed in handling the material from one machine to the next.

Linear materials flow

Time elapsed to finish: 3 minutes

```
 - - - - - - - - - - - - - - - - - - - - ->
     *       *       *       *       *
    /*\     /*\     /*\     / \     /*\
   / \     / \     / \     / \     / \
    1       2       3       4       5
```

In the above case, five workers are producing and completing one unit every three minutes using machines 1 to 5.

U-shaped materials and labour flow

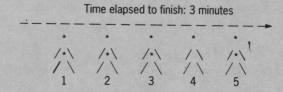

In the above case the worker starts by setting machine 1 to go and walks to machine 2 setting that off to go until reaching the last machine, taking off the completed unit and setting this machine to go. At the end of the six minutes one employee has completed the walking cycle and completed one unit and will start the cycle again at machine 1 which is ready to re-load and start again. In output per employee terms the first case would produce 20 units per hour with five employees, that is four units per employee. The second approach produces only ten units per hour with one employee, or ten units per employee, which is 2.5 times greater than the linear flow case.

Further reading
Monden (1994).

Table 2.11 Work-in-progress to value added ratios for major car companies

Company	Work-in-progress to value added ratio, 1991
Nissan	13.90
Toyota	24.14
Honda	46.50
Mazda	10.02
BMW	15.15
Volkswagen Audi	12.03
Ford UK	13.93
Peugeot	17.50

Note: Work-in-progress = that part of a company's stock levels which is within the production process (rather than bought-in items or finished products).
Value added = labour costs plus profit pre-tax plus depreciation charges (see Key Concept 1.6).

As we shall see in Chapter 4, it is possible to make approximate flow performance comparisons between companies in a similar line of business, using information from their annual report and accounts. In Table 2.11 we outline the work-in-progress to value added ratios for some of the major car companies.

One would expect a high flow factory to achieve a high value added in relation to work-in-progress, so dividing value added in a year by the average level of work-in-progress gives a reasonable proxy for rate of flow. The figures presented in Table 2.11 do not suggest that Japanese firms are uniformly superior to their European counterparts. Honda leads Toyota at the head of the table, but most of the rest have performance close to the average, with Mazda and Nissan under-performing some of their European competitors.

Quality control

In the 1940s, the US government and certain American companies such as Western Electric and General Dynamics developed a statistical quality control (SQC) system. SQC was based on taking samples from individual process stages, and testing the items produced to check the dimensional closeness of fit to a given length or diameter, and effectiveness of components in performing their prescribed functions at different stages in the assembly process.

Under SQC, if the proportion of parts or sub-assemblies which do not function or do not meet the required dimension exceeds a set norm, then production is stopped until the reasons for the failure can be established and corrected. This type of statistical control system is based on a sampling system which is semi-continuous, because samples are drawn off either a set number of times per day or after a set number of units have been produced (see Figure 2.9).

The diagram below represents the methodology of the statistical quality control system. If the number of defects in a sample is greater than a set norm (say 5%), then this sample is unsatisfactory, and the process stage is stopped. If, on the other hand, testing establishes a defect rate of below 5%, this will fall within the acceptable tolerance.

Duran and Demming, the originators of SQC, saw two main benefits from its introduction: cost reduction, as fewer resources are wasted on defective components and products, and enhanced reputation with customers, as a result of improved product quality.

It has become fashionable recently to talk of total quality control systems, or total quality management (TQM), in which your objective is to continually improve the management of quality until you approach zero defect rates. Yashiro Monden (1994) explains the difference be-

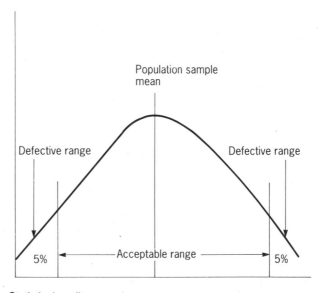

Figure 2.9 Statistical quality control.

tween the Toyota system of quality control and statistical quality control as follows:

> In SQC, the acceptable quality level which determines products that are passed but are of the minimum acceptable quality is fixed at 0.5 or 1.0 percent. Either level, however, is unsatisfactory from the point of view of the companies that aim for very high producer quality, for example one in a million. At Toyota, for example, the goal of quality control is to obtain one hundred per cent good units and a defect rate of zero.
>
> *Monden, 1994*

For Monden, there are only two circumstances when statistical quality control is appropriate. One is when you are operating a continuous process, such as a chemical works or press shop, where if you check the first and the last quantity/unit and these are satisfactory this indicates that there are no problems with any of the intervening units. The other is when it is safe to assume that your machines will deliver a correct unit every time. Apart from these instances, defects are bound to surface from time to time. In order to stop defective parts from passing through the production system, Monden suggests the following:

- Ensure that suppliers deliver components etc. in small batches, and ensure that each batch is of the required quality.
- Ensure that no defective unit passes from one stage in the production cycle to the next stage. This is achieved by undertaking an automatic or manual check at each stage.
- If one unit is found to be defective, then stop the machine and take immediate corrective action.

This particular system of quality control places increased stress into the system, because the avoidance of error and line stop is made a priority. As Monden explains (1994): 'When a defect occurs, the line stops, forcing immediate attention to the problem and investigation into its causes, and initiation of corrective action to prevent similar defects from occurring again.'

Improved yield rates (i.e. fewer defects) aid cost recovery by reducing labour time and machine costs at each stage of the production process. At each stage of the production cycle, conversion costs are applied to the product or service as it is being manufactured or executed. If, at the end of a number of stages, the product or service fails, then the firm has wasted costs because these are not recoverable from sales (see Key Concept 2.11).

KEY CONCEPT 2.11
Product conversion costs

We can depict the production process as a set of stages in which labour time (wages and salaries) and machine cost (depreciation) are added to raw materials and components as they are converted into the final product.

Process stage 1	1	2	3
Labour costs	$£ \rightarrow$	$+ £ \rightarrow$	$+ £$
Depreciation	$£ \rightarrow$	$+ £ \rightarrow$	$+ £$

As materials are passed from one process stage to another, labour and depreciation costs attach themselves on the basis of the labour and machine time spent on conversion. If a product passes through all three stages and is then found to be faulty, the labour and depreciation costs added at all three stages are wasted. Under these circumstances, the firm has added costs which cannot be recovered from sales, because the product is unsaleable. Costs will have to be recovered either through setting a higher price on those units that can be sold (adversely affecting demand) or through reworking faulty units (which increases costs still further).

Improved quality control systems also contribute to cost recovery by enhancing the reputation of the product with the consumer. Maintaining customer loyalty for the product is a particularly important objective when product markets are reaching maturity (see Chapter 1), and improved quality (at no extra cost) helps establish the conditions for replacement demand to be maintained.

The importance of labour costs

We have seen that each of the three cases we have considered – design and development, improvements to the flow conditions of the business, and improved quality control – contributes towards the reduction of cost and increased possibilities of cost recovery. In addition, all three cases illustrate the importance of reducing labour costs, as design and development cost is mostly labour time, improved flow is all about taking labour time out of manufacture, and quality control is predominantly about reducing the wasted labour time added to a defective product or service.

In most firms, labour costs represent the most important costs which must be controlled by management. To develop this analysis, we need to distinguish between total costs of manufacture and the value added concept of internally controllable costs.

Total costs of manufacture are defined as sales minus profits, and this measure of costs includes, in order of significance: purchases of materials and components, direct labour costs, indirect labour costs, and other overheads. An alternative definition of costs might distinguish between external costs and costs which are internally controllable. The value added calculation, as we saw in Chapter 1, is sales – purchases of materials and services. Value added represents the internal costs of conversion, and can be broken down into its constituent parts:

$$\text{Value added} = \text{Wages, salaries, pensions}$$
$$+ \text{ profit pre-tax and net interest charges}$$
$$+ \text{ depreciation.}$$

In UK firms, labour costs generally account for 65–70% of value added, with depreciation charges accounting for another 5%. The importance of labour costs cannot be avoided because they take by far the greatest share of the value added (conversion cost added) to a product or a service. Cost reduction from improved design and development, better organization of production, or improved quality control can only be significantly achieved by taking labour time out of the product or service.

We have said much in this chapter about the potential contribution of improved internal resource management to cost reduction, and we turn now to consider some of the factors which might limit cost reduction. These include product characteristics, physical characteristics, and the institutional framework.

Product characteristics

As we have seen, changing the design of a product can reduce the number of labour hours needed to manufacture it. However, the nature of each product requires that a minimum expenditure of labour hours goes into its construction. It takes, for example, a minimum expenditure of about 150 labour hours to build a car (Williams *et al.*, 1993); no matter how efficient your production process, you cannot take out any more labour time. Similarly, in television manufacture it is possible to design out labour time, but unless radical innovations can be made in electrical componentry, the rate at which this can be done in future will slow down considerably.

Physical characteristics

Within production operations, improvements to flow will eventually reach physical limits. Rearranging flow into U-shaped lines may make it possible to reduce labour time, but there are limits to what one worker can do in a given time when walking from one machine to another. In addition, improvements to flow which increase the potential for greater output must also confront the physical limits of the product market.

Institutional framework

The structure of industrial relations plays an important role in regulating the use of labour time. In Japan, for example, company-based trade unions play an important role in facilitating a process of work intensification. In Europe, however, management attempts to take labour time out are much more vulnerable to industrial dispute. Under these conditions, management may abandon the attempt to improve the organization of production, or negotiate a compromise. These issues are explored further in Chapter 6.

Relocation of production

Product characteristics, physical characteristics and institutional factors all establish limits to management capacities to effect reductions in labour time. When these limits are reached, management will look for alternative methods of cost reduction. In Europe, social settlements with the workforce have generally involved increased costs to the employer, from reductions in the working week and increases in hourly wages. As Case Study 2.3 shows, these differences in social settlement can be very marked.

CASE STUDY 2.3
Labour costs in motor vehicle manufacturing

As is shown in the table below, employers in Europe, Japan, and North America pay, on average, similar hourly labour costs, while these costs are much lower in South Korea. Hours worked, however, are longer in Korea, and lower in Europe, than in Japan or the USA.

Average working hours and employer wage cost per hour in motor vehicle manufacturing, 1991

Country	Hours worked average	Employer labour cost per hour ($)
Japan	2200	20.5
USA	2000	21.2
Europe (average)	1600	19.3
S. Korea (1989)	2400	6.5

Source: Verband der automobilindustrie, Frankfurt; International Labour Office.

Looking at employer costs per hour in dollars, it is clear that, on average, employers in Europe, Japan and the USA have roughly the same employment costs. The difference lies predominantly with the hours each worker works per year – on average, the level of hours worked in American and Japanese firms is 25 to 35% higher than European firms. The implication is that, if it takes 150 worked hours to make a typical car, each individual worker could make 14.7 cars per year in Japan, 13.3 in the USA, and 11 in Europe.

In contrast, Korean workers supply 2400 worked hours per year – 45% greater than the European average, and 10% higher than Japan. In addition, labour costs are only $6.50 – a third of the level in Japan, Europe and the USA.

Recently Japanese manufacturers have been relocating production to countries like Korea and Malaysia, to take advantage of lower employer wage costs and longer working hours. It is ironic that these were the reasons why it was cost effective to produce in Japan in an earlier period (in 1970, Japanese employers' hourly labour costs were only half those of the USA). Some European producers are also shifting component manufacture and assembly of cars into Eastern Europe, where again labour costs are much lower and working hours longer.

In many manufacturing industries, the tendency is for business to shift labour-intensive production towards those regions which have lower labour costs and poorer working conditions. Just as Malaysia and Korea are attractive to Japanese firms, so Mexico is to US firms, and

Eastern Europe to West European firms. In Mexico and Eastern Europe wages are one-tenth of those paid in Texas and in central Europe.

The recent creation of NAFTA (North American Free Trade Agreement) will open up trade relations, and at the same time expose the social settlements of Canada and the USA to competition from a developing country (Mexico) with a population of 85 million with a national income of just $3000 per head. Initially, US and Canadian firms which relocate production to Mexico will benefit from lower labour costs, but in the long run it may be a zero sum game, if rival firms are all chasing lower hourly labour costs. These issues are explored further in Chapter 8.

Conclusion

In this chapter we have considered the traditional economic theory of production costs and the relationship between unit costs of production and volume of output. While firms can in practice reduce unit costs of manufacture and expand output, the traditional approach does not explain the processes by which cost reduction and cost recovery are achieved.

We have explored the role of product design, improved flow, and quality control in creating opportunities for firms to simultaneously pursue the objectives of cost reduction and cost recovery. We have also, however, identified various limits to cost reduction and cost recovery, such as physical and institutional factors, which limit management's ability to continually reorganize labour tasks to make full use of the workers' time. When these limits have been met within the confines of a particular national economy, then, in the search for further cost reduction, managers may well look increasingly in the future to alternative low labour cost economies for the location of production.

Further reading

Chapter 5 of Andrew Dunnett's text *Understanding the Market* (Longman, 2nd edn, 1992) gives a good summary of the theory of economies of scale.

On the policies of cost reduction and cost recovery, see *Fait Accompli: Volvo and Renault*, by Karel Williams, Colin Haslam, and Sukhdev Johal (University of Manchester Labour Studies Paper No. 7, 1993).

On total quality control systems at Toyota, see *The Toyota Production System* by Y. Monden, especially Chapter 10, and on the contribution of R. & D. to cost reduction, see 'Real World R & D', by M. Iansiti (*Harvard Business Review*, May/June 1993).

Finally, for an extended consideration of Henry Ford's achievements at Highland Park, see 'Ford versus Fordism: the beginning of mass production', by Karel Williams, Colin Haslam, and John Williams (*Work, Employment and Society*, December 1992).

Exercises

1 A company, Excel plc, is suffering from a deterioration in profit margin on sales.

   What short-run and longer-term policies might you consider in order to reduce costs and improve profit margin on sales?

2 What do you understand by the term 'flow' with regards to labour and materials?

   How can flow improvements reduce manufacturing costs?

3 Distinguish between the terms 'statistical quality control' and 'total quality control'.

   What are the main benefits which flow from improvements in quality?

4 In what ways can techniques applied for 'cost reduction' also improve a firm's ability to 'recover' costs?

5 What do you understand by the term 'economies of scale'?

   Why did British Steel fail to obtain the full benefits promised by economies of scale?

References

Bryer, R. and Brignall, T. (1982) *Accounting for British Steel*, Gower, Aldershot.

Cockerill, A. *et al.* (1974) University of Cambridge Occasional Paper no. 42.

Iansiti, M. (1993) Real world R & D; jumping the product generation gap, *Harvard Business Review*, May/June.

Kodama, F. (1992) Technology fusion and the new R & D, *Harvard Business Review*, July/August.

Monden, Y. (1994) *The Toyota Production System*, 2nd edn, Chapman & Hall, London.

Nicols, K. (1992) Better, cheaper, faster products – by design, *Journal of Engineering Design*, vol. 3, no. 3.

Ohmae, K. (1982) *The Mind of the Strategist*, McGraw-Hill, New York.

Ohno, T. (1988) *The Toyota Production System*, Productivity Press, Cambridge, Mass.

Pryke, R. (1981) *The Nationalised Industries*, Martin Robertson, Oxford.

Scherer, F.M. (1975) *Economics of Multi-Plant Operation*, Harvard University Press.

Whitney, D. (1989) Manufacturing by design, *Harvard Business Review*, July/Aug.

Williams, K. *et al.* (1986) Accounting for the failure of nationalised industries. *Economy and Society*, May.

Williams, K., Haslam, C. and Williams, J. (1992) Ford versus Fordism: the beginning of mass production, *Work, Employment and Society*, Dec.

Williams, K., Haslam, C. and Williams, J. (1993) The myth of the line, *Business History Review*, June.

Williams, K., Haslam C., Williams, J. and Johal, S. (1994) Deconstructing car assembly productivity, *International Journal of Production Economics*, forthcoming.

Financial calculations and business enterprise

3

This chapter explains and assesses a number of different financial calculations which are made by business in relation to budgeting, stock control, allocation of overhead costs, break-even, and investment appraisal. A major theme is that many of these calculations have been designed to protect shareholder interests, and do not necessarily generate decisions which secure the long-term interests of the business. Attention is drawn to the contrast between the Western emphasis on cost maintenance and the Japanese emphasis on cost reduction.

Introduction

The main focus of this chapter is on the accounting rules which, more than any economic theory, determine both the analysis of costs within the firm and its pricing policies. The chapter explores the roles played by budgeting and costing in controlling the activities of the firm, and suggests that these procedures may often conflict with the needs of the business by emphasizing cost maintenance rather than cost reduction. Finally, the advantages and disadvantages of different accounting procedures for evaluating investment proposals are assessed.

The separation of ownership and control

In the traditional, neo-classical, economic theory of the firm, it is assumed that the single financial objective of the business is to maximize profits. As we saw in Chapter 1, this objective is achieved at an output level where marginal cost is equal to marginal revenue. The theory is based on a model of the firm in which a single owner of the business controls its day-to-day activities, operating with perfect knowledge of the firm's costs and markets, and perfect foresight as to how competitors might respond to its decisions.

KEY CONCEPT 3.1
Ownership and control

Neo-classical theory abstracts from the organizational complexity of large firms by implicitly assuming that all firms are run by entrepreneurs who combine the functions of owners and managers. Modern corporations (or public limited companies), however, are legal entities which raise capital by issuing shares to shareholders, whose liability for any debts the company may incur is limited to the extent of their shareholding. (For further detail on the limited liability principle, you are referred to our companion volume, *Law in a Business Context*.) While shareholders elect the Board of directors of the company they typically delegate operational control to professional managers who, although they may have substantial shareholdings, in no sense own the firms which employ them.

Many alternative, 'managerial', theories of the firm, such as those of Baumol (1959) and Marris (1964), focus their attention on divisions within the large firm between managers and shareholders, and on possible conflicts between the objectives of these groups. Many of these theories suggest, on the basis of Berle and Means's study of US corporations (1932), that shareholdings are dispersed among a large number of individuals, and that these individuals have little capacity to control how a corporation is run. Shareholders, these alternative theories suggest, have to delegate not just operational but strategic control to professional managers, who as a result have considerable discretion to pursue their own objectives. Shareholders' interests in maximizing receipts from dividends may lose out to managers' interests in boosting their salaries and ploughing profits back into the business to finance new investment without reference to the capital market.

Many writers feel that the Berle and Means model overstates the significance of the separation of ownership from control in the modern corporation (you are referred to our companion volume, *Business in Context*, for a fuller discussion). Two points from this debate are particularly significant for our purposes:

1 Most shares in large UK companies are owned not by individuals but by financial institutions such as insurance and pension funds, which may be more interested in long-term capital gains or in short-term trading profits than in dividend payments. These institutional shareholders have considerable capability to intervene in the corporation's strategic decision-making if their interests require it (Cosh and Hughes, 1987).
2 Corporate managers are constrained in their decision-making not just by the potential intervention of powerful institutional shareholders, but by the wider financial environment in which they operate (Thompson, 1986). As we shall see later on in the chapter, the financial accounting system, developed to safeguard the interests of shareholders, plays an important conditioning role, while, as we shall see in Chapter 7, the lending practices of banks, and the ways capital markets value company shares, also place significant constraints on management discretion.

The traditional concept of the entrepreneur as both owner and con-troller of the business abstracts from a number of legal and structural changes that have established, in practice, a separation of ownership and control in business operations generally. Under these changed conditions, control, on a day-to-day basis, is exercised by management on behalf of a dispersed set of shareholders (Key Concept 3.1).

With the advent of limited liability and the need by firms to obtain funds in excess of that provided by the owner of the firm or close family, many firms dispersed part shares of ownership of the firm's capital to shareholders. For example, firms such as ICI are owned by a dispersed set of shareholders who have a right to dividends distributed out of the profits of the organization and in most cases a right to vote at the Annual General Meeting.

Some shareholders can use their influence to alter the composition of the Board of Directors. However, once a system of management is established it is difficult to change in the short run because of the difficulty that small shareholders have in getting to the Annual General Meeting (AGM). Professional managers generally control the day-to-day operational activities of the business concerned.

In addition to the legal framework of limited liability, structural changes, in terms of the size and complexity of business organization under conditions of oligopoly rather than perfect competition, have ensured that a management role is required for the co-ordination of business operations. The organization and control of complex struc-tures would be beyond the capabilities of one individual.

Acknowledgement that there is in practice a separation of ownership and control encouraged the development of a number of alternative theories of the firm. All of these establish that there is no one overriding objective of profit maximization, but a possible range of financial objec-tives which could lead to less than maximum profits being earned. We look at some of these alternative theories briefly.

Managerial theories

Here it is argued that managers are in control of day-to-day activity of the firm and that managements do not have the same interest in or need for profit maximization that we associate with the single entre-preneur. Managements will have a certain level of discretion and freedom to alter the goals and objectives of the firm they are managing. Managers will wish, it is argued, to pursue those objectives which at least stabilize or improve their own position within the organization over a period of time in either financial or status terms.

W.J. Baumol (1959) argued that management would wish to establish the objective of maximum sales revenue, sacrificing some profit in order to maximize sales and so improve their pay or status within the organization. We can illustrate the implicit trade-off between revenue and profit in Figure 3.1. A profit maximizing owner would set output where the difference between total revenue and total costs is at a maximum (Pm). However management may well aim for a sales

Financial calculations

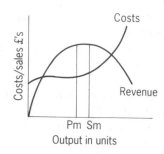

Figure 3.1   A comparison of a profit maximizing and a sales maximizing firm.

maximization position which also maintains sufficient profit for the distribution of dividends to the shareholder (Sm). In order to increase market sales some revenue and hence profit per unit may have to be lost because the price charged to sell extra output falls.

Baumol's theory is a static one which tends to replace one unitary objective (profit maximization) by another (sales maximization). Marris (1964), however, establishes management objectives as those of growth maximization subject to a minimum profit constraint. In this more dynamic model of the firm Marris argues that management seeks a balanced rate of growth in both the output and capital base of the firm. Balanced growth requires that management pays attention to a number of related financial variables which help to secure a long-run career position within the organization. The prime aim is to improve the rate at which the firm is growing over time, but at the same time generating sufficient profits to finance expansion as well as to keep shareholders happy.

Behavioural theories

Some economists (H. Simon, 1955; Cyert and March, 1963) have suggested that in an uncertain environment firms cannot establish the conditions that are necessary for achieving financial maxima but instead management will try to establish satisfactory levels of profitability, sales, dividends and capital growth from one year to the next.

In practice the financial results of the business are the result of the interaction of various interest groups or sub-groups within the organization. An example is where the firm produces financial plans or budgets that specify, in financial terms, the planned trajectory of the firm over the next year or years. These financial plans represent the interaction of a number of sub-groups within the organization such as production engineers, sales personnel, marketing management, accountants, etc., who will all contribute to the shaping of the financial plan and actual financial performance of the business.

Within an uncertain environment, the organization's calculations and decisions about future sales, profits and dividends etc. will be subject to the limits of information and resources available at any particular time. As a result, management cannot have universal and perfect financial rationality as implied by the marginalist rules of neo-classical economics. Rather management's understanding of the future financial position of the firm at certain levels of output is 'bounded' by the imperfect and often incomplete information available to it at particular moments in time (K. Williams *et al.*, 1983).

So far we have established that, in neo-classical economic theory, the unitary financial objective of profit maximization will not operate in practice because the conditions for its operation cannot be established. Fundamentally the separation of ownership (shareholders) from control (management) in large business operations establishes conditions in which complex financial objectives are both set and achieved. It is not possible to establish that all shareholders, or all managers, behave in a way designed to maximize profit. Many shareholders, for example, will be interested in the growth of dividends paid over time rather than establishing whether those dividends are at a maximum level, while, as we have seen, managers may have a vested interest in growth.

Apart from this fundamental point it must also be said that for the profit maximization rule to be established in a technical sense we must be able to identify marginal costs and marginal revenues. That is identification of the costs and revenues that are associated with the production of each and every extra unit of output. In fact, it would be administratively impossible, in terms of the resources and costs involved, to identify marginal cost and marginal revenue, and the practice of identifying marginal costs and revenues is not undertaken by firms. In 1939, surveys carried out by Hall and Hitch established that firms, in practice, apply a mark-up to average total costs of production to establish the price at which the output of particular products should be sold.

Price = Average variable costs + Average fixed costs + Profit mark-up. The financial information needed for mark-up pricing can readily be obtained from the accounting records and information system of the firm. (R. Hall and C. Hitch, 1939.)

Most important, for the purpose of this chapter, the previous point emphasizes the importance of the role and principles of accounting in the financial calculations that firms make. Overall the financial calculations of any business enterprise are based upon the principles of accounting. It is accounting convention and accounting methods which determine the following:

- The presentation of annual report and accounts which detail the financial profit of the firm in the annual profit and loss account and the level of shareholder funds in the balance sheet.
- The price at which a product should be sold to recover costs and make a contribution to profit.
- The future profitability of projects or strategic investments in new capital equipment.

As we have said, the main feature of the development of the limited liability company was that many people could now invest directly in business operations and take financial rewards in the form of dividends or capital gain. Although some shareholders may be managers as well, the majority of shareholders will not be involved in the day-to-day activities of the business. However, to protect and safeguard the 'financial interest' of the shareholder a system of accounting for the owner of capital has developed. The accounts of limited companies are required by law and are basically prepared for the shareholders in their capacity as owners but with specific provisions to safeguard creditors of the business.

The accounting concept of 'going concern' was established as a means to ensure that the business accounts were constructed on the basis of assuming continuity of operations and preservation of the business capital (shareholders' funds). Financial accounting concepts and conventions have developed as a means for recording, in as consistent a way as possible, the annual profit of the business, whereas cost and management accounting is concerned either to utilize the historical financial accounting records for day-to-day operational control purposes or to calculate strategically the future profitability of a commitment of investor funds to a capital investment project.

In financial terms, profit is the result of accounting calculations and conventions related to such things as the valuation of stocks and the calculation of depreciation expense etc. Accounting profit is therefore not a standard universal measure but subject to how accountants use the conventions at their disposal for the treatment of costs and expenses in the accounts of the business. This concept of profit and its calculation is very different from the concept of profit as specified under conditions of certainty in neo-classical economics (K. Williams *et al.*, 1983 and G. Thompson, 1986).

In traditional economic theory it is argued that resources will be applied most efficiently where those resouces are put to use so as to earn the greatest level of profit. Profit is used in economic theory as a means to demonstrate that resources are being efficiently utilized or as a signal to attract resources to where maximum profits can be obtained.

In practice, however, it is accounting conventions which determine the level of profit recorded by the business in the accounts, and where resources such as capital and labour might be most profitably allocated. We will therefore consider in the rest of this chapter how financial accounting calculations affect the allocation of resources in the firm both strategically and operationally. For purposes of simplicity we will take twelve months to represent the operational time period – given that it is the period over which the financial summary profit and loss accounts extend, and the strategic time period to be that greater than one year.

Accounting calculations and decision-making

In any business organization it is accounting practice and convention that determine the nature of a firm's profits (retained profits or net profit pre or post tax). These profits are the result of accounting calculations or double entry records that are summarized and presented in the trading and profit and loss account of the business (for a more detailed review of these practices see the accounting text in this series). Essentially the trading and profit and loss account records the difference between revenue and expenses of the business incurred during the year. The accounting concepts of 'matching' and 'accruals' have been developed to ensure that expenses incurred by the business are matched with revenue earned during the year.

Profit = Revenue (Sales) − Expenses (Purchases, Interest, Depreciation, Rent and Rates, Tax, Dividends etc.)

The calculation of profit is therefore based not on the economic concepts of marginal cost or marginal revenue but on a whole set of accounting rules and conventions that are the stock of accounting literature and professional accounting exams. Profit is therefore something which is subject to the forms of calculations used by accountants when they calculate expenses such as depreciation and tax etc.

Accounting information in the profit and loss account and the balance sheet are also based on what we call historic costs. All accounting information in the annual accounts is based on financial information relating to the previous year's sales earned, or last year's depreciation charge etc. In addition to the calculation of profit in the profit and loss account, the balance sheet shows values for assets etc. that are also based on the historic cost of purchase and are, for example, depreciated on the basis of their original cost. In the mid-1970s a major debate on the relevance of historic cost accounting in times of inflation resulted in recommendations for inflation cost accounting to be introduced. We will not go into any detail here but it must be recognized that in times of inflation the use of historic cost information for decision-making becomes more problematic (Berry and Jarvis, 1994).

Limited companies have to report their profit and loss position and their balance sheet position each year to Companies House. These financial results are presented in a summary annual report and accounts which are available for public inspection in Companies House and are sent to the shareholders as of right. In the balance sheet of the firm we can obtain a 'snapshot' of the position of the firm at the year end. A typical balance sheet would include the following.

Shareholders' Capital

Shareholders' issued shares,
Retained profits.

Represented by;

Fixed assets

Land and buildings − accumulated depreciation
Plant and equipment − accumulated depreciation
Motor vehicles etc. − accumulated depreciation

Plus net current assets

Current assets
Stocks
Debtors
Bank balance
Cash

Minus current liabilities
Creditors
Loans
Overdrafts

As we shall see in Chapter 4, a range of calculations can be under-taken, from a company's published annual report and accounts, to assess the market, productive, and financial performance of the business. In addition, financial data from the accounts can be used in calculations which it is hoped will enhance decision-making, and, in particular, the control of costs and recovery of profit from the price charged for the product or service. In the following sections we will consider some of the accounting calculations used by management accountants – to plan and control the future activity of the business (budgeting), to determine the product's cost and price, and to allocate capital funds to the most profitable investment opportunity.

The budgeting process

In the 1920s and 1930s in the USA, the role of the accountant shifted from that of 'mere recording of information' to that of providing information for the strategic future planning and control of the business. This emphasis on keeping costs under control was externally sponsored by shareholders, who had seen profits collapse in the 1920s depression, particularly in the Great Crash of 1929.

When British managers, sponsored by the Anglo American Productivity Council, visited the USA after the war, they returned to Britain impressed with the budgetary control and standard-costing systems operating in American firms. The Anglo American Productivity Council reports of the early 1950s recommended wider adoption of these aids to management in Britain 'to enable it to decentralise responsibility' and to 'plan and co-ordinate production to the last detail' (Hutton, 1953).

The US system of budgeting was recommended to British firms – emulation of American techniques, it was argued, would improve the management and control of resources within the business. Many companies surveyed in the 1980s and 1990s now apply some if not all these budgeting techniques, which are designed to plan, co-ordinate and control the business.

In general terms, a firm which uses budgets will use the current year's financial information on sales, production costs, cash flow, etc., to establish plans (of expected achievement) for the coming year. Individual budgets (for sales revenue, materials and labour costs, cash flow, etc.) estimate what is expected to happen in the course of the coming year, and can be combined into one overall budget, known as the master budget. This is a financial representation of the future activity of the business in the coming financial or calendar year, which, it is argued, helps management to plan and co-ordinate the activities of the business.

Financial control

To illustrate how control of costs is achieved, we will consider the production budget and in particular the estimation of future labour costs for the coming year. Estimates of future budgeted labour costs in production take this year's labour costs and inflate them by the expected rate of wage increase, and the production department lists the budgeted labour costs for each stage of the production process (see Case Study 3.1).

As the year progresses, the company records actual labour costs incurred at each stage in the production process, and these appear in the spreadsheet for the production department. In our case study (3.1), these actual figures show up on a monthly basis to the right of the budgeted figures and also as a cumulative figure for the year to date. The process of comparing the actual costs incurred with the expected standard (the budgeted cost) is known as variance analysis. Where, for example, the actual costs are greater than those expected, there is an adverse variance, shown as a positive percentage difference in the variance column.

This practice of comparing actual results with a standard is known as management by exception, in which attention is focussed on adverse variances, so that they can be reduced. The overall objective of this practice is to reduce variances between budgeted labour (or materials) costs and the actual costs of labour (or materials). Control is achieved through the process of identifying, and then correcting, those costs which turn out to be higher than was expected at the start of the year. In this way, costs can be 'maintained' at the planned level, to preserve the budgeted profit. Contracts to supply a particular product are normally drawn up in advance, and the price set when the contract is signed. Once the price is contractually agreed, the firm then needs to maintain costs within those set by the price so that at the end of the day a contribution to profit is made.

ABZ plc is a company which manufactures a single product which is sold to the car manufacturers Ford, General Motors and Rover. The product requires materials to be fabricated into a final component through a number of stages of manufacture. The spreadsheet shown below gives an indicative outline of the information required to control the direct production labour costs which go into the manufacture of this component.

CASE STUDY 3.1
Budgets and cost control at ABZ

cc Name	Current month Nov 199X			Year to date 11 months			Comments
	Budget £000	Actual £000	Variance %	Budget £000	Actual £000	Variance %	
Weld Robot 1	4.6	4.7	2.17	55.7	60.6	8.80	
Weld Robot 2	4.3	7.8	81.40	48.8	55.6	13.93	Machine breakdown
Weld Robot 3	5.9	5.3	−10.17	70.2	68.4	−2.56	Wage cost not as high as expected
Bending machine 1	14.3	12.8	−10.49	164.6	170.6	3.65	
Sawing 1	14.7	13.1	−10.88	158.7	156.7	−1.26	
Box Line 1	6.8	7.2	5.88	74.8	77.7	3.88	
Box Line 2	5.6	5.7	1.79	78.6	80.1	1.91	
Total	56.20	56.60	0.71	651.40	669.70	2.81	Overall just 2.8% adrift after 11 months

Overall, the variance between the budgeted and the actual outcome is not large for ABZ. In the current month the overall adverse variance between the budget and that planned is only 0.71%. For the current year to date the variance is again slightly adverse, with the actual level of labour cost expenditure just 2.81% above that planned at the start of the year.

ABZ plc also uses the spreadsheets to give a running picture of the profit margin for the year, based on a budgeted share of costs and profit. These are shown below.

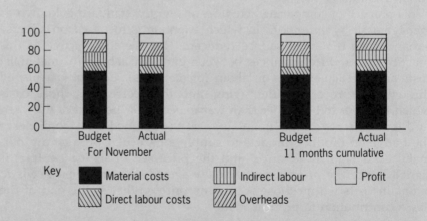

The above histogram shows a monthly total and running total of all costs of production for materials, direct labour, indirect labour, and overheads. The histogram brings down the direct labour costs from the spreadsheet shown above, and indicates the extent to which the budgeted profit is being maintained during the month in question and for the cumulative yearly total.

The objective of maintaining costs incurred at or around the level set by the budget was achieved by ABZ plc in Case Study 3.1, because there was no significant variation between the actual labour costs incurred and the estimated costs or standard costs set by the budget at the start of the year. When translated into cumulative profit/loss, we see that ABZ plc has maintained overall costs at the level expected and has preserved the contribution towards profit.

We have stressed, in Chapters 1 and 2, the importance of reducing cost levels, yet it is clear that standard costing is more concerned with maintaining cost levels around a standard than with promoting cost reduction. The difference between this approach to the management of costs and the approach of many Japanese companies is that Japanese firms seek to continually reduce costs and use their accounting system to reflect the contribution to cost reduction from newly designed products as well as from improvements to in-house manufacturing. In Figure 3.2, we contrast target cost reduction, as a system which continually takes cost out through improved design and development and changes to the organization of manufacture, with the cost maintenance emphasis of standard costing.

In Case Study 3.2, we reproduce a typical spreadsheet used by the Nissan Motor Corporation. This illustrates how the accounting spreadsheet can be used to combine variance analysis with information relating to the contribution made to cost reduction by newly developed models and improvements to in-house manufacturing. This spreadsheet combines information on the progress of cost recovery and cost reduction.

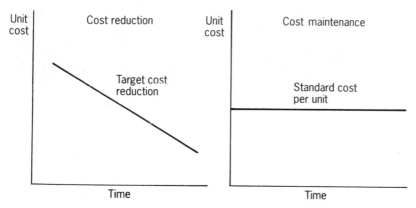

Figure 3.2 Cost reduction versus cost maintenance.

CASE STUDY 3.2
Nissan Motor Corporation: divisional income statement

Nissan's divisional income statement brings together the information needed to monitor the conditions of cost recovery and the behaviour of actual against expected profit.

Number of units sold
Total revenue

Net sales

Marketing costs

Operating profit (A)

Expected number of units
Expected profit (B)

Difference
(A) − (B)

Sales increase/decrease

Production change

Sales rate changes

Fluctuation in exchange rate

Shipping costs

Total

Changes in invoice price

Discounts

Change in marketing costs

Profit/loss account of fixed assets

Cost reduction from in-house manufacturing

Fluctuations in purchasing price

Cost reduction of newly developed models

Research and development

Where the expected profit is at variance from the actual profit earned, then the company breaks down the contribution made to this variance by market conditions (sales increase/decrease), discounts given, cost reduction contribution from in-house manufacturing, and the contribution to cost reduction from newly developed models.

Further reading
Williams *et al.* (1992)
Norgan and Prasanna (1989)
Koshikawa *et al.* (1989)

In this section, we have considered how management accountants construct budgets to co-ordinate, plan, and control manufacturing costs. We have seen that the general approach in the West is one of maintaining costs so that a profit is guaranteed for the shareholder, and preserved against cost incursion. In contrast, the approach to cost reduction adopted by many Japanese firms is a pro-active approach in which the fundamental interests of the business in cost reduction and cost recovery are directly addressed. As Toshiro Hiromoto has stressed:

> Japanese management accounting does not stress optimising within existing constraints. Rather, it encourages employees to make continual improvements by tightening those constraints . . . Instead [it] establishes target costs derived from estimates of a competitive market price. These targets are usually well below currently achievable costs.
>
> *Hiromoto, 1988*

Stock control

A similar discrepancy between Western and Japanese calculations emerges in relation to stocks. There are costs involved in both holding stocks (e.g. the financial cost of the capital tied up in stocks and handling costs) and ordering them (e.g. the clerical time taken to process orders). Holding costs increase as stock levels increase; if larger average stocks are maintained, however, fewer orders need to be placed, and this reduces ordering costs. Western management accounting promotes the calculation of economic order quantity (EOQ), to determine the optimal order size, where the total cost relevant to stocks (i.e. holding costs plus ordering costs) is kept to a minimum (see Key Concept 3.2).

KEY CONCEPT 3.2
*Economic order
quantity (EOQ)*

In the diagram below, ordering costs fall as order quantity increases, because, with a given annual demand, the number of orders which have to be placed each year is reduced. Holding costs rise, however, because the average stock held is increased. Total relevant costs (holding costs plus ordering costs) are at a minimum where holding costs equal ordering costs, and this determines the EOQ.

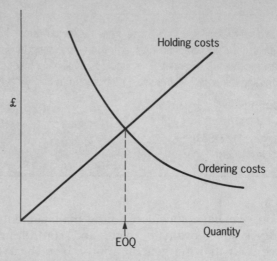

EOQ can be worked out according to the formula:

$$EOQ = \sqrt{\frac{2 \times D \times O}{H}}$$

Where *D* is annual demand (in units),
        O is order cost (per order),
        H is holding cost (per unit).

Standard texts focus on the financial opportunity costs of holding stock, and see other holding costs as only minimally important. Typically, however, overhead costs associated with stockholding (indirect labour, warehousing, etc.) are twice as large as financial costs. In addition, if stock levels are reduced, there may be a variety of dynamic gains associated with reduced cycle, set up and lead times, as well as a once-off financial saving at the time of de-stocking. Ordering costs, too, may be capable of being reduced if purchasing policies are changed – with closer supplier relations reducing the need for formal paperwork, for example.

Practical applications of EOQ in the West tend to emphasize maintaining costs at a constant level, in order to optimize around a given structure of costs. Japanese firms like Toyota, in contrast, see their aim as to change the structure of costs, in order to reduce the costs associated with stocks. It is not that the EOQ model is incorrect, but that firms which emphasize continual improvement in their production and purchasing systems can bring the level of EOQ down over time.

Further reading
Williams *et al.* (1989).

As can be seen from Key Concept 3.2, Western applications of EOQ accept as given the costs associated with stocks, so that the objective is to maintain stocks at a standard level in relation to demand. Indeed, UK and US financial accounting systems view stocks as assets rather than liabilities, and managers often see stocks as playing a positive role in shielding production systems from fluctuations in demand, and preventing imbalances.

Many Japanese managers, in contrast, aim to reduce stocks as a priority, and see stock reduction as a means of exposing and tackling the fundamental problems (like high machine set-up times, or production bottlenecks) which high stock levels disguise. One approach, developed at Toyota in the 1950s, is just-in-time (JIT) production. Here, small quantities of supplies are delivered 'just in time' for the next stage of the production process, reducing the need for buffer stocks. JIT is not, however, merely a low-inventory production system, but a holistic approach which emphasizes *kaizen* – continual improvement in productive efficiency. If only minimal buffer stocks are maintained, for example, it is essential that the quality of each part is assured. JIT therefore implies total quality control, challenging conventional views of supplier relationships and work organization. The result, as we saw in Chapter 2, can be a positive contribution to both cost reduction and cost recovery.

The accounting calculation of cost and price

When considering the pricing and output decisions of firms, economists have refined their analysis to move away from the marginalist framework of neo-classical economics which we explored in Chapter 1. Rather than charge the maximum price the market will bear, to maximize

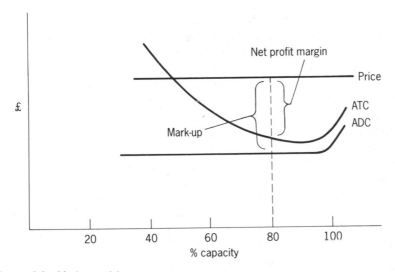

Figure 3.3 Mark-up pricing.

short-run profits, it is now suggested that firms will fix their price at a level which is low enough to deter new entrants into the market, by applying a mark-up to average variable costs (see Figure 3.3). This allows prices to change as costs change, but discourages price variation in response to short-term changes in demand conditions. In this later work, by writers such as Andrews and Brunner (1975) and Eichner (1976), we move towards a more realistic understanding of business calculation, which sees accounting rules and regulations, rather than economic theory, as being the main determinants of price.

In this section we consider the accounting rules and procedures which determine the costs and price of a product. We have seen how vitally important it is for the firm to recover the costs incurred in the manufacture of its products. In order to calculate price, the accountant must firstly establish the cost of the product, which involves using a variety of techniques to 'attach' costs to a product. In general terms, the accountant will classify a product's cost as follows:

Direct materials + direct labour + direct fixed and variable overheads = prime cost of manufacture + indirect fixed and variable overheads = total cost of manufacture.

Once these costs are 'attached' to the particular product in question, the total cost of manufacture is divided by estimated volume sales for the coming year to establish the unit total cost. The final stage in the pricing calculation is to add on a profit mark-up to obtain the final unit price.

Total cost of manufacture/volume output = unit total cost
Unit total cost + profit mark-up = price charged per unit.

Allocation of overheads

One of the main problems in determining the cost of a product is how to allocate the overhead costs of the business between its different products. It is relatively easy to identify the direct costs of manufacture, but much more difficult to allocate indirect overheads to a particular product. According to John Sizer (1977), 'there is no one way of apportioning overhead costs and calculating overhead absorbtion rates. There are a number of possible bases and the cost accountant has to decide which is the most suitable in the circumstances.'

The accountant under these circumstances makes an arbitrary decision on how to allocate the overhead cost to the product in order to set a price which will recover the required profit margin. Accountants generally argue that the information they supply on a product's cost and profit margin can improve decision-making, by establishing which products will make a loss, and which will be profitable. We need, however, to be more cautious.

We can illustrate this last point with a basic example in which the choice is between the production of product A and product B shown below:

	Product A £	Product B £
Sales revenue per unit	60.00	70.00
Direct labour costs	5.00 (5 @ £1)	10.00 (10 @ £1)
Direct material costs	25.00	30.00
Direct overheads	10.00	10.00
Indirect overheads	10.00	20.00
Profit contribution	10.00	nil

On the face of it, the above calculation of costs in relation to the sales price per unit suggests that we should produce product A rather than product B. The fixed overheads in this example were allocated to each product on the basis of the direct labour hours in each product – five in the case of product A, and ten in the case of product B. However, the use of direct labour hours as a means to absorb the overheads has been questioned by management accountants Johnson and Kaplan (1987). They argue that it is inappropriate to allocate overheads on the basis of direct labour costs, as these only account for a relatively small proportion of total costs. Johnson and Kaplan suggest refining the process by which costs are attached to the product, by introducing activity based costing systems (ABC). Activity based costing systems are the latest in a whole series of management accounting calculations which search for the holy grail of the 'true cost' of a product's manufacture. The issue of how to accurately define a product's costs has been around for a long time, as the quote below, from a book written in 1920 and called *The Management Problem*, illustrates:

> In a works where there is no satisfactory costing system it is possible and highly probable, if several classes of articles are being made, to be actually manufacturing at a loss without the weakness being traceable or even discernible until the financial position of the business has been seriously undermined.
>
> *Elbourne, 1920*

The ABC system of attaching costs takes into account those factors which 'drive' a product's costs, known as 'cost drivers'. In the above example, we might, using ABC, now adjust our calculations, because we believe that the process of producing product A drives up much more of the indirect overhead than we have allocated to it. We might now have the following:

	Product A £	Product B £
Sales revenue per unit	60.00	70.00
Direct labour costs	5.00 (5 @ £1)	10.00 (10 @ £1)
Direct material costs	25.00	30.00
Direct overheads	10.00	10.00
Indirect overheads	20.00	10.00
Profit/loss	nil	10.00

According to this new presentation, it is product B that now makes the profit contribution, whereas it now appears that product A should be dropped because it makes a loss. All this would seem to the casual observer to be a rather random affair in which several different 'correct' choices could be made depending on the rules that the accountants are employing at a particular moment in time. The resulting decision will be unsatisfactory, because it will reflect the rather arbitrary system being used to allocate costs to the products.

There may also be a conflict between the calculations undertaken by the management accountants and the requirements of the business. You can, for example, establish a target price which you think is appropriate for your market. Whether or not it is possible to make a contribution to profit at this price will depend, however, on sales performance. As we have suggested earlier in this chapter, we may need to redefine the objectives of the firm, to reflect the importance of cost reduction.

The relationship between costs, volume, and profit

The simplest method of illustrating the relationship between costs, volume, and profit is the break-even chart, which depicts the relationship between total costs and revenue earned as output expands over a period of time. The traditional economic presentation of this relationship is shown in Figure 3.4.

In Figure 3.4 the total revenue curve is shown to increase at a decreasing rate, illustrating that the firm can only sell more output by reducing the price at which that output is sold. In the case of the total cost curve this is shown as at first increasing (X to Y) but at a slower rate as the firm increasingly utilizes the 'lumpy' investment constructed to produce this product, that is, where growth in production increasingly fills the production capacity installed. Over the portion Y to Z the curve is shown to be relatively flat as the firm operates in the minimum efficient scale portion of the plant where unit costs are constant. In this diagram there are two break-even points shown (*) that is where total costs are equivalent to total revenue. Break-even point is where

$$\text{Total costs} = \text{Total revenue}$$

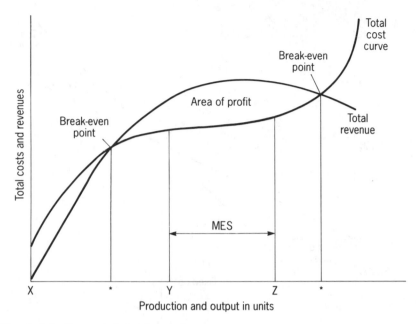

Figure 3.4 Economist's version of a break-even chart.

The accountant's calculations of the break-even point and the relationship between volume and profit are based on linear curves rather than non-linear economic relations. The total costs curve is made up of the fixed plus variable costs of the product's production, while the revenue curve is constructed by calculating total revenue over a certain volume of sales range.

Consider the example where product A has the following cost and revenue characteristics.

> Fixed costs of production are £120 000.
> Variable costs per unit are £20.
> Sales price per unit £40.
> Plant capacity is 10 000 units.

The break-even chart (Figure 3.5) is constructed below and this illustrates that the break-even point is at an output level of 6000 units. If sales volume is above this level of output then a profit will be earned by the firm, but output levels below 6000 units will incur a loss. The break-even point therefore represents a position in which no profit is made and costs are just covered by revenue earned by the firm.

It is also possible to calculate the break-even point using this formula.

Break-even point (in units) = Fixed Costs (£)/Sales Price per unit
− Variable Cost per unit.

In this case £120 000/£40 − £20 = 6000 units.

In the above example if the firm were to increase the sales price per unit then the break-even point will fall, whereas if the variable costs

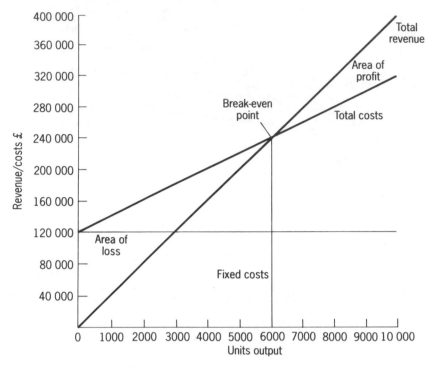

Figure 3.5 Break-even chart.

increase or fixed costs increase due to say excess material costs (above those planned) and increased construction costs the break-even point will rise.

As a means of illustrating the relationship between volume of future sales and the costs/profit relationship, the accountant's break-even chart is a reasonably useful financial tool. However, there are a number of problems associated with using the technique as a means for management decision-making and the allocation of resources.

Firstly the calculation assumes that the costs curves are linear. When this assumption is relaxed, as in the economist's version of the total cost and revenue curve, then there may well, in fact, be two break-even points and a range of output within which it is possible to obtain a profit contribution beyond which a loss may be incurred.

Secondly the break-even chart relates only to one product and when in practice is necessary to compare the various break-even levels and profit contributions from a range of products produced. Finally there is the implicit assumption that the firm can estimate the future level of product demand with utmost certainty. As we have seen in the chapter on markets, such calculations about the future level of demand for a product are fraught with uncertainty. Miscalculations of demand can be critical, especially when the break-even point can only be achieved after significant growth in demand for product. Obviously the higher is the break-even point for the product being manufactured (i.e. break-even point as a percentage of the theoretical plant capacity) the greater the risk that the plant will not reach a level of volume sales each year that delivers a positive contribution to profit. In the case of highly capital-intensive investments made in industries such as steel or car manufacture, fixed costs of manufacture are very high indeed and as a result break-even output levels operate at very high levels of plant capacity.

The break-even chart is a useful technique for assessing the relationship between costs, volume, and profit. However, after noting some of the issues relating to the assumptions of break-even analysis, it will be clear that the information required to construct the chart can only be obtained within an organization. For outsiders, the annual report and accounts of a company can be used to make an approximate calculation of the degree to which a company is operating at or below break-even in a given year. This alternative calculation again uses the concept of value added.

Firstly, we calculate value added as:

Wages plus salaries plus social costs + depreciation + profit pre net interest and tax

Secondly, we measure the extent to which labour costs and depreciation charges are covered by value added. We can then work out the percentage operation above or below break-even point, according to the following formula:

$$\frac{\text{Value added} - (\text{labour} + \text{depreciation})}{\text{Value added}} \times 100$$

Case Study 3.3 illustrates this calculation for the Ford Motor Company, based on its published UK accounts. The calculation demonstrates that as volume sales have fallen for the Ford Motor Company, it has progressively moved into a situation where it is operating well below a break-even point where value added generated would just cover the labour and depreciation costs.

CASE STUDY 3.3
Ford UK

1988 was a good year for Ford UK. It sold 779 000 vehicles in the UK and overseas markets, and the value added generated from these sales (sales revenue minus purchases) was double that required to cover the wages and depreciation costs. As a result, Ford made a record profit contribution of £673 million before tax.

It can be seen that in 1991, however, Ford was running well below break-even and was only recovering 68% of the labour costs and depreciation charges incurred by the business. That year, the company made a loss before tax of £935 million. The last column of the table below shows that, in 1991, value added would need to have been 47.2% higher for the firm to have achieved break-even.

Year	Value added (£m.)	Labour costs (£m.)	Depreciation (£m.)	% of operations above or below break-even
1988	2291	872	201	+53.2
1989	2189	1000	251	+42.9
1990	1393	1295	301	−14.6
1991	1173	1290	437	−47.2

As we shall see in Chapter 4, a company which is operating at a level which is below break-even point will usually have no alternative than to shed labour if it is to normalize labour's share of value added. For Ford to have normalized labour's share of value added at 70% in 1991 would have required a drop in the total wage bill to £903 million (0.70 × 1290) – a reduction in the workforce of 36%.

Capital investment decision-making

In addition to establishing the relationship between future volume growth, costs, revenue, and profit, management accountants are also concerned to establish whether or not an application of shareholder funds to new investment projects will reveal a profit for the shareholders. Capital investment decisions, on the replacement of new assets or investment in new product lines, depend on whether or not future income (net cash inflow minus net cash outlay) makes a contribution to profit after the original borrowings (including the costs of borrowing) are paid back. As we shall see in the next section on capital investment decision-making, small investment projects that go wrong may not compromise the future viability, but strategic investments which commit a large proportion of shareholder capital can compromise the future of the business when they go wrong.

Payback

One of the simplest forms of accounting calculation used by management accountants to decide whether an investment project should be undertaken, is the payback financial calculation. This calculation involves assessing the future net cash flows likely to be obtained from an investment. The net cash inflow is calculated as the difference between the future cash inflows and cash outflows. For example, where a firm wishes to evaluate the financial attractiveness of different investment choices it will compare each option in terms of the criterion – how quickly do net cash flows pay back the original investment outlay?

Consider the following simple example in which there are two projects being evaluated, project A costing £2000 and project B costing £4000. Each of these investment projects is expected to have the following net cash flow profiles.

Table 3.1 Costings for projects A and B

		Investment/outlay £	Net cash inflows £			
Years		0	1	2	3	4
Projects	A	−2000	+1000	+500	+500	+500
	B	−4000	+500	+1000	+1000	+1500

In the above illustration investment project A would incur an investment outlay of £2000 and over four years the net cash flow would
account for £2500. In case B an investment outlay of £4000 would reveal
net cash flows totalling £4000 by year four. In terms of how quickly
each project obtains a net cash flow that 'pays back' the initial investment outlay, project A would seem to be more attractive because the
payback would be three years whilst that of project B would be four
years.

The advantages of payback are that it is simple to understand and
that it emphasizes the importance of achieving cost recovery in as short
a period as possible. In addition, payback can be used to encourage
cost reduction, because if costs are taken out of the product, this will
ensure a more rapid payback.

However, even with such a simple form of accounting criterion such
as payback there are a number of problems. Firstly, although on a strict
financial payback calculation project A is more attractive than B, it may
be the case that project B would deliver other benefits which cannot be
considered in purely a strict financial calculation. Project B may be, for
example, an important component in an overall set of projects which
would eventually contribute strategically to an improvement in the
future market position of the firm. Or project B may well contribute to
the efficiency of the overall production system, for example reducing
the level of stocks held as work-in-progress. But this benefit is not
taken into account in the financial calculation of payback.

The decision to invest in particular projects would also need to take
into account other factors that may not be easily represented in financial
terms but would also need to be considered in the decision-making
process.

Finally, the use of payback as a means of judging the recovery of
investment outlay only makes sense when the company is not starved
of cash.

Discounted Cash Flow (DCF)

Another objection to simple payback rules is that they do not take
adequate account of the 'time value of money' (see Key Concept 3.3),
and pay no attention to cash inflows after the investment outlay is paid

back. To answer these criticisms, Joel Dean introduced, in the early 1950s, the concept of discounted cash flow. This, Dean argued, gives managers a decision-making technique which would result in the allocation of scarce capital funds to the most profitable investment projects (Dean, 1954).

KEY CONCEPT 3.3
The time value of money

This concept provides the basic rationale for the discounting calculation. Where an investment requires the commitment of capital funds in return for an income flow over a number of years, it is assumed that the investor would prefer this income flow to be equivalent to or greater than that which the investor would have obtained from investing the capital fund at the market rate of interest. It is for this reason we argue that the investor would prefer to receive £100 now rather than in one year's time because this £100 could be invested now so as to earn interest on this sum.

Discounting establishes whether the present value of a future income stream is not less than the original capital outlay and that the investor receives an income stream which fully compensates for the interest returns forgone.

It is argued that the commitment of investment funds by the individual or firm involves an opportunity cost (see Key Concept 3.4). That is, committing investment funds to one particular purpose involves the sacrifice of not being able to place these funds elsewhere. Once a decision is made to invest in a particular project then these funds are essentially locked in to that project. This would particularly be the case when the investment funds are allocated for the purchase of fixed plant and equipment.

What is the sacrifice the firm or investor makes when funds are committed to an investment project? It is clear that at the decision-making stage a firm could place its surplus funds, available for investment purposes, either in a bank where they could gather a compound market rate of interest or in the hands of divisional managers for investment in new physical investment projects. Before the decision to allocate funds to particular purposes is made we are assuming that a choice such as this exists.

KEY CONCEPT 3.4
Opportunity cost

Because the resources at our disposal are scarce in relation to our wants, we have to make choices. As individuals, we all have to choose how to spend our limited income. Shall I buy a colour television, or save up for a holiday abroad instead? Economists talk of opportunity cost to emphasize the way choosing something involves a cost in terms of the opportunities you have to forgo. Thus if I decide to buy a colour television, its opportunity cost is the holiday abroad I can no longer afford.

For firms, the opportunity cost of using retained profits to finance an investment project is the interest that could be earned by lending them out on the money markets instead. This is not just an abstract possibility – in the late 1970s and early 1980s, for example, net income from cash reserves accounted for more than 10% of GEC's total pre-tax profits.

It may be that investing surplus funds in the bank or gilt-edged stock would reveal a net cash-flow return to the investor which is greater than that which could be obtained from investments in physical plant and equipment designed to produce a particular product for the market. As such we would argue that the funds would, financially, be better invested in financial rather than physical assets. Managers use the DCF calculation as a means to establish whether or not funds should be used for physical plant and equipment investment or placed in alternative financial assets.

The discounted cash flow (DCF) calculation starts with the presumption that a pound received now is worth more than a pound received in one year's time. This is because the pound received now could be invested at the market rate of interest and therefore be worth more than one pound in a year's time. For example, if we assume that the market rate of interest is 10% and a person or firm has the choice of receiving £100 now or in one year's time. The £100 received now could be invested at 10% and be worth £110 in one year's time.

	Year 0	Year 1
Investment at 10%	100	110

Looking at this problem another way we could say that a person would be indifferent to receiving £100 now or £110 in one year's time (assuming that inflation was zero).

In this simple example it is the principle of compound interest that is used to establish what £1 invested now would be worth in some future time period at a given rate of interest. Compound interest calculations are based on the following formula.

$$FVn = Vo(1 + i)^n$$

Where FVn = Future value of an investment over n years.
  Vo = Initial investment sum.
  i = Interest rate.
  n = number of years over which investment is to be made.

It is easy to obtain the compound future value of an investment with a given rate of interest from compound interest tables or from simple computer software statistical packages. For example where a person invests £100 over four years at a 10% interest rate then the future value of this investment would be £146.40

$$FVn = 100 (1 + 0.10)^4$$
or FVn = 100 × 1.464 (from compound tables based on rate of interest and number of years the investment is made for).

In contrast to compounding which establishes the future value of an investment at a particular rate of interest, discounting involves establishing the present value of future net cash flows received. This calculation is used to establish whether future cash flows from an investment project are sufficient to do the following.

- Pay back the initial investment outlay.
- Recover the interest that could have been earned on the investment funds had they been invested at the market rate of interest.

To calculate the present value of future cash flows we use the formula:

$$PVo = \frac{FVn}{(1 + i)^n.}$$

Where PVo = The present value of future net cash flows

FVn = The future value of net cash flows in each future year n

$(1 + i)^n$ = The compound discount factor based on the year in which net cash flow is obtained (n) and market rate of interest (i).

Again it is possible to obtain present value discount factors from statistical tables or from computer software packages.

Once the present value of future net cash flows from an investment project have been calculated they then need to be compared with the initial investment outlay. This final step involves calculating the *net present value* of the investment. To illustrate this financial decision-making tool consider the example below. Here the firm could choose to invest £10 000 of investment funds in a bank at a market rate of interest of 10% or invest in a project which delivered the net cash flow profile over a period of five years as shown in Table 3.2. Note also that in many cases the discount rate of interest will be based on a cost of capital (Key Concept 3.5) calculation which involves taking the weighted average cost of capital invested in the firm by shareholders and creditors.

The present value figure for the end of year one amounts to £1818.2 and it represents the amount that we could invest at the start (year zero) and in one year's time obtain £2000 at 10% cost of capital. Likewise, the figure of £1862.7 in year five represents that amount we could invest now (in year zero) and at 10% compound over five years receive £3000.

Table 3.2 Net present value calculation

End of year	Net cash flow £		Discount factor or present value factor	Present value £
Year 1	2000	*	0.9091	1 818.2
Year 2	3000	*	0.8264	2 479.2
Year 3	3000	*	0.7513	2 253.9
Year 4	3000	*	0.6830	2 049.0
Year 5	3000	*	0.6209	1 862.7
			Total present value	10 463.0

However, it is only when we summate the present value column that we see that the total present value of future net cash flows is in excess of the original investment outlay of £10 000. That is the Net Present Value (NPV) of the project is as calculated below.

NPV = Original investment − The summation of present
   outlay   values of future net
             cash flows

$$NPV = \int PVo - Io$$
$$= £10\,463 - £10\,000$$
$$= +£463$$

In this example the present value of future net cash flows from this investment is sufficient for the following.

- Cover the interest that would have been received on £10 000 had it been invested in financial assets.
- Contribute a positive NPV of £463 i.e. contribute to profit.

The cost of captial is the discount factor used by the firm to establish whether a new investment project will cover the cost of capital that is applied. It usually represents the weighted average cost of capital for the firm as a whole or for a division within the firm.

D. Solomons (1965) defined the cost of capital as 'the expected earnings yield on the current market price of an all equity company or the weighted average cost of capital in a company financed by both debt and equity'.

The cost of capital is therefore an average rate of interest which is paid out to shareholders or holders of debt within the firm. Any investment should therefore make a contribution to income which will cover the cost of funding both the firm's debt and equity.

KEY CONCEPT 3.5
The cost of capital

In the above example we have calculated the net present value (NPV) of a particular project investment. In this case the NPV of the project was found to be positive, demonstrating that a positive contribution to profits would indeed be made. However at any moment in time decision-makers will have a number of possible option choices. As a result it is necessary to compare the relative merits of each investment option open to the business. To do this accountants calculate the NPVs of a number of options and then rank these options in terms of their profitability or NPV.

For example we may have two possible project options to choose from, project A and project B. In the table below (Table 3.3) we show the net cash flow profiles expected from each project and the initial cash outflow attributable to each project. We also assume that the cost of capital is 10%.

Table 3.3 Comparison of Project A and Project B

Outlay year 0	Net cash inflows year	1	2	3	4	5
Project A (£10 000)		6 000	5 000	4 000		
Project B (£50 000)		10 000	10 000	20 000	20 000	20 000
Discount factors 10%		0.9091	0.8264	0.7513	0.6830	0.6209
Present values						
Project A		5454.6	4 132	3 005.2		
Project B		9091.0	8 264	15 026.0	13 660	12 418
Net present value						
Project A	12 591.8 − 10 000 = +2591.8					
Project B	58 459.0 − 50 000 = +8459					

In terms of a simple ranking of each project using the contribution to profits or level of NPV we would rank the projects as follows:

Project	NPV	Rank
A	+2591.8	2
B	+8459.0	1

However accountants usually construct a ranking that relates NPV to the initial investment outlay in the form of return on capital investment ratio. If we were to do this for the above example we would arrive at the following ranking of the projects.

	Project	NPV/Initial investment outlay	Rank
2592/10 000 =	A	25.9%	1
8459/50 000 =	B	16.9%	2

CASE STUDY 3.4
Net present value and the case of British Steel

In the BSC's 1972 Strategic Evaluation Exercise (SEE) the BSC financial planners utilized the NPV discounting method as recommended by the government in the White Paper setting up the corporation. In this exercise the BSC evaluated the NPVs of ten different investment options. These all involved the expansion of steelmaking capacity to a greater or lesser extent. All the options involved constructing new steelmaking plant and equipment. In some options this would require a modest commitment of resources, while in others a very large commitment of financial resources would be needed.

The results of the BSC's calculations of NPV are summarized in the table below and ranked on the basis of the NPV earned by the firm from each different option choice.

Rank	Option	NPV £m.
1	6	604*
2	11	567
3	4	541*
4	10	514
5	7	511
6	12	494*
7	8	490
8	9	476
9	5	441
10	2	416

From this list the BSC management eventually chose Options 6, 4, 12 as the final three. Although Option 6 was the most profitable option in terms of NPV the others in this list of three were ranked 3 and 6 respectively. Finally the option choice made by BSC managers was that of Option 12, ranked 6th in NPV terms.

According to Bryer and Brignall (1983), the BSC management argued that the decision should not be made on financial NPV terms alone but on other considerations. In management's opinion Option 12 should be retained because it was characterized as a 'high capacity: radical plant pattern'. As we have seen from our chapter on technology the economies of scale assumption also played a major part in shaping the final option that BSC management would adopt.

Bryer and Brignall criticize management of the BSC for not adopting the 'correct' option, that is, the one which promised the best NPV per unit of capital investment made.

> . . . given the Government's concern with the optimal allocation of resources, it could justifiably be argued that the comparison should have been made using Present Value earned per unit of capital outlay.

In addition Bryer and Brignall criticize the BSC management's use of NPV on a number of other counts. Firstly that they did not carry out a sufficiently wide sensitivity analysis, and that the effect of varying some of the basic assumptions was not examined. It was clear that the BSC's option choice involved a great deal of risk relative to Option 4 because Option 12's NPV profile was negative well into the early 1980s. Option 4 was a more conservative choice, because it obtained a positive NPV contribution much earlier.

Further reading
Bryer and Brignall, *Accounting for British Steel* (Gower, 1983).

In this case although the absolute level of NPV earned favours project B we would favour adopting project A using an accounting ranking procedure that relates expected NPV to the initial capital investment outlay.

However if we look at project A we can see that it requires, in comparison to project B, a relatively small capital outlay which promises returns which are reasonably large and more immediate. Whereas project B involves the commitment of a large initial investment outlay in the expectation that net cash flows will improve in the more distant future. It may be, however, that project B involves investing in new plant and equipment etc. which would secure an improved market share for the product being produced. Whereas with project A we may have invested in existing plant and equipment to 'patch up' or 'modify' the existing equipment or product mix. This latter strategy promises more immediate returns but it may compromise the future market viability of the business.

This criticism of the use of NPV for decision-making has been made by Hayes and Abernathy (1980). They argue that the discounted cash flow calculations have a tendency to bias investment option choices. The mathematics of the discounting calculation can be compared to that of a 'reversed telescope' in which distant returns are depreciated more heavily. According to Williams *et al.* (1986), 'Large-scale strategic investment in, for example, new process technology should capture earnings in the long run but these distant and uncertain returns are worth less in terms of present value'.

It is for these reasons that Hayes argues that decisions made using NPV tend to be more conservative. NPV supports a 'patch and mend' mentality which defends existing process plant and technology. This strategy is attractive in NPV terms because it offers short-run returns which are substantial in relation to modest investment outlay. However Hayes points out that preoccupation with the short run may inhibit innovative decision-making and the exploitation of new process technology which may well be essential if the firm is to have a sustained long-run market presence.

So on the one hand we have the accountants' use of the NPV calculation and on the other we have the American business school interpretation which privileges a more 'enlightened' use of the NPV model (Hayes and Abernathy, 1980). The former is biased in favour of short-term returns while the latter suggests modifying the use of NPV by taking into account factors other than purely the financial present values.

In the case study on the British Steel Corporation (BSC) opposite we show that the BSC used NPV calculations as a means to evaluate the profitability of ten different investment opportunities open to the firm in 1972. This case study illustrates how the strict use of NPV by accountants leads to one set of conclusions whilst management's 'enlightened' use of NPV can lead to a radically different set of investment choices.

This case study illustrates how malleable the NPV calculation was in the hands of BSC management. It also illustrates that BSC management was not preoccupied with a purely financial rationale for their investment strategy. In fact the BSC management decision might well have been supported by Hayes and Abernathy (1980), in that it was adventurous, and conditioned by other factors such as going for market share and achieving this with an innovative investment strategy.

One of the main problems facing the BSC's investment option choice,

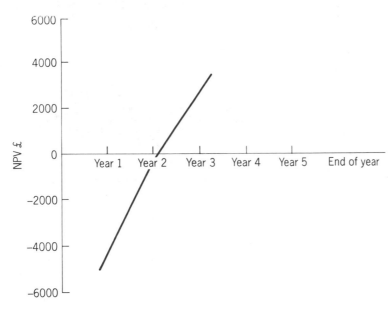

Figure 3.6 NPV profile for Project A.

namely Option 12, was the nature of its NPV profile over the strategic planning time period. If we return to our previous example in Table 3.1 it is apparent that in the early years of the investment planning period the net present value is negative, that is, investment expenditure minus present value up to and including the year considered. However, over a period of time the net present value improves and becomes a positive value. In this simple example, Option A has an NPV profile which becomes positive between year two and year three in terms of net cash-flow years, while project B has an NPV profile which becomes positive in years four to five. The NPV profile for each project is plotted in Figures 3.6 and 3.7.

These figures illustrate that investment projects often have different NPV profiles and that these are determined by the relationship between the level of investment outlay and the present value of future cash flows earned from the investment project. If the investment project involves a very small fraction of the company's capital assets then any failure to obtain the necessary level of cash inflow will not compromise the profitability of the organization as a whole. However, where the investment project involves the allocation of a very large and substantial level of the firm's capital for strategic purposes, any failure to obtain the necessary net cash flows will have a powerful negative effect on the firm's annual profit and loss account.

In the case of the British Steel Corporation, investment Option 12 involved a substantial strategic commitment of financial resources to an investment plan which did not show a positive contribution to profit until the mid-1980s, fifteen years after the start of the plan. A number of fundamental uncertainties will exist over this period, and these may

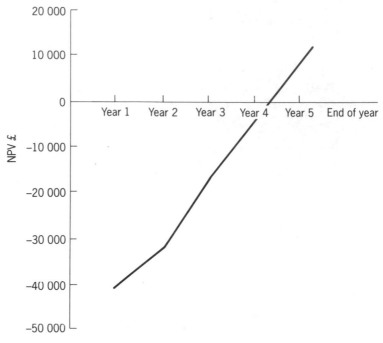

Figure 3.7 NPV profile for Project B.

operate to set the financial net cash inflows off target. In addition any problems associated with the construction of the new steelmaking facilities would also have an adverse effect on the realization of positive NPV.

NPV is a purely internal calculation made by the firm to assess the future profitability of a particular investment plan. As such it also tends to ignore the reactions of competitors. Investments made by the firm in new process technology may be 'matched' by competitors doing the same thing with the net result being overcapacity. This has happened in both the European steel and car industries over the last decade. In addition the information revealed from the NPV calculation depends on the discount rate or cost rate of capital used by the firm. If competitors have access to funds with a lower cost of capital, then their discount rates will also be smaller. The net result is that firms using the NPV calculation can arrive at totally different decisions about similar investment projects.

When a firm has decided to invest strategically it is essential that expected market sales materialize, and that the operational costs of running the investment on a day-to-day basis are budgeted for correctly. It is these two components that determine the annual net cash flow. In addition, construction times and investment costs need to be accurately estimated and executed as planned. With nuclear power reactors, construction costs have been on average above those estimated due to technical problems associated with reactor build. At the Dungeness B Advanced Gas-cooled Reactor (AGR) this involved a construction overrun of approximately 100% or nearly double the original estimate. In such circumstances even where net cash flows are estimated correctly these cannot recover a positive NPV because they have to be set against a much larger than expected investment outlay.

Where the difference between the expected and actual financial variables is adverse and significant, the firm is left in a situation where profit starts to deteriorate. It is at this stage that the operational financial calculations of the annual report and accounts become paramount and take precedence over the strategic.

Strategic and operational financial calculation

Where a firm makes successful strategic financial calculations this will tend also to be revealed in the annual profit and loss account. The firm would see improvements in the profit to sales ratio or profit to capital employed. In this case the relationship between the strategic and operational is a virtuous one financially. For the investment planner it is always important to consider this relationship because in many cases the firm's strategic calculations can operate to frustrate the achievement of an annual profit.

We have examined the nature of strategic financial accounting calculations and in particular the NPV discounted cash flow calculation. In many cases the firm will commit only a small percentage of available financial resources to an investment project. However, cases such as the BSC and Eurotunnel projects have involved, or will involve, a massive commitment of financial resources. With all projects involving a large commitment of financial resources it is vital that the firm establishes a number of fundamental things.

Firstly it is necessary for the firm to establish whether returns from existing investments can cover the cost of the new investment outlay in the early years when the cash flow from the new investment will be negative. Unless the business is a 'greenfield' operation, the existing facilities will have to carry the new investments financially. It is therefore necessary to consider how robust the financial contribution from existing facilities to the new investment will be over a period of time.

Secondly, the firm's calculations concerning future revenue (cash inflow) and future costs (cash outflow) must be made as accurately as possible. Although the NPV calculation can be used to justify the strategic investment opportunity, it is the annual profit and loss account which will financially represent the operational success or failure of the investment. In the case study that follows on the Eurotunnel project, the future financial benefits of the investment are shown in terms of future profit and loss accounts from the year 1993 to 2041.

When a strategic investment project like the Eurotunnel is undertaken, any divergence from the expected financial scenario would have an adverse effect on the business annual report and accounts. If this were to happen the firm would find it very difficult to defend the annual profit level and maintain shareholder interest and confidence.

Where the firm is successful in executing its planned investment strategy then the annual profit and loss account will reveal this fact and confidence in the firm's abilities will usually be maintained. The firm in these circumstances will benefit from a virtuous circle of increased productivity and financial gain.

Failure carries with it a number of operational financial problems which will also have adverse knock-on effects for the firm more generally. When annual profit and loss starts to deteriorate because of strategic miscalculations, the firm will usually try to protect profit by shedding labour and eventually closing down plant and equipment. This connection, between market sales, labour and annual profit, can be made by considering the concept of value added (see Chapter 4).

CASE STUDY 3.5
Eurotunnel – the financial projection

In November 1987 the Offer for Sale document for Eurotunnel shares was issued. This document included financial calculations designed to attract funds and demonstrate the future profitability of the tunnel project. In this document a number of calculations were made, some of which we examine here.

Capital costs

It was expected that the tunnel would involve the investment of approximately £5 billion over a six-year period. This capital expenditure would conisist of money spent on construction costs (60% of the total) and administration and finance charges (40% of the total).

	£ million
Construction costs (July 1987 prices)	2788
Corporate and other costs	642
Provision for inflation	469
Net financing costs	975
Total capital costs	4874

Profitability

The tunnel was expected to open in 1993 and for the period up to 2041 the Eurotunnel consortium estimated the profitability each year of its operations. In the table below we have reproduced a sample of these calculations of annual future profit and loss.

In the event, the Tunnel did not open until 1994 (a year late), and the original revenue estimates had to be revised downwards because of the start-up delays and fierce price competition from the ferry operators. Relationships between Eurotunnel and Transmanche Link (the building contractors) were strained, and actual construction costs were almost double the original estimate. Revised estimates made in 1993 suggested that the Tunnel would not break even until 1998.

It is clear that these expected profits figures depend crucially on a number of very important calculations. Firstly, that the expected construction times and cost schedule can be met and that there are no major problems or delays associated with construction, which would serve to increase the level of capital spend relative to the future earnings that have been projected after 1993. Secondly, that the expected growth rate in passenger traffic is achieved so that revenues earned are not over-estimated and finally, that the level of operating costs is kept to a level that was planned. With these calculations of future profitability there are a great many

Table 3.4 Eurotunnel profit and loss projections

Years			£ million			
	1993	*2000*	*2013*	*2023*	*2033*	*2041*
Turnover	488	1254	3236	6184	11356	17824
Operating costs	(86)	(235)	(631)	(1207)	(2246)	(3604)
Depreciation	(103)	(171)	(234)	(271)	(328)	(383)
Interest	(229)	(234)	39	173	370	616
Profit after tax	63	374	1476	2986	5605	8880

uncertainties. What is certain, however, is that any problems associated with executing the strategy will be reflected in the actual annual profit and loss accounts in future years.

Source: Eurotunnel, 1987.

Conclusion

In this chapter we have argued that traditional economic concepts of costs and pricing abstract from the rules and procedures adopted by accountants within the firm. In assessing some of the predominant financial calculations undertaken by business, however, we found that management acounting systems are based on financial reporting conventions which are designed to promote shareholder interests, and that they may fail to adequately address the fundamental problems of business. Standard costing systems, for example, are concerned more with cost maintenance than with regulating cost reduction, while different methods of allocating costs to products come to quite different conclusions about which products earn the most profit. In contrast to systems which sum costs and then add on a profit mark-up, we have outlined how target pricing systems operate, and how target cost reduction would require the firm to reduce its break-even point.

Finally, we explored management accounting calculations which promise optimal allocation of capital funds, noting that pay-back emphasizes a quick return on the outlay in line with the market and financial conditions the firm faces, while discounted cash flow techniques promise an allocation of capital to the most profitable of investment projects. Again, we found that neither of these forms of calculation could be relied upon to generate investment decisions which best meet the long-term interests of the business.

Further reading

On the budgeting process and management accounting more generally, see Colin Drury's *Management and Cost Accounting* (Chapman & Hall, 3rd edition, 1992). On the differences between Japanese and Western management accounting you might consider Hiromoto's 'Japanese management accounting: another hidden edge', *Harvard Business Review*, July/Aug 1988, or Williams *et al.* 'How far from Japan?', *Critical Perspectives on Accounting*, No. 2 (1991).

On the problems associated with using NPV and DCF techniques, see Hayes and Abernathy 'Managing our way to economic decline', *Harvard Business Review*, May/June 1982, or, more recently, a good set of small case studies by Regine Slagmulder and Werner Bruggeman (1992), 'Investment justification of Flexible Manufacturing Technologies', *International Journal of Operations and Production Management*, vol. 12, no. 7/8.

A text which critically evaluates the usefulness of management accounting techniques is *Relevance Lost*, by Johnson and Kaplan (Harvard Business School Press, 1987). On new cost accounting techniques such as activity based costing (ABC) see also the *Journal of Management Accounting*: November 1989, pp. 42–4, September 1990, pp. 37–42, and March 1991, pp. 42–4.

Y. Monden and K. Hamada's 'Target costing and kaizen costing in Japanese automobile companies' (*Journal of Management Accounting*, vol. 3, pp. 17–34, 1991) covers Japanese management accounting. A more comprehensive text is *Japanese Management Accounting: a World Class Approach to Profit Management*, by Y. Monden and M. Sajuai (Productivity Press, 1989).

Exercises

1 What do you understand by the term 'separation of ownership and control'?

   In what ways will the objectives of management differ from those of the single owner-controller of a small business?

2 Discuss the main benefits assumed to flow from the use of budgets within an organization.

3 What do you understand by the term 'standard costing'? What are the main objectives of a standard costing system?

4 What are some of the main problems associated with 'attaching' costs to a product?

   To what extent is the cost of something the result of an arbitrary allocation of costs?

5 A firm purchases a component from an outside supplier at a cost of £14 per unit. Total annual demand for this component is 10 000

units. Total holding costs are £1.50 per unit, and ordering costs are £12 per order.

(i) What is the economic order quantity?
(ii) What other factors might need to be taken into account in deciding order size?

6 'Break-even analysis is a useful accounting tool we can use to understand the relationship between costs, volume and profit.' Discuss.

7 From the following accounting information:

Sales price per unit	£100
Variable cost per unit	£60
Fixed costs	£1 200 000
Plant capacity	50 000 units

You are required to undertake the following:

(i) Calculate the break-even point.
(ii) Draw the break-even chart.
(iii) Calculate what happens to the break-even point when:
 (a) variable cost increases by £10.00 per unit while all other factors remain constant; and
 (b) the sales price falls by £20.00 per unit, all other factors remaining constant.
(iv) Explain how you could estimate the degree to which a firm is operating above or below break-even from its annual report and accounts.

8 A firm has a choice between investing in project X or Project Y. Project X would involve a cash outlay of £100 000 for the updating of existing facilities. Project Y would involve the introduction of a new flexible manufacturing system. The projects have the following net cash flow profiles.

Project	Outlay (£)	Net cash flow at end of year (£)				
		1	2	3	4	[5]
X	(100 000)	25 000	30 000	40 000	30 000	20 000
Y	(150 000)	60 000	50 000	40 000	20 000	20 000

Assume that for discounting purposes the cost of capital is 10%. You are required to:

(i) Calculate the NPV for each project.
(ii) Recommend, on the basis of the NPV, which project should be adopted.
(iii) Discuss some of the issues, not addressed in the NPV calculation, which you might wish to raise in connection with the decision.

References

Andrews, P. and Brunner, E. (1975) *Studies in Pricing*, Macmillan, London.

Baumol, W.J. (1959) *Business Behavior, Value and Growth*, Macmillan, London.

Berle, A. and Means, G. (1932) *The Modern Corporation and Private Property*, Macmillan, London.

Berry, A. and Jarvis, R. (1994) *Accounting in a Business Context*, 2nd edn, Chapman & Hall, London.

Cosh, A.D. and Hughes, A. (1987) The anatomy of corporate control. *Cambridge Journal of Economics*, Dec.

Cox, B. (1979) *Value Added*, Heinemann, London.

Cyert, R.M. and March J. (1963) *A Behavioral Theory of the Firm*, Prentice Hall, Hemel Hempstead.

Dean, J. (1954) Measuring the productivity of capital, *Harvard Business Review*, Jan/Feb.

Drury, C. (1992) *Management Cost Accounting*, 3rd edn, Van Nostrand Reinhold, Wokingham.

Eichner, A. (1976) *The Megacorp and Oligopoly*, Cambridge University Press, Cambridge.

Elbourne, E. (1920) *The Manufacturing Problem*, The Library Press, London.

Eurotunnel Offer for sale (1987) Eurotunnel, London.

Hall, R. and Hitch, C. (1939) *Price Theory and Business Behaviour*, Oxford Economic Papers.

Hayes, R. and Abernathy, W. (1980) Managing our way to economic decline. *Harvard Business Review*, July/August.

Hiromoto, T. (1988) Japanese management accounting: another hidden edge, *Harvard Business Review*, July–Aug.

Hutton, G. (1953) *We Too Can Prosper*, Allen & Unwin, London.

Johnson, H. and Kaplan, R. (1987) *Relevance Lost: the Rise and Fall of Management Accounting*, Harvard Business School Press, Boston.

Koshikawa, T. *et al.* (1989) Japanese Management Accounting: a comparative perspective, *Management Accounting*, Nov.

Marris, R. (1964) *Theory of Managerial Capitalism*, Macmillan, London.

Norgan, M. and Prasanna, S. (1989) Japanese Management Accounting; its contribution to the Japanese economic miracle, *Management Accounting*, June.

Simon, H. (1955) A behavioral model of rational choice. *Quarterly Journal of Economics*, **69**.

Sizer, J. (1977) *An Insight into Management Accounting*, Penguin, Harmondsworth.

Skinner, R.C. (1970) The determination of selling prices. *Journal of Industrial Economics*, July.

Solomons, D. (1965) *Divisional Performance, Measurement and Control*, Richard D. Urwin, USA.

Thompson, G. (1986) *Economic Calculation and Policy Formation*, Routledge, London.

Williams K. *et al.* (1983) *Why are the British Bad at Manufacturing*? Routledge, London.

Williams, K., Williams, J. and Haslam, C. (1989) Why take the stocks out? Britain vs Japan, *International Journal of Operations and Production Management*, vol. 9, no. 8.

Williams, K. *et al.* (1992) Management Accounting: the Western problematic against the Japanese application, *mimeo* (University of Manchester).

Wood, E.G. (1978) *Value Added – the Key to Prosperity*, Business Books, London.

Performance evaluation

4

The main emphasis in this chapter is on how company accounts may be used to assess different aspects of business performance. Measures such as real sales growth, productivity, stock turnover, and liquidity ratios are described and assessed, and particular attention is given to value added and its distribution as a major indicator of corporate well-being.

Introduction

In Chapters 1 and 2, we emphasized the importance of recovering costs from market sales, and the need to apply productive resources to the aims of cost reduction and recovery. When a firm is successfully taking advantage of a growing market, then sales revenue and value added generated by the firm will improve. Under these market conditions, the productive ratios of the business, for example real sales or value added generated per employee, and the financial ratios, for example, liquidity, profit to sales, and cash flow, will all appear satisfactory.

In Chapter 3, we saw the use that can be made by management of the information which companies must provide in their annual financial report and accounts. In this chapter, we examine the use which can be made of these publicly available reports in interpreting a firm's market, productive and financial performance. We will consider the relationship between the market, productive, and financial ratios of the business, making use of the Profit and Loss Account, Balance Sheet, and Source and Application of Funds Statement. We show, with information covering the past five to ten years for a variety of companies, how it is possible, using the accounts, to develop an understanding of the trajectory of each business.

Evaluating market performance

One of the most important aspects of the performance of a firm relates to its success in recovering costs from sales of its final product or service sales and its overall market share. Tesco plc's annual report and accounts for 1990, for example, draws attention to the fact that, 'As a result of a significant increase in selling space and a strong sales performance in existing stores, and the acquisition of Hillards in 1987, [Tesco's] market share has increased significantly from 6.7% to 8.7% over the past 5 years.'

Sales breakdown by activity and geographic area

We start our evaluation of company performance by considering the breakdown of sales revenue by activity and by geographic area, which many companies disclose in the notes to their accounts. From the information which the company reveals on sales by activity, it is possible to assess the extent to which some activities have become more important than others. For example, over a period of time the company may be running down particular aspects of the product mix of the business and concentrating on specific areas, or the firm may be diversifying from a dominant product type into new unrelated areas of business.

ICI, before it was broken up into ICI and Zeneca, reported the sales and profit breakdown by activity in 1991. These figures are converted, in Table 4.1, into a percentage share of total sales and total profit by division.

The figures in Table 4.1 show that by far the greatest share of sales revenue in ICI came from the Petrochemicals and plastics product

Table 4.1 ICI sales and profit shares by division, 1991

	Share of sales %	Share of profit %
Pharmaceuticals	10.6	42.7
Specialities	8.6	0.3
Paints	12.4	9.4
Fertilizer	6.5	1.0
Agrochemicals and seeds	10.3	9.6
Pigments	5.3	8.7
Explosives	3.9	4.4
Fibres	5.3	1.6
Petrochemicals and plastics	21.9	9.0
Industrial chemicals	15.2	13.3

Table 4.2 Domestic and overseas sales by Ford UK, 1986–91

Year	Home market sales (£m.)	Export sales (£m.)	Home market sales as share of total sales	Export sales as share of total sales
1986	3187	1187	72.8	27.20
1987	3854	1357	73.9	26.10
1988	4366	1570	73.5	26.50
1989	4850	1882	72.0	28.00
1990	4454	3055	59.3	40.70
1991	3351	2840	54.1	45.90

division, but in terms of profit, the Pharmaceuticals product division generated 43% of the profits from only 11% of the sales revenue.

In addition to the breakdown of sales revenue by activity, it is also possible from the annual report and accounts to obtain information on the geographic breakdown of sales. There are two aspects to this breakdown which are worth considering: those sales made overseas from home-based operations (i.e. exports), and those sales made by the overseas operations of the firm.

The Ford UK accounts present a ten-year run of figures showing the breakdown of sales between domestic and overseas markets, six years of which are shown in Table 4.2.

Table 4.2 shows that, in the late 1980s, Ford UK's exports accounted for 25 to 30% of total sales. In 1990 and 1991, however, the export share increased to 40 to 45% as Ford's sales pattern shifted after the takeover of Jaguar (which sells more in export markets than in the UK).

Whereas Ford UK exports directly from the UK, Hanson Trust, as we saw in Chapter 1, prefers to purchase firms overseas rather than directly export. Overseas operations in Hanson Trust have accounted for a steady 50–60% of sales revenue in the company over the last ten years. More generally, if we were to split the sales revenue of the top 25 UK manufacturers by domestic versus overseas operations, we would find that overseas operations now generally account for an increasing share of total sales revenue by UK-registered companies (Williams *et al.*, 1990).

Growth in sales

Sales growth is a useful calculation which can be used to compare the performance of different firms selling in similar markets, especially when the comparison is made over a period of years. In this calculation, we take the total sales revenue or net sales revenue figures from the company's Profit and Loss Account. When we take raw financial data from the accounts of a company over a period of time, we call them the 'nominal' financial data. This nominal financial information includes the effects of any price increases passed on by the company to the customer. We will at times in this chapter refer to 'real' sales, or 'real' value added. This real data is obtained by deflating the nominal, so taking out the effects of inflation each year (see Key Concept 4.1).

KEY CONCEPT 4.1
Nominal and real financial information

The nominal figures are those which are taken straight from the annual report and accounts of a company, or from annual national or sectoral statistics, and reflect price levels in that year. Real financial information 'deflates' the nominal information by a price index which strips out the effect of inflation.

The Retail Price Index (all items) is updated each month, and can be found in government publications like the *Monthly Digest of Statistics* or the *Annual Abstract of Statistics* (see Key Concept 10.4 for further details). The table below shows the Retail Price Index with a base year of 1980 = 100.

	Retail price index 1980 = 100
1980	100
1981	111.9
1982	121.4
1983	127.1
1984	133.4
1985	141.5
1986	146.3
1987	152.4
1988	159.8
1989	172.3
1990	188.6
1991	199.7
1992	207.1

In order to calculate real sales from the nominal sales obtained from a set of accounts, we divide the nominal sales by the Retail Price Index expressed as a decimal, as shown below.

	Nominal sales (£ m.)	Retail Price Index (1980 = 1.00)	Real sales (£m.) (1980 prices)
1980	258	1.00	258
1981	267	1.12	238
1982	278	1.21	230
1983	312	1.27	246
1984	334	1.33	251
1985	348	1.42	245
1986	354	1.46	242

1987	357	1.52	235
1988	365	1.60	228
1989	378	1.72	220
1990	382	1.89	202
1991	399	2.00	200
1992	422	2.07	204

In this hypothetical example, we can see that although nominal sales increased by over 60% between 1980 and 1992, real sales fell over the same period by more than 10%.

The principle of deflating nominal figures is as follows. Sales revenue in a given year is made up of sales volume × price per unit sold. So in 1991 and 1992 we could have:

	1991	1992
Sales revenue =	Volume × price/unit	Volume × price/unit
	100 × £10.00	100 × £12.00
Sales revenue =	£1000	£1200

All that has changed is the price per unit, and this has increased nominal revenue by £200. In real terms, however, the number of units sold has not changed. If inflation had been 20% for the period 1991 to 1992, then real sales would in 1992 have been the same as 1991 – i.e. £1000 in 1991 prices. That is: £1200/1.20 (the inflation index as a decimal).

When we deflate the nominal sales figures obtained from the annual report and accounts, we have real sales figures which give an indication of how volume sales have been increasing or decreasing.

Table 4.3 takes nominal sales revenue from Ford UK's accounts, and then converts it into real sales revenue (1982 prices) using the method shown in Key Concept 4.1. This is represented in the last column as an index, with 1982 as the base year. The table shows that from 1982 to 1984, Ford UK's real sales increased by only 4%, but that in the general UK economic upturn of the late 1980s volume growth was strong, with a 46% increase in real sales over the decade to 1990. In 1991, however, the level of real sales fell to a level which was only 13% above that of 1982. This alternation of positive and negative real growth in sales is typical of a cyclical market.

As we saw in Chapter 1, growth in real sales was slower in Ford UK than in Hanson Trust. Hanson's growth was, however, achieved by taking over other firms' operations, while Ford UK concentrated on its core activity of making cars, and achieved organic growth in sales, particularly in the UK home market.

The calculation of value added

We turn now to the calculation of value added, which is the net output of the business. As we saw in Chapter 1, value added can be measured

Table 4.3   Real sales growth at Ford UK

Year	Sales nominal in (£m.)	Retail Price Index as a decimal	Real sales (£m.) (Col. 2 divided by Col. 3)	Real sales revenue index (1982 = 100)
1982	3287	1.21	2717	100.0
1983	3585	1.27	2823	103.90
1984	3752	1.33	2821	103.83
1985	4045	1.42	2849	104.86
1986	4374	1.46	2996	110.27
1987	5211	1.52	3428	126.17
1988	5936	1.60	3710	136.55
1989	6732	1.72	3914	144.06
1990	7509	1.89	3973	146.23
1991	6191	2.00	3096	113.95

Table 4.4   Ford UK value added

Year	Labour costs (£m.)	Profit pre-tax (£m.)	Depreciation (£m.)	Nominal value added (£m.)	Real value added	Index of real value added (1982 = 100)
1982	710	194	192	1096	906	100
1983	743	178	231	1152	907	100
1984	785	60	165	1010	759	84
1985	756	160	164	1080	766	85
1986	791	109	182	1082	741	82
1987	828	317	192	1337	880	97
1988	872	673	201	1746	1091	120
1989	1000	483	25	1508	877	97
1990	1295	−274	301	1322	701	77
1991	1290	−935	437	792	396	44

in either of two ways – as sales less purchases, or as labour costs (including social charges) plus depreciation plus profit pre-tax.

Value added, as we have seen, represents the value that is recovered from selling the product after the suppliers of components and services have been paid. What is left over after paying for the purchases is the fund of money out of which wages and salaries and the depreciation of capital equipment must be paid, after which it can be established whether or not the firm has made a profit. Once corporation tax and dividends have been paid, profits can be retained to be used as a source of funding for future investment.

In Table 4.4 we calculate the value added for Ford UK in nominal terms, by adding together labour costs, pre-tax profit, and depreciation from the company accounts. Then, using the method outlined in Key Concept 4.1, we convert nominal value added into a real figure by using the Retail Price Index as a deflator, and in the final column we express real value added as an index number, with 1982 as the base year.

Table 4.4 shows that real value added fell by 18% between 1982 and 1986, but recovered in the upswing of the late 1980s, reaching in 1988 a level 20% above that of 1982. In the subsequent recession, however, real value added collapsed by 60% between 1988 and 1991.

Evaluating productive performance

As well as analysing an organization's success or failure in the market place, we can also assess its productive performance by measuring the productivity of labour and fixed assets. In addition, we can look at stock turnover to indicate the extent to which the firm is reorganizing its production to improve flow.

Productivity and the organization of production

In economic analysis, productivity is measured by relating a physical measure of output to a physical measure of labour or capital input, such as cars per employee. In many manufacturing organizations, it is not possible to identify a single physical unit of output which is produced by the firm, and in these cases output has to be measured in financial terms, such as value added per employee.

In the case of Ford UK, we do have a reasonably clear physical measure of output, and vehicles produced per employee can be calculated, as in Table 4.5.

Table 4.5 shows that Ford UK increased productivity in physical units per employee by 65% from 1982 to 1988. We can see that this productivity gain was made up of an increase in output of 13% and a reduction in employees of 31%, with the reduction in the workforce making the main contribution to productivity gain. Labour productivity fell in the recession, however, to 13 vehicles per employee in 1991, mirroring the falls in real sales (see Table 4.3) and real value added (see Table 4.4).

Although the physical productivity calculation in Table 4.5 is useful in assessing how Ford has performed over the last ten years, it has limited applicability when we are comparing one firm with another. This is because no two firms are the same, and in most cases there may be no single physical homogeneous unit of output.

Table 4.5 Vehicles per employee at Ford UK

Year	Vehicles sold (000s)	Employees (000s)	Vehicles sold per employee
1982	687	70	9.81
1984	653	59	11.07
1986	656	49	13.39
1988	779	48	16.23
1991	677	52	13.02

As we shall see in Chapter 5, academic researchers have used a physical productivity measure – cars per employee – to compare car manufacturers, suggesting that Toyota produces twice as many cars per employee as Ford US. This calculation of physical units per employee at first seems a sensible one, until it is recognized that Toyota is a much less vertically integrated firm than Ford US (see Key Concept 4.2).

KEY CONCEPT 4.2
Vertical integration and disintegration

Some firms are more vertically integrated than others, in that they add more value to the raw materials and components they purchase. We can estimate this difference in vertical integration by calculating a ratio of value added to sales. The higher the ratio, the greater the degree of vertical integration. If we have two firms, firm A with a 30% ratio of value added to sales and firm B with a ratio of 15%, then firm A adds twice as much value to the product as firm B.

We can represent this calculation in the diagram below.

Firm A

70% of final sales value bought-in	30% value added in-house to sales

——————————————————————————————— — — — — — — — 100%

Firm B

85% of final sales value bought-in	15% added in-house to sales

——————————————————————————————— — — — — 100%

If the sales price for each unit sold is the same, firm A adds more value added to the product than firm B. As we have seen, most of the value added (or cost added) to a product or service is labour cost. For every one unit produced, firm A might be using twice the labour of firm B. But we cannot say that firm B is twice as productive because it is using half the labour per unit than A. This is because the firms we are comparing have different degrees of vertical integration. The end result is that both are producing a unit of output at the same sales price per unit.

Further reading
Williams et al. (1990).

Table 4.6 Real value added per employee at Ford UK, 1982–91

Year	Value added in real terms (£m.)	Employees (000s)	Real value added per employee (£)
1982	906	70	12 943
1984	759	59	12 864
1986	741	49	15 122
1988	1091	48	22 729
1991	396	52	7 615

Table 4.7 Real value added per £ of fixed assets at Ford UK, 1982–91

Year	Value added (£m.)	Fixed assets (£m.)	Value added generated per £ of fixed assets
1982	1096	806	1.36
1984	1010	839	1.20
1986	1082	964	1.12
1988	1746	1207	1.45
1991	792	2198	0.36

To get around the problem of firms generally producing a variable output mix and also having differing degrees of vertical integration, we can use instead a financial measure of net output (value added) in relation to labour and capital input for productivity calculations. The financial measure of value added per employee automatically corrects for the degree of vertical integration and represents all physical output in one financial variable – value added.

Table 4.6 illustrates this calculation for Ford UK, using the value added figures from Table 4.4 and employment from Table 4.5. It shows that value added generated per employee is flat from 1982 to 1984, because real value added falls at the same rate as employment drops. By 1986 real value added is still at the 1984 level, but employment loss has resulted in the productivity (value added per employee) increasing. In the general economic upswing up to 1988, real value added per employee was some 75% higher than that of 1982, but in the recession, value added per employee collapsed.

In addition to using real value added generated per employee to indicate the productivity of labour, we can also calculate value added generated per £ value of fixed assets, to indicate the productivity of fixed assets. This calculation for Ford UK is illustrated in Table 4.7.

It can be seen from Table 4.7 that fixed assets at Ford UK generated £1.36 of value added in 1982, but that this fell by 18% between 1982 and 1986. Nineteen eighty-eight was a peak year for Ford UK, and the value added generated by fixed assets returned to 1982 levels, only to collapse again in the subsequent recession.

Stock turnover

We now consider stock turn ratios, which can be calculated from a company's annual report and accounts, by dividing annual sales turnover by the average level of stocks over the year. The ratios represent the average number of times the stock 'turns over' each year, and can be used to evaluate the organization's relations with suppliers, its internal organization of production, and its distribution linkages.

Stocks represent a financial burden for the firm, as capital is tied up in stocks which could otherwise be used more productively, so a high stock turn ratio generally indicates good performance in managing internal operations and external relationships. Different types of organization have different stock requirements, however – manufacturers generally have a long lead time from raw material purchase to finished output, for example, whereas supermarkets have a relatively quick cycle time or lead time from purchase of food to final point of sale. This is illustrated, for Sainsbury's and Ford UK, in Table 4.8.

Table 4.9 demonstrates the general difference in stock turnover between a food retailer and a manufacturer. On average, stock turns over 22 times a year at Sainsbury's, or once every 2.2 weeks. In Ford UK, because of the long lead time from raw material coming into the factory to final product coming off the line, stock takes 10 or 11 weeks to turn over. It should be remembered that stocks tie up the labour

Table 4.8 Stock turn in Sainsbury's and Ford UK, 1987–90

Year	Weeks of stock held in Sainsbury's	Stock turn for Sainsbury's	Weeks of stock held in Ford UK	Stock turn for Ford UK
1987	2.28	22.8	9.81	5.3
1988	2.18	23.9	9.56	5.44
1989	2.41	21.6	10.83	4.8
1990	2.23	23.3	11.82	4.4

Note: Stock turn is sales turnover/average stock

Average stock is (opening stock + closing stock)/2

Weeks' stock held is 52/stock turn ratio.

costs that have gone into the production of that stock – at Ford in 1990, an amount equivalent to 23% of a year's sales revenue (11.82 as a percentage of 52) is tied up in stocks.

In addition to calculating an overall stock turnover ratio, it is often possible to disaggregate stocks into their component parts of raw material, work-in-progress, and finished stock. To check if the firm is improving relations with its suppliers, improving the internal flow of materials, and improving linkages to distributors, we can work out ratios as follows:

$$\text{Raw material stock turn} = \frac{\text{Sales revenue}}{\text{Average raw materials}}$$

$$\text{Work-in-progress stock turn} = \frac{\text{Sales revenue or value added}}{\text{Average work-in-progress}}$$

$$\text{Finished stock turn} = \frac{\text{Sales revenue}}{\text{Average finished stock}}$$

Where the raw material stock turn is increasing (or the number of weeks' stock held is falling), this indicates that suppliers are delivering more frequently. If the work-in-progress stock turn is increasing, this may be because integration between machines is more effective, or because the design and development team have reduced the number of components and hence the number of stages in production (see Chapter 2). Finally, where the finished stock turn is increasing, this might be the result of better co-ordination between orders received and production, or of de-stocking following an expansion in market demand.

Evaluating financial performance

We turn now to consider the financial ratios of a business, and how the sales and productive performance of the business can improve, maintain, or, in some cases, destabilize them. In order to demonstrate the connections between financial performance and the market/productive conditions of the business, we will again utilize the concept of value added, and particularly the share of labour in value added.

Labour's share in value added

It is generally the case that the greatest share of the value added generated by the firm is used to pay labour. If market sales fall, labour's share in value added will rise. This has the effect of squeezing profits, particularly as firms generally write off a constant proportion of their fixed assets as depreciation each year.

Table 4.9 explores the behaviour over time of labour's share in value added in three of the companies we have been considering in this chapter: Ford UK, Hanson Trust, and Tesco plc.

The three cases in Table 4.9 represent different types of organization –

Table 4.9   Labour's share of value added (%): Tesco, Hanson and Ford

Year	Tesco PLC	Hanson Trust	Ford UK
1983	70.51	75.22	64.5
1984	69.30	73.43	77.7
1985	67.66	67.55	64.07
1986	63.28	57.95	56.99
1987	59.47	51.85	53.56
1988	57.67	53.72	38.06
1989	57.05	47.57	45.7
1990	54.86	43.17	92.9

a retailer of food and drink, a conglomerate specializing in growth through acquisition, and a manufacturing company. Labour's share in value added was around 70% in each company in 1983/4, but in each case this level fell as the economy recovered in the mid-1980s.

We have seen, in Case Study 1.2, how Tesco plc now retails from larger premises. It has, at the same time, shifted into higher value added, higher profit margin activities, like in-store bakeries and pre-pared meals – a far cry from the 'pile them high, sell them cheap' philosophy of the 1970s. As a result, the value added by Tesco for every £1 of goods sold rose from 12.6 pence in 1980 to 18.3 pence in 1990. This represents an increase in the value added generated per £1 of sales of 45%. If Tesco had generated its 1980 value added per £1 of sales in 1990, its profits pre-tax in that year would only have been £60 million, rather than £362 million. Thus Tesco has successfully shifted into a higher value added market segment, reducing labour's share of value added to increase the profit margin on items sold.

With Hanson Trust we also see a reduction in labour's share of value added. This is the result of a programme of acquisitions which em-phasized the purchase of basic operations such as aggregates, coal and gold mining, cement, and forestry. These acquisitions delivered a five-fold increase in sales revenues (and hence value added) for only a 3.7-fold increase in labour costs. Profits were increased, at the expense of labour's share in value added.

Demand conditions in the UK were favourable for Ford UK after 1983, and vehicles sold in the UK increased by 22% from 1983 to 1989, while employment fell by 31%. This combination of growing sales and reduced employment served to reduce labour's share of value added to 45% in 1989. At this stage, as we shall see, Ford UK was generating internally a record level of cash flow and profit. The recession hit car sales hard, however, and labour's share in value added at Ford rocketed upwards.

The Ford case illustrates a fundamental point: when sales volume falls, value added generated will also fall, labour's share of value added will increase, and profits will decline. In this situation, if there is no prospect of an immediate sales recovery, job losses are inevitable when the firm has to renormalize labour's share of value added.

Cash flow

Cash flow is what remains of value added after labour's share is deducted, and Table 4.10 illustrates the effect of changes in labour's share on cash flow in Tesco, Hanson Trust, and Ford UK.

The calculation of cash flow in Table 4.10 is equivalent to that in the funds flow statement published with the profit and loss account and balance sheet in the annual report and accounts. This statement discloses which funds are generated from internal cash flow (profit and depreciation) and which are externally sourced from borrowings.

Cash flow is the lifeblood of any organization, and what is left after dividends and tax have been paid is the major source of funding

Table 4.10 Cash flow as a percentage of value added

Year	Tesco (%)	Hanson (%)	Ford (%)
1983	29.5	24.78	35.50
1984	30.7	26.57	22.30
1985	32.3	32.45	35.93
1986	36.7	42.05	43.01
1987	40.5	48.15	46.44
1988	42.3	46.28	61.94
1989	43.0	52.43	54.30
1990	45.1	56.83	7.10

Table 4.11 Dividends and capital investment as a percentage of cash flow

Year	Hanson Trust		Tesco PLC	
	Capital investment as % of cash flow	Dividends as % of cash flow	Capital investment as % of cash flow	Dividends as % of cash flow
1988	19.7	26.6	141.1	14.6
1989	16.2	20.5	140.5	15.6
1990	16.9	34.2	145.3	15.0

for capital investment projects. A strong cash flow indicates a high capacity to maintain dividends and finance capital investment. Many organizations do not have the high share of cash flow in value added that Tesco and Hanson can obtain, and after paying dividends they have very little, if any, cash left over for internal capital investment programmes. Under these circumstances, firms have to seek investment funding from increased bank borrowing, exposing them to interest charges which can depress future profits.

We have seen how successful Tesco and Hanson have been in generating cash over the past decade, and Table 4.11 shows how they have allocated these funds.

Table 4.11 reveals considerable differences in priorities between Hanson and Tesco over the years 1988–90. In this period, Hanson Trust applied only 16–20% of its cash flow to the organic development of its assets base. Tesco, in contrast, spent 40–45% more on capital investment than it generated from internal cash flow, borrowing externally to bridge the gap. As a percentage of internally generated cash flow, Tesco was investing in organic growth at a rate which was 8.5 times that of Hanson Trust.

Dividends paid out of internally generated cash flow to Hanson's shareholders were twice those paid by Tesco. This is typical of Hanson, whose main objective is to satisfy shareholders with a good distribution of profit to dividends (Adcroft *et al.*, 1991). In addition, rather than apply cash for the purposes of capital investment, Hanson has built up a massive cash surplus in the balance sheet to maintain the liquidity ratios of the business, so that borrowing to fund takeovers is not a problem. In the case of Tesco, on the other hand, little cash is employed in the balance sheet, because most of the funds generated from operations are applied immediately to the expansion of retail square footage and hence retail sales.

Break-even

It is clear from the above discussion that profit is the volatile residual which remains after labour costs and depreciation have been covered, so it is extremely vulnerable to reductions in demand under cyclical market conditions. This vulnerability can be measured using the calculation we developed in Chapter 3 of the extent to which an organization is operating above the break-even point:

$$\text{Per cent operating above or below break-even point} = \frac{\text{Value added minus (labour plus depreciation)}}{\text{Value added}}$$

Table 4.12 presents this calculation for Tesco plc. It is clear from Table 4.12 that the value added generated by Tesco has increasingly been covering its labour costs and depreciation charges. In 1980, Tesco had a margin of safety of only 19%, which means that if sales and value added were to have fallen by 19%, Tesco would have just achieved

Table 4.12   Tesco: per cent operations above break-even point

Year	Total labour costs (£m.)	Depreciation (£m.)	Value added (£m.)	Per cent operations above break-even point
1980	138.64	17.56	193.20	19.15
1981	170.80	22.68	249.48	22.45
1982	191.23	25.82	284.05	23.59
1983	211.05	27.21	299.26	20.38
1984	234.11	30.71	337.82	21.61
1985	264.89	35.59	391.48	23.25
1986	300.09	43.11	474.20	27.63
1987	332.89	50.89	559.78	31.44
1988	391.95	61.80	679.75	33.25
1989	458.59	69.2	803.79	34.34
1990	543.94	85.5	991.44	36.51

break-even (just covering labour and depreciation), but would have made no contribution to profits. By 1990, Tesco had increased the margin of safety to 37%, close to that of its main rival, Sainsbury's.

Where a firm is operating above the break-even point, two factors can lead to a reduction in the margin of safety and contribution to profit – a reduction in sales volume, and a reduction in price (if this fails to generate an offsetting increase in sales volume). Even though, in 1990, Tesco had a large margin of safety, the company could still have suffered a loss of profit in the event of a price war. Price is a critical variable in food retailing, especially in a recession, and the super-markets are vulnerable to competition from discount warehouses. If prices were to drop by, say, 20%, the margin of safety would drop to 16%, and the contribution to profit and cash flow would be much reduced at Tesco plc.

Liquidity

We turn now to the calculation of a firm's liquidity, which draws on information from a company's balance sheet (unlike the measures of financial performance in the previous sections, which draw more on the revenue side of the published report and accounts). We have seen that where a firm operates in a cyclical market, value added is also likely to fluctuate. The result in cash flow terms is often a cycle of surpluses and deficits. If firms want to maintain capital expenditure programmes in the face of these cyclical fluctuations, they need to seek external funding, particularly in times of deficit. This exposes the firm's balance sheet to scrutiny by the lender. As we shall see in Chapter 7,

UK banks are particularly concerned about liquidity, which they see as essential to maintain the security of their loans.

Liquidity ratios measure the relationship between current liabilities and current assets (see Key Concept 4.3), and banks assess these ratios to establish credit ratings for the firms they are considering lending to.

KEY CONCEPT 4.3
Liquidity ratios

The current liquidity ratio of a firm is its current assets (closing stock, debtors, and cash at hand or in the bank) divided by its current liabilities (trade creditors, and liabilities payable within the next financial year).

It is often considered that the current assets of a business should be sufficient to cover the current liabilities twice over – i.e. that its current liquidity ratio should be 2:1.

In addition to the calculation of a current ratio, many accounting texts also recommend the calculation of a quick assets ratio, sometimes known as the 'acid test'. In this calculation, the stock figure is deducted from the numerator of the current ratio, as the timing of revenues from sales of stock is often uncertain.

It is often considered that current liabilities should be covered by current assets less stocks – i.e. that the acid test ratio should be 1:1.

Table 4.13(a) compares the current liquidity ratios of Tesco and Sainsbury's, while Table 4.13(b) gives a similar comparison for Toyota, Mazda, and Ford UK.

In both retail companies, the liquidity ratios are well below the 2:1 level, indicating an inability to cover short-term liabilities. Under such

Table 4.13 Current liquidity ratios

a) Tesco and Sainsbury's

Year	Tesco plc	Sainsbury's
1988	0.51:1	0.38:1
1989	0.50:1	0.38:1
1990	0.37:1	0.44:1

b) Toyota, Mazda, and Ford UK

Year	Toyota	Mazda	Ford UK
1987	1.83:1	0.94:1	1.34:1
1988	1.76:1	0.87:1	1.25:1
1989	2.21:1	0.96:1	0.80:1
1990	1.92:1	0.97:1	0.88:1
1991	1.84:1	1.05:1	0.90:1

circumstances, it is likely that any loans would need to be secured on property or on preferential loan stock.

The experience of the three car assemblers is quite different. Mazda and Ford UK had similar current ratios of roughly 1:1 in 1991, but whereas Mazda had maintained its liquidity ratio over time, Ford's position had deteriorated considerably since 1987. A more striking a comparison is with Toyota, which had a current ratio of almost 2:1. Toyota had managed to achieve this 'ideal' ratio because the company had generated a surplus of cash which was held under current assets in the balance sheet.

While liquidity ratios have much influence with external providers of credit, particularly in the UK, the future generation of cash flow may be of even greater significance, as this is what will determine whether or not a loan can be serviced. Detailed cash flow statements are not generally provided for anyone outside the organization, but they would be made available to the bank before a decision on lending was made.

It is possible, however, for outsiders to establish the trajectory of the firm using labour's share of value added. Where labour's share of value added is rising over time, this suggests that the firm's cash flow position is more likely to be deteriorating than improving.

Shareholder calculations

We have seen, in this chapter, how value added calculations can be used to highlight the share of net output distributed to the various stakeholders in the business. By far the greatest share of the value added fund is distributed to the employees, and it is they who bear the major burden of any adjustment when value added falls. As labour's share of value added increases, this presses on the 'interests' of the shareholder.

In this final section we consider the calculations of the shareholder, and how these are reflected in the annual report and accounts. As we shall see in Chapter 7, most shares nowadays are held by financial institutions – insurance companies, unit trusts, and pension funds –

Table 4.14 Composition of shareholdings in Tesco and Sainsbury's in 1990 (percent share)

Year	Tesco plc		Sainsbury's	
	Corporate/ institution	Individual	Corporate/ institution	Individual
1990	85.8	14.2	53.0	47.0

rather than by individuals. Some company reports disclose the pattern of share ownership, and Table 4.14 compares Tesco and Sainsbury's in this respect.

Table 4.14 shows that almost half of Sainsbury's shares are still in the hands of individuals, whereas Tesco reflects the more general condition where 80% or more of the shares are held by corporate institutional shareholders. The latter manage investments in company shares on the basis of the performance of their investment. It is the job of the unit trust or pension fund manager to monitor the performance of their shareholdings in different organizations, and it is for their benefit that company annual reports and accounts give information on measures such as earnings per share, dividends per share, and price earnings ratio.

Earnings per ordinary share is generally calculated as the net profit for the year after tax, divided by the number of ordinary shares. This measures the full potential dividend per share if all profits after tax were distributed to ordinary shareholders. In practice, however, earnings per share will usually exceed dividends per share, because the company has to consider the need to retain profit for business expansion, as well as the short-term interests of the shareholders. This is illustrated for Tesco plc in Table 4.15.

We have seen in Table 4.9 that labour's share of value added fell at Tesco in the late 1980s, and this was reflected in increased earnings per share, as shown in Table 4.15. Tesco has maintained a 26–28% distribution of profits to dividends, but the dividend per share more than doubled (from 1.9 pence in 1986 to 4.3 pence in 1990) on the back of the increase in earnings per share.

For the fund manager in a unit trust or pension fund, the two most important indicators which will be monitored are the price earnings ratio and the dividend yield. The price earnings ratio is the market price of the share divided by earnings per share. It can be seen from Table 4.15 that the price earnings ratio for Tesco was declining, which means that the stock market would have been downgrading the market

Table 4.15 Tesco earnings per share, dividends per share, price earnings ratio and dividend yield

Year	Earnings per share (pence)	Dividends per share (pence)	Dividends per share as percentage of earnings per share	Price earnings ratio on year end market price per share	Dividend yield (%)
1986	7.03	1.93	27.45	15.79	1.74
1987	9.51	2.43	25.55	16.44	1.56
1988	10.69	2.85	26.66	14.22	1.88
1989	12.35	3.50	28.34	12.39	2.29
1990	16.36	4.30	26.28	11.98	2.19

value in relation to earnings per share. As the capital value of the shares deteriorates in relation to earnings per share, however, the dividend yield (dividends as a percentage of the market value of the shares) improves.

The dividend yield and the price earnings ratios are two powerful calculations which can materially affect the future of an organization. When these ratios weaken, institutional shareholders may start to sell the company's shares on the stock market, where ownership of the company can be traded so that the firm changes hands.

In these circumstances, it is not surprising to find external pressures being internalized by the organization, so that management actions start to reflect the 'interests' of the external shareholder. Discounted cash flow and standard costing techniques, for example, are employed to ensure that the shareholders' rate of return on investment is maximized and that costs are maintained to keep profits under control, as we saw in Chapter 3.

Conclusion

In this chapter we have established how it is possible to utilize published company accounts to evaluate the market, productive, and financial performance of the business. We have explored a number of different indicators of performance which can be identified from the accounts, and have indicated their uses and limitations. What stands out is the crucial importance of the value added concept, both in establishing the conditions for cost recovery and profit contribution, and in measuring productivity.

Analysis of company accounts shows that no two companies have the same results, even in the same line of business. We can use it, however, to consider how a particular company has performed over the last five to ten years, whether this performance is on a positive or negative trajectory, and how the firm compares with other firms in a similar line of business. This helps us to improve our understanding of a firm's performance, and to learn from the differences between firms.

We saw that, generally, good marketing and productive performance is reflected in good financial results, but that UK firms are increasingly taking decisions in the short-term interests of their shareholders, which may conflict with the long-term needs of the business.

Further reading

There are a number of case studies which use the framework outlined in this chapter.

Firstly, at a sectoral level *Factories or Warehouses*, by Karel Williams *et al*. (University of East London Occasional Paper No. 6, 1992) analyses Japanese manufacturing foreign direct investment in the UK.

Hanson versus ICI, by Andy Adcroft *et al*. (University of East London

Occasional Paper No. 2, 1991) considers the Hanson bid for ICI and the nature of financial engineering.

Leyland Daf: A Good Deal Gone Bad, by Karel Williams *et al.* (University of East London Occasional Paper No. 12, 1993) uses company accounts to analyse the power relation between Leyland Daf (NV) (in Holland) and Leyland Daf UK.

Finally, *Fait Accompli: A Machiavellian Interpretation of the Renault-Volvo Merger*, by Karel Williams *et al.* (University of Manchester Labour Studies Occasional Paper No. 7, 1993) uses company accounts and company publications to consider the different problems of Volvo and Renault in relation to cost recovery, and their different reasons for seeking a merger.

Exercises

1   What calculations can you make from a set of company accounts which could be used to explain the market performance of that company?

2   What do you understand by nominal and real sales revenue? Using the information below, and the Retail Price Index figures from Key Concept 4.1, calculate the real sales revenue for J. Sainsbury plc, and index this sales revenue with a base year 1982 = 100.

J. Sainsbury plc

Year	Sales revenue (£m.) million	Square footage total sales area million square feet
1982	1950.5	3.3
1983	2315.8	3.6
1984	2688.5	3.9
1985	3135.3	4.3
1986	3575.2	4.7
1987	4643.5	5.0
1988	5009.5	5.5
1989	5915.1	6.0
1990	7257.0	6.4

3   Using the table above, calculate the real sales revenue per square foot/week (assume 52 weeks per annum) earned in Sainsbury plc and compare this productivity with that of Tesco plc for the same period (using data from the table below).

Tesco plc

Year	Sales (nominal) (£m.)	Square footage of Tesco stores million square feet
1982	1994.4	7.2
1983	2276.6	7.4
1984	2594.5	7.4
1985	3000.4	7.4
1986	3355.3	7.5
1987	3593.0	7.0
1988	4119.1	8.2
1989	4717.7	8.5
1990	5401.9	9.1

4 For the Volkswagen-Audi Group, calculate:

(i) The vehicles produced per employee (as physical units of annual output divided by number of employees), from the data below:

Volkswagen-Audi

Year	Output in 000 units	Employees in 000s
1983	2127	232
1984	2145	238
1985	2398	259
1986	2758	276
1987	2774	260
1988	2854	252
1989	2941	251
1990	3030	261
1991	3237	277
1992	3433	273

(ii) Compare and contrast its labour productivity (vehicles per employee) with that of Ford UK (from Table 4.5).

What other factors much be taken into account when you are comparing two firms in terms of their productivity?

5 For the Volkswagen-Audi Group calculate, from the following information, the value added in million of DM for each of the years shown, and then labour's share of value added and cash flow's share of value added.

Volkswagen-Audi

Year	Sales revenue (million DM)	Labour costs (million DM)	Depreciation (million DM)	Profit pre-tax (million DM)
1984	46 671	13 227	2961	1494
1985	52 202	13 913	3411	2589
1986	52 794	14 747	5380	1595
1987	54 635	15 192	5498	1610
1988	59 221	15 143	6321	2136
1989	65 352	16 107	7151	2987
1990	68 061	17 056	7308	2392
1991	76 315	18 872	7599	1795
1992	85 403	20 753	7977	602

(i) What were the effects on cash flow and profit generated by Volkswagen-Audi when labour's share of value added increased?

To what extent would Volkswagen-Audi have been able to sustain employment levels if output and value added had fallen further in 1993?

(ii) Calculate the level of vertical integration (see Key Concept 4.2) in Volkswagen-Audi (using the information contained in the table above) and in Ford UK (using the information contained in Tables 4.4 and 4.5).

To what extent was the Ford UK company more or less vertically integrated than Volkswagen-Audi?

(iii) Calculate from the table above the degree to which Volkswagen-Audi was operating above break-even in 1985, 1989, and 1992.

6 What do you understand by the term 'liquidity'?

What calculations can we make from a set of company accounts to evaluate the liquidity of a business?

(i) Calculate Hanson Trust plc's current ratio from the balance sheet information shown below, and comment on the degree to which Hanson Trust has maintained liquidity.

Hanson Trust plc

Year	Current assets (£m.)	Current liabilities (£m.)
1983	961.7	563.2
1984	1 443.4	752.3
1985	2 062.0	907.0
1986	5 551.0	2486.0
1987	5 014.0	2083.0
1988	6 158.0	2463.0
1989	7 454.0	3269.0
1990	8 993.0	4226.0

1991	9 955.0	4751.0
1992	11 204.0	6386.0

(ii) Using the information below, update Table 4.9 on labour's share of value added at Hanson, and comment on the recent trend in profit's share of value added.

Hanson Trust plc

Year	Employment costs (£m.)	Depreciation (£m.)	Pre-tax profit (£m.)
1991	1216	206	1316
1992	1375	246	1286

7 What is the relationship between sales revenue, value added, cash flow and employment generated in a business?

To what extent do you think it is possible to maintain the interests of all the stakeholders (shareholders, employees and managers) when the firm is in a mature cyclical market?

8 What do you understand by the term 'productivity'?

In what ways can you use a set of company accounts to evaluate labour and capital productivity?

References

Adcroft, A. *et al.* (1991) Hanson and ICI; the consequences of financial engineering, *UEL Occasional Papers*, no. 2.

Williams, K. *et al.* (1990) The hollowing out of British industry, *Economy and Society*, vol. 19, no. 4.

Williams, K. *et al.* (1994) Deconstructing car assembler productivity, *International Journal of Production Economics*, forthcoming.

Williams, K. *et al.* (1994) *Cars: Analysis, History, and Cases*, Berghahn, Oxford.

Management practice and the limits of management

This chapter outlines how management theory and practice in the USA and UK have developed over the course of the century, away from concern with operational detail towards a more generalized 'strategic' function. In the face of large apparent differences in performance, managers are now being encouraged to pursue 'excellence' by emulating 'best practice' in other countries, notably Japan. A number of social, institutional, and market factors are identified, however, which condition business performance and limit the scope of management action.

Introduction

We have seen in Chapter 3 how traditional theories of the firm posit a single business objective, that of profit maximization, which is dictated by the external forces of market competition. We also gave some attention to managerial and behavioural theories of the firm. These newer theories take on board the fact that there has been a separation of ownership and control in the modern corporation, and that the objectives of managers may differ from those of shareholders, so opening the way for managers to pursue goals other than profit maximization.

In this chapter, we start by reviewing key developments which have shaped the practices of management and elevated the management function from an operational to a strategic role. These newer, more strategic approaches, we suggest, neglect the level of detail which would be needed to enhance productive performance, while they overestimate the extent to which management can influence its competitive environment. Reports which compare the performance of average firms with 'excellent' firms are then examined, and attention is drawn to the way certain themes, such as team working and flow management, keep reappearing. Finally, attention is drawn to the significance of structural factors, beyond the control of management, in explaining differences in business performance.

What do managers do?

Peter Drucker, in his book *The Practice of Management* (1955), suggests that traditional economic theories, such as that of perfect competition, do not take the role of management seriously. He suggests that

> The economist's 'business man' – the picture that underlies the prevailing economic 'theory of the firm' and the theorem of 'maximisation of profits' – reacts to economic developments. He is still passive, still adaptive . . . Basically this is a concept on the 'investor' or 'financier' rather than that of a manager.

Drucker takes the view that management has an active role to play in the organization of the firm's resources so as to achieve a particular set of objectives.

> Managing goes a long way beyond passive reaction and adaption. It implies responsibility for attempting to shape the economic environment, for planning, initiating and carrying through changes in that economic environment, for constantly pushing back the limitations of economic circumstances on the enterprise's freedom of action – it is management's specific task to make what is desirable first possible and then actual.
>
> *Drucker, 1955*

What writers such as Drucker put forward is a model of the manager as hero, battling against the external forces of market competition. Good managers, it seems, are like good generals, mobilizing the resources at their disposal against external threats. The military analogy is developed by Michael Porter:

> Knowledge of these underlying sources of competitive pressure provides the groundwork for a strategic agenda of action. They highlight the critical strengths and weaknesses of the company, animate the positioning of the company in its industry, clarify the areas where strategic changes may yield the greatest payoff, and highlight the places where industry trends promise to hold the greatest significance as either opportunities or threats.
>
> *Porter, 1979*

Every modern management text emphasizes the ability of management to use strategic concepts to positively change the strategic direction of the business. These concepts are typically reinforced by case studies to demonstrate the positive application or the inappropriate use of the strategic concept by management, and management success is defined as the effective application of management knowledge to influence the internal operations and external environment of the business.

US management history

Before we consider the development of 'corporate strategy', we will review various facets of American management practice from the early

Table 5.1 Output increases in US manufacturing, 1879–1929

Year	Output index (1929 = 100)	Average growth per annum (%)	
1879	10.2	3.9	1869–79
1889	18.3	7.2	1879–89
1899	27.5	4.6	1889–99
1909	43.4	5.3	1899–1909
1919	61.0	3.7	1909–19
1929	100	5.8	1919–29

Source: S. Fabricant, *Output of manufacturing industries*, National Bureau of Economic Research (1940).

part of this century, to establish the historical development of the management function.

The period of US economic history from 1879 to 1929 was one of rapid growth in output across a whole range of manufacturing enterprise, particularly in steel, textiles, industrial equipment and commercial goods. As Table 5.1 shows, US manufacturing output increased tenfold over the period. Output growth averaged 5% per annum between 1879 and 1929 – double the rate achieved between 1929 and 1990.

We have seen in Case Study 2.2 how Ford transformed car production at Highland Park between 1909 and 1916, implementing cost reduction to create the market conditions which would allow a phenomenal increase in output. Cost reduction was achieved, not so much as an automatic result of economies of scale, but through a judicious and continuous process of reorganization of production and redesign of the product.

The management of operations at Ford was dynamic, and subject to constant change in the struggle to take cost out. The company did not have a sophisticated costing system, and Henry Ford was known to despise accountants. As Case Study 5.1 shows, an early management text by Arnold and Faurote considers in great detail the operational activity required to run the Highland Park factory on a day-to-day basis.

Arnold and Faurote's concern with the management of operational detail is also reflected in the work of F.W. Taylor, and of consultants such as C. Knoeppel. F.W. Taylor's contribution to operational management is best known as 'scientific management'. In his work *The Principles of Scientific Management* (1929), Taylor outlined 'how work should be done', elaborating the principles of time and motion study, as well as exploring issues relating to the cutting of metals and the functional organization of business.

Taylor's focus on how work should be done makes sense in the light

In 1915, Arnold and Faurote undertook a detailed survey of Henry Ford's manufacturing methods, and one cannot help but be impressed by the detailed descriptions of manufacture activities applied to the Model T. This detailed analysis stands in stark contrast to later strategic management cases which are much more generalized, and have little to say about manufacturing detail.

In what follows we examine the stock-chaser role in the Highland Park plant, and how stocks are managed at the operational level. We have taken the language and references directly from the Arnold and Faurote text.

> Probably the average Ford factory visitor has the same general broad conception of the 'How' of making 1000 automobiles (it is now more than 1100 automobiles) per day. The man who really knows anything of the entrails of a machine shop, who knows that nothing, of advantage at least, ever 'happens' in a machine shop, has plenty to think about as he stands at the 'start to run' end of the Ford chassis assembling lines. This man of experience asks himself how the component production is evened up to assembling requirements. Here are, say, from 1000 to 4000 separate pieces of each chassis component to be supplied daily, infallibly, and consistently. How is this done?
>
> In brief, first, by unremitting record-keeping of every finished component produced. Hour by hour, with endless toil and pains, an absolutely correct record is kept of the Ford component production and of factory output.
>
> The factor of safety of component supply is placed by the official production head at a sufficiency for 25 000 cars, a month's assembling supply at the production rate of 1000 cars per day. This is official, but as will be seen from the 'shortage-chaser' story, the factory practice does not follow the production-head schedule, but quite to the contrary, places a maximum component supply at a sufficiency for 5000 cars, three days' assembling, with a danger line at components enough for 3000 cars.

The authors go on to say that 'Seeing is believing. When a Ford car assembled-component assembler suddenly discovers that his requisition on finished stores for components wanted at once is not filled because there are no such components in finished stores, no grand conclave of factory accountants is summoned.'

Instead, the Ford operations at Highland Park were co-ordinated by stock-chasers, both for the day and the night shift. In total some 800 individuals were employed for the purposes of controlling the flow of materials within the Highland Park plant.

> At 6.30 the day shortage chaser, henceforth specified as the 'shortage chaser' only, at first inspects the night reports, making notes of impending shortage; next he notifies the 'checkers' who direct the movements of components reported at or below the 3000 danger limit; this is done at 7.00 am, the shortage chaser making a personal delivery of his own pencil memoranda to the proper 'checkers'. Next the busy shortage chaser goes in person to each assembling station reporting shortages and informs himself by personal observation of shortages – this because the final reports were made to component-production officials at 2.30 pm the previous day. Being then advised of the actual conditions by personal observation, the shortage-chaser goes to the foreman of the machine department producing the most needed components.

This excerpt describes in detail the operational processes involved in managing a complex flow of components, and demonstrates that Ford Highland Park was operating with very low stocks in the factory. In a later period, Toyota introduced the *Kanban* stock control system, which removed the role of the stock-chaser. The results of both systems were to maintain flow conditions with minimal work-in-progress.

Further reading
Arnold and Faurote (1915).

of the evidence we assessed in Chapter 2, that most conversion cost is labour cost. His approach required a full understanding of existing operational details, on the basis of which a standard time for accomplishing work tasks could be established. Taylor emphasized the importance of 'objective' measurement, because, as he saw it, 'Both sides [the workforce and management] must recognise as essential the substitution of exact scientific investigation and knowledge for the old individual judgement or opinion' (Taylor, 1929). Once information on the use of labour time was made available, Taylor suggested, it could then be appropriated as a form of management knowledge and used to plan and schedule what was to be done in the working day.

Taylor's preoccupation with measurement and its presentation to management for the purposes of exercising control of operations mirrors Ford's work at Highland Park. Here, records of time elapsed for particular operations were used by management to establish the labour costs for a particular operation, and this was recorded in great detail in Ford's cost books. Attention to operational detail at Highland Park focussed on factory layout and the use of machinery, as well as on working time. Ford engineers were concerned, for example, to combine operations performed at one machine so that a bundle of tasks could be completed at one work station, and to lay out machines, regardless of function, according to their sequence of use (Bornholt, 1913).

In order to co-ordinate, plan and control management, much emphasis was given in inter-war America to the need for detailed information on operations. Journals such as *Industrial Management* reflected the desire to improve the functioning of management through the use of 'management information systems'. In 1919, Charles Knoeppel, founder of the consultancy firm C.E. Knoeppel and Co Inc, presented a series of articles on 'graphic production control'. These articles explained how graphical charts could be used to visually represent manufacturing activity. This information was presented for two reasons – firstly, to establish 'analysis' (which, according to Knoeppel, was 'The determination of what is to be done, the manner of doing, and what it should cost in time and money – the standard to work to'), and, secondly, 'Control' ('the means provided for enabling the shops to either measure up to the standard determined upon, or to investigate variations in such a way as will result in a constructive attempt to subsequently attain it'). 'With *Analysis* and *Control* utilized to the fullest,' Knoeppel suggested, '. . . the manufacturing world can be assured that it will secure the maximum operating efficiency.'

Knoeppel's work combined analysis of standard labour times with measures of the cost of performing operations, by multiplying labour time by the labour rate per hour to establish standard costs which can be used as a control device by management. As a result, 'graphic production control not only controls production, but leads indirectly to better organization and furnishes costs, both standard and actual, as a by-product' (Knoeppel, 1919).

At this stage of US management history, there is no doubt that the main focus of management, academics and consultants was on internal resource management issues. As US firms reaped the benefits of earlier output expansion, however, co-ordination and control became more of a corporation-wide issue.

As early as 1917, Charles Knoeppel was already presenting possible solutions to the problems of large-scale business co-ordination and management, arguing that 'No business can be as successful as it is possible to be with two or three heads running things. There must be a single co-ordinating and directing function' (Knoeppel, 1917). His recommendation was that, to avoid duplication and poor co-ordination, large organizations should adopt divisional rather than functional organization structures (see Key Concept 5.1).

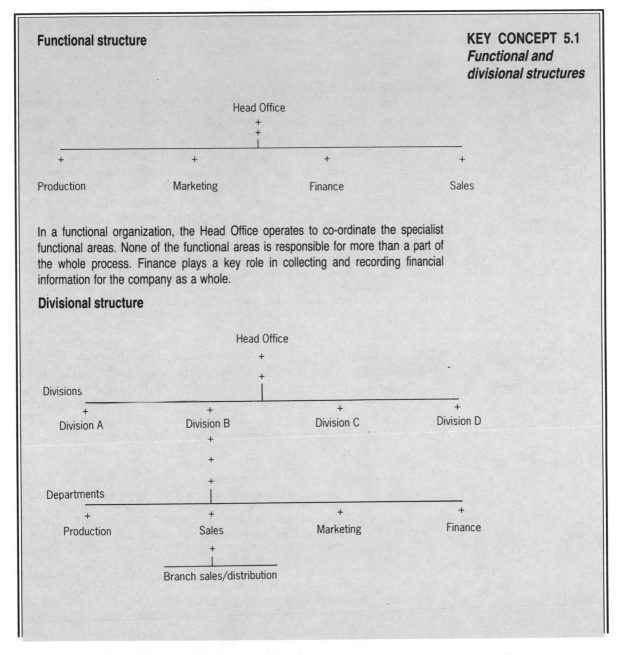

Functional structure

KEY CONCEPT 5.1
Functional and divisional structures

In a functional organization, the Head Office operates to co-ordinate the specialist functional areas. None of the functional areas is responsible for more than a part of the whole process. Finance plays a key role in collecting and recording financial information for the company as a whole.

Divisional structure

In a divisional organization, the functional areas of the business are separated by a divisional layer. Divisions can be defined in terms of a particular activity/product range, or geographically, in relation to particular regions of a national or international market.

The divisional form was introduced into US business around the period 1915 to 1920. The example that is commonly used to illustrate this concept is that of General Motors. Where Ford is remembered for his productive innovations, General Motors is credited with establishing the organization structure for controlling and administering large-scale business. We consider the importance attached to divisional structure, and the contribution made by structure to the development of organization strategy, in the next section.

Structure before strategy?

In 1962 and 1964, two influential books were published – first Alfred Chandler's *Strategy and Structure*, and then Alfred Sloan's *My Years With General Motors*. Both these texts identify the divisional form of organization structure as a key ingredient in modern business success.

In the divisional form of organisation (see Key Concept 5.1), divisions are an extra layer of management, located between the Head Office and the functional departments. In Chandler's words,

> The executives in charge of these divisions . . . have under their command most of the functions necessary for handling one major line of products or set of services over a wide geographical area, and each of these executives is responsible for the financial results of his division and for its success in the market place. This administrative form is often known in business parlance as the 'decentralised' structure.
>
> *Chandler, 1962*

Within a decentralized (or divisionalized) organization, the divisions take responsibility for operational day-to-day administrative functions, leaving Head Office free to concentrate on more long-term business planning and on regulating the outcomes of these longer-term policies. The overall planning and co-ordinating function is labelled 'business strategy', and again the language used, this time by Sloan, has military overtones:

> The departmental and divisional offices may make some long-term decisions, but because their executives work within a comparable framework determined by the general office, their primary administrative activities also tend to be tactical or operational. The general office makes the broad strategic or entrepreneurial decisions as to policy and procedures and can do so largely because it has the final say in the allocation of the firm's resources – men, money and materials.
>
> *Sloan, 1964*

Chandler considered three examples: General Motors, Du Pont, and Jersey Standard. In Case Study 5.2, we outline some of the main aspects of GM's divisionalization process and the context within which this took place.

There is no doubt that the creation of the divisional structure was an important innovation in organizational development. Most importantly, it brought about two distinct changes: first, the separation of operational management from strategic goal and policy setting, and, second, the development of budgeting and strategic management accounting to regulate divisional performance.

CASE STUDY 5.2
Divisionalization at General Motors

General Motors was formed in 1908 by William Durant. Its expansion up to 1920 was the result of a number of judicious deals which brought together a number of separate smaller companies – Buick, Olds, Cadillac, Oakland, Chevrolet – under the auspices of one holding company, General Motors.

The first steps towards divisionalization of General Motors started as early as 1911 and 1912. The banks which had lent to General Motors promoted the establishment of a central administration to preserve and control the use of their funds. An accounting office was established to standardize accounting procedures to maintain accurate assessments on costs, profits and losses that might occur. Then, in 1919, Durant also established General Motors Acceptance Corporation (GMAC), which was a financing operation designed to give credit to customers so that they could purchase a car without a large one-off commitment of cash.

According to Chandler, the underlying problem facing General Motors was the poor co-ordination and administration of a collection of 'autonomous' even 'uncontrollable' operations under the management of Durant. By the end of 1920 Durant was forced to go, when the banks no longer had confidence in him.

In November 1920, Pierre Du Pont took over the presidency of General Motors and immediately adopted Alfred Sloan's policy for restructuring the organization. Sloan's basic aim was to establish an organization structure in which a 'general office could co-ordinate, appraise and plan programmes and policies for the divisions'.

Sloan's policy was twofold – first, 'decentralize' operations so that divisions had a degree of independence, and second, give Head Office overall regulatory financial powers over the divisions. So although 'decentralization' was established by giving control and responsibility for day-to-day operations to divisional managers, this was subject to checks and balances from the Head Office.

In Sloan's book, *My Years With General Motors*, the first page outlines the elements which he believed most powerfully influenced the development of General Motors: 'These elements are the decentralized organization structure and the system of financial controls and the related profit-responsibility concept.'

To create the framework of financial regulation within which divisional managers were allowed to operate, responsibility for restructuring General Motors' financial reporting system was given to Donaldson Brown, the Treasurer from Du Pont. Brown established a comprehensive budgeting system for the control of sales revenue and production costs, along the lines outlined in Chapter 3. Capital allocations were systematized, and strict controls were placed on the use of cash.

In general terms, the divisional structure was overlaid with a financial budgeting system which acted, in Sloan's words, as 'the discipline of management by method'. By delegating responsibility for day-to-day operations to divisional managers, Head Office management were free to concentrate on formulating policy and objectives for

General Motors. But although responsibility was delegated to divisional managers, they were subject to the discipline of the financial reporting system which required them (and their profit centres) to meet a target profit on the assets employed set by Head Office.

Further reading
Sloan (1964);
Chandler (1962);
Wolff (1964).

In 1929, the Great Crash resulted in massive write-offs in the value of shares, and shareholders questioned the effectiveness of firms' cost control and profit-reporting procedures. Reflecting this concern, C. Knoeppel's 1933 text *Profit Engineering* argued that 'A post depression text or business should be motivated by profit mindedness.' Budgeting, Knoeppel suggested, could perform the dual role of first, satisfying the interests of the shareholders by protecting their returns on investment, and, secondly, making a positive contribution to Head Office strategic management in terms of planning and controlling the business:

> Profits being vital and necessary if business is to render the service, it should never be left to accident, hope and blind chance. They should be planned on in advance and so controlled, all of the time, as to assure that they will be made. In other words profit should be the first deduction from the dollar on income, and the business should be budgeted to operate off the balance.
>
> *Knoeppel, 1933*

What Knoeppel proposed was the use, by Head Office, of historic accounting information to strategically plan ahead, because otherwise 'they will continue to rush past all danger signals like a train on a stormy night'. Management texts published in the UK at this time gave a similar message. The whole of A. Dent's 1935 publication, *Management Planning and Control*, for example, is devoted to the detail of the budgeting process, and how this can enhance management co-ordination, planning, and control.

The influence of companies such as General Motors and Sears Roebuck as role models to be emulated cannot be over-estimated. In particular, General Motors' ascendancy over Ford in the US car market of the 1920s is generally attributed to the efficacy of GM's policy-directed and financially managed business. Much of the emulation was uncritical, however, and 'learning from GM' often became a substitute for in-dependent thought. As H. Wolff, noting the success of Alfred Sloan's book *My Years With General Motors*, warned:

> There is a real danger that the success of this book may presage a new round of wholesale imitation of General Motors. It is easy to envisage a new crop of eager executives bounding into the boardroom, proclaiming: 'What's good enough for General Motors is certainly good enough for World-Wide Widgets Unlimited'.
>
> *Wolff, 1964*

The Americanization of management

American management practices diffused across the Atlantic, particularly after the Second World War. The diffusion process in the UK was promoted by the Anglo American Productivity Council (AAPC), which sponsored visits by British executives to US firms to observe their management practices. Seventeen reports were published, each of them making recommendations as to how British business might benefit from the adoption of American management practice. These reports emphasized the importance of international differences in the management of operations as well as in overall methods of managerial control.

On the management of operations, the AAPC drew attention to a number of points of operational detail. In its *Report on Internal Combustion Engines*, for example, shop layout was considered. The visitors note in their summary report that

> machines were not always laid out in lines, but were sometimes grouped together round an operator. Thus the principle of effective utilisation of labour has a considerable influence on shop lay-out. If the cycle time of a machine permits the operator to undertake a further task, the appropriate machine is placed near him.

On the design of tools, the AAPC noted that considerable labour time can be saved if tools are designed to undertake a number of operations at one setting. Ingenious methods to improve and manage the flow of materials around the factory were also reported:

> In production lines, machines were not laid out to make an attractive shop, but to reduce to a minimum the distance travelled by the material between successive operations. The result was commonly a crowded floor and a tortuous production line, but the primary objective of reducing handling was achieved.

More generally, American companies were praised for the attention they gave to production design (e.g. the standardization of parts) and cost reduction (e.g. the substitution of cheaper for more expensive materials).

The general impression of the AAPC teams was that attention to the operational detail was a major factor explaining high levels of produc tivity in US, and that 'at least the majority of British plants had much to learn about the full utilisation of man power and the efficient use of machine tools.'

Turning now to the AAPC investigations of financial corporate management, it is significant that the *Report on Management Accounting* sold more copies than any of the others. This report emphasized that in successful US firms, the central role of the accountant was to provide a 'control' function for senior management. In most of the companies visited,

> the controller is normally responsible for all accounting and costing functions, for budgeting, for measuring performance against approved

operating plans and standards for reporting and interpreting the results of operations to all levels of management.

AAPC, 1950

In addition to establishing the 'strategic' position of the accounting function, the AAPC also emphasized that the management accounting function should be set within the context of the divisionalized/decentralized oganizational structure, along the lines of those adopted at General Motors in the 1920s. By the 1940s, the AAPC found, centralization of strategic control and decentralization of responsibility, regulated by the financial management system, had become commonplace in the USA.

The conclusions of the AAPC report on management accounting present a strong case for the emulation of 'best' American management practices. In particular, it was suggested, British managers should, like their American counterparts, plan for the furture by paying more attention to forecasts and budgets: 'The nearer management is to the shop floor and the customer, the more it needs figures to guide its immediate action, and consequently it is more interested in current actual results compared with the budget.'

The British visitors to the US sponsored by the AAPC were greatly impressed with American management practices and techniques, and considered that these practices went a long way towards explaining the US firms' superior productivity performance. Graham Hutton (1953) summarized this point as follows:

> In short, viewing American management as whole, the Teams saw ways of bringing the less effective average of British performance up to higher standards set by the best British managements, which in many cases challenge comparison with the best managements in America.

From structure to strategy

The development of American business management is most often reduced to certain essential elements – particularly divisionalization and management accounting. Once an appropriate structure is in place, the firm needs to develop a strategy for mobilizing and managing the resources of the firm. As we saw at the start of this chapter, post-war writers like Drucker and Porter see strategy formulation as the prime function of senior managers in the modern corporation. If the correct strategy is chosen and executed, it is suggested, this will deliver above-average performance against competitors. In short, executives can use management strategy to push back competitive forces and create opportunities for the business.

In 1979 and 1980 Michael Porter constructed a synthetic model to interpret the strategy formulation process (Porter, 1979, 1980, and 1985). This was made up of two overlapping concepts: industry structure and 'generic strategy'.

The first of these concepts, 'industry structure', describes what Porter considers to be the 'underlying economics' of the business (see Key Concept 5.2). Traditional economic analysis is used to classify the relation of the business to its competitors, suppliers, distribution network, and substitute products. This classification is presented as a check-list, against which you can position your own business within its industry. Understanding your industry structure means understanding the competitive forces you are up against. According to Porter, 'The strategist, wanting to position his company to cope best with its industry environment and to influence that environment in the company's favour, must learn what makes the environment tick.'

Porter's model, some of which is presented below, identifies different elements of industrial structure.

KEY CONCEPT 5.2
Porter's elements of industry structure

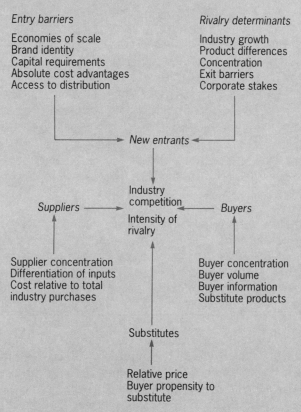

Using this model, you can position your firm in relation to these elements. If your firm is a large organization producing car components, for example, your suppliers of materials might be tied into you because they supply 80% of their sales to you alone, while you might depend on a single major car assembler for 45% of your sales. The substitute product range might not be able to compete with you on cost, but new entry might be possible from overseas suppliers.

It is clear that different organizations and different products will have different industrial structures, and that embedded in these structures are power relations which can promote or hinder the organization's objectives.

Further reading
Porter (1980).

Once a firm has established its position in relation to competitors, other products, suppliers, buyers and new entrants, it must sustain competitive advantage in the long run, by means of its 'generic strategy' (see Key Concept 5.3).

KEY CONCEPT 5.3
Porter's generic strategy

Porter's generic strategy is presented as a 2 × 2 matrix, characterized according to competitive scope and competitive advantage:

	Competitive advantage	
	Lower cost	Differentiation
Broad target	Cost leadership	Differentiation
Narrow target	Cost focus	Differentiation focus

Competitive scope

Each 'generic' strategy represents a particular route towards competitive advantage. Cost leadership, for example, requires the firm to seek out the lowest costs and price within the industry, by obtaining economies of scale. A 'differentiation' strategy, in contrast, involves developing characteristics which customers view as especially significant, such as design, quality, after-sales service, etc. These enable the firm to charge a premium price.

Finally, we have those generic strategies which focus on a particular product or market segment, and might be termed 'niche marketing'. Focusing strategies deliver positive returns from a particular product segment rather than competitive advantage across the overall product market. A firm can focus on cost or differentiation by concentrating on particular price or non-price factors.

Porter argues that 'generic strategies' cannot be combined, so that the firm which is 'stuck in the middle' will possess no competitive advantage. Positively choosing the 'generic strategy' which best fits the organization's position relative to the 'industry structure' will, Porter claims, lead to an increased probability of superior performance.

From Americanization to Japanization

As we have seen, post-war British industry looked to the USA for new management practices, emphasizing corporate strategy and structure. Adoption of these new practices, it was thought, would enhance productivity in the firm and the national economy. Recently, however, confidence in American business and management practices has been damaged, as a result of the high-profile failure of US corporations to sustain profits and employment, and the emergence of a large trade deficit between the USA and Japan. General Motors, for example, lost nearly $4 billion in 1991, and IBM lost $5 billion in the following year.

These two companies, in an earlier period, had epitomized corporate managerial excellence, but they are now in trouble. The problems facing IBM are explored in Case Study 5.3.

Forty thousand jobs were lost at IBM in 1992, and in December of that year they announced that a further 25 000 jobs would go. To discover what had happened at IBM, we need to consider both the past performance and the present market and productive conditions of the computer business.

IBM made its name with the production and installation of mainframe computers, and with after-sales training and service provision for customers. Customers were locked into IBM because the hardware and software was IBM-specific, and the cost of changing over to another company was high. Following Porter's analysis of industrial structure and generic strategy, we might have expected IBM to have strengthened its competitive advantage, especially given its power to influence suppliers and consumers, and its dominant position against rivals.

In 1985, John Akers took over as Chairman of IBM and immediately pursued a strategy of decentralization, capacity-cutting, and a shift in focus away from hardware towards software and service provision. Fundamentally, these 'off the shelf' strategies were not up to the job of recovering IBM's faltering profits and cash flow. Essentially the policy at IBM was that of cost-cutting to maintain cost leadership in the mainframe business.

Overall world market sales of mainframe computers, peripherals, personal computers, and software services rose from $212 billion in 1984 to $649 billion in 1992 – a threefold increase. In terms of product segments, the main changes have been the loss of market share by minis and mainframe computers (down from 28.5% in 1984 to 13.5% in 1992), with corresponding gains in sales of personal computers and services and software provision.

The nature of the product has changed, and manufacturing now 'involves little more than assembling microprocessor and memory on printed circuit boards in a suitable case. Disk drives, keyboards and displays are bought as standard components' (*Financial Times*, 8 Nov. 1991). Manufacturing the hardware has become more like manufacturing a video recorder or television, and most software is now standardized. As a result 'A £2 million machine of five or six years ago now costs £10 000. The improvement in performance for a given price furthermore is growing at some 20 to 25 per cent a year' (*Financial Times*, 5 June 1991).

In terms of product development, the cost of manufacture for each unit has fallen, but current market conditions make cost recovery uncertain. Porter considers the generic strategy of cost reduction to be a rational policy, and he would be supported by the traditional economic theory of demand, which assumes that cost and price reductions will deliver compensatory increases in sales. But as we saw in Chapter 1, markets are maturing and growth is not automatically assured even when costs per unit fall.

Sales growth, which was sustained at an annual average rate of 20 per cent or so throughout the 1980s, has slowed abruptly because of the recession in the US, parts of Europe and Australasia. This has masked the fact, however, that the market is maturing rapidly and in many business sectors is close to saturation. This replacement market already represents 50 per cent of business across the board. By 1995 it will represent close to 80 per cent of all personel

CASE STUDY 5.3
Whatever happened to IBM?

computer sales. In the US, unit sales are up by perhaps 3 per cent this year while prices are falling at between 25 and 60 per cent a year.

Financial Times, 8 Nov. 1991

The case of IBM demonstrates that when the trajectory of market maturity meets a generic strategy of cost reduction per unit, neither competitive advantage nor future profitability and cash flow are assured. As Abernathy and Wayne (1974) notes, 'other results that are not planned, foreseen, or desired may grow out of such a market penetration/cost reduction progression'.

Further reading
'What went wrong at IBM', *The Economist*, 16 Jan. 1993;
'New order forces the pace of change,' *Financial Times*, 8 Nov. 1991;
Abernathy and Wayne (1974).

There is an emerging academic and practitioner debate which questions the rationality of American management practices, and in some cases goes on to compare them adversely with Japanese management practices.

Some academics, as we saw in Chapter 3, now question the efficacy of 'management accounting' and the contribution it can make to improved strategic decision-making. Hayes and Abernathy (1980), for example, question the strategic rationality of using discounted cash flow techniques for investment decisions. DCF, they argue, privileges short-term profit returns and does not taken into account what competitors might be doing. The solution, they argue, is to use the DCF calculation in a more 'enlightened' way, taking into account the reactions of competitors. Similarly, Johnson and Kaplan (1987) question the extent to which management accounting provides product cost and price data which accurately reflect the 'true' cost of manufacture. They then recommend a refinement of the existing system of costing, so that, instead of applying absorption rates to direct labour, firms use alternative cost drivers to absorb product costs.

The positions outlined in the previous paragraph suggest that the market and productive failings of US business can best be reversed through a refinement of existing decision-making techniques. Other writers have gone on from this position to argue that US firms should learn from their competitors (especially in Japan), rather than refine existing management systems. The general proposition is that Japanese management practices are different from American practices, and that these differences explain the success of Japanese industry. To improve productivity, it is suggested, we should emulate Japanese management practices. History indeed repeats itself, as in an earlier period the Americanization of business policy also promised the transformation of productivity.

'Japanization' is a term that is often used to represent a set of management practices, work methods and institutional conditions which are specific to Japanese firms and which have made a significant contribution to Japanese economic success. Some of these techniques and work methods, such as U-shaped lines, total quality management, line stop methods, company-based unions, and just-in-time, have been considered in Chapters 2 and 3, but we could also add strong relations with suppliers, team working, individualized payment systems, and long-term support from financial institutions. We do not have enough space in this text to consider these techniques in detail, but we will instead examine a specific industry case, which, it has been argued, represents all that is good about Japanese management and all that is bad about American management. This case is that of 'lean production' in the car industry (Case Study 5.4).

CASE STUDY 5.4
The Japanese car industry – lean producers?

A recent text by Womack, Jones and Roos (WJR), *The Machine that Changed the World*, introduced the concept of 'lean production'. This is presented as a recipe for success in the car industry, as against old-style mass production systems as represented by Henry Ford.

In an earlier period, the authors argue that the dominant management practices which shaped the industry were the production practices of Henry Ford, and the management and marketing practices of General Motors. These practices then diffused throughout the industry after World War One. After World War Two, however, Toyota led a transition to 'lean production', and this in turn was diffused from Toyota into its suppliers and also into other Japanese car makers.

Technically, lean production is carried out by multi-skilled workers using flexible equipment and just-in-time production, with small lots of stock inside and outside of the main factories, and little indirect labour. According to WJR, lean production has a substantial cost advantage over mass production 'because it uses less of everything compared with mass production – half the human effort in the factory, half the manufacturing space, half the investment in tools, half the engineering hours to develop a new product in half the time'.

The claim of 'lean production' is that unbuffered low stock operations result in higher productivity and robust financial performance. To what extent, though, are Japanese manufacturers low stock unbuffered organizations? In Chapter 2 we identified the ratio of value added to work-in-progress as a reasonable measure of the flow conditions of a business. These calculations showed that Honda and Toyota were strong performers, but that BMW and Peugeot came above Nissan and Mazda. There was no clear pattern of overall Japanese superiority.

On productivity, WJR made use of plant-level studies undertaken by J. Krafcik. These studies compared the productivity, measured in hours taken to assemble a car, of assembly operations at General Motors' Framingham plant and Toyota's Takaoka plant. Williams *et al.* (1992), in their critique of the lean production concept, argue that this calculation of productivity is biased in favour of Toyota, because the Takaoka plant was run at or near full capacity utilization. In addition, the use of assembly labour hours only considers a small percentage (15%) of overall labour hours that go into a car. It is far more meaningful, they argue, to consider the total hours that go into a motor vehicle at a sectoral level than to attempt plant-level comparisons involving different spans of operation and different market conditions. More realistic sectoral comparisons are shown in the table below.

We can see from this table that the Japanese car producers have been successful in taking labour hours out of their product, but that in 1989 they reached a level which

	Sectoral build hours per vehicle	
	USA	Japan
1969	187	279
1975	174	176
1984	165	141
1989	174	132

was just 32% per cent below that of the Americans, not the 2:1 difference claimed by WJR.

At company level, we argued in Chapter 2 that a better measure of productivity is value added per employee. This is illustrated for 1989, the last year of peak output for the US companies, in the table below.

	Value added per employee ($, 1989)
Toyota	83 932
Ford	83 516
Chrysler	73 078
Honda	68 246
Nissan	59 881
General Motors	53 143

Toyota stands out as an exceptional case in years when the US producers suffer from a market downturn and loss of value added generated. In a good year, however, US firms can achieve a level of value added per employee which is similar to the average Japanese car manufacturer, and, in the case of Ford, equal to Toyota.

In general terms the case for lean production and the superiority of Japanese management practices is not proven. Williams *et al.* (1992) consider that non-management factors on both the supply side and demand side explain Japanese advantage – low costs and wages in the supplier network, longer working hours, and favourable demand conditions in the home market.

Further reading
Womack, Jones and Roos (1990);
Williams K. *et al.* (1992).

The superiority of Japanese management techniques and excellence in terms of productivity performance should not be accepted uncritically. As Case Study 5.4 suggests, the gap between Japanese and American firms is not large, and cost differences may reflect factors such as a steep wage gradient between final assembler and component suppliers, hours worked, and market demand conditions.

Despite the dubious nature of many of the claims made about lean production, recent management consultancy benchmark studies (see Key Concept 5.3) have reiterated the existence of a large efficiency gap between 'world-class' lean producers and other plants. The Arthur Andersen report, *The Lean Enterprise Benchmarking Project* (1992), like the Womack, Jones and Roos text, concludes that Japanese firms are world-class, and outperform their (in this case) UK counterparts.

> Benchmarking is a form of company analysis which compares the performance of one company against another, or a group of companies against another group. Generally, firms are grouped and classified on the basis of their performance, according to productivity, quality, defect rates, stock levels, or workforce skills.
>
> Once performance against each criterion is established, the results are aggregated and the range between best and worst performers calculated. The average firm is identified, and the best and worst performers positioned in relation to the average.

KEY CONCEPT 5.4
Benchmarking

According to the Andersen study executive summary, 'The world class plants show a 2:1 productivity differential and a superiority in quality of 100:1.' A previous summary point notes that 'All world class plants are Japanese, but not all Japanese plants are world class. Some UK plants have either high quality or high productivity but none have both' (Andersen, 1992). Having identified a gap, the report recommends 'using the resulting crisis to commit the firm to closing the gap – through a shared vision of an integrated business aligning the business process, organization and technology with the business strategy.'

There is a striking similarity between the Andersen Report of 1992 and the Anglo American Productivity Council reports of the post-war period. The earlier AAPC reports identified a large productivity gap between the UK and USA, and suggested that this gap could be narrowed through a thorough application of American systems and methods of management. Forty years on, the Andersen report identifies a similar productivity gap between the UK and Japan, and argues for the adoption of Japanese management methods.

The similarity in the messages about emulating world-class management practices is striking: 'World class plants involve more of their employees more intensively in problem solving' (Andersen Report, 1992). 'It is impossible to reject the conclusion that there is better teamwork in America during normal working' (Hutton, 1953). 'It is time to concentrate on the organisation of production . . . this starts by integrating every production step into an uninterrupted flow' (Andersen Report, 1992). 'The best management cannot do its best if the smooth flow of operations and materials is interrupted' (Hutton, 1953).

The limits to management

We have seen how management thinkers, from Drucker to Porter to Arthur Andersen, have viewed management as an agent which can, through its actions, significantly improve the environmental conditions of a business. In this final section we consider the limits to management action, which dictate that not all firms can achieve 'excellence'.

The main focus of this section is the extent to which better management can, in practice, deliver higher productivity. For the Anglo American Council on Productivity in the early 1950s, low productivity was a result of poor production engineering. For the National Institute of Economic and Social Research in the 1980s, the cause was poor training and workforce skills. For others, it is not enough research and development, or poor management. We might ask the question, 'Can they all be right'? The foundation on which inferiority is interpreted, whatever cause is identified, is productivity analysis, which concentrates on the productivity of labour.

In order to compare different firms, and assess their respective productivity, business economists often construct a calculation which makes a series of adjustments for differences between the companies, and then ends up with the so-called 'bottom line'. In the case of Womack, Jones and Roos, the bottom line is a 2:1 difference in favour of Japanese car assembly. As we have seen, comparisons for part of a production process can be misleading, and it may be more meaningful to construct an alternative bottom line for the company as a whole. This is demonstrated in Case Study 5.5.

CASE STUDY 5.5 *Differences in car assembler productivity – a case of now you see it, now you don't*	In this case we will consider the labour productivity of the Toyota Motor Corporation and that of Ford. We start from a calculation of what is termed the 'crude productivity', based on total vehicle output divided by the number of employees.

Crude vehicles per employee, 1991

Toyota	Ford
44.3	18.5

On this first calculation, it would seem that the difference in productivity is around 2:1 in Toyota's favour. But we have not yet adjusted for the differences between the two companies. The first difference we can note is that Totoya workers work 10% longer hours than Ford. Correcting for this difference would reduce Ford employment by 10%, and 10% fewer workers would increase the crude productivity from 18.5 to 20.5.

The second adjustment we could make relates to capacity utilization differences. In 1991, Toyota was operating at 120% of capacity and Ford at 70% of capacity. Crediting Ford with the extra output to bring it up to the Toyota level of capacity utilization would increase the crude productivity to 31.6 cars per employee.

A third adjustment we could legitimately make is to correct for the differences in vertical integration (see Key Concept 4.2). In Toyota the value added to sales ratio is 14%, while at Ford it is 36%. Ford therefore requires 2.6 times more workers than Toyota, because Ford is doing more of the work in its own factories. To correct for this difference, we would need to reduce Ford's employment to a level which corresponded to Toyota's degree of vertical integration. This would increase in crude productivity for Ford to 48 vehicles per employee.

The result of these three, inherently rational, adjustments is to move productivity for Ford close to that of Toyota. As we adjust the crude productivity figures, we can, according to Williams *et al.* (1994)

> add an interpretation and commentary which reflects the pattern of differences rather than imposes the preconceptions of the external discourse [be it economics, management, engineering or accounting] which supplies the explanation in productivity discourse; thus the end result of lateral thinking is not a bottom line but a story line which grows and is open ended.

Further reading
Williams *et al.*, 1994.

In Case Study 5.5 we have shown how it is possible to 'correct' a crude output per employee figure for differences in working hours, capacity utilization and vertical integration. Making these three adjustments to the crude productivity figures for Ford relative to Toyota, for example, completely eliminates the productivity gap between them. The by now conventional assumption that Japanese car manufacturers have a large margin of superiority over their US rivals is seen to depend on dubious calculations which take no account of structural differences – particularly relating to vertical integration – which significantly affect the figures.

If we were to compare Volvo with Toyota, we would likewise have to correct for the degree of vertical integration, but in this case differences in working hours would be more significant. Swedish car workers worked an average of 1388 hours in 1991, less than two-thirds of the average Japanese employee's 2200 hours. The extra hours worked in Japan result in Japanese factories employing fewer workers for a given output, because of the greater physical output per employee.

Adjustments to crude productivity figures are necessary to correct for institutional differences that exist between different national economies – only after making these adjustments can we legitimately say that the residual difference is explained by differences in management systems/techniques. It is clear that the adjustments we have made relate not to managerial but to structural variables. Hours worked, for example, differ between national economies because particular institutional 'social settlements' have resulted in shorter working hours in one country rather than another. Similarly, differences in vertical integration reflect national differences in the structure of core–periphery relationships, affecting the extent to which components are outsourced rather than produced in-house. Finally, market demand conditions in Japan have resulted in steady growth which has served to maintain output at or near full utilization of capacity – in direct contrast to the US car market, whose cyclicality has resulted in substantial under-utilized capacity.

If all car firms faced exactly the same market conditions, in economies with the same social settlements and the same institutional structures, then we might be able to determine the extent to which 'better management practices contribute to higher productivity'. If we accept that structural differences between national economies are major determinants of differences in crude productivity, then we must also accept that a high proportion of the perceived 'productivity gap' is beyond management's control and influence.

Conclusion

It is often suggested in business management texts that improvements to and emulation of best management practice will allow the firm to create a window of strategic opportunity. These texts stress the importance of management techniques in explaining superior performance. In an earlier period, it was argued that emulation of best American management practice would enhance the productivity and profits performance of UK firms. More recently, the promise of superior performance from emulating best management practice is still made, but Japanese management practices are now the order of the day.

We have argued that the singular importance attached to 'managerial techniques' as an explanation of superior productivity performance, to the exclusion of social, institutional and market factors, results in an imperfect understanding of the conditions which materially affect the fortunes of a business. Weak companies will not be able to sustain product renewal cycles, and may continually lose market share. In addition, it is not possible for all weaker firms to emulate the market leader, because there can be only one market leader. In particular, companies which have smaller market share, engage employees on shorter working hours, or build more of the product in-house, cannot emulate market leaders whose employees work longer hours and which subcontract more work. All firms face particular circumstances and constraints, which often limit the scope of management action and are beyond the influence of management.

According to Williams *et al.* (1994),

> the firm represents a dispersed network of choices about what to make or buy, how to delegate operations management inside and outside the firm, and how to pay for distribution. These firms are not centres of economic efficiency but networks of social decisions which cannot be easily remade because they are tied in to durable national settlements which involve other actors including organised labour, political interests and financial institutions.

Further reading

Early management practices at Highland Park are analysed in 'The Myth of the Line', by Karel Williams, Colin Haslam, and John Williams (*Business History*, June 1993), and in D. Hounshell's *From the American System to Mass Production* (Johns Hopkins University Press, 1984).

On divisional structure, it is worth looking at D. Solomons' *Divisional Performance Measurement and Control* (Irwin, 1965). H. Wolff's 'The great GM mystery' (*Harvard Business Review*, Sept–Oct. 1964) is also worth reading as it summarizes A. Sloan's *My Years with General Motors*. On the role of strategic management accounting, see the Anglo American Council on Productivity's report on management accounting (1950).

On strategy, it is worth reading Michael Porter's *Competitive Advantage* (Free Press, 1985). The *Harvard Business Review* contains a number of articles on the influence of Japanese management techniques – for example, T. Hiromoto in July/Aug 1988. More specifically, the text by Womack, Jones and Roos (*The Machine That Changed the World*, Rawson Associates, 1990) establishes the concept of 'lean production' as it applies to Japanese car manufacturers. Techniques of Japanese management practice are well developed in Y. Monden's text, *The Toyota Production System* (2nd edn, Chapman & Hall, 1994).

For a critical review of the 'lean production' concept, see Karel Williams *et al.*, 'Against lean production', in *Economy and Society*, August 1992. In addition, see Williams *et al.* (1993) 'Beyond Management' (mineo available from University of Manchester Accounting Department).

Exercises

1 What lessons can we learn from a consideration of Henry Ford's management practices at Highland Park in the early part of this century?

2 To what extent would you agree with the argument that management has become less concerned with operational detail and more about strategic matters?

3 What are the main benefits assumed to flow from the adoption of a divisional form of organization structure? Illustrate your answer with any relevant case study material.

4 In what ways did American management practices influence the management of UK firms in the 1960s and 1970s?

5 According to Porter, the choice of a 'generic strategy' which best fits the organization's 'industry structure' will always lead to above-average performance. To what extent do you agree with this position?

6 'There are many variables which limit the effectiveness of management strategy, and many of them are beyond management's control.' Discuss.

7 'Cost recovery, not cost reduction, is the most important business policy a firm should pursue.' Discuss. (See also Chapters 1 and 2.)

References

Abernathy, W. and Wayne, K. (1974) The limits to the learning curve, *Harvard Business Review*, Sept/Oct.

Anglo American Productivity Council (1950) *Report on Internal Combustion Engines* and *Report on Management Accounting*.

Arnold and Faurote (1915) *Ford's Methods and Ford's Shops*, Engineering Magazine Co New York.

Arthur Andersen (1992) *The Lean Enterprise Benchmarking Project*, Andersen Consulting, London.

Bornholt (1913), in *Iron Age*, 4 December.

Chandler, A. (1962) *Strategy and Structure*, MIT Press, Cambridge, Mass.

Dent, A. (1935) *Management Planning and Control*, Gee, London.

Drucker, P. (1955/1989) *The Practice of Management*, Heinemann, Oxford.

Haves, R. and Abernathy, W. (1980) Managing our way to economic decline. *Harvard Business Review*, July–Aug.

Hutton, G. (1953) *We Too Can Prosper*, Allen & Unwin, London.

Johnson, H. and Kaplan, R. (1987) *Relevance Lost: the Rise and Fall of Management Accounting*, Harvard Business School Press, Boston.

Knoeppel, C. (1919) Graphic production control, *Industrial Management*, Feb.

Knoeppel, C. (1933) *Profit Engineering: Applied Economics in Making Business Profitable*, McGraw-Hill, London.

Porter, M. (1979) How competitive forces shape strategy, *Harvard Business Review*, March/April.

Porter, M. (1980) *Competitive Strategy*, Free Press, New York.

Porter, M. (1985) *Competitive Advantage*, Free Press, New York.

Sloan, A. (1964) *My Years with General Motors*, Doubleday, New York.

Taylor, F.W. (1929) *Principles of Scientific Management*, Harper & Bros., New York.

Wolff, H. (1964) The great General Motors mystery, *Harvard Business Review*, September–October.

Womack, J., Jones, D. and Roos, D. (1990) *The Machine that Changed the World*, Rawson Associates, New York.

Williams, K., Haslam, C., Williams, J. and Cutler, T., with Adcroft, A. and Johal, S. (1992) Against lean production, *Economy and Society*, August.

Williams, K., Haslam, C., Williams, J. and Johal, S. (1994) Deconstructing car producer productivity, *International Journal of Production Economics*, forthcoming.

The labour market environment

6

This chapter reviews key features of the UK labour market –
employment, labour costs, skills, and industrial relations – and
contrasts them with conditions elsewhere in Europe and in
Japan. Institutional factors are seen to be at least as important
as competitive forces in explaining international differences.
The policy implications are explored in the context of recent
debates about 'Social Europe'.

Introduction

At the heart of the personnel function in modern business is a recognition that workers are people, and that management has to win their
support for the achievement of company goals. Yet traditionally,
labour economics has gone to considerable lengths to deny the human
attributes of labour, treating workers as a 'factor of production', a
commodity whose behaviour, like that of any commodity, is determined by the impersonal forces of supply and demand.

The traditional neo-classical approach to labour economics sees
changes in pay as performing an important role in matching labour
supply to labour demand. Each employer in a competitive labour
market is assumed to pay a wage rate which is determined by the
relationship between supply and demand in the labour market as a
whole, so that the marginal cost of hiring labour (the cost of taking on
one extra worker) equals the wage, and each firm's demand for labour
is inversely related to the wage rate. If product demand changes, then
demand for labour will shift to raise wages in expanding industries,
and reduce them in contracting industries. In the long run, it is
assumed, these wage differentials bring about movements of labour

between the sectors until competitive equilibrium is reached, and wage cuts will be needed if unemployment is to be reduced.

Critics of the competitive approach point to the lack of realism of many of its assumptions: that labour is homogeneous, for example, or that job switching is costless, or that institutional factors in pay determination can be ignored. An alternative approach suggests that structured barriers to labour mobility create distinct segments within the labour market, which are a major cause of the persistence over time of pay inequalities. In some firms, 'internal' labour markets develop, where jobs are filled by internal promotion rather than open entry, and workers are offered higher pay and greater job security in order to reduce labour turnover. Internal labour markets may arise to protect firms' investments in job-specific skills, or in response to union demands. Alongside these 'internal' labour markets, however, are 'external' labour markets, where pay and working conditions are generally poor. In external labour markets, workers are hired and fired according to current market conditions, or alternatively workforce stability is achieved by recruiting disadvantaged workers, who, under conditions of sexism or racism, have limited alternative job opportunities. The result, overall, is a labour market where pay inequalities are socially structured, and bear little relation to differences in productivity.

These competing perspectives on labour markets – competitive and structural – have influenced much of the recent debate about the impact of the labour market on economic performance in Britain. We explore this debate in the context of four related aspects of contemporary labour markets – employment, labour costs, skills, and industrial relations – and draw attention to labour's share in value added as a key influence on economic performance. The chapter concludes with an assessment of the conflict between Britain and her European partners over the extent to which European integration should extend to labour as well as capital.

Employment

This section explores the basic trends in demand for labour and labour supply over the post-war period, and focusses on the mismatch between the two which has been such a pervasive feature of the past two decades.

Demand for labour

A firm's demand for labour is derived from demand for its products, which depends fundamentally on its success in anticipating and satisfying consumer wants as expressed in the market-place. As we saw in Chapter 1, this means understanding the variety of characteristics that modern consumers require, and competing successfully with other firms in selling products which incorporate these characteristics.

At the national level, governments can stimulate or restrain consumer spending through their fiscal and monetary policies, within the constraints imposed by the essentially cyclical nature of demand in mature product markets. This will have a direct effect on demand for labour in retailing and other services. In a closed economy, there would also be a substantial impact on demand for labour in manufacturing, but where foreign trade is significant this effect is spread over a number of different national economies. In Britain in recent years, as we shall see in Chapters 8 and 10, stimulation of consumer demand has been associated more with an increase in manufacturing imports than with an increase in manufacturing jobs.

An important subsidiary influence on labour demand is the effect of technological and other changes on labour productivity. Improvements in the way production is organized, or a substitution of capital equipment for labour, each result in fewer workers being required to produce the same output. In British manufacturing industry, output per person hour has been rising at a long-term rate of 4–5% per year (Gordon, 1992). This means that, for manufacturing employment to remain constant, manufacturing output has to rise at the same rate. If manufacturing output should fall, as it did dramatically in 1973–5, 1979–81, and 1989–92, then the fall in manufacturing jobs will be ever more severe.

Labour supply

There are number of cultural and political factors which determine labour force participation (the proportion of the population who are in paid employment or seeking it) and hours worked. There are, for example, extensive legal restrictions on child labour, while at the other end of the age spectrum provision of retirement pensions limits the need for older adults to seek paid employment. Some young adults delay entry into the labour market by staying on in the education system, while some adult family members (usually women) withdraw from the labour market to spend time looking after dependants and maintaining the family home.

There have been many changes over the years in labour force participation by different social groups. The school leaving age has been raised, for example, and more young people are staying on in the education system, encouraged by the growing use of educational qualifications by employers as a screening device in selecting applicants for high-paid jobs. Some older people are retiring earlier, encouraged in some cases by government schemes to ease the burdens of redundancy and unemployment for younger workers. By far the most significant trend in recent decades, however, has been increased labour force participation by women, who by 1993 constituted 49% of all employees in employment (compared with 34% in 1951). Labour force participation by women has risen particularly dramatically among the over-30s, and this is associated with an increasing tendency for married women with children to return to the labour market when their children are old enough to go to school.

Family life requires a series of interrelated decisions about labour force participation (to provide income which is needed to purchase consumption goods), unpaid work (to maintain the home and bring up the children), and consumption patterns (involving the allocation of time as well as money). In these circumstances, it is more appropriate, for married men as well as married women, to focus on the household rather than the individual as the main locus of decision-making about labour supply. This requires an understanding of the different positions of women and men within the family as well as in the labour market.

In Britain, as in most industrial countries, men have traditionally taken on few of the responsibilites for childcare and housework, and women have been discriminated against in access to higher-paid jobs. It is not surprising, therefore, that women with children have lower labour force participation rates than other groups. What has changed is that their withdrawal from the labour force has become temporary rather than permanent, and a number of interrelated developments on the supply and the demand sides of the labour market have helped bring this about. The following are particularly significant.

- The high level of aggregate demand in the 1950s and 1960s encouraged employers to recruit new sources of labour.
- The changing composition of demand away from heavy industry and towards services has expanded many jobs which have traditionally been done by women, while many traditionally 'male' jobs have declined.
- New products such as vacuum cleaners, washing machines, convenience foods, freezers, and microwave ovens have reduced the time which needs to be spent on unpaid housework.
- The expectations of married women have changed.

The growth in female employment in post-war Britain has been almost entirely a growth in part-time jobs, as Table 6.1 indicates. Part-time

Table 6.1   Employees in employment (GB, millions)

	Manufacturing			Services		
	1977	1987	1993	1977	1987	1993
Males	5.1	3.5	3.0	6.0	6.4	6.5
(of which part-time)	(na)	(0.1)	(0.1)	(na)	(0.8)	(1.0)
Females	2.1	1.5	1.2	6.7	7.9	8.7
(of which part-time)	(0.5)	(0.3)	(0.3)	(3.0)	(3.8)	(4.4)
Total	7.2	5.0	4.2	12.7	14.2	15.2

Source: Employment Gazette.

Note: All figures relate to June.

employment is much more significant in Britain than in other industrial countries (Beechey and Perkins, 1987), and a quarter of all employees (female and male) are employed part-time.

In explaining the growth of part-time employment, both supply and demand factors are again significant.

- It is easier for women with children to combine part-time jobs with domestic responsibilities, particularly where community childcare facilities are underdeveloped.
- Where jobs require unsocial hours to be worked, or where there are considerable fluctuations in demand, employers value the flexibility that part-time jobs can bring (e.g. evening or Saturday work in retailing).
- Where employees work less than 16 hours per week, employers are exempt from the provisions of the Employment Protection Act, making it easier for them to lay off workers when demand is slack.
- Employers can pay part-timers at lower hourly rates than full timers, and save on National Insurance contributions.

For most workers who are employed on a full-time basis, basic working hours are fixed. There have, however, been a number of reductions since the mid-nineteenth century (when a 60-hour working week was common), and recent negotiations in the UK engineering industry suggest that a $37\frac{1}{2}$-hour working week may become standard. Changes in the level of economic activity have been one of the most significant environmental influences on the basic working week. In periods of rising unemployment, as in the early 1980s, trade unions often shift their emphasis from pay bargaining to bargaining over hours, in an attempt to protect jobs and reduce unemployment. Employers, however, are resistant to changes which adversely affect their profitability, and are more willing to accept reductions in hours if these are accompanied by improved labour productivity. The end result is often an increase in work intensity or a change in working patterns, rather than an increase in jobs.

Traditionally, the main element of flexibility within full-time employment is overtime working, paid at premium rates. The extent of overtime working tends to vary with changes in the level of economic activity. When demand expands, employers often prefer to offer increased overtime rather than recruit extra workers. There are two basic reasons for this.

- They can meet increased demand without having to expand overhead labour costs.
- If the increase in demand proves to be short-lived, it will be easier to cut back again on overtime working than to declare workers redundant.

Since the recession of the early 1980s, many UK employers have made a determined effort to cut back on overtime working. As we shall see later in the chapter, some have preferred instead to introduce greater flexibility in working hours.

Unemployment

In the 1950s and 1960s, there was a reasonable match between labour demand and labour supply in the UK economy as a whole. This resulted from two factors: an unprecedentedly long post-war boom, and a social settlement which gave primacy to the pursuit and main-tenance of full employment (see Key Concept 6.1). There was some frictional unemployment (temporary unemployment while switching jobs), and there was some regional unemployment, in that demand for labour was more intense in Southern England and the Midlands than in Northern England, Scotland, Wales, and Northern Ireland. National unemployment rates (the proportion of the workforce who are out of work but entitled to unemployment benefit) were rarely above 2%.

KEY CONCEPT 6.1
Full employment

Full employment is a concept which is often referred to, but seldom defined. Beveridge's (1944) description comes close to what most economists understand by the term: 'Full employment means that unemployment is reduced to short intervals of standing by, with the certainty that very soon one will be wanted in one's old job again or will be wanted in a new job that is within one's powers.' In other words, full employment does not mean zero unemployment, but allows for some measure of 'acceptable' unemployment, e.g. frictional unemployment while switching jobs.

Beveridge suggested that full employment would exist when the number of unfilled vacancies exceeded the numbers registering as unemployed (thus ignoring problems due to job vacancies being in a different region or requiring different skills). He thought that full employment would correspond to an unemployment rate of 3% (an estimate which Keynes felt to be too low). In fact, the average UK unemployment rate for the two decades after the war was below 2%, and in the more prosperous regions like the South East and West Midlands the unemployment rate was seldom above 1%.

Deficiencies in the compilation of official statistics make it difficult to define full employment with any precision. The unemployment figures, for example, have since 1982 counted only those unemployed people who claim benefit at an Unemployment Benefit Office. The unemployment count thus excludes the voluntarily unemployed and temporarily stopped. It also excludes significant numbers of people who are unemployed but are not entitled to benefit, either because they have not paid the requisite contributions, or because the government has changed the entitlement rules. The official job vacancy figures, too, give only a partial picture, as vacancies notified by employers to Job Centres or Careers Offices are thought to represent less than half of total vacancies.

Over the past two decades, however, there has been an increasing mismatch between labour supply and labour demand, as successive recessions have taken their toll, as UK manufacturing performance has deteriorated, and as government policies no longer give priority to full employment. Labour's share in manufacturing value added rose above 70% in 1979, and firms responded by laying off workers on a massive scale. In the recovery of the 1980s, there was a dramatic fall in labour's share, but increased profits, as we shall see in Chapter 7, went into increased dividends and acquisitions, rather than new investment to recover the market shares that had been lost to foreign competitors.

Employment in the service sector continued to rise (except in 1980–82 and 1990–93), but most of the gains were in part-time jobs for women, whereas most of the losses in manufacturing were in full-time jobs for men. Table 6.1 (above) presents the basic data for the period since 1977. Over the 17 years from 1977 to 1993, both male and female employment in manufacturing declined by 42%. In the service sector, however, male employment increased by 7%, while female employment rose by 30% (mainly part-timers).

Given these significant changes in the composition of demand for labour, it is not surprising that unemployment has increased, not just at times of recession, but in a long-term sense as well. According to the official figures (which considerably understate the true picture, because of new rules restricting entitlement to unemployment benefit), national claimant unemployment rates rose above 10% in 1982–86 and 1992–93, and even at the height of the 'boom' of the late 1980s did not fall below 5%.

Unlike the 1979–82 recession, which hit the peripheral regions much more than Southern England, the 1989–92 recession created high levels of unemployment in all regions, so that by 1993, as Table 6.2 shows, no region had an unemployment rate below 8%.

Table 6.2 Claimant unemployment rates by region, June 1993

South East	10%
East Anglia	8%
South West	10%
West Midlands	11%
East Midlands	9%
Yorks and Humber	10%
North West	11%
North	12%
Wales	10%
Scotland	10%
N Ireland	14%
UK Average	10%

Source: Employment Gazette.

Labour costs

In the 1980s, governments, following the competitive model, echoed their predecessors in the 1920s in suggesting that British workers were pricing themselves out of jobs. Lower labour costs, this argument ran, would make British industry more competitive, and thus create jobs. This section explores recent trends in pay inequalities, and policy debates relating to low pay, before going on to assess comparative labour costs and their relationship to British manufacturing decline.

Pay inequalities

One of the features of the UK labour market is the extent to which pay inequalities have widened in recent years. As Table 6.3 shows, for much of this century the relative earnings of full-time manual men remained remarkably stable. Since 1977, however, the inequalities widened dramatically.

Male manual workers, of course, represent only a part of the total workforce, but this is the only group for which reliable statistics have been collected over such a long period of time. The distribution of earnings for all full-time employees (i.e. including women and non-manual workers) is more dispersed than that for male manual workers alone. From Tables 6.4 and 6.5, it can be seen that overall earnings

Table 6.3 Dispersion of average weekly earnings of full-time manual men

Year	Lowest decile as % of median	Highest decile as % of median	Lowest decile as % of highest decile
1886	69	143	48
1906	67	137	49
1938	68	140	48
1960	71	145	49
1977	71	144	49
1993	63	159	40

Source: 1886–1960 Thatcher (1968). 1977–93 *New Earnings Survey.*

Note: For an explanation of deciles and medians, see Chapter 4 of Slater and Ascroft (1990).

Table 6.4 Dispersion of average weekly earnings of all full-time adult employees

Year	Lowest decile as % of median	Highest decile as % of median	Lowest decile as % of highest decile
1984	58	177	33
1993	58	201	29

Source: New Earnings Survey.

Table 6.5 Proportion of full-time workers earning less than 66% of the median wage, EC member states, 1990

Belgium	5%
Denmark	0%
France	14%
Greece	16%
Irish Republic	18%
Italy	15%
Netherlands	11%
Portugal	12%
Spain	19%
UK	20%
W Germany	13%

Source: Bazen and Benhayoun (1992).

distributions for full-time workers have widened in recent years, and that they are more unequal in Britain than in any other EC country.

We have seen that job growth in post-war Britain has been largely a growth of part-time employment. Data limitations and variability in hours worked make it difficult to incorporate part-timers in an overall earnings distribution. Most part-timers are, however, women employed on hourly rates which increasingly are below those of their full-time counterparts. Their inclusion would further widen the overall dispersion of hourly earnings.

Low pay and unequal opportunities

As Table 6.6 shows, low pay affects women more than men, and part-timers more than full-timers. It is concentrated on industries such as

Table 6.6 Proportion of employees on adult rates earning less than £3.40 per hour, GB, April 1993

	%
Female full-timers	8
Male full-timers	3
Female part-timers	24
Male part-timers	28

Source: New Earnings Survey.

agriculture, clothing manufacture, retailing, hairdressing, and catering – industries with a predominance of small firms, and low levels of unionization.

Given the predominance of women in the ranks of the low paid, equal opportunities policies have a major role to play, not just in promoting greater equity of treatment between women and men, but in tackling low pay as well. The main legislation here is the Equal Pay Act, which made it illegal for employers to pay women less than men for doing the same job. This Act was passed in 1970, and fully implemented by 1976. The scope of the Act was extended in 1984, following pressure from the European Commission, to provide equal pay for jobs of equal value.

The relationship between changes in the legislation and changes in women's pay, relative to men, is remarkable. As Table 6.6 shows, relative female pay rose by 12 percentage points in 1970–76, the period over which the Equal Pay Act, as originally worded, was implemented. Gender inequalities in pay then stabilized over the period 1976–87, only to narrow again, by six percentage points over the next six years, as the equal value amendment started to bite. They remain wider in Britain than in other European countries, however, because of the absence of any general system of labour market regulation (Rubery, 1992).

The competitive model predicts that dramatic rises in women's pay would result in some substitution of male for female labour, or greater job losses in firms employing mainly women than in firms employing mainly men. In fact, as Table 6.7 reveals, the full-time employment of women to men continued to grow relative to men from 1970 to 1976, and even accelerated after 1987.

More effective equal opportunities policies, though highly desirable in their own right, would not in themselves solve the low-pay problem, because of continued high levels of job segregation (which limits the scope for establishing comparability of job content), the predominance of low pay among part-time workers, and the significant (and increasing) proportion of men in low-paid jobs. Demands are therefore

Table 6.7 Relative pay and employment of women and men in full-time jobs

Year	Hourly earnings, women as % of men	Employees in employment, women as % of men
1970	63	42
1976	75	43
1987	74	51
1993	80	58

Source: New Earnings Survey; Employment Gazette.

growing, particularly within the trade union movement, for a national minimum wage, such as exists in most other industrial countries. Such demands have been resisted by the government, which, following the competitive model, favours wage cuts to price 'marginal' workers into jobs.

Experience in other countries suggests that, if the institutional conditions are favourable, minimum wages can, by improving the utilization of labour, be brought in with minimal loss of jobs. This provides powerful evidence that pay inequalities are socially structured, rather than determined competitively. It remains the case, however, that, at the level of the firm, there is an important relationship between labour costs and employment. As we have seen in Chapter 4, in most industries a company's wage bill forms a significant proportion of its value added. If labour's share of value added rises above a critical level as a result of market failure, then in most cases a firm will have no alternative but to lay off workers if it is going to survive (see Case Study 6.1).

CASE STUDY 6.1
A national minimum wage

A national minimum wage makes it illegal for employers to pay their workers at below the established rate.

From a neo-classical perspective, the main problem with minimum wages is that they interfere with the pay flexibility needed to generate full employment. If a minimum wage is imposed at a level above the market equilibrium (at W_2 in Figure 6.1(b)), then firms will offer fewer jobs (Q_2 instead of Q_1). A minimum wage is also seen as creating an element of 'stickiness' in the labour market, reducing the scope for pay flexibility to reallocate labour in line with shifts in product demand.

The structural approach is more complex. It sees firms which employ large numbers of low-paid workers as being caught in a low-productivity trap. Lacking any incentive to develop new products or new production methods, or even to use their existing workforce more effectively, they depend on cheap labour as their only source of competitive advantage. A minimum wage, in this situation, could have a positive impact on industrial efficiency. Inefficient firms, if they had to pay higher wages, would have to innovate in order to survive. Some jobs would be lost as marginal firms were

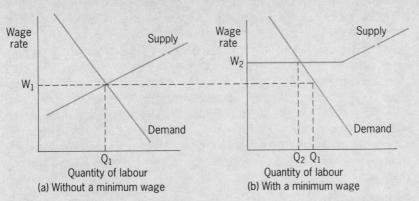

Figure 6.1 Quantity of labour demanded (a) without a minimum wage and (b) with a minimum wage.

driven out of business, but others would be created as a result of the expanded product demand which would result from improved efficiency in the surviving firms, and from the boost to investment which greater labour market stability would encourage.

Britain was one of the pioneers of minimum wage legislation (with the Trade Boards Act of 1909), but her approach was, and has remained, a piecemeal one. Trade Boards, consisting of employers, workers' representatives, and independent members, were created to determine minimum wages in a small number of trades, following widespread publicity about the evils of sweated labour in the East End of London. The Act was passed in the face of economic arguments that any state interference in wage determination would create unemployment – supporters argued that sweating (the employment of family labour at below-subsistence wages) was an exceptional case, and that the sweat shops were in effect being subsidized by the rest of the economy. The system (renamed Wages Councils and Agricultural Wages Boards) was expanded after each of the World Wars, but never covered more than a fifth of the workforce.

Most other countries came to minimum wage fixing later than Britain, but the coverage of their legislation was, in general, more comprehensive. Ten out of the 12 EU countries, for example, have legislation covering all, or almost all, the workforce. Research evidence from the USA (Brown *et al.*, 1982) and France (Bazen and Martin, 1991) suggests that minimum wages in those economies increase youth unemployment, but have no effect on adult jobs.

Divergence between Britain and the other industrial countries has become particularly pronounced over the past quarter century. Most countries, in this period, extended the protection given to low-paid workers, but in Britain Wages Councils were progressively weakened, and eventually abolished in 1993. Interest in minimum wage fixing for Britain has, however, revived in recent years. This reflects growing awareness of the widening of pay inequalities since the 1970s, and of the limited effectiveness of equal pay legislation in improving the position of women workers. There has been pressure, too, within the European Union for all member countries to establish 'equitable remuneration'.

In the 1992 general election, low pay was, for the first time, a major item on the British political agenda. The Labour Party proposed a national minimum wage, to be set initially at half median male earnings (£3.40 per hour). They suggested that this would stimulate industrial efficiency (following the structural approach), and would not destroy jobs. The Conservatives, drawing on neo-classical theory, argued that a national minimum wage would price low-paid workers out of jobs, adding to unemployment.

The analysis which has been developed in Chapter 4 suggests that whether or not a firm responds to a minimum wage by sacking workers depends crucially on labour's share in value added. If, as in the clothing industry, labour's share is consistently above 80%, the imposition of higher minimum wages would squeeze profits, and inhibit firms' ability to make the investments in new technology and training which would be needed to improve efficiency. In cases such as this, constructive responses to a minimum wage would depend on the introduction of complementary measures to encourage investment, such as concessionary finance and a more active industrial policy.

Further reading
Neale (1992a).

Unit labour costs

From the view of the employer, labour costs include not only the wages and salaries that are paid direct to employees, but the related 'social charges', such as National Insurance contributions, which have to be paid as well. Column (a) in Table 6.8 shows that in 1960 there was little difference in hourly labour costs between the main European economies, though these costs were significantly higher in the USA and lower in Japan. Over the next quarter century, rapid growth in continental Europe and Japan brought their hourly labour costs closer to those in the USA, while Britain lagged behind. By the late 1980s, Britain had become, compared with the other major industrial economies, a low labour cost country.

For an employer, what is most meaningful is labour costs per unit of output – or labour costs per hour divided by output per hour. International comparisons of labour productivity are, as we have seen in Chapter 3, notoriously hazardous, but calculations at the level of the manufacturing sector as a whole get over some, at least, of the problems of inter-plant or inter-firm comparison. Column (b) in Table 6.8, based on one recent estimate, suggests that manufacturing labour productivity is now lower in Britain then in the other major industrial economies.

Comparison of columns (a) and (b) suggests a broad correspondence between hourly labour costs and labour productivity. This is what one might expect, given that high productivity businesses can afford high pay levels, and that firms in low labour cost economies have less incentive to improve productivity. The evidence from column (c), which has been calculated from columns (a) and (b), is tentative, and too much significance should not be read into the precise figures, though

Table 6.8 Comparative unit labour costs in manufacturing (GB = 100)

	(a) Hourly labour costs		(b) Output per hour		(c) Unit labour costs	
	1960	1989	1960	1989	1960	1989
Britain	100	100	100	100	100	100
France	94	113	93	124	101	91
Japan	30	127	50	124	60	102
USA	296	130	255	158	116	82
W. Germany	98	195	110	116	89	168

Source: (a) Swedish Employers' Confederation; Neale (1992b). (b) O'Mahony (1993).

they do suggest that Britain is about in the middle of the range of unit labour costs in the major industrial countries.

What is worrying, from the evidence in Table 6.8, is not so much that unit labour costs in Britain are too high, but the extent to which Britain has become a low labour cost, low productivity economy. Hourly labour costs are, of course, significantly above those in the newly industrializing countries of East Asia (see Case Study 2.3) which have, in recent years, achieved similar productivity levels to the developed economies. The danger, for an economy like Britain's, is that firms are finding it increasingly difficult to compete with Germany and Japan in high value added products (which command a premium price on world markets), while they are becoming increasingly vulnerable to competition from lower labour cost countries in the more price-sensitive markets for low value added products.

Skills

To use any technology effectively, a firm needs an appropriate mix of skills in its workforce. In choosing which products to make, and how to go about making them, the firm will be constrained by the capacities of its existing workforce, and by the prospects of recruiting new workers with the requisite skills. Changes in technology will have effects on productivity and company profits, not only directly through changes in productive efficiency, but indirectly through changes in work organization.

Harry Braverman, in his influential book *Labor and Monopoly Capital* (1974), presents a mass of historical evidence indicating that, with

---

KEY CONCEPT 6.2
Labour process

The term 'labour process' was coined by Karl Marx in 1867, to describe the way raw materials are transformed by human activity into useful objects (Marx, 1976). The capitalist labour process, Marx suggested, differs from other labour processes in two ways.

- Workers work under the control of the capitalist.
- Their products belong to the capitalist.

Because capitalists aim to produce commodities whose value exceeds that of the commodities used in their production, they are encouraged to develop production methods which subordinate workers to their direct control.

Contemporary academic interest in the labour process has been stimulated by Harry Braverman, who extended Marx's analysis to cover twentieth century developments (1974). Doubts have been expressed about the validity of Braverman's tendency to reduce all production decisions to a desire on the part of management to de-skill the workforce, but Braverman has successfully drawn attention to the fact that they involve considerations of control as well as of technical efficiency.

mechanization, jobs have become fragmented, and workers de-skilled. This, he suggests, is due more to a desire on the part of management to take control over the labour process (Key Concept 6.2) away from craft workers than to considerations of technical efficiency. Subsequent research suggests, however, that Braverman has underestimated both the ability of skilled workers to resist de-skilling and the extent of which some new technologies might create new skills as well as destroy old ones.

Fragmentation of jobs and the replacement of craft workers by machines and machine minders have certainly been characteristic of work processes involving the mass production of standardized products, though in some cases (notably the Swedish car industry in the 1970s) employers have allowed autonomous group working in an attempt to cut down the absenteeism and turnover costs resulting from worker dissatisfaction with repetitive jobs. When flexible manufacturing systems are used to produce differentiated products for fragmenting markets, however, de-skilling may be a totally inappropriate strategy for management. Effective use of micro-electronic systems requires at least a core of the workforce to have well-developed hybrid skills, combining, for example, craft and technician skills, engineering and design skills, mechanical and electronic skills, or operator and diagnostic skills. Where these systems are being continuously developed, management may need employees to update their skills continually, and to be able to identify and rectify faults rapidly.

When the capacities of new manufacturing systems to produce a flexible product mix are exploited, the levels of skill and training required may be very high indeed. Mostly, this effect occurs at the top of the occupational hierarchy. Jaikumar, in a study of flexible manufacturing systems in Japanese factories (1986), points to the crucial role of engineering teams, and notes that 'engineers now outnumber production workers three to one'. It is nonetheless the case that firms in Britain which have been unwilling to train and retrain their production workers are not able to take full advantage of the flexibility of modern manufacturing systems. Where firms try to make full use of this flexibility, unforeseen problems may occur on the shop floor, and because workers are not sufficiently skilled (or not allowed) to solve them the resulting delays can be extremely disruptive and costly (Senker and Beesley, 1986). Alternatively, some firms may make operational decisions which result in less flexibility than was expected at the planning stage.

Skills can be acquired informally (at home, or through relevant on-the-job experience) or formally (through the education system, or through training schemes). There is evidence that skills which are acquired informally are insufficiently recognized and rewarded by British employers. In a survey of four manufacturing and two service industries carried out in 1980–81, for example, it was found that a significant number of jobs done by women were not classed as skilled, yet required at least six months on-the-job experience and particular qualities such as manual dexterity and sharp eyesight. Yet women who did such jobs were paid no more than inexperienced casual workers (Craig *et al.*, 1985).

Skill differences between Britain and other industrial countries are most pronounced at the level of intermediate formal qualifications (apprenticeships, City and Guilds certificates, and secretarial qualifications, for example). The National Institute of Economic and Social Research did a series of surveys in the 1980s which explored the differences between Britain and other industrial countries in some detail (Prais, 1989). While the variations revealed in these surveys are complex, three findings stand out as particularly significant.

- International differences in the number of qualified personnel and in the quality of the qualifications are more significant at intermediate than at degree level.
- Mathematical attainments by average and below-average pupils are significantly lower in British than in West German or Japanese schools, limiting their opportunities to go on to vocational courses.
- Both the numbers undergoing vocational education and training and the standards required are significantly lower in Britain than in West Germany, Japan, or France.

KEY CONCEPT 6.3
Human capital

Neo-classical theory sees individuals as embodying not just the capacity to work, but 'human capital', the product of deliberate 'investment' in education, training and on-the-job experience. The acquisition of human capital involves an immediate cost in terms of pay and other opportunities forgone, but it also involves a subsequent return in terms of higher pay. In choosing between different types of human capital investment, individuals, it is suggested, will be influenced by the rate of return they can expect. Changes in demand for 'quality' labour will affect pay and thus expected returns, bringing about appropriate adjustments in human capital investment and thus supply.

Neo-classical theory uses the concept of 'human capital' (see Key Concept 6.3) to explain both the pay differentials which skilled workers can command and levels of training provision. Economists using this approach sometimes suggest that market forces can be relied upon to bring about appropriate levels of skill acquisition. The problem here is that, in a market-based system, firms are unwilling to train employees in transferable skills, for fear that 'free-riding' competitors will be encouraged to 'poach' their skilled workers, rather than offer training themselves.

KEY CONCEPT 6.4
Externalities

Externalities are positive or negative impacts which transactions have for people who are not parties to the transaction.

When you smoke a cigarette in a public place, for example, you create external nuisance and health costs for other individuals who have to breathe in the smoke.

Similarly, when a firm pollutes a river, it creates external costs for people downstream who use that river for their drinking water.

When, on the other hand, a firm offers its employees training in transferable skills, it creates external benefits for the local economy as a whole, because it expands the pool of skilled labour from which all firms can recruit. Similarly, if a fishing boat limits its catch to sustain fishery resources, it creates benefits in terms of sustained harvests for all fishing boats in future years.

Externalities represent a misallocation of resources, because producers of negative externalities do not have to take account of the external costs of their activities, while bestowers of external benefits are not rewarded for this. Generally speaking, un-regulated markets over-produce goods and services which create harmful externalities, and under-produce goods and services which create beneficial externalities.

To compensate for such market failures, neo-classical economics suggests that action should be taken to 'internalize the externality'. Taxes can be imposed where producers create negative externalities, for example, while subsidies can be given to reward the creation of positive externalities.

International experience confirms the suggestion that training is a positive 'externality' (see Key Concept 6.4), and that some form of state intervention is required to ensure that training provision is matched with skill requirements. This can take the form of direct state provision (as in France) or of a legal requirement on employers to provide apprenticeships (as in Germany). In countries like Britain, where vocational training is largely market-based, there is considerable under-investment in skills.

The National Institute research programme has explored the relationship between training provision and labour productivity in Britain and West Germany. Comparative studies of metal working (see Case Study 6.2), furniture manufacture, clothing and hotels (Prais, 1989) suggest that, in these sectors, both labour productivity and training provision are significantly higher in Germany than in Britain. The National Institute researchers argue that the differences in labour productivity are in large part caused by differences in workforce skills.

CASE STUDY 6.2
Labour productivity in metal working

International comparisons of labour productivity are notoriously difficult to interpret. Different industries use different production methods, so comparisons of national aggregates (involving different industry mixes) have little meaning. Even where the study is narrowed down to a particular product, there may be variations in the quantity and quality of labour, in the choice of technique, in work patterns, and in plant utilization. The effects of these variations are difficult to disentangle from the effects of any differences in the expenditure of effort.

One study which claims to avoid most of these potential pitfalls was done at the National Institute of Economic and Social Research in 1983–84 (Daly *et al.*, 1985). The National Institute researchers compared simple matched metal products (screws, springs, hydraulic valves, and drill bits) made by six British and six West German firms. The choice of simple products reduced the need to take account of quality variations, and made it possible to measure output in physical terms. It also enabled the researchers to isolate the contribution of operator efficiency to productivity from that of design and technical staff.

In each of the comparisons, the German firms had higher levels of labour productivity, ranging from 10% to 130%. There were no significant differences in direct labour levels between the two countries (though there was some evidence of inefficient use of indirect labour in feeding materials to machines in British plants), and there was little difference in machine running speeds. The machinery used in the British firms was no older than that in the German firms, though technically it was often less advanced, because of a lack of technical competence among British decision-makers, and an unwillingness to contemplate long payback periods. Machine breakdowns were more frequent in Britain than in Germany, and took longer to put right.

About half of the German shopfloor workers had apprenticeship-type qualifications, whereas the British proportion was only a quarter. These differences were most apparent at the supervisory level. Few of the forepersons in the British plants had formal qualifications, while in the German plants nearly all had been trained not just in routine setting and maintenance of machines, but in staff supervision, work organization and light repair work as well. Absence of appropriate skills at all levels, reported one numerically-controlled machine tool manufacturer, meant that 'almost half the machines sold in Britain are not used as they might be, because their full capacity is not understood'. German users, in contrast, were better able to diagnose faults when machines broke down, and to undertake repairs themselves – a major factor in their superior maintenance record.

Daly *et al.* conclude that 'lack of technical expertise and training... is the main stumbling block', but as Cutler (1992) points out, what is crucial is the sophistication of the capital equipment employed, which may reflect financial calculations more than technical expertise.

Further reading
Prais (1989);
Cutler (1992).

The National Institute research has been widely quoted, not least by politicians seeking to boost training provision in Britain. The methodology of the research has been criticized, however, notably by Cutler (1992), who argues that the policy conclusions cannot be justified by the evidence. The National Institute case studies, for example, reveal considerable differences between the British and German industries in the sophistication of the machinery used, yet the significance of these differences in physical capital is downplayed. Although enhanced skills, among 'key' workers at least, may be a necessary condition of improved performance in many British firms, they are unlikely to be sufficient.

Lack of appropriate skills may be more of a problem with British managers than with British workers. Fewer than one in seven British managers have received an education in management, and in their jobs they receive on average only one day's formal training per year (Constable and McCormick, 1987). This contrasts with a much greater emphasis on management education and training in other industrial countries, and is part of the explanation of the poor record of British firms in adapting to changed market conditions and in making effective use of the opportunities provided by new technology.

It is not, however, sufficient just to improve the formal qualifications of British managers. One of the most important lessons of an influential study of Japanese firms in Britain is that Japanese managers are more effective because they combine qualifications with detailed knowledge of their company's products, processes and systems (White and Trevor, 1983). The British custom of rapidly promoting qualified managers to senior non-operational positions, while entrusting operational decisions to managers with practical experience but few technical qualifications, is inappropriate to the modern business environment.

Industrial relations

At the end of the 1970s, just over half of full-time employees were trade union members, but almost three-quarters had their pay determined by collective bargaining. Since then, trade union involvement in pay determinations has lessened as a result of legislative changes (which have weakened union bargaining power) and structural changes in the economy (which have caused union membership to decline). Successive workplace industrial relations surveys have shown not only an increase in individual bargaining, but a decentralization of collective bargaining itself, with the emphasis shifting away from multi-employer national agreements, towards company or plant-level agreements (Beatson, 1993).

Reduced trade union power has been a prime goal of Conservative government policy since 1979. One result, in the late 1980s and early 1990s, was a reduction in strike activity, but the economic significance of this is often exaggerated – even in peak years (e.g. 1972, 1979, or 1984), the average worker lost only a single day's work as a result of industrial stoppages. There is, too, little research evidence to support government claims that industrial relations reform has boosted economic performance by enhancing labour productivity and reducing wage inflation. Investment in new technology and skills, is, if anything, greater in unionized workplaces than in non-union workplaces. And, while there was some erosion of the pay differential between union and non-union workplaces in the late 1980s, greater decentralization of pay bargaining encouraged real wage levels to rise rapidly, despite high levels of unemployment (Metcalf, 1993).

While it is easy to exaggerate the extent of trade union opposition to new technology in Britain, there is no doubt that the industrial relations system can limit what changes in technology or work organization can take place. Just-in-time (JIT) production systems are a case in point. As we saw in Chapter 3, JIT developed at Toyota in the 1950s, and is now seen by many Western firms as the answer to their production problems.

What is ignored in much of the current enthusiasm for JIT in the West is the extent to which the Toyota production system is embedded in a particular labour market structure, which limits its transferability to a different institutional context. A large discrepancy in wage levels between the core firms and the peripheral subcontractors provides financial incentives for Japanese manufacturers to rely on outside suppliers for operations which have been performed 'in-house' by most Western firms. JIT is an attempt to resolve the resulting problems of co-ordination, which results in the dumping of problems onto the peripheral small firm sector and its low-paid temporary workers (Chalmers, 1989). Higher levels of pay within core plants have been accompanied by coercive control over the labour process to speed workflow, made possible by the repression of militant industrial unions in the 1950s, and their replacement by tamer, company-based unions (Dohse *et al.*, 1985). The oppressive consequences of this regime for assembly line workers have been graphically documented by Kamata (see Case Study 6.3).

CASE STUDY 6.3 ***Working for Toyota***	The Toyota production system depends for its effectiveness on the maximum possible 'synchronization' of operations, both within the assembly plant and between component supply and assembly; this in turn depends on the almost total subordination of working time to management-determined production requirements. If production slows down because of malfunctioning machinery, the conveyor is speeded up to compensate; if a worker is unexpectedly absent from work, his or her colleagues must work compulsory overtime, or give up holiday entitlements. Basic wages form only a small proportion of the pay packet – the rest is made up of bonuses which depend on how much the work team has exceeded its production target. The resulting stress is enormous. Workers suffer chronic back pain and repetitive strain injury. Industrial injuries, fatalities and even suicides caused by the pressures of the job are high.

As Satoshi Kamata, a sociologist who worked on the assembly line at Toyota has put it: 'While management journalism may applaud Toyota's high profit and the "kanban method" which they see as supporting it, the human cost of Toyota methods – suicides, injuries, job fatalities, and occupational disease – increase at a horrifying rate.'

Further reading
Kamata (1984).

In Britain, wage differentials between large and small firms are less pronounced than in Japan, limiting the potential financial rewards of out-sourcing. At the same time, management attempts to establish JIT in conjunction with work intensification have proved more problematic (Turnbull, 1988). Lower stock levels make production systems more vulnerable to industrial disputes, and trade unions are able to halt output, at little cost to themselves, with limited actions like overtime bans. In this context, management can essentially choose between three possible courses of action:

● To abandon attempts to improve the organization of production.

- To force through changes in the industrial relations system so as to weaken the power of trade unions to resist work intensification (e.g. via 'no strike' agreements with compliant unions).
- To negotiate, with trade unions, ways of implementing improvements in production organization which do not involve a worsening of working conditions on the shop floor.

In the mid-1980s, the latter avenue was the one which was least explored in the UK. It is, however, arguably the approach which would be the most appropriate to the industrial relations environment of the UK, and which would offer the greatest opportunities of mutual benefit for management and shop floor workers alike.

Labour market flexibility v. Social Europe

In the early 1980s, employers faced with increased pressure from the global recession and from intensified international competition defended profit through a drastic reduction in the level of employment. In the medium term, recent research suggests that some employers, stimulated by the additional pressure of reductions in the basic working week, have attempted to pursue greater flexibility in working patterns (NEDO, 1986).

Flexible working practices, the NEDO Report (1986) suggests, involve a conscious attempt by employers to achieve greater numerical flexibility by creating a group of 'peripheral' workers whose activities can be expanded or contracted at fairly short notice. For 'core' workers, who employers see as central to the future of the organization, the emphasis is on increasing functional flexibility, so that workers can be re-deployed more easily between different tasks and locations. The aim in each case, Atkinson suggests, is to develop competitive advantage through increased ability to respond to changes in the product market environment.

The Atkinson model has been described by Anna Pollert (1987) as resting on 'an uncertain basis of confused assumptions and unsatisfactory evidence'. While there have undoubtedly been moves in the direction of greater job flexibility in recent years, their significance should not be exaggerated. In many cases, Pollert suggests, they represent not so much a radical break with the past as a continuation of long-established trends (such as overtime working by men in manufacturing industry, and part-time employment of women in service industries). The motive is often to cut short-term costs rather than to improve a long-term market position. Indeed, moves to greater 'functional flexibility' are constrained by limited budgets set aside for retraining, and a preoccupation with 'numerical flexibility' can serve to divert attention from the negative impact of skill shortages on UK industrial performance.

In order to match the hours of core workers more closely to output and capacity utilization requirements, without the cost penalties of overtime working, attempts have been made in recent years to introduce flexible working hours, where the hours worked vary from one week to another, or from one day to another.

Perhaps the most radical departure from customary practice has been the replacement of employment contracts by commercial contracts, through practices such as franchising and sub-contracting. More and more organizations, particularly in the public sector, are concentrating resources on core activities, and devolving to outside organizations activities which are not firm-specific. One advantage for the core organization is greater financial security. This is achieved, however, by shifting the burden of risk and uncertainty to the sub-contractor or franchisee, a process which involves high levels of dependence for the latter, and employment which is frequently insecure and low-paid. As part of this process, the 1980s have seen a revival of homeworking, in many cases under highly exploitative working conditions. This has been a feature not just of traditional spheres such as the clothing industry, but of high-tech areas such as computer programming and systems analysis as well (Huws, 1984; Mitter, 1985).

Alongside these employer-led initiatives, the government has, as we have seen, encouraged deregulation of the labour market and decentralization of pay bargaining, to reduce employee protection and promote pay flexibility. These changes, the government claims, attract foreign investment to Britain, and thus create jobs. In fact, as we shall see in Chapter 8, the number of jobs created by incoming investment has been limited, and the main effect of these policies has been to widen disparities in pay and working conditions between different groups of workers.

There is nothing inherently anti-worker in the idea of job flexibility. Functional flexibility could, for example, lead to more varied and rewarding jobs – significantly, many trade unionists are now beginning to demand that new technology be used, not to control workers, but to enhance their skills and their opportunities for creative work (Cooley, 1987). Flexibility in working time could, in appropriate circumstances, offer workers more choice, and make it easier for women and men to share childcare and well-paid employment. Indeed, writers such as André Gorz (1985) and James Robertson (1985) see greater flexibility in working time as the key to a more satisfying, equitable and sustainable future. At present, however, such scenarios seem remote. Brian Towers has observed (1987) that 'employers enthusiastically advocating labour flexibility are mostly looking for short-term means of reducing labour costs'. The negative consequences, for peripheral employees above all, are considerable. As the research workers who carried out the NEDO study conclude, 'The entire "flexibility debate" has been conducted in terms of what flexibilities capital requires from labour; labour's own needs for flexibility have been squeezed off the agenda' (Atkinson and Meager, 1986).

In part, the drive for labour market flexibility in Britain has been motivated by a desire to emulate labour market conditions in Japan. As such, it is probably doomed to failure – the Japanese system, as we have seen, depends both on a destruction of employee and trade union rights far in excess of what has occurred so far in Britain, and on a degree of protection in the domestic market, to underpin job security for core workers, which the British government has no intention of introducing.

British labour market policies in recent years have come increasingly into conflict with those of her European partners. In 1989, all EC members, except Britain, adopted the 'Social Charter', which contained provisions to restrict working hours, to establish rights for part-time workers, and to guarantee the rights of all workers to basic information, consultation, and training. This Charter was seen as an essential social counterpart to the Single European Market – necessary both to promote social cohesion and to protect the high-wage economies from 'unfair competition' (Adnett, 1993). The British government, however, viewed the Social Charter as an inefficient constraint on the operation of market forces.

CASE STUDY 6.4
Hoover

In January 1993, Hoover, the US-owned domestic appliance manufacturer, negotiated with the AEEU, MSF, and GMB/APEX a new pay and working conditions agreement at its Cambuslang plant in Scotland. Under the agreement, the unions, fearing closure of the plant, accepted a pay freeze for 1993, following a similar freeze in 1992. They also agreed to more 'flexible' working practices, including banning any industrial action until a disputes procedure is exhausted, removing demarcations between electricians and mechanics, and excluding new staff from the occupational pension scheme until a fixed-term contract of two years is completed.

Soon after the agreement was signed, Hoover Europe announced that it would close its Dijon plant in France (destroying 600 jobs), and shift its operations to Cambuslang (creating 400 jobs). Hoover cited low labour costs in Britain as the main reason for its decision. French trade unions and the French government denounced Hoover's decision to relocate as a form of 'social dumping', and blamed it on the lack of employee protection or a minimum wage in Britain. The British government saw the episode as proof that its encouragement of unregulated labour markets and low pay did attract foreign investment and jobs. Despite their disagreements on whether Hoover's move was desirable or not, both sides interpreted it as a symptom of Britain's refusal to accept the Social Chapter of the Maastricht Treaty.

It is, however, extremely doubtful that British acceptance of the Social Chapter would in itself have altered Hoover's decision. Although the Social Charter provides that 'workers shall be assured of an equitable wage', the Maastricht Treaty specifically states that pay levels lie outside EU competence. Similarly, under Maastricht, although all workers have the right to 'adequate' social security benefits, the level and financing of those benefits is determined by Member States, not at European Union level. Only a much more stringent harmonization of social conditions in Europe would discourage a transnational employer such as Maytag (the US owner of Hoover) from shifting production to take advantage of labour market differences.

Further reading
Industrial Relations Review (1993).

By the time of the Maastricht Treaty (1992), the 'Social Chapter', as the Charter was now called, was much watered down, but the British government still refused to endorse it. It is often claimed that Britain's opt-out from the Social Chapter has been instrumental in encouraging the development of Britain as a low-wage sweatshop economy, but, as Case Study 6.4 shows, this over-estimates the effectiveness of current European social policies. If Britain is to re-create a social settlement which guarantees well-paid jobs for the majority of her workers, then this would require not only acceptance of the social dimension of Europe, but support for a much greater degree of social protection than was agreed by her European partners at Maastricht.

Conclusion

Traditional (neo-classical) economic theory greatly exaggerates the capacity of market forces to match workers and jobs, to pay everyone in accordance with their productivity, and to ensure an effective organization of work. In reality, a number of organizational and environmental influences interact to divide labour markets into relatively self-contained segments, and to render the labour process indeterminate. As a result, mismatches between workers and jobs are endemic, and there is often little relationship between pay and productivity. In this situation, market forces frequently perpetuate rather than remove inefficiencies and inequalities.

British government policies designed to promote labour market flexibility have reduced the bargaining power of employees in relation to employers, and widened inequalities in pay, but they have done little to create new jobs. The Social Chapter of the Maastricht Treaty has created, for Britain's 11 European Union partners, certain minimum standards for workers, but these fall far short of what would be needed to guarantee full employment or protect well-paid jobs.

Further reading

The Economics of the Labour Market, by David Sapsford and Zafiris Tzannatos (Macmillan, 1993) provides a good introduction to the neo-classical approach. For an understanding of the structural approach and its policy implications, *Labour Market Policy*, by Nick Adnett (Longman, 1989) is invaluable.

Shirley Dex's *The Sexual Division of Work* (Wheatsheaf, 1985) and Swasti Mitter's *Common Fate, Common Bond* (Pluto, 1986) both explore the significance of gender differences at work, while the latter provides, in addition, a succinct summary of recent trends in the international division of labour.

Farewell to Flexibility?, edited by Anna Pollert (Blackwell, 1981) is a useful exploration of the limitations of the 'flexibility' concept, while the December 1992 issue of the *British Journal of Industrial Relations* focusses on the social dimension of European integration.

Exercises

1 Using the current issue of *Regional Trends*, choose two UK regions and compare their recent experiences of changes in manufacturing employment, service employment, and unemployment.
   How would you explain your findings?

2 Using the current *New Earnings Survey*, update Tables 6.3 to 6.6.
   What is the significance of your findings?

3 White and Trevor suggest that the British response to the example of Japanese management 'must come from the systems of management training and development within the leading British companies' (rather than from the formal education system).
   What would you suggest the main features of such a response might be?

4 Choose a recent industrial relations dispute, and compare and contrast the bargaining strengths and weaknesses of the employer and the union.

5 In what circumstances might an employer consider creating an internal labour market?

6 Why might a neo-classical economist have predicted that implementation of the Equal Pay Act would encourage employers to reduce female jobs?

7 Implementation of the Equal Pay Act was in fact accompanied by increased female employment.
   How would you explain this?

8 To what extent is a European social policy a pre-requisite for Economic and Monetary Union?

References

Adnett, N. (1993) The Social Charter: unnecessary regulation or pre-requisite for convergence?, *British Review of Economic Issues*, June.

Atkinson, J. and Meager, N. (1986) Is flexibility just a flash in the pan?, *Personnel Management*, September.

Bazen, S. and Benhayoun, G. (1992) Low pay and wage regulation in the European Community, *British Journal of Industrial Relations*, December.

Bazen, S. and Martin, J. (1991) The impact of the minimum wage on earnings and employment in France, *OECD Economic Studies*, Spring.

Beatson, M. (1993) Trends in pay flexibility, *Employment Gazette*, September.

Beechey, V. and Perkins, T. (1987) *A Matter of Hours*, Polity, Cambridge.

Braverman, H. (1974) *Labor and Monopoly Capital*, Monthly Review Press, New York and London.

Brown, C., Gilroy, C., and Kohen, A. (1982) The effect of a minimum wage on employment and unemployment, *Journal of Economic Literature*, June.

Chalmers, N. (1989) *Industrial Relations in Japan: the Peripheral Sector*, Routledge, London.

Constable, J. and McCormick, R. (1987) *The Making of British Managers*, British

Institute of Management, London.

Cooley, M. (1987) *Architect or Bee?*, Hogarth, London.

Craig, C., Garnsey, E. and Rubery, J. (1985) Labour market segmentation and women's employment: a case study from the UK, *International Labour Review*, May–June.

Cutler, T. (1992) Vocational education and British economic performance. *Work, Employment and Society*, June.

Daly, A. *et al.* (1985) Productivity machinery and skills in a sample of British and German manufacturing plants. *National Institute Economic Review*, Feb.

Dohse, K. *et al.* (1985) From Fordism to Toyotism, *Politics and Society*, vol. 14, no. 2.

Gordon, R. (1992) Productivity growth reconsidered: discussion, *Economic Policy*, October.

Gorz, A. (1985) *Paths to Paradise*, Pluto, London.

Huws, U. (1984) *The New Homeworkers*, Low Pay Unit, London.

Industrial Relations Review (1993) Hoover's flexibility deal at Cambuslang, *Pay and Benefits Bulletin*, 323, March.

Jaikumar, R. (1986) Post-industrial manufacturing, *Harvard Business Review*, November–December.

Kamata, S. (1984) *Japan in the Passing Lane*, Unwin, London.

Marx, K. (1976) *Capital*, vol. 1, Penguin, Harmondsworth.

Metcalf, D. (1993) Industrial relations and economic performance, *British Journal of Industrial Relations*, June.

Mitter, S. (1985) Industrial restructuring and manufacturing homework: immigrant women in the UK clothing industry, *Capital and Class*, Winter.

National Economic Development Office (1986) *Changing Working Patterns: How Companies Achieve Flexibility to Meet New Needs*, NEDO, London.

Neale, A. (1992a) Who pays? Enterprise calculation and a national minimum wage, *University of East London Occasional Papers on Business, Economy and Society*, no. 7.

Neale, A. (1992b) Are British workers pricing themselves out of jobs? Unit labour costs and competitiveness, *Work, Employment and Society*, June.

O'Mahony, M. (1993) Capital stocks and productivity in industrial nations, *National Institute Economic Review*, August.

Pollert, A. (1987) The 'flexible firm': a model in search of a reality, *Warwick Papers in Industrial Relations*, no. 19, December.

Prais, S. (ed.) (1989) *Productivity, training, and skills*, National Institute of Economic and Social Research, London.

Robertson, J. (1985) *Future Work*, Temple Smith/Gower, Aldershot.

Rubery, J. (1992) Pay, gender, and the social dimension to Europe, *British Journal of Industrial Relations*, December.

Senker, P. and Beesley, M. (1986) The need for skills in the factory of the future, *New Technology, Work and Employment*, Spring.

Slater, R. and Ascroft, P. (1990) *Quantitative Techniques in a Business Context*, Chapman & Hall, London.

Thatcher, A. (1968) The distribution of earnings of employees in Great Britain, *Journal of the Royal Statistical Society*, 2.

Towers, B. (1987) Managing labour flexibility, *Industrial Relations Journal*, Summer.

Turnbull, P. (1988) The limits to 'Japanisation': Just In Time, labour relations, and the UK auto industry, *New Technology, Work and Employment*, Spring.

White, M. and Trevor, M. (1983) *Under Japanese Management*, Policy Studies Institute, London.

The financial environment

7

This chapter reviews the different roles of banking institutions and capital markets in supplying external finance to businesses in different industrial economies. It highlights the critical role which has been played by UK financial institutions in promoting takeover activity. This financial environment has encouraged managers to pay out increased dividends to shareholders rather than invest in the future, and to expand by acquisition rather than by organic growth. A shift from productive to financial engineering has resulted in a 'hollowing-out' of UK manufacturing industry.

Introduction

Most financial calculations take place in a specific organizational context, formed by the separation of ownership from control in the modern corporation. As we saw in Chapter 3, accounting practices, designed to protect shareholder interests, play an important role in conditioning management decision-making. The financial environment of the business will also affect the decision-making process, and we examine in this chapter the influence on the business of external institutions such as banks and capital markets.

We start the chapter by looking briefly at some of the factors which determine the balance between internal and external financing of investment. In a UK company, investment is overwhelmingly financed out of internal funds, and we explore some of the implications of this situation for company performance. We explore the terms and conditions under which external finance is provided to the firm, and how this can influence the behaviour of non-financial companies. We focus chiefly on the UK banking system and stock market, which are the main sources of external finance for UK business. However, we also draw attention to different institutional arrangements for financing business development in other countries.

The organization of business finance

The financial and organizational structure of single-owner firms is comparatively simple. A single person both raises the finance to set up the business (by putting up his or her savings as capital, and perhaps borrowing from relatives and friends or from a bank), and runs the organization.

In the modern UK economy, most production is carried out by large corporations, or limited companies, whose financial and organizational structures, as we saw in Chapter 3, are much more complex. Here the company is a legal entity in its own right. It raises capital by issuing shares, which entitle the shareholder to a dividend (a share in the company's distributed profits). To encourage potential shareholders to put up capital for a venture over which they may have little control, their shares can be bought and sold at any time on the Stock Exchange, and their liability for any debts the company may incur is limited to the extent of their unpaid shareholding. Shareholders can influence who is elected to the Board of Directors of the enterprise, but day-to-day control is delegated to management.

'Going public' is a crucial step in the development of any business organization, because it overcomes the capital constraints which limit the activities of single-owner firms. The costs of administering new share issues are considerable, and most firms do not raise a substantial

Table 7.1   Sources of capital funds of UK industrial and commercial companies

	1985–86	1987–88	1989–90	1991–92
Total funds (£bn. per year)	47	87	79	76
of which:				
Undistributed income (%)	66	51	41	63
Bank borrowing (%)	17	25	28	−3
Market capital issues (%)	14	15	8	19
Other (%)	3	9	23	21
	100	100	100	100

Source: Financial Statistics.

proportion of their funds for ongoing investments from the stock market. As Table 7.1 shows, capital issues account for less than a fifth of total funds raised by UK firms.

Most firms borrow from banks to finance their working capital – the short-term funding they need to cover their operating costs or raw material purchases. Bank borrowing can also be an attractive source of finance for longer-term capital investment if the return from that investment exceeds the interest charges. This is, however, risky for the firm, as interest is a fixed cost payable irrespective of whether profits are being made. Where profitability is low and interest rates are high, a firm may find that it cannot afford a loan, or is unable to obtain one because banks doubt its financial security. As we shall see later on in the chapter, banks in the UK are less willing, relative to those in competitor countries, to provide long-term loans for industry. The terms on which funds are provided to firms will affect their decisions regarding their use of such funds. High interest rates coupled with short-term payback conditions may well make firms avoid seeking funds from the banking sector.

The vast majority of company investment in Britain is financed by internally generated funds. These include depreciation provisions, which should be set aside for the eventual replacement of existing capital equipment, but which can in practice be used to finance current investment expenditure. They also include retained profits (profits which are not distributed to shareholders, after allowing for depreciation and stock appreciation). Companies are not obliged to distribute all their profits to shareholders, and while the latter may object if retained profits are boosted at the expense of dividends, finance from retained profits can easily be increased if the total value of profits is rising. However, where profit rates are declining as they were for most UK firms in the 1960s and 1970s (Figure 7.1), then the capacity to finance new investment from this source is severely constrained.

Figure 7.1 Return on capital* by UK industrial and commercial companies (excluding North Sea), 1960–92.

Source: British Business; Bank of England Quarterly Bulletin.
* Pre-tax rate of return on capital stock at replacement cost.

Internal and external finance

Heavy reliance on internally generated funds has been actively sought by many UK managers for the relative freedom it gives them from external control. It does, however, pose a number of problems, of which the most important is that investment expenditure is heavily dependent on current profit performance. Most seriously, if a company hits bad times, and it relies heavily on internally generated funds, its ability to finance the investment which may be necessary to turn it round is severely curtailed, unless it can obtain extra credit from a bank. A subsidiary problem is the tendency, in an inflationary period, for historic cost accounting conventions to understate the cost of replacing capital equipment and stocks. This problem was particularly significant in the inflationary period 1973–76, when published accounts exaggerated the level of retained profits because of stock appreciation and low depreciation provisions. The net result was that firms had not made sufficient provision for the actual cost of replacing capital stock, which was based on inflated, not historic cost, values.

International comparisons of investment finance are difficult to make, because of differences in accounting conventions and in tax legislation. Data such as those in Table 7.2, which are based on net flows of funds over a period of time, avoid most of the possible inconsistencies. The differences which are revealed are dramatic. In Japan and France for

Table 7.2 Net financing of private physical investment by enterprises (% shares, 1970–85)

	Japan	USA	UK	W. Germany	France
Retentions	65	90	107	73	62
Loans	42	26	5	12	37
Bonds	1	12	−2	−2	1
Shares	4	−3	−4	1	5

Source: Mayer (1988).

Notes: A net source of funds is new issues less acquisitions of the same type of liability, so that funds for the accumulation of financial assets are excluded. A negative figure represents an excess of acquisitions over new issues (the net outflow of share capital from UK companies, for example, reflects the extent of cash expenditure on acquiring shares in other companies).

Columns do not add to 100%, because trade credits and other financial sources are excluded, and because of statistical discrepancies.

example, two fifths of investment spending is financed by borrowing (mainly from banks), whereas, at the other extreme, it is quite common in the UK for all investment expenditure to be internally financed.

There are a number of important consequences which follow from the overwhelming reliance of UK firms on internally generated funds.

The effect of share prices on corporate investment

In neo-classical theory, a firm's share value is assumed to reflect the present discounted value of future distributed profits. A dramatic fall in share values, as occurred in October 1987, would, according to this theory, reflect a decline in confidence in future profits, which would have the effect of discouraging investment. In fact, econometric analysis reveals that the 1987 stock market crash had very little effect on company investment (Bond and Devereux, 1988).

In our view, the finding that investment behaviour is largely independent of movements in share prices is not surprising, for two reasons. First, because the stock market is not a major source of funds for new investment, there is little reason for firms to be influenced in their investment behaviour by movements in share prices (though they may be influenced in their takeover activity). Second, share prices are influenced by the speculative activities of shareholders themselves. As we shall see later in this chapter, Stock Exchange speculation increasingly reflects autonomous expectations of short-term movements in share prices, rather than realistic forecasts of business profits over a long period. The result is an effective de-coupling of the performance of share values from the performance of the real economy, and in particular the long-term profit performance of the firm.

The effect of interest rates on corporate investment

Neo-classical theory suggests that there is an inverse relationship between business investment and the general level of interest rates, on the assumption that the interest rate reflects the cost of financing investment. We would not disagree with the general view that higher interest rates discourage company investment, though we would draw attention to the empirical evidence that this effect is often not significant in practice (Savage, 1978).

Our view of the causal mechanism is, however, different from the neo-classical one. In the UK, retained profits are far more significant than bank loans as a source of finance for investment, and the direct effects of a change in interest rates are likely to be swamped by those of a change in retained earnings. Because firms often rely on bank loans to cover their working capital needs, a rise in interest rates will increase the costs of financing working capital, and this will have a depressing effect on profits. The effect of interest rates on company investment in the UK context is thus more indirect (via the effect on profits) than direct.

The effect of value added on corporate investment

Because the overwhelming majority of the funds used to finance capital investment in the UK are internally generated, it follows that there must be a significant relationship between the amount of investment a firm undertakes and its current financial performance. We have already, in Chapter 3, drawn attention to the value added fund – the difference between a firm's revenues and the costs of its raw materials and bought-in components. In most industries, the most important charge on the value added fund is the cost of hiring labour, and when sales are slack, there is often a tendency for labour's share of value added to rise, squeezing the share of value added which is available to finance new investment. If we regress labour's share of value added against gross fixed capital formation in manufacturing in the following year, we obtain a strong negative correlation (r = −0.930 in 1976–85, see Williams *et al.*, 1988). This suggests that there is a strong relationship between variations in labour's share of value added and the level of gross fixed capital investment in the UK manufacturing sector.

The main lesson of Mayer's work (1987, 1988) on the sources of investment funds for industrial and commercial companies is that the level of fixed capital formation in the UK is determined by the current individual success of the firm in the market place. This must be the case where the firm's ability to generate sufficient internal funds sets the constraints on the level of physical investment. The peculiarities of the UK financial system are such that it would be possible to float off the real from the financial economy, without any substantial effect on the real economy.

Bank lending

One of the most significant differences between business finance in Britain and in other industrial countries is the traditionally low level of involvement by British banks in medium and long-term loans to industry. Historically, this is related to the earlier development of capital markets (markets for securities such as shares and bonds) in Britain than in most other industrial countries, and the reduced demand for longer-term bank lending that this implied. We shall be exploring the operation of capital markets in the next section. Low bank involvement in longer-term loans to British industry is also related, however, to the lending practices of British banks. To understand these, we need to know something of the structure of the banking system, and especially the different lending practices of retail and wholesale banks.

KEY CONCEPT 7.1 *Fractional reserve banking*	Banks make most of their profits from the interest they obtain by lending money to customers, or by investing in securities. Because only a small proportion of deposits will be required at any time in cash form, they can make loans, creating new deposits, up to a multiple of the original cash deposit.

A simple example will illustrate how fractional reserve banking creates deposit money. Suppose there is only one bank (the arithmetic is more complicated with many banks, but the principle is the same), which knows from experience that it needs only 10% of its assets in cash form. If a customer deposits £1000 this will allow the bank to lend out £900 (leaving a cash reserve of £100). The recipient of this loan can buy goods and services to the value of £900, which then returns to the bank as new deposits in the recipients' accounts. The bank can now lend another £810 (90% of the £900). This credit creation process continues until total deposits reach £10000, of which 10% (the original £1000) is available as a cash reserve. From the original deposit of £1000 the bank has created additional deposits of £9000, as shown in the simplified balance sheet below.

Liabilities		*Assets*	
Initial deposit	£1 000	Cash	£1 000
Created deposits	£9 000	Loans	£9 000
Total deposit	£10 000	Total assets	£10 000

In practice, the balance sheet of a commercial bank is more complicated than this. On the liabilities side, deposits are divided into current accounts, deposit accounts, certificates of deposit, and non-sterling deposits. On the assets side, there is a spectrum of assets ranging from those which are high in liquidity (ease of conversion to cash) but low in profitability, to those which are low in liquidity but highly profitable. The precise balance of liquidity and profitability will depend on both the bank's commercial sense, and on government monetary policy as implemented by the central bank, the Bank of England.

The asset structure of a commercial bank

<--------more liquid

Cash   Bills   Market loans   Long-term marketable securities   Advances

more profitable-------->

Retail banks

Retail (or 'High Street') banks offer deposit and loan facilities to personal and business clients, in branches located throughout the country. They perform two main functions.

- Money transmission (distributing cash, and allowing deposits to be transferred between accounts by the use of cheques and credit transfer arrangements).
- Financial intermediation (bringing together lenders and borrowers).

These two functions are linked by the practice of fractional reserve banking – the creation of new deposits, in the form of loans and overdrafts, so that cash and other liquid assets held by the banks form only a small proportion of their total assets (Key Concept 7.1).

The money transmission activities of retail banks perform an important service for all businesses, and, in addition, retail banks have traditionally provided most of the external finance for small businesses, through overdraft facilities. Here the bank sets a limit to the amount which the firm can borrow, but actual borrowing (and the interest charged) varies according to day-to-day requirements.

Wholesale banks

The wholesale banks (some of which are specialized subsidiaries of retail banks) are concentrated in the City of London. They are not involved in money transmission, but specialize in buying and selling sterling and foreign currency deposits on the money markets, and in lending large sums both in Britain and overseas.

Within the wholesale banking sector, merchant banks and overseas banks have in recent years become increasingly important providers of external finance to large and medium-sized firms, and they have pioneered the development of longer-term bank loans in Britain. Wholesale bank loans are usually on a fixed term basis, most of them ranging between two and seven years.

Availability of bank lending

There is considerable dispute about why banks in Britain are less prepared than those in other industrial countries to lend money to finance industrial investment. The Wilson Committee Report on the functioning of financial institutions (1980) concluded that, for medium and large firms, low levels of investment in Britain were due more to a lack of profitable investment opportunities than to a lack of adequate funding. Certainly in the late 1970s, when the banks were searching out ways of profitably recycling oil revenues deposited by the oil-exporting countries, there was no shortage of money to lend, and the fact that many of the new loans went to Brazil and Mexico reflected the strong demand by such newly industrializing countries for low-conditionality external finance rather than any perverse desire on the part of the banks to starve British firms funds.

Critics of the Wilson Committee, however, suggest that supply side factors are important. Carrington and Edwards, for example, point to the shorter periods over which bank loans have to be repaid in Britain than elsewhere, and stress the negative impact this has on firms' ability to earn positive cash flows from their investments (1981). Poor investment performance in Britain, in their view, depends more on inappropriate conditions under which funds are supplied than on deficiencies in demand.

The issue of whether demand or supply factors are more important in explaining poor investment performance by British firms is clearly complex, yet closer scrutiny of the conditions under which bank finance is supplied certainly suggests that banking practices may have a significant effect on investment behaviour. In overdraft arrangements with companies, for example, it is common for retail banks to set out written agreements giving the bank security on a firm's assets in the event of the company being liquidated or defaulting on the conditions of the loan. The effect of this 'liquidation approach' is for banks to err on the side of 'conservatism' in their lending – they make loans available only if they are sure of getting their money back in the event of liquidation, and they tend to cut back on lending to firms which want to invest for rapid expansion. Such financial 'conservatism' by the banks may well reinforce a reluctance on the part of managers to consider investment projects which produce profits in the longer term.

American wholesale banks in Britain have, in contrast, pioneered a 'going concern' approach to lending. Here, the main focus is on the bank's assessment of a company's ability to repay loans out of future cash flows as a going concern. This requires greater technical expertise on the part of the banks, and formal agreements to provide them with advance warning of any deterioration in the company's financial situation and enable them to take appropriate action to guard against possible default. British banks have, in the 1980s, followed the American example, helping to lessen their traditional obsession with security. As a result, the overall emphasis of British bank lending to industry has belatedly begun to shift away from overdrafts and towards medium-term loans.

Financial deregulation

In 1979, the UK government abolished foreign exchange controls, and over the following seven years it instigated a number of changes which gave financial institutions greater freedom from government and central bank control, and which removed most of the distinctions between banks and building societies (see Key Concept 7.2). Many observers hoped that deregulation, by introducing more competition into the provision of financial services and encouraging the innovation of new products, would stimulate more bank lending to industry. In fact, the main effect of financial deregulation was to expand consumer credit, in particular mortgage finance for owner-occupiers. Far from helping domestic industry, the credit explosion brought about a massive trade deficit, and created a speculative bubble in house prices. The adverse consequences of these developments for the macro-economy are explored further in Chapter 10.

KEY CONCEPT 7.2
Financial deregulation and 'Big Bang'

Financial deregulation refers to a progressive relaxation of controls by which the government and/or central bank regulates financial institutions and of barriers to competition between those institutions. The following measures were undertaken in the UK between 1979 and 1986:

October 1979 – abolition of foreign exchange controls
June 1980 – abolition of Supplementary Special Deposit scheme (the 'Corset')
August 1981 – abolition of Reserve Asset ratio, and of publication of Minimum Lending Rate
July 1982 – abolition of restrictions on hire purchase
October 1983 – collapse of building society interest rate cartel
December 1986 – abolition of Bank of England guidance on mortgage lending.

'Big Bang' is the name given to the Stock Exchange reforms of October 1986. These abolished the traditional distinction between stockbrokers (who made contact with the public) and stockjobbers (who traded company securities and established market prices), and created a system where trading is done by telephone rather than face-to-face.

Bank/company relations

In countries like Germany and Japan, banks play a major role as long-term suppliers of finance to business, and, to lessen the risks, they develop close relationships with company management – exchanging information, participating in the development of corporate strategy, and pressing for changes in policy or personnel when mistakes have been made (Corbett, 1987; Schneider-Lanne, 1992).

In Britain, however, it has been traditional for banks to adopt arm's-length relationships with their clients. This has been particularly apparent with overdraft arrangements, where, once the bank has been satisfied that repayment would be secured in the event of the firm's liquidation, there is little bank involvement in monitoring company performance. With the recent development of medium-term loans by the wholesale banks, the monitoring of company performance in relation to the terms of loan agreements has become more critical, but such monitoring takes place more at the level of scrutinizing financial ratios than of supervising the production and marketing decisions of the company.

The main exceptions to this occurred in response to the financial difficulties experienced by many firms as a result of the 1979–82 recession. In many cases the banks protected their loans by calling in the receiver. With some larger firms, on the other hand, the banks, encouraged by the Bank of England, took on a more interventionist role, offering to reschedule loan repayments on condition that the company reduced its debts by closing down or selling off some of its operations. As yet, however, banks in Britain have shown little interest in becoming more involved in ongoing strategic decision-making by their clients, and companies have not been willing to provide the information which such an involvement would require. As a result, bank provision of funds for long-term investment remains low.

The determination of interest rates

The interest rate which is charged when a bank lends money reflects a number of factors, including the following.

- The spread between rates charged to borrowers and rates offered to lenders. This reflects the degree of competition between financial institutions.
- The term of the loan. Long-term loans will usually bear higher interest rates than short-term loans, reflecting their lower liquidity

for the lender, though they may occasionally bear lower rates if short-term rates are unusually high and are expected to fall.

- The risk of default. Lenders assess the risk that creditors will default on their loans, and make an allowance for this in the interest rate that they charge, with high risk creditors paying a higher rate than low risk ones.
- The general level of interest rates. Interest rates generally rise and fall over time, reflecting changes in the supply and demand of loanable funds, and government monetary policy.

Before the 1970s, interest rates in the UK were determined administratively. The Bank of England set a Bank Rate (subsequently called Minimum Lending Rate) which represented the interest it would charge if commercial banks needed to borrow money from it to maintain their liquid reserves. Most of the interest rates charged by the commercial banks were directly related to this interest rate, so interest rates generally rose or fell with Bank Rate.

In the immediate post-war period (1945–51), Bank Rate was set deliberately low at 2% per year, as part of a government policy to encourage industrial investment and to reduce the cost of the government borrowing which was needed to finance a programme of nationalization. Such a policy could be maintained only in the context of strict controls over the ability of individuals and firms to acquire foreign exchange. Without these controls, savings would have left the country to benefit from higher interest rates abroad, and the supply of domestic loans would have been restricted.

Financial deregulation in the 1970s and early 1980s encouraged two interrelated developments – London's emergence as the world centre of the Eurodollar market (Key Concept 7.3), and the determination of interest rates by competitive forces in the international money markets rather than administratively. These developments have created a situation where small shifts in interest rates can cause a rapid movement of funds from one currency to another.

As a result of these changes in financial markets, it is possible for the government to influence either interest rates or exchange rates, but not to control both simultaneously. In this institutional context, the government could not push interest rates below the levels prevailing in international markets, without suffering a shift in funds away from sterling and thus a fall in the rate at which sterling is exchanged against other currencies. (We shall be exploring the issue of exchange rate determination in Chapter 8.)

Eurocurrencies are bank deposits and loans in currencies other than that of the country where the transactions take place. They originated in the late 1950s when West and East European holders of dollars opened accounts in Western Europe rather than in the USA, to avoid Federal Reserve Board control over interest rates and capital exports (and, in the case of East European countries, possible political interference). Eurodollars were followed by EuroDeutschmarks and other Eurocurrencies,

KEY CONCEPT 7.3
Eurocurrencies

all of which shared the same characteristic of freedom from regulation. It was on the Eurocurrency markets that the oil-exporting countries deposited most of their increased revenues following the oil price rises of 1973–74, and it was these same markets that recycled the money to middle-income countries in Latin America and East Asia later in the decade.

The City of London rapidly became the world centre of Eurocurrency markets, largely as a result of the efforts of the Bank of England to ensure the dismantling of regulatory controls. This encouraged many foreign banks to set up branches in London, competing with each other for dollar deposits. Before long foreign banks began to compete for sterling deposits as well, breaking down traditional agreements and controls on domestic interest rates.

Most Eurocurrency deposits are short-term, and many are passed on to other banks to boost the profits of the lender and to satisfy the short-term liquidity requirements of the borrower. Loans to non-bank borrowers are large in scale and often made on a medium or long-term basis, with variable interest rates to lessen the risks of borrowing short and lending long.

Eurocurrency markets have revolutionized banking practice and the availability of finance throughout the world. They are, however, a source of potential instability, as the international debt crisis illustrates. The developing countries which had borrowed from the Eurocurrency markets at a time of booming export earnings and low interest rates were squeezed in the early 1980s by declining exports and high interest rates. Many debtor countries, notably Mexico and Brazil, were unable to repay their loans on time, and their debts had to be rescheduled. Additional loans to discourage debtor countries from defaulting were accompanied by harsh conditions, and living standards in the debtor countries suffered. The banks, meanwhile, had to write off some of their debts, creating severe pressures on their liquidity. The risks these pressures created affected all major banks (not just those most directly implicated in the debt problem), because of the extent of inter-bank lending and borrowing in the Eurocurrency system.

In the 1980s, the Bank of England abandoned the practice of announcing a Minimum Lending Rate, and allowed short-term interest rates to fluctuate, within an undisclosed band, in response to market forces. The effect of this change should not be exaggerated, for the Bank retained a powerful influence on interest rates, not least through its 'open market operations' (buying and selling short-term paper debt). What was more significant was the willingness of the government to allow greater fluctuation in interest rates over the medium term. This reflected a shift in emphasis away from interest rate stability as a target of government policy, towards allowing interest rate variation as an instrument in achieving other government objectives.

As we shall see in Chapter 10, government policy in the late 1970s and early 1980s was strongly influenced by the monetarist idea that the rate of growth of money supply should be controlled. If money supply is growing faster than the target rate, then bank lending, which creates the deposits which form the most significant part of the money supply, has to be restricted. In the absence of direct controls over lending, which the banks have strenuously resisted, this can be achieved only by allowing interest rates to rise. If, as is often the case, demand for credit is interest inelastic, it is possible for interest rates to rise to very high levels without money supply being significantly affected, as in the early 1980s.

By the mid-1980s, the government was adopting a more relaxed stance in relation to monetary targets, but it had become increasingly willing to allow interest rates to fluctuate in order to maintain a more stable exchange rate. The main implication of these changes for business is that now, more than ever before, the cost of borrowing depends on changing conditions in the money and foreign exchange markets. Financial deregulation benefited British firms by narrowing the spread between interest charged to borrowers and interest paid to lenders, but they suffered from the increased volatility of interest rates which accompanied this.

Interest rates as a determinant of investment

The interest rate on a loan is an important representation of the cost of borrowing money to finance investment, but it is also, according to both neo-classical and Keynesian theory, a major determinant of investment activity. This applies to a certain extent even where investment is financed internally, for the interest rate will indicate the opportunity cost (Key Concept 3.4) of the investment in terms of the return which could have been earned by say depositing the money in a bank or building society instead.

At any point in time, there will be a range of investment projects a firm could undertake. Some will have a high expected Internal Rate of Return (Key Concept 7.4), others a low internal rate of return. If firms embark on all investment projects where the expected internal rate of return exceeds the interest rate, then there will be an inverse relationship between the amount of investment and the interest rate. This is illustrated in Figure 7.2, where the investment demand schedule (sometimes called the marginal efficiency of capital schedule) shows how much investment firms would carry out at different interest rates, assuming other influences on investment remained constant. This schedule implies that a rise in interest rates from r_1 to r_2 would result in a fall in investment from I_1 to I_2.

The internal rate of return of an investment project is the discount rate for which the Net Present Value of the project (see Chapter 3) would be zero. It thus gives a representation of the project's expected yield over a period of time.

KEY CONCEPT 7.4
Internal rate of return

In practice, as we saw in Chapter 3, firms, in making investment decisions, need to consider not just expected long-term returns, but short-term cash flows as well. These will be affected by the period over which the loan has to be repaid, as well as by the interest rate. Indeed econometric evidence suggests that changes in interest rates have had

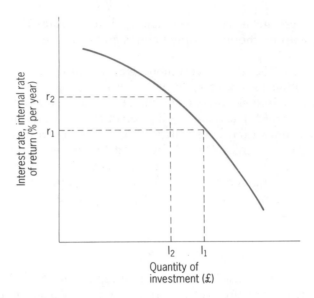

Figure 7.2   Investment demand schedule.

little effect on the amount of fixed investment by UK business (Savage, 1978). These are a number of possible reasons for this.

- The effect of changes in interest rates may be swamped by other, more significant, changes, for example in business expectations of future profits (a point which was stressed by Keynes, but ignored by some of his followers), or in capacity utilization (which determines whether or not new investment is needed).
- A change in interest rate will in itself alter the monetary values of different items of capital equipment, and thus the expected rates of return on different investment projects, so invalidating the notion of a stable relationship between investment and the interest rate.
- As we have seen, only a very small proportion of company investment in the UK is financed by loans.

Capital market finance

As we saw in the previous section, it is often claimed that a major reason for the relatively low involvement of banks in medium and long-term lending to British industry is the highly developed nature of the capital market (or Stock Exchange) in Britain. Yet the data in Table 7.2 suggest that the Stock Exchange makes little net contribution to investment finance in the UK. To understand the role of capital markets in the UK economy, we need to appreciate the two interrelated functions which they perform – to issue new securities, and to trade in second-hand securities.

The new issue market

The new issue market is where companies (and central and local government) seek money from the general public, either directly or via financial intermediaries, against the issue of some form of security. For companies, the main form of security issued nowadays is the ordinary share, though before the 1970s debentures were often more significant (Key Concept 7.5). When a company issues new shares, the costs it incurs (from publishing a prospectus, employing financial institutions to issue and underwrite the shares, and offering the shares at a discount on the existing share price) can be prohibitively expensive for all but the largest firms, and this is an important contributory factor in the preference of most UK firms for financing new investment from internally generated funds. New share issues have become extremely significant in the financing of takeover activity, however, and we shall be exploring this at the end of this section.

An ordinary share entitles the holder to a dividend out of the distributed profits of the company. This dividend depends on the current profitability of the company, and on management policy over the proportion of profits which is retained. There is no obligation for the company to pay a dividend, and if shareholders want to dispose of their shares, they have to sell them on the secondary market. Ordinary shares are thus risky assets whose liquidity (ability to be turned into cash) depends on the fortunes of the company.

Preference shares are different from ordinary shares, giving holders the right to a specified dividend which must be paid before dividends on ordinary shares are calculated. They are less risky, but often less profitable for the holder, than ordinary shares.

Debentures are long-term loans which are repaid at maturity, carrying a fixed rate of interest. They are secured on the assets of the company, so that if the company goes into liquidation, debenture holders have a priority claim to repayment. In the 1960s, when real interest rates were low, debentures were much favoured as a source of external finance for large companies. In the late 1970s and early 1980s, higher and more volatile long-term interest rates made the issue of new debentures unprofitable. In the late 1980s, however, there was a revival in issues by companies of long-term debt, following lower interest rates and the 1987 stock market crash. Much of this debt now consists of Eurobonds, which are securities issued in exchange for Eurocurrencies (Key Concept 7.3).

KEY CONCEPT 7.5
Company securities

The secondary market

Shares are long-term securities which cannot be repaid by the company. The liquidity which savers require if they are to hold long-term assets is provided by the secondary market, where shares can be sold to another party. Since deregulation of the Stock Exchange in 1986 (the so-called 'Big Bang'), share transfers are arranged through dealers who buy and sell securities both on their own behalf and as agents for members of the general public, and set the prices. Share prices rise when purchases exceed sales, and fall when sales exceed purchases.

Shareholders and shareholder behaviour

In the nineteenth and early twentieth centuries, shareholders were, almost exclusively, wealthy individuals. Nowadays, however, the most important shareholders are not individuals but financial institutions such as insurance companies, pension funds, investment and unit trusts. These financial institutions have long dominated the ownership of debentures and preference shares, and the proportion of listed UK ordinary shares that they owned rose continuously from a fifth in the late 1950s to a half in 1980. There has been a revival in direct share ownership by private individuals in the 1980s, stimulated by the government's policy of selling off public sector enterprises such as British Telecom and British Gas. Many of the individuals who were attracted into the stock market by these privatizations sold their shares for a quick profit, however, and within a short space of time the financial institutions became the dominant shareholders in these as in other large companies.

The behaviour of individuals who bought shares in privatized companies suggests that many individual shareholders are motivated more by the prospects of speculative gain than by long-term investment considerations. It might be supposed that financial institutions such as pension and life assurance funds would adopt a less short-term approach, concerned as they are with improving capital values over a long time period. As Table 7.3 shows, however, financial institutions are much less committed than they were to holding company shares in a stable portfolio. This table shows, for example, that pension funds had an average shareholding period of 23 years in the 1960s, but that in

Table 7.3   Implied average period* for holding shares by financial institutions

	UK and overseas shares			UK 1984–86	Overseas 1984–86
	1963–67	*1968–71*	*1973–77*		
Insurance companies	23.8	14.9	7.9	6.3	2.7
Pension funds	23.3	9.8	6.1	6.0	2.4
Investment trusts	9.6	6.9	4.6	2.9	2.2
Unit trusts	9.8	3.3	2.2	2.1	1.2
All institutions	15.4	8.5	5.2	5.1	2.1

* Market value of ordinary shareholdings divided by sales activity.

Source: derived from Bain (1987).

the mid-1980s this had fallen dramatically, implying a fourfold increase in the turnover of shares.

Given this change in the behaviour of financial institutions, it is perhaps understandable that 'the majority of transactions (in financial markets) involves a reshuffling, mostly by professional operators, of existing assets' (Goodhart, 1987). Such reshuffling would not be harmful if it resulted in share prices being adjusted in line with informed analysis of changed company prospects. Concern is frequently expressed, however, that share dealings and prices are influenced more by the latest half-year profit figures, and by stock market 'sentiment', than by informed analysis of future yields. As Keynes warned more than half a century ago, professional traders have become largely concerned 'not with making superior long-term forecasts of the probable yield of an investment over its whole life, but with foreseeing changes in the conventional basis of valuation a short time ahead of the general public' (1936). The prime motive for buying shares thus becomes speculative capital gain (from short-term movements in the market price) rather than long-term dividend yield.

Shifting stock market sentiment and speculative activity by traders combine to ensure that periods of rising share prices ('bull' markets) alternate with periods of falling share prices ('bear' markets). When speculation pushes share prices up to levels which are artificially high in relation to asset values or earnings potential, the resulting 'crash' can be severe, as 1929 and October 1987 testify. In this situation, individual share market prices will frequently give a distorted valuation of a company's ability to earn profits in the future.

Short-term attitudes by financial institutions often have negative consequences for business investment. When a firm faces short-term financial difficulties, for example, UK financial institutions will often sell their shares in it, rather than work with it to resolve the difficulties (Bracewell-Milnes, 1987). A low share price will, in turn, reduce the firm's ability to raise new capital, and at the same time possibly increase its vulnerability to the threat of takeover. In this sort of financial environment, a firm may will be forced into making short-term defensive responses. It might be tempted, for example, to cut back on activities such as research and development or training, in an attempt to boost its short-term profits and improve its dividend payout. This would bring short-term relief if it stops shareholders from exchanging their shares to a takeover bidder but it may well damage the firm's long-run competitive advantage. Such defensive short-term preoccupation with maintaining dividend yield may only bring temporary relief where the firm's real productive and market requirements are sacrificed.

As Table 7.4 shows, research and development (R. & D.) expenditure has for some time been growing at a much slower rate in the UK than in other industrial countries. As a result, the innovation record of most UK industry has been poor, and there has been much concern in recent years about the damaging long-term effects on international competitiveness.

Table 7.4 Business enterprise R. & D. financed by industry, 1975–87

	% Annual increases (constant prices)
Japan	9.3
W Germany	6.6
US	5.4
France	5.1
UK	3.6

Source: DTI (1990).

During the 1979–82 recession, of course, company profitability was low (see Figure 7.1), and a high proportion of the value added fund went to labour in the form of wages and salaries, so there was little scope to finance increased R. & D. expenditure. Nevertheless, in this period, UK (and US) companies cut R. & D., output and jobs, to protect short-term returns to shareholders, while in Germany and Japan firms often preferred to cut dividends, to protect R. & D. and investment (Cox and Kriegbaum, 1989).

In the mid-1980s, as profitability recovered, most UK companies preferred to increase distributions to shareholders rather than boost R. & D. expenditure to update their product ranges. The official study from which Table 7.4 is taken suggests that this reflected short-termism (a preference for short-term gains over long-term improvement in performance) on the part of UK financial institutions. Many managers feared that, if they invested in R. & D. rather than paying out increased dividends, this would earn the displeasure of their major shareholders, and the share value of their company would fall, making it more vulnerable to takeover.

Mergers and takeovers

A firm which wishes to grow has the choice of doing so internally, by investing in new fixed assets, or externally, by amalgamating its assets with those of another firm. Amalgamation can take the form of an agreed merger, where the Boards of Directors of each company agree terms, or a hostile takeover, where one firm acquires another by buying more than 50% of the shares of another, despite the opposition of that firm's Board of Directors. In practice, it is often not possible to identify how willing each of the partners are to a merger agreement, so the dividing line between a merger and a takeover is a difficult one to draw, and the terms are often used interchangeably.

Merger activity tends to take place in waves, but over a long time span it can have a significant impact on the structure of asset ownership. In the UK, for example, the share of the largest 100 firms in UK manufacturing net output doubled from 21% in 1949 to 42% in 1976

Table 7.5 Expenditure on mergers and acquisitions by industrial and commercial companies within the UK

	1985–86	1987–88	1989–90	1991–92
Total annual expenditure (£bn.)	11	20	18	8
of which:				
Cash (%)	31	55	80	67
Ordinary shares (%)	55	38	14	32
Preference shares and loan stock (%)	14	7	5	1
	100	100	100	100

Source: Financial Statistics.

(Prais, 1976), and most research studies suggest that at least a half of this increased concentration was a result of merger activity.

The unusually high level of takeover activity in the UK reflects a market-based system of corporate finance, based on a dispersed group of 'outside' shareholders. In the largest UK manufacturing firms, the Board of Directors typically owns only less than 1% of the shares, and the financial institutions who own most of the shares are frequently prepared to sell control to a takeover bidder if the short-term capital gain is sufficiently high. At the same time, as Table 7.5 indicates, the stock market is often prepared to facilitate share issues to finance acquisitions, so that a takeover bidder does not need to put up all the cash. In this financial environment, the threat of takeover is an ever-present one.

Most economic theories suggest that mergers result from a rational calculation of economic advantage. Neo-classical theory, for example, suggests that firms amalgamate to improve their profitability, either through economies of scale (enabling cost reductions) or through greater market dominance (enabling price increases). Managerial theory gives a different emphasis, suggesting that a firm will bid for another one if it thinks it can run the business more efficiently than its existing management. Takeovers, in this view, result from a discrepancy between the value a bidder places on the firm and the value placed on it by its shareholders, as indicated by the valuation ratio (Key Concept 7.6). Either way, it is assumed that takeovers operate in such a way as to impose corporate control by shareholders, and eliminate poor managerial performance.

The valuation ratio is the ratio of the stock market valuation of a firm to its asset value.

$$\text{Valuation ratio} = \frac{\text{number of shares} \times \text{share price}}{\text{book value of assets}}$$

KEY CONCEPT 7.6
The valuation ratio

If the stock market values a firm's prospects highly, then its share price, and thus its valuation ratio, will rise. If shareholders are dissatisfied with a firm's financial performance, then they will sell shares, causing the share price, and with it the valuation ratio, to fall.

In Marris's economic theory of managerial capitalism (1964), the valuation ratio plays a crucial role in explaining takeover activity. If one firm values another firm's assets at a higher level than the stock market values the shares, it will be tempted to mount a takeover bid. Management failure to secure satisfactory profits will cause the valuation ratio to fall, making the firm more vulnerable to takeover. In Marris's view, the threat of takeover is an important constraint on management freedom to pursue growth at the expense of profits.

Empirical studies suggest that firms with low valuation ratios are slightly more vulnerable to takeover than firms with high valuation ratios, but that only very large firms are significantly less threatened by takeover than other firms (Singh, 1971 and 1975).

Research into the motives and effects of merger behaviour suggests that most mergers in the UK do not involve the precise calculation of financial benefit implied by neo-classical and managerial approaches alike. Newbould, for example, in a classic study of the 1967–68 merger boom (1970), found that mergers were usually rushed affairs, and that managers rarely had the time to analyse alternatives. Few managers were prepared to rationalize the combined assets of the merged firms to the extent that the achievement of economies of scale would imply, and high valuation ratios in 'victim' firms did not deter takeover activity. Most managers involved in mergers were primarily interested in extending or defending the market dominance of their firms, in response to increased uncertainty in their corporate environment. The trigger factor was usually intensified international competition (Case Study 7.1), or mergers by other firms operating in the same market.

More recent research, by Jenkinson and Mayer (1992), confirms that hostile takeover bids continue to be based more on the strategies of the acquiring firms than on any managerial failures on the part of their targets.

When a takeover bid is announced, shareholders in the target firm typically benefit from a 25–30% jump in share prices, and after successful completion of a hostile takeover, most executives in the target firm are typically replaced. There is no research evidence to suggest, however, that financial performance improves after the merger. More often than not, profitability deteriorates, as managers are diverted from addressing the fundamental problems their firms face into sorting out the problems of organizational restructuring which mergers, agreed or contested, create (Sawyer, 1987).

In Germany and Japan, share ownership tends to be concentrated on a small number of other firms, banks, and families, and institutional arrangements make it difficult for outsiders to 'buy' control over a firm

(Jenkinson and Mayer, 1992). In these circumstances, contested take-over bids are extremely rare, and the mergers that do occur tend to be both well thought out and to result in improved financial performance. Corporate control in these countries is exerted by 'insiders' who are closely involved with the company, and who have a stake in its long-term development. This encourages firms to invest for the future, without having to worry about shareholder short-termism.

Many observers see the short-termism of the financial environment as a major barrier to improved UK industrial performance. As Crafts (1992) has put it: 'the effectiveness of German banks as monitors of company performance, and the apparent ineffectiveness of the British takeover mechanism in eliminating poor performance and creating post-merger gains makes the German system unambiguously superior.'

The late 1960s were a period of intense merger activity in the UK. The most prominent mergers were those between Leyland and British Motor Holdings to form British Leyland in the motor vehicle industry, and between GEC, AEI and English Electric to form the enlarged GEC in the electrical engineering industry. The similarities between the two sets of mergers were striking.

CASE STUDY 7.1
GEC and British Leyland

1   Both the electrical engineering and motor vehicle industries in the UK had failed to respond adequately to intensified international competition.
2   In each case, a smaller firm (Leyland, GEC) effectively took over a much larger firm (BMH; AEI and English Electric), financing the acquisition by shrewd share exchange deals involving little cash expenditure.
3   Both mergers were actively supported by the government, on the grounds that the superior management teams of the smaller firms would be able to improve the performance of the larger ones, and compete more effectively in international markets.

Despite these similarities, there were significant differences between the two firms in post-merger performance.

The GEC amalgamation, unusually for a UK merger, resulted in dramatic improvements in company profitability. These were achieved largely by plant closures which removed excess capacity, and by the successful introduction of a unified management system based on making each remaining plant a profit centre subject to strict financial controls. The very factors which produced financial success brought about other problems, however. The GEC workforce fell by about 40 000 between 1967 and 1971, largely as a result of the plant closures, but employment continued to decline after 1971 as the company failed to achieve significant increases in output. This, in turn, reflected the inhibiting effect of GEC's stringent financial controls on innovation and new product development.

In British Leyland's case, it was hoped that Leyland's marketing skills could be combined with BMH's production capacity to provide an effective answer to the challenge of foreign competition. In the event, the new management team found it hard to translate the skills of selling buses and trucks to the much more fashion-conscious volume car market, and they underestimated the problems of integrating the different components of the British Leyland empire. Insufficient funds were available to modernize production facilities, and salvation was sought in unattractive new models which failed to generate sufficient sales to even recover their development costs. There was no improvement in the already poor profitability record of volume car production, and by 1975 losses were so great that the firm had to be taken into public ownership to save it from bankruptcy.

Further reading
Cowling *et al.* (1980);
Williams *et al.* (1983);
Earl (1984).

Financial engineering and the hollowing out of British manufacturing

Labour productivity grew faster in the UK, during the 1979–89 business cycle, than in many other industrial countries, but this reflected a one-off increase in the utilization of labour and capital, achieved by laying off workers and scrapping plant, rather than a qualitative improvement in performance (Nolan, 1989). When profits recovered, from 1982 to 1988 (see Figure 7.1), firms channelled them into increased dividend payments, overseas investment, and takeover activity, rather than into new product development or improvements in the organization of production.

It is tempting, given the evidence we have reviewed in this chapter, to blame poor UK manufacturing performance on the short-termism of the financial institutions, but part, at least, of the responsibility lies with company management. Williams *et al.* (1990) have detailed how management in many UK manufacturing firms has turned its attention away from productive achievement, and towards 'financial engineering'. GEC was an early example (see Case Study 7.1): an emphasis on stringent financial controls improved company profitability in the late 1960s and 1970s, but the company made a deliberate decision to cut back on new product development, preparing the ground for massive import penetration by foreign electrical and electronic products in the 1980s. Although GEC was a manufacturing firm, it came to see more financial opportunities in closing its manufacturing operations, and investing the gains elsewhere, than in developing them.

The archetypal financial engineer of the 1980s was Hanson plc. Hanson grew by acquiring other companies, rationalizing them by cutting out 'unnecessary' expenditure (including, in many cases, R. & D.), selling off part of the assets at a higher price than they were acquired for, using the capital gains to finance the next cycle of acquisitions, and retaining a portfolio of manufacturing operations characterized by low technology and cyclical or declining markets. Hanson is unambiguous that its sole objective is to maximize earnings per share; not surprisingly, it was the darling of the Stock Exchange in the 1980s. Its earnings, however, have come more from dealing – from buying and selling companies, by speculating on differences between US and UK exchange and interest rates, and by utilizing tax havens like Panama – than from its manufacturing operations. As Case Study 7.2

illustrates, Hanson's style of financial engineering has had damaging consequences for manufacturing output and employment.

CASE STUDY 7.2
ICI and Hanson

ICI in the early 1990s was a UK-based transnational firm, which, unusually for a British manufacturer, had a good R. & D. record, and competed successfully with its global rivals in markets worldwide. In common with its competitors in this cyclical industry, profits, particularly in the bulk chemicals division, were depressed by recession and overcapacity in the European industry. As a result, ICI shares were unpopular on the Stock Exchange.

In May 1991, Hanson acquired shares in ICI 'for investment purposes', and it was widely rumoured that this was the first stage in a takeover bid. City appetites were whetted by the prospect of a Hanson bid, and in particular by the possibility that Hanson might sell off the profitable pharmaceuticals division, and slim down its remaining chemicals business.

A Hanson takeover would have been welcomed by the City, but would probably have been disastrous for the real economy. On past form, Hanson would have cut back on R. & D. expenditure, shut down plants, and made thousands of ICI's UK workforce redundant, to achieve a higher rate of return on the remaining assets, and sales would have been lost to ICI's European rivals.

In the event, ICI embarked on its own restructuring programme to boost its standing in the City and defend itself against Hanson. Hanson eventually backed off, and set their sights elsewhere, but ICI's own financial restructuring resulted in a demerger which floated off the pharmaceuticals division as a separate company, Zeneca.

Further reading
Adcroft *et al.* (1991).

State finance

It is sometimes suggested that the UK financial institutions are at fault, not in starving industry of funds, but in providing funds and failing to use the potential influence this gives them to stimulate and guide industrial development. Fine and Harris, for example (1985), argue that by responding too readily to company demands for 'easy' credit, UK commercial banks have blocked the need for state intervention, which might have guided industrial development along more co-ordinated lines.

Certainly the UK government, unlike those elsewhere in Europe and in Japan, has only been minimally involved in the active promotion of industrial investment, despite Keynes's suggestions (1936) that the state should take greater responsibility for organizing investment to avoid the harmful effects of speculation. As we shall see in Chapter 10, there has been little consistency over time. In the 1960s, for example, the emphasis was on investment grants for regions of high unemployment and funding industrial reorganization. In the 1970s, an increasing proportion of state funds were allocated to bailing out 'lame ducks' like British Leyland and to 'prestige' projects like Concorde. In the 1980s, state funding of private industry was cut, and became focussed on selective support for individual profitable enterprises, particularly to promote new technology.

Finance for small business

More than half a century ago, a government report identified a so-called 'Macmillan Gap' in financial provision for companies that were too small to raise capital on the Stock Exchange (Macmillan Committee, 1931). Soon after the war, the Industrial and Commercial Finance Corporation (now part of 3i, and financed by retail banks) was set up to help fill that gap. The ICFC has played a valuable, if small, role in providing start-up capital and medium-term loans for small businesses. The Stock Exchange, however, continued to ignore smaller companies, and small firms remained dependent for most of their external finance on short-term loans from retail banks, with all the disadvantages we identified earlier in this chapter.

The Wilson Committee, concluding in 1980 that supply of finance was not a constraint on investment, made a significant exception of smaller firms. Since its report was published, a number of measures have been taken to improve the financial situation of small firms. The most important of these are the following.

- The establishment of an Unlisted Securities Market, enabling small and medium-sized firms to obtain share capital on the Stock Market at a much lower cost than would be incurred with a full listing.
- The introduction, on an experimental basis, of a Loan Guarantee Scheme, with the government guaranteeing 70% of bank loans to small firms.
- The development by retail banks of medium-term loans, at fixed interest rates, for small businesses.
- Various fiscal incentives, such as reduced rates of corporation tax for small firms, and an 'Enterprise Allowance' for unemployed people starting up their own business.

Much attention was given to the financial needs of small firms in the 1980s, as part of the government's belief that establishing an 'enterprise culture' would reduce unemployment. Experience has been disappointing, as most of the small firms that were set up as a result of the new policies either remained static in employment terms or went out of business.

Conclusion

Managerially-controlled corporations in the UK finance a high proportion of their investment from retained earnings. The institutions which provide external finance are, however, extremely influential in conditioning their economic behaviour. Financial institutions are less directly involved with their business clients in the UK than in many other industrial countries, and this may also contribute to poor UK business performance. In the UK, the banks and the capital markets allocate funds to companies mainly on the basis of short-term financial criteria, and there is little opportunity for external scrutiny and guidance of firms' long-term development plans. In addition, UK managers in recent years have emphasized financial rather than productive engineering. As a result, firms are encouraged to pursue short-term gains rather than to embark on investments whose returns are long-term, and to grow by acquiring the assets of other firms rather than by developing new products, processes and markets.

Further reading

The Economics of the Financial System, by A.D. Bain (second edition, Basil Blackwell, 1992) gives a comprehensive account of the UK financial system. For more recent developments, you should refer to the Money and Finance section of the most recent edition of *Prest & Coppock's the UK economy*, edited by M.J. Artis (Oxford University Press, new edition every two or three years).

Exercises

1 Using data presented in recent issues of *Financial Statistics*, outline the main changes which have taken place over the past five years in the sources of capital funds of UK commercial and industrial companies. How would you explain these changes?

2 In what ways might the adoption by banks of a liquidation approach to business loans affect the investment behaviour of firms?

3 Why do long-term loans usually bear higher interest rates than short-term loans?
   In what circumstances might the reverse be the case?

4 In what ways have the development of Eurocurrency markets affected interest rates?

5 What have been the main changes in the structure of share ownership in the UK in recent years, and how have these affected business?

6 Why do so few UK mergers result in improved business performance?

7 Periods of intense merger activity are often associated with 'bull' markets on the stock exchange.
   What reasons can you suggest for this association?

8 What economic arguments can you see for and against greater

government involvement in the allocation of investment funds to private firms?

References

Adcroft, A., Cutler, T., Haslam, C., Williams, J. and Williams, K. (1991) Hanson and ICI: the consequences of financial engineering, *University of East London Occasional Papers in Business, Economy & Society*, no. 2.

Bain, A. (1987) Economic commentary, *Midland Bank Review*, Summer.

Bond, S. and Devereux, M. (1988) Financial volatility, the stock market crash and corporate investment, *Fiscal Studies*, April.

Bracewell-Milnes, B. (1987) *Are Equity Markets Short-sighted?* Institute of Directors, London.

Carrington, J.C. and Edwards, G.T. (1981) *Reversing Economic Decline*, Macmillan, London.

Corbett, J. (1987) International perspectives on financing: evidence from Japan. *Oxford Review of Economic Policy*, Winter.

Cowling, K. *et al.* (1980) *Mergers and Economic Performance*, Cambridge University Press, Cambridge.

Cox, J. and Kriegbaum, H. (1989) *Innovation and Industrial Strength in the UK, West Germany, United States and Japan*, Policy Studies Institute, London.

Crafts, N. (1992) Productivity growth reconsidered, *Economic Policy*, October.

DTI Innovation Advisory Body (1990) *Innovation: City attitudes and practices*, Department of Trade and Industry, London.

Earl, P. (1984) *The Corporate Imagination*, Wheatsheaf, Brighton.

Fine, B. and Harris, L. (1985) *The Peculiarities of the British Economy*, Lawrence and Wishart, London.

Goodhart, C.A.E. (1987) The economics of 'Big Bang'. *Midland Bank Review*, Summer.

Jenkinson, T. and Mayer, C. (1992) Corporate governance and corporate control, *Oxford Review of Economic Policy*, Autumn.

Keynes, J.M. (1936) *The General Theory of Employment, Interest and Money*, Macmillan, London.

Macmillan Committee (1931) *Report of the Committee on Finance and Industry*, HMSO, London.

Marris, R. (1964) *The Economic Theory of Managerial Capitalism*, Macmillan, London.

Mayer, C. (1987) Financial systems and corporate investment. *Oxford Review of Economic Policy*, Winter.

Mayer, C. (1988) New issues in corporate finance. *European Economic Review*, June.

Newbould, G. (1970) *Managers and Merger Activity*, Guthstead, Liverpool.

Nolan, P. (1989) 'The Productivity miracle?' in Green, F. (ed.) *The Restructuring of the UK Economy*, Harvester Wheatsheaf, Hemel Hempstead.

Prais, S.J. (1976) (2nd impression 1981) *The Evolution of Giant Firms in Britain*, Cambridge University Press, Cambridge.

Savage, D. (1978) The channels of monetary influence: a survey of the empirical evidence. *National Institute Economic Review*, February.

Sawyer, M. (1987) Mergers: a case of market failure? *British Review of Economic Issues*, Autumn.

Schneider-Lanne, E. (1992) Corporate control in Germany, *Oxford Review of Economic Policy*, Autumn.

Singh, A. (1971) *Takeovers*, Cambridge University Press, Cambridge.

Singh, A. (1975) Takeovers, economic natural selection, and the theory of the firm. *Economic Journal*, Sept.

Williams, K. *et al.* (1983) *Why are the British Bad at Manufacturing?* Routledge, London.

Williams, K. *et al.* (1988) *Do Labour Costs Matter?* Mimeo, University of Aberystwyth Economics Department.

Williams, K., Williams, J. and Haslam, C. (1990) The hollowing out of British manufacturing and its implications for policy, *Economy and Society*, November.

Wilson Committee (1980) *Report on the Functioning of Financial Systems*, HMSO, London.

8

The international environment

This chapter explores key elements in the modern international trading system, exchange rate determination, and balance of payments accounting. Analysis of recent trends in the UK balance of payments focusses attention on poor manufacturing trade performance, and the failure of North Sea oil, financial services, and inward investment to compensate for the loss of jobs in other fields. UK manufacturers are especially vulnerable to intensified international competition, as European integration deepens and world trade barriers are reduced.

Introduction

Modern business operates in an increasingly international context. Flows of trade between different industrial economies are becoming more and more intricate, as businesses feel the need to expand their export markets if they are to benefit from product differentiation without losing the cost advantages of large scale production. Greater sophistication in telecommunications and computerized information systems is making it possible for transnational firms to reorganize their production and marketing systems on a continent-wide or even global basis. Similar developments have made financial markets international, with financial centres competing with each other to lend money or issue securities to customers who are free to choose where in the world they make their transactions.

We start this chapter with an overview of the main changes in international trading patterns, and then examine balance of payments accounts and exchange rate determination. Analysis of the UK's trading situation focusses on the enormous shifts which have taken place in the composition of the UK's current account in recent years, and particularly on the significance of the deterioration in the manufacturing trade balance. Assessment of recent shifts in patterns of international investment is followed by an analysis of the role of capital flows on the UK economy. The chapter ends with a discussion of the chequered progress towards European union.

International trade

Continued industrial growth requires increased inputs of raw materials and expanding markets. Early on in the development of an economy, this leads to an expansion of foreign trade, and businesses which succeed in foreign markets often increase their competitive advantage as they experience increasing unit cost advantages from the resulting growth in sales. In the early nineteenth century, Britain developed a virtual world monopoly in mass-produced manufacturing goods, and this was made possible by a pattern of trade where she produced a surplus of manufactured goods in exchange for primary products (food and raw materials) from abroad.

KEY CONCEPT 8.1
Comparative advantage

Ricardo's theory of comparative advantage states that it is differences between countries in the relative production costs of commodities which determine patterns of specialization and trade, not absolute cost differences. Suppose, to take Ricardo's example, Portugal can produce a unit of wine with 80 hours of labour, and a unit of cloth in 90 hours, while England can produce the wine in 120 hours and the cloth in 100. Portugal has, on these figures, an absolute advantage in both wine and cloth, but Britain could not import both on a long-term basis, for she would have nothing to offer in exchange. Profitable trade can take place on the basis of the different relative costs, however. Because in Portugal one unit of wine exchanges for 8/9 unit of cloth, while in England it exchanges for 12/10 units of cloth, Portugal has a comparative advantage in wine, and England in cloth. If Portugal produces two units of wine and England two units of cloth, then the same total output in the two countries can be produced in thirty less hours. Provided a mutually acceptable basis for exchanging Portuguese wine for English cloth can be found, both countries will benefit from specialization and trade.

Labour hours involved in production

	Before specialization			After specialization		
	Wine	Cloth	Total	Wine	Cloth	Total
Portugal	80	90	170	160	–	160
England	120	100	220	–	200	200
			390			360

Ricardo identified differences in technology as the main source of production cost differences. In the twentieth century, two Swedish neo-classical economists, Heckscher and Ohlin, modified Ricardo's theory by suggesting that different factor endowments, rather than different technologies, were the main source of comparative advantage. If, they suggested, all countries have equal access to technology, then countries where labour is relatively abundant (and therefore cheap) would be encouraged by free trade to specialize in labour-intensive goods, while countries which are well-endowed with capital would specialize in capital-intensive goods. The analysis of the sources of comparative advantage is different in each case, but the policy conclusion is the same – prosperity will increase if barriers to trade, which prevent full specialization on the basis of comparative advantage, are removed.

David Ricardo, an early nineteenth century English political economist, attempted a justification for this trading pattern with his theory that world output would be maximized if each country specialized in producing the goods in which it had a comparative advantage (Key Concept 8.1). On the basis of this theory, he argued that a regime of free trade would maximize the gains from trade. What Ricardo's theory left out, however, was any indication of how the gains from trade might be distributed. As it happened, development of manufacturing industry brought about dynamic gains from improved efficiency of resource use and new product development, gains which were ignored by the static comparative advantage approach.

Productivity gains in the industrial countries eventually took the form of increased wages. In the primary producing countries, however, the benefits of productivity increases in the export sector were transferred abroad in the form of reduced prices, and the terms of trade (the rate of exchange between exported and imported goods) moved in favour of the industrial countries. There was more than a hint of self-interest, then, in the free trade policies which were espoused by the British government in the mid-nineteenth century.

In the late nineteenth century politicians in countries like Germany and Japan realized that if they adhered to the rules of the free trade game, they could never build up their own industries and the benefit from the increased incomes these would provide. They decided instead to develop their own industries behind protective barriers, forgoing the short-term advantages of free trade in order to develop more powerful advantages in the long term. In Japan's case, a distinctive policy of consciously channelling resources into areas of greatest potential long-term advantage has continued to the present day. Meanwhile, most of the economies that continued to specialize in primary products remained poor, both initially as colonies of the industrial countries and subsequently as independent nations. The main exceptions, the oil exporters, became rich not so much through free trade but because in the 1970s they took collective action, through the Organization of Petroleum Exporting Countries (OPEC), to raise revenues by restricting oil supply to the world market.

After the Second World War, there was an enormous expansion of international trade, most of which took the form of two-way trade in manufactured goods between industrial market economies. As we saw in Chapter 1, markets for many consumer goods have become more sophisticated, with non-price factors becoming ever-more significant as determinants of demand as disposable incomes increased. Some consumers have turned to imports to satisfy their particular requirements, and domestic firms have had to differentiate their product range in order to limit losses in their market share to importers. As domestic product markets have fragmented, many firms have been encouraged to seek out new export markets, in order to increase their returns on new product development.

Expanding two-way flows of imports and exports between industrial countries have been accompanied, and encouraged, by reciprocal reductions in tariffs (negotiated through GATT, the General Agreement on Tariffs and Trade), and by the creation of regional free trade areas (especially the European Union, or EU). About three-quarters of all manufacturing exports from industrial market economies now go to other industrial market economies.

Growth in manufacturing exports from most industrial market economies has slowed since 1973. This period has, however, seen big increases in manufacturing exports from some developing countries, most notably Singapore, Hong Kong, Taiwan, South Korea, Brazil, and Mexico. Much of the manufacturing growth in these Newly Industrializing Countries has involved labour intensive processes such as clothing manufacture and electronics assembly, and comparative advantage in labour costs is obviously a relevant factor here. It is worth noting, however, that South Korea and Brazil are now competing successfully against industrial economies not just with these sorts of products, but with more capital intensive products such as steel, ships, cars, and aircraft.

Recession in industrial market economies in the mid-1970s encouraged a partial return to protectionism (mostly in the form of non-tariff barriers such as subsidies for domestic producers or informal import quotas) as the governments of those countries sought to keep down domestic job losses. Much of this 'new protectionism' was aimed specifically at developing countries. Despite this, as Table 8.1 indicates, the developing economies now export more manufactured goods than primary products, and account for almost a fifth of world manufacturing exports.

In understanding recent changes in manufacturing trade, it is often more useful to focus on the changing organizational, technological and market environments of modern manufacturing than on the comparative costs of classical theory. In particular, we have observed two things.

- Where product markets are differentiated and fixed costs of production are high, firms need buoyant export markets both to compensate for lost market shares at home and to maintain a level of output which reduces average fixed costs to a minimum.
- Where product life cycles are short, firms need increased exports to

Table 8.1 Value of merchandise exports by country group

	High-income economies	Low- and mid-income economies
Merchandise exports (1991, $bn.)	2650	686
Real growth in merchandise exports (1980–91, % per year)	+4.1	+4.1
Manufacturing as % of total merchandise exports		
– 1970	79%	36%
– 1991	86%	64%

Source: World Bank (*1993 World Development Report*).

Note: High-income economies are those with a per capita GNP of more than $7910 in 1991. They include all OECD members as well as Singapore, Hong Kong, and Israel.

maximize the returns from sales of existing products which are needed to finance new product development.

As we saw earlier in the book, some Japanese firms have recently begun to utilize the opportunities of flexible manufacturing systems to increase their penetration of export markets by creating products which are more clearly differentiated from those of their competitors, and tailored to meet local demands. In this situation, the gains from trade for the consumer come not so much from lower prices but from greater product variety.

The Single European Market, NAFTA, and GATT

In 1957, France, West Germany, Italy, Belgium, Holland and Luxembourg signed the Treaty of Rome. This sought to establish a 'Common Market', by removing tariffs on trade between member countries, and establishing a common external tariff and a Common Agricultural Policy. The European Community (EC) was subsequently enlarged to include also Britain, Ireland, and Denmark (1973), Greece (1981), Spain and Portugal (1986) and, as a by-product of German reunification, the former East Germany (1990). Austria, Finland, Norway, and Sweden were, at the time of writing, negotiating with a view to joining the European Union (as the EC is now called) by 1996.

Formation of the 'Common Market' led to an increase in the significance of intra-EC trade, compared to trade with non-EC countries, illustrated for the UK in Table 8.2. A number of non-tariff barriers remained, however, including border controls, differences in technical standards, and differences in levels of indirect taxation. The Treaty of Rome was amended in 1987 to provide for the removal of all barriers to

Table 8.2 Area composition of UK trade, 1973–92 (% of total)

	Exports		Imports	
	1973	1992	1973	1992
EC	36	56	36	52
Other developed economies	40	24	38	31
Oil exporting countries	6	6	9	2
Rest of World	18	14	16	14
Total	100	100	100	100

Source: Annual Abstract of Statistics.

Note: EC includes the original 'six', plus Denmark, the Irish Republic, Greece, Spain, Portugal, and East Germany throughout.

trade, and to create a 'Single European Market' by 1992. According to official EC estimates, achievement of the Single European Market would boost GDP by around 5–6%, as a result of lower prices and efficiency gains (Cecchini, 1988). The Cecchini Report was criticized, however, for exaggerating the positive impact of removing trade barriers, and for failing to address the unequal distribution of gains between different member countries (Cutler *et al.*, 1989).

According to the Cecchini Report, the creation of a liberal free market in post-1992 Europe would encourage merger and takeover activity to obtain economies of scale, which would benefit consumers and producers alike, throughout the Community. We have seen, however, that it is often difficult to achieve economies of scale in practice (Chapter 2), and that the logic of mergers and takeovers is often financial rather than productive (Chapter 6). Although achievement of a Single European Market is presented as a benefit to all member nations, these benefits can only be realized where national firms have the resources and abilities to exploit the opportunities now open to them. Many British manufacturers, for example, have found that the physical and financial resources they can commit to winning market advantage from freer trade are more limited than those of their continental rivals. From the point of view of the firm, changed trade regulations may be a necessary condition for improvement in sales, but they are not sufficient.

In 1993, the USA, Canada, and Mexico set up a North American Free Trade Agreement (NAFTA). The aims of NAFTA are more limited than those of the European Union, but, if realized, will result in the elimination of trade and investment restrictions between the three countries over a 15-year period. NAFTA will speed up the process whereby US manufacturing firms migrate across the Mexican border to take advantage of low labour costs there. In the medium term, other Latin American countries may join the Agreement, to create a regional free trade area of a size that would dwarf the Single European Market.

At the same time as regional free trade trade areas like the Single European Market and NAFTA have been forming, protracted negotiations have been taking place, under the auspices of GATT (the General Agreement on Tariffs and Trade), to set up a world trade deal. Agreement was eventually reached in December 1993 to cut tariffs (import taxes) and trade-distorting subsidies on a wide range of industrial goods and agricultural products, and to begin a process of liberalizing trade in services. The OECD has forecast that world output will increase by \$274 billion (1%) by the start of the next century as a result of implementation of a world trade treaty. As with regional free trade, however, an unequal distribution of benefits from freer trade can be expected.

Exchange rates

Foreign trade necessarily involves the exchange of one currency for another. If, for example, a British firm purchases computer equipment from a US supplier, its pounds have to be exchanged into dollars. If, on the other hand, an American family come on holiday to Stratford-on-Avon, they will have to exchange dollars for pounds. Foreign exchange markets exist to establish rates of exchange between currencies which equate total purchases and sales of each currency. Suppose, for example, that the current exchange rate between sterling and the US dollar is £1 = \$1.50. If, at this exchange rate, purchases of dollars exceed sales, and sales of pounds exceed purchases, then the exchange value of the pound in relation to the dollar will fall until purchases again equal sales, at, say £1 = \$1.49.

The post-war period has been characterized by three distinct exchange rate regimes: pegged exchange rates, floating exchange rates, and the European Exchange Rate Mechanism.

Pegged exchange rates

The Bretton Woods Conference in 1944 established a new international monetary system under US leadership. The dollar was convertible into gold at a fixed price of \$35 per ounce, and other currencies were given a par value against the dollar. Monetary authorities were obliged to use their gold and foreign currency reserves to maintain the market value of their currency within 1% of the par value. Par values could be adjusted from time to time, but only in the case of a 'fundamental disequilibrium' between imports and exports. The International Monetary Fund (IMF) was formed to act as a sort of Central Banker for the entire international economy outside the Communist bloc. The IMF held a pool of currencies and gold deposited by member countries, from which it could extend short-term credit to countries whose currencies were under pressure.

Under the pegged exchange rate system, the Bank of England would respond to a rise in UK imports of US goods by using its dollar reserves to buy sterling, to counter downward pressure on the exchange rate. In the event of a continued drain of reserves to support the exchange rate, the authorities had to take action to reduce imports (by restraining domestic demand, for example), to increase inflows of private capital (by raising interest rates, for example), or to decrease outflows of private capital (by controlling access to foreign exchange, for example). Only in exceptional circumstances (as in 1967, when speculation against sterling forced a devaluation from £1 = $2.80 to £1 = $2.40) was action taken to change the exchange rate itself.

Floating exchange rates

The pegged exchange rate system broke down in the early 1970s, following the inability of the US monetary authorities to satisfy foreign demands for dollars in the wake of the Vietnam War. In the regime which followed, exchange rates were determined mainly by market

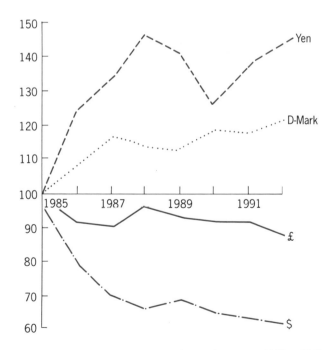

Figure 8.1 Effective exchange rates 1985–93 (annual average, 1985 = 100).

Source: IMF, *International Financial Statistics.*
Note: Effective exchange rates measure changes in the value of a currency against a basket of other currencies, weighted according to their importance in the countries' trade.

forces. Monetary authorities attempted to inject some stability into a turbulent situation, by using reserves or manipulating interest rates, but the period was characterized by some dramatic changes in exchange rates. This is illustrated for the four major currencies in Figure 8.1.

Proponents of exchange rate flexibility argue that it enables international prices to adjust to national differences in costs, thus maintaining purchasing power parity in the face of differential inflation rates (see Key Concept 8.2). In practice, however, exchange rates are more volatile than the purchasing power parity approach would suggest, particularly in the short term. This reflects an increased demand for foreign exchange to acquire foreign assets, encouraged by liberalization of capital markets (see Chapter 6). Demand for foreign assets is determined more by expectations of future performance than by experience of past inflation, and this will often cause market exchange rates to diverge from the purchasing power parity rate. The divergence is intensified if financial institutions use their market power to shift funds between currencies in order to speculate against countries which the market judges to be 'weak'. This occurred on a massive scale in 1986–7 and again in 1992–3.

KEY CONCEPT 8.2
Purchasing power parity

If trading partners experience different rates of inflation, nominal exchange rates would have to change for real exchange rates to be maintained at a constant level. Thus if, over a period of ten years, the price of goods in the UK rose by 100%, but the price of goods in Germany remained unchanged, to maintain the same rate of exchange between UK goods and German goods, the exchange rate of the £ against the D-mark would have to halve.

Purchasing power parity theory suggests that exchange rates change to maintain the purchasing power of each currency, so that in periods where inflation is rising faster in the UK than in other countries, the exchange rate of the £ will fall, and vice versa. In the long term, exchange rates do tend to move in the direction that purchasing power parity theory suggests (though not necessarily to the extent that the theory would predict). Over shorter time periods, however, other influences predominate, and the activities of foreign exchange speculators are often the most significant determinant of changes in exchange rates.

The Exchange Rate Mechanism

The Exchange Rate Mechanism, or ERM, was established by the European Community in 1979. It assigned each member currency a central rate against other EC currencies, and a target band within which the currency was allowed to fluctuate. Although there were, initially, frequent realignments within the ERM, the new system had, in the late 1980s, created a degree of stability between European currencies which contrasted with intense fluctuations against the dollar and yen. This stability, it was suggested, would facilitate intra-EC trade, and lay a foundation for eventual full monetary union.

The UK government in the early 1980s was unconvinced by the economic case for joining ERM, and it rejected the political goal of monetary union. The pound therefore remained outside the ERM, and was free to fluctuate against other European currencies as well as against the dollar and yen. In the mid-1980s, however, the Chancellor of the Exchequer decided to informally tie the pound to the D-mark, and in 1990 the UK formally joined the ERM at a high central rate of £1 = DM2.95, on the assumption that this would help to bring UK inflation under control.

The events of September 1992 revealed the fragility of the new framework. Full ERM membership at a high exchange rate reduced UK inflation, as the government had hoped it would, but at the cost of a major recession and a collapse in the housing market. Foreign exchange dealers doubted the government's capacity to implement its declared intention to resist realignment, and they speculated massively against sterling. The government tried to defend the pound with unprecedented rises in interest rates, but it failed, and 'temporarily withdrew' from the ERM, accompanied by Italy. Within a month, the exchange rates of both the pound and the lira had fallen by 20% against the D-mark.

The problems which erupted in September 1992 sprang from many different causes, including high German interest rates following re-unification, and a failure of the UK government to realign its currency within the ERM. More fundamentally, however, they revealed a major weakness of rigid exchange rate regimes in a world of global financial markets characterized by vast daily exchanges of currency, and where there is still divergence in underlying economic performance. What September 1992 exposed was the powerlessness of governments and central banks to defend fixed exchange rates against determined speculation by foreign exchange dealers.

This powerlessness was demonstrated again in July 1993, when speculators forced five of the remaining eight ERM currencies on to their floor against the D-Mark, threatening the whole European Monetary Union project. Agreement was reached to widen the bands for the weaker currencies, allowing them to fluctuate by up to 30%.

Exchange rates and business

Variation in exchange rates can lead to considerable uncertainty for firms. The price of imported components and raw materials will vary, making production costs difficult to predict. Sales revenue from exports, too, will be affected if the exchange rate changes between when a contract is fixed and when the goods are actually supplied.

If the exchange value of sterling depreciates, this lowers the (foreign currency) price of UK products in export markets, and raises the (domestic currency) price of imports to the UK market. Depending on the price elasticities of demand, this raises demand for the products of UK firms, which, if there is spare capacity, results in increased sales and increased profits.

At the same time, however, depreciation increases the costs of UK producers – initially by raising the price of imported raw materials and components, and subsequently by increasing import prices generally and thus stimulating higher wage demands. Although exchange rate depreciation improves the price competitiveness of domestic firms in the short term, past experience in the UK suggests that this advantage is eroded within three to four years by increased domestic inflation.

More fundamentally, in markets where competitive advantage depends more on new product development and effective marketing than on price, currency depreciation may be of only limited benefit to firms, even in the short term. It is worth noting that Japanese exports to the US continued to flourish in the late 1980s, despite a massive appreciation of the yen in relation to the dollar (see Figure 8.1). This was partly a result of the ability of many Japanese firms to cross-subsidize exports from sales in a protected domestic market, but it also reflected the competitive edge of many Japanese manufacturers in terms of non-price factors such as quality and reliability.

Balance of payments accounts

A country's balance of payments is an accounting record of all transactions between its own residents and residents of other countries in a given period, usually a year. It follows the principles of double-entry bookkeeping, and always balances, as every transaction involving the exchange of one currency for another is balanced by another transaction in the opposite direction.

A summary of the UK balance of payments for 1989–93 is shown in Table 8.3. The visible trade balance (sometimes called the balance of trade) shows the value of exports less imports of commodities (food, fuel and other raw materials, and manufactured goods), while the invisibles balance brings together exports less imports of services (banking, travel, etc.), profits on overseas investment, and transfers

Table 8.3 UK balance of payments summary (£ billion)

	1989	1990	1991	1992	1993
Visible trade (balance)	−24.7	−18.8	−10.3	−13.4	−13.4
Invisibles (balance)	+2.2	+0.5	+2.6	+3.4	+2.8
Current balance	−22.5	−18.3	−7.7	−10.0	−10.7
Net transactions in UK external assets and liabilities	+19.4	+11.0	+6.7	+6.3	+8.9
Balancing item	+3.1	+7.3	+0.9	−3.7	−1.8

Source: Economic Trends.

(such as payments to EC institutions). The current account balance is the sum of the visibles balance and invisibles balance. A negative figure, as in the period since 1983 in the UK, indicates a current account deficit, with expenditure on imports exceeding earnings from exports.

When there is a surplus or deficit on current account, this must be balanced by an equal and opposite deficit or surplus on transactions in external assets and liabilities. This covers international capital flows such as direct and portfolio investment, banking transactions, and government asset transactions (including the use of official reserves).

Because of the double-entry methodology of the accounts, the current balance and the asset transactions balance should sum to zero. In practice they rarely do, because of incomplete statistical coverage, particularly in relation to short-term capital flows. To compensate, the statisticians introduce a 'balancing item'.

Traditionally, it has been thought that no country can run a persistent deficit on its current account without having to take action to remove it. Recently, however, it has been argued that persistent current account deficits can, in certain circumstances, be sustained by ensuring that they are financed by inflows of private capital rather than by running down official reserves. These issues are explored further in the context of recent UK experience later in this chapter.

The role of the International Monetary Fund

The International Monetary Fund (IMF) is an international institution, founded at the end of the Second World War, which attempts to harmonize the exchange rate and balance of payments policies of member governments. Each government has a quota of Special Drawing Rights (international money created by the IMF), which can be used for balance of payments settlement. Governments can in addition borrow up to 25% of their quotas in foreign currencies from the IMF to finance balance of payments deficits. Further borrowing from the IMF is possible, but only on condition that the government adopts economic policies which meet the IMF's approval. The conditionality clauses of IMF programmes are highly controversial, with critics claiming that the IMF gives too much emphasis to short-term monetary adjustments (such as cuts in public expenditure), and gives insufficient attention to long-term structural factors which give rise to deficits (such as dependence on uncertain revenues from primary product exports).

The IMF has also been involved in attempts to find solutions to the international debt crisis. This crisis arose because developing economies which had borrowed heavily in the 1970s to finance ambitious development programmes were squeezed in the early 1980s by rising interest rates and declining export markets (Key Concept 7.2). Some Latin American governments were unable to repay their debts on time, and such was the scale of the debt that their creditors (commercial banks in the USA and Western Europe) faced the prospect of severe liquidity problems, and in some cases bank failure. The IMF stepped in to persuade the creditors to reschedule their debts, in return for which it negotiated tough austerity programmes with the debtor countries. The IMF's policies have been heavily criticized for placing most of the burden of adjustment on the debtor countries, even where the problem has been caused by factors outside their control (Griffiths-Jones, 1987; George, 1988). In some cases, debtor countries have found the IMF conditions too onerous, and have unilaterally limited their debt repayments. The threat of a major default, and consequent bank failure, has receded, but it remains real.

UK trade performance

For most of this century, the UK's visible trade balance has been in deficit, largely as a result of dependence on imported food and raw materials. Deficits in visible trade were usually counter-balanced by surpluses on invisibles, so that the current account, taking one year with another, remained roughly in balance.

In the post-war boom, the main problem with the balance of payments was a tendency for the current account to move into deficit at the height of the business cycle. This, under the pegged exchange rate regime then operating, required the government to restrain aggregate demand, thus slowing down economic growth.

Recent experience, as Figure 8.2 shows, represents a significant departure from this historical pattern. Visible trade moved into surplus in 1980–82, creating an overall current account surplus which lasted throughout the early 1980s. In the late 1980s, however, a series of large visible trade deficits pushed the current account into chronic deficit.

To understand the reasons for this change in experience, we need to look beneath the crude breakdown of visibles and invisibles, to examine changes in the composition of UK trade. Three elements are particularly significant here: manufacturing, oil, and services. We examine each of these in turn.

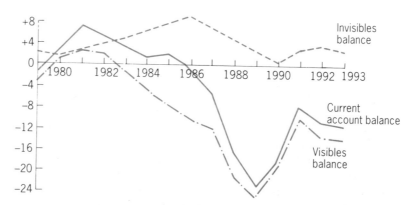

Figure 8.2   UK current account balance, 1979–93.
Source: Balance of Payments Pink Book.

KEY CONCEPT 8.3
Gross domestic product

Gross domestic product (GDP) is an indicator of the national income of a country. It is the monetary value of the output of all marketed goods and services in an economy in a given period (usually one year). GDP can be measured in any of three different ways – by adding incomes from employment, value added, or final expenditure on domestic goods and services.

Gross national product (GNP) is another commonly used indicator of national income. It includes net property income from abroad as well as GDP.

GDP and GNP are alternative measures of money flows in an economy, and are useful in indicating both the size of those flows at a point in time and changes over time. They are also sometimes presented as indicators of 'welfare' or 'progress', but there are a number of important objections to this. In particular:

- Non-marketed activities, such as housework and childcare within the family, voluntary work, or subsistence farming in less developed countries, can form a significant part of total output, yet they are not counted as national income.
- Crude national income figures reveal nothing about how money incomes are distributed between different sections of the population, and how this affects different people's well-being.
- Present national income accounting conventions take no account of the degradation of 'free' environmental resources, and the welfare costs this imposes on present and future generations.

Traditionally, the UK has relied mainly on manufacturing exports to pay for the imports of food and raw materials that have been needed. This pattern of specialization reached its zenith around 1950, when 10% of UK gross domestic product (see Key Concept 8.3) went into net manufacturing exports, to help pay for an even larger deficit in non-manufacturing trade. The long-term trend from then on was for manufacturing surpluses to decline in real terms, until by the early 1980s the UK was, for the first time in centuries, importing more manufactured goods than she exported. Case Study 8.1 gives a more detailed picture of what was happening in the motor vehicles industry.

CASE STUDY 8.1
UK trade in motor vehicles

Up to the early 1960s, UK motor vehicle manufacturers supplied the vast majority of the UK domestic market, and earned in addition substantial export revenues. Since the mid-1960s, however, importers have achieved dramatic increases in their shares of the UK market, while UK manufacturers have failed to maintain their position in export markets. These trends – of increasing import penetration and falling export sales ratios – are illustrated graphically in the figure below.

There are four main elements in this changing picture

1   The failure of British Leyland/Austin Rover (the main UK car producer until the 1970s) to develop new models which were sufficiently attractive to customers, and its strategic miscalculation to retreat from European markets.
2   The integration by Ford and General Motors (Vauxhall-Opel) of their European operations, and the concentration of much of their new investment on plants in Germany and Spain.

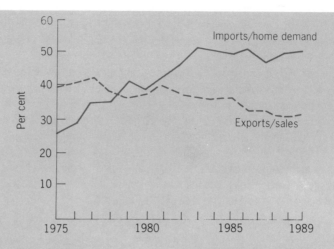

3   The decisions of both Ford and GM to enter the small car market (traditionally dominated in the UK by British Leyland/Austin Rover) with new models, many of which are assembled in Spain.
4   The further fragmentation of UK car markets by imports from producers based elsewhere in Europe or in Japan.

The net result of these and other processes has been the transformation of the UK from being a substantial net exporter of motor vehicles in the 1960s to being a substantial net importer in the 1980s. The DTI statistics on which the graph is based have not been collected since 1989, but it is unlikely that the picture changed much in the early 1990s. The UK car industry now includes Japanese transplants (Nissan at Sunderland, Honda at Swindon, Toyota at Derby) but any positive effects on UK trade are counter-balanced by their high import content, and their expanded share of the UK market, at the expense of home producers.

Further reading
Dicken (1992);
Williams *et al.* (1987);
Williams *et al.* (1991).

The credit boom of the late 1980s sucked in more and more imports, and by 1989, as Table 8.4 shows, the manufacturing deficit had soared to £17 billion (around 5% of GDP). From 1989 to 1991 the manufacturing deficit eased somewhat, but this was more a response to the restraining influence on imports of the recession than a result of improved manufacturing performance.

As a result of development in the North Sea, the UK had become a net exporter of oil by 1980. Although new reserves have since been discovered, in Dorset for example, oil is a finite natural resource, and UK physical production peaked in 1985. Declining output, coupled with declining oil prices, combined to reduce the oil surplus from £8 billion in 1985 to less than £2 billion per year from 1989–92.

Table 8.4 Selected components of the UK current account, 1976–92 (£ billion)

	Manufacturing balance	Oil balance	Services balance
1976	+4.9	−3.9	+2.2
1977	+5.9	−2.8	+3.0
1978	+5.0	−2.0	+3.5
1979	+2.7	−0.7	+3.9
1980	+5.4	+0.3	+3.7
1981	+4.5	+3.1	+3.8
1982	+2.1	+4.6	+3.0
1983	−2.7	+7.0	+3.8
1984	−4.4	+6.9	+4.2
1985	−3.8	+8.1	+6.4
1986	−6.2	+4.1	+6.2
1987	−8.3	+4.2	+6.2
1988	−15.3	+2.8	+4.0
1989	−17.3	+1.3	+3.4
1990	−11.6	+1.5	+3.8
1991	−3.6	+1.2	+3.7
1992	−7.4	+1.5	+4.1

Source: Balance of Payments Pink Book.
Note: Manufacturing = semi-manufactured + finished goods.

The surplus on services increased in the early 1980s, largely as a result of financial deregulation, which increased the City of London's attractiveness as an international financial services centre. The surpluses peaked in 1985 at £6$\frac{1}{2}$ billion, however, and have deteriorated substantially since then.

It was suggested, in the early 1980s, that declining manufacturing trade was the inevitable outcome of improvements in oil and financial services. Because the current account tends to balance in the long run, the argument ran, increased surpluses in one sector must be counterbalanced by increased deficits in another. As we have seen, however, the improvements in oil and financial services were short-lived, while manufacturing has been in persistent long-term decline. Seen in the context of experience over the past two decades as a whole, rather than the exceptional circumstances of the early 1980s, it is clear that declining manufacturing trade cannot be explained by improvements in non manufacturing trade. Rather, it reflects the generally poor international competitiveness of UK manufacturing products, in both the domestic and export markets. The consequences of this for employment are particularly severe, as the jobs which were created in financial services and in the oil sector were far fewer in number, and far more localized geographically, than the jobs which have been lost in manufacturing.

Price and non-price factors in UK trade performance

Numerous studies of the poor trade performance of British manufacturing firms draw attention to the significance of non-price factors such as poor marketing and poor product quality. Failure to appoint sales representatives or to set up dealerships and after-sales service facilities in key export markets, and poor delivery times, are common. This often reflects marketing strategies which pay more attention to defending short-term profit than to promoting market growth (Doyle *et al.*, 1986).

In markets where purchasers are prepared to pay a premium price for product quality and delivery, exchange rate depreciation will not necessarily have a positive effect on trade performance. In the UK machine tools industry, for example, Brech and Stout (1981) found that sterling depreciation encouraged 'down-trading' (switching from high unit value to low unit value products). A falling exchange rate made it easier to make short-term profits by selling more older, low-value, products, and discouraged many producers from investing in (higher value) new product development. Over time, however, any gains in value added from improved price competitiveness were whittled away, not just by rising domestic costs, but by losses in non-price competitiveness.

International capital movements

The classical model of international trade implicitly assumes that factors of production are mobile within, but immobile across, national boundaries. In reality international movements of labour and, especially, of capital have played significant roles in the development of market economies. The latter take three main forms.

- Portfolio investment
- Direct investment
- Bank lending and borrowing.

Portfolio investment

Portfolio investment is investment in securities issued by foreign governments or companies. Historically, this type of international investment became significant in the late nineteenth century, when British rentiers often invested more abroad (usually in government or government-guaranteed stocks) than they did at home. Its popularity declined after the 1930s, when a number of Latin American governments defaulted on their debts, but has revived again in recent years. Most portfolio investment nowadays takes the form of active trading by financial institutions in the shares of foreign companies and in the gilt-edged securities of foreign governments, and this has been encouraged by more relaxed government attitudes to foreign exchange control. Many investors have seen an international spread of securities as a way of diversifying their risks and avoiding too close a dependence on the financial performance of one particular national economy. Even so the events of October 1987 demonstrated the domino effect brought about by capital markets that have become so interlinked that a crash in one national market will affect all the others.

Direct foreign investment

Direct foreign investment involves an investor in one country purchasing and acquiring a controlling interest in assets in another country, or adding to (or deducting from) such a controlling interest. It can be financed by a transfer of cash, by an exchange of shares, or from profits made by local subsidiaries which are not remitted back to head office. Direct investment is used largely for the establishment or expansion of branch plants overseas by transnational corporations, or the acquisition of overseas companies.

There are many reasons why a firm might wish to establish production facilities overseas. Dunning (1979) suggests that a firm will be interested in international production when three conditions are satisfied.

- The firm has *ownership advantages* over competitors, such as privileged access to technologies or supplies.
- There are *internalization advantages* which encourage the firm to exploit these ownership advantages by direct investment rather than by licensing arrangements. The firm may prefer to have direct control over a technology it has developed, for example, to protect returns on its research and development investment.
- There are *locational advantages* of producing in another country, rather than exporting to it from its domestic base, resulting from lower production or distribution costs, for example, or from the possibility of getting round trade barriers.

Direct foreign investment has grown rapidly since the war, helped by technological innovations in communications which made it much easier for an international head office to control foreign branches at a distance. Transnational operations have grown particularly rapidly in technologically advanced manufacturing industries, in high volume consumer goods industries, and in business services like banking. As Table 8.5 shows, most direct foreign investment originates in industrial market economies, though the predominant role of US firms has been eroded in recent years by competition from Japan in particular.

Industrial market economies are the main destination, as well as the main source, of direct foreign investment. There has in recent years, however, been an increase of direct foreign investment in developing

Table 8.5   Origin of direct foreign investment (percentage of world total)

	1960	1985
USA	47	35
UK	18	15
Japan	1	12
W Germany	1	8
Switzerland	3	6
Netherlands	10	6
Canada	4	5
France	6	3
Other developed market economies	9	7
Developing economies	1	3
	100	100

Source: UNCTC (1988).

economies, particularly Newly Industrializing Countries like Singapore, Hong Kong, Brazil and Mexico.

The relationship between direct foreign investment and international trade is an intricate one. There is intense international rivalry between large firms in sectors like electronics and cars, and often if a firm is to survive in the face of increased competition from imports in its home market, it has to develop markets overseas. In some cases, firms will prefer to produce at home, and export to a new market. In other cases (where trade barriers or transport costs are significant, for example) they will prefer to allow a local firm to produce their products under licence, or to set up their own production facilities locally. In the latter case, direct foreign investment will usually be accompanied by exports of capital equipment and components – almost a third of all exports from UK firms go to 'related concerns' abroad, for example.

International trade between different branches of the same firm is an important source of competitive advantage for transnational firms, as it enables them to exploit differences in national economic conditions. Transnational firms can, for example:

- Manipulate transfer prices to minimize their tax burden (see Key Concept 8.4).
- Take advantage of different financial conditions to obtain finance where interest rates are low, to lend cash reserves where interest rates are high, to alter the timing of profit remittances from branches to head office, or to actively speculate in foreign currencies.
- Reorganize their production globally so as to minimize production costs.

A transfer price is the administered price used in a company's management accounting system to represent the value of goods and services which are transferred from one division of the firm to another. Transfer prices can be market-based (reflecting the market price of comparable external goods and services), cost-based (reflecting actual internal costs), or negotiated (between the divisions and company headquarters). These methods can produce quite different results, and for transnational corporations there may be considerable scope to set transfer prices artificially low or high so as to reduce taxes and duties payable to national governments.

Consider a car manufacturer which exports engines from its branch in Mexico, to be assembled with other components in the United States into a car which sells mainly in the United States. If there are duties payable on the import of engines from Mexico to the United States, then the cost of duties to the firm will be minimized by setting the transfer price low. If tax on profits is higher in the United States than in Mexico, however, then the burden of profits tax will be reduced by setting the transfer price high, which will exaggerate the proportion of global profits which can be shown to accrue in Mexico. The transfer price which is most advantageous to the company will depend on the levels of duty and tax levied in each country. In many countries such manipulation of transfer prices is illegal, but the law is often difficult to enforce, for governments cannot easily determine what an undistorted transfer price would be.

KEY CONCEPT 8.4
Transfer prices

Globalization of production

Most of the early transnational corporations operated as loose federations of relatively autonomous national units, but since the 1960s many of them have developed structures which enable them to integrate production and distribution on a global scale. Global organization makes it possible for transnational corporations to exploit national differences for their own advantage. Through direct foreign investment, or through international subcontracting, transnational corporations can now restructure their activities to produce where costs are lowest, and sell where profits are highest.

Labour market considerations have played an important role in these calculations. One of the pioneers here was Ford, which integrated its European operations as long ago as the late 1960s. One of the principles adopted at that time was that of 'dual sourcing'. To achieve economies of scale, each plant specialized in only a limited range of activities. To bypass possible disruption from labour disputes, key activities were duplicated at plants in two different countries. If, for example, there was a strike affecting the production of Capri bodies at Halewood, then output at Saarlouis could be stepped up to compensate.

A more significant consideration nowadays is labour costs. Low wage levels were an important factor in encouraging Ford in the 1970s to set up a new assembly plant for the European market at Valencia, and a new engine plant for the North American market at Mexico City. Labour cost differences have been particularly significant in the clothing industry and in assembling electrical goods and electronic components. In industries such as these, important elements of the production process are both labour intensive and highly standardized, and here transnational corporations have relocated or subcontracted production to developing countries which can provide cheap disciplined labour and appropriate industrial inputs (see Case Study 2.3).

In cases where labour requirements vary significantly at different stages of the production process, the resulting flows of components and final products can become extremely intricate (Case Study 8.2). Alongside the old international division of labour, where rich countries specialized in manufacturing and poor countries in primary products, a new international division of labour has emerged where certain developing countries have become major manufacturing exporters. As Case Study 8.2 indicates, however, changes in technology and in labour markets can be destabilizing, as they encourage continual shifts in the location of this type of production.

CASE STUDY 8.2
Integrated circuits

At the heart of the micro-electronic revolution are tiny devices called integrated circuits (chips), whose components are all made from a single piece of semiconducting material. Production of integrated circuits involves four distinct stages, each with their own distinctive locational requirements.

1 *Circuit design.* Scientists and engineers produce complex, multilayered circuit patterns which are then photographically reduced and incorporated into masks. This work is highly knowledge intensive, and much of it is done in California, though newer centres have emerged in Japan and Western Europe.

2 *Wafer fabrication.* Layers of silicon are 'doped' with chemical impurities, to control the flows of electrical current through the circuit. These semiconductors are then etched with the patterns in the masks, baked, and tested. This stage requires both technical and assembly workers, a 'pure' production environment, and good access to raw materials such as silicon. Initially wafer fabrication was also centralized in California, but recently there has been a shift to peripheral areas of West Europe. Central Scotland has, over the past decade, become a major wafer fabrication centre.

3 *Chip assembly.* Circuits are bonded to external electrodes, using extremely fine wire, and then baked to seal them in a protective coating. This is a low-technology, labour-intensive process, and most of it is done by low-paid women workers in South East Asia.

4 *Testing.* Finally, reliability is tested by dipping components in chemicals and applying electrical currents to them. Traditionally, this involved shipping the chips back to the US, but recently testing has also been carried out in South East Asia.

While it is significant that integrated circuits have heralded a new stage in the internationalization of production, it is ironic that they have also brought into being working conditions which hark back to the nineteenth century. Young Asian women are chosen for chip assembly because their high levels of manual dexterity are learnt informally at home, because they have few alternative opportunities for paid work, and because their governments restrict their rights to organize in a trade union (all of which limit their ability to win pay rises). Health and safety problems abound, from peering through microscopes for hours on end and using hazardous chemicals.

The new international division of labour which has emerged is far from static. Wages in Singapore have risen in response to labour shortages, and firms there have begun to diversify into new areas like testing and sub-systems assembly, and, in one case (PCI), to set up a branch plant in Europe. Routine assembly work has been further decentralized to economies such as Malaysia and the Philippines, where wages are even lower. Meanwhile, developments in computer aided manufacturing have encouraged some firms to automate chip assembly, so that it can be shifted back to the US to improve delivery times without increasing inventory costs.

Further reading
Mitter (1986);
Henderson (1989).

Bank lending and borrowing

As we saw in Chapter 7, banking activities have become more international in scope in recent years, and flows of borrowing and lending across national boundaries have become much more frequent. Some of this borrowing and lending is extremely short-term – London banks will lend deposits overnight to New York and Tokyo, for example, and receive them back (with interest) the following morning. Some, however, is much longer-term, for example the recycling of OPEC oil surpluses to Newly Industrializing Countries via the London Eurocurrency markets in the late 1970s.

Loans set up under the Eurocurrency system are often extremely intricate, with deposits passing from bank to bank before they reach the ultimate borrower. As a result, the precise extent of bank lending and borrowing across national boundaries is often difficult to measure, and international banking activities are difficult for national monetary authorities to control. Many observers fear that this situation is particularly vulnerable to financial crisis, as difficulties experienced by any participant bank (as a result of default by a major debtor, for example) will be transmitted rapidly through the Eurobanking system as a whole.

International capital flows and the UK balance of payments

Thanks to the dominant role of the City of London in the economy and to the legacy of colonialism, the UK has a long history of involvement in the export of capital and in international finance. In analysing this involvement, it is important to distinguish between different types of international transaction, and between stocks and flows (see Key Concept 8.5).

A stock is an amount of something at a point in time, whereas a flow occurs during a period of time. Thus wealth is a stock, while income is a flow. Investment can be measured both as a stock or as a flow, and so it is particularly important not to confuse the two meanings. Each year, for example, there is a flow of direct investment by UK firms overseas, which in 1992 was valued at £8.6bn. At any point in time, however, there will be a much greater stock of direct investment by UK firms overseas, which has built up over the years – at the end of 1992, this stock was valued at £163.8bn. To complicate things further, a stock of investment at any point in time yields a flow of income over the life of that investment – in 1992, the UK earnings from direct investment overseas came to £14.1bn.

Flows of portfolio investment by UK residents in shares and bonds overseas have increased rapidly since the abolition of foreign exchange controls in 1979, as have the overseas transactions of UK banks. By the end of 1992, the stock of foreign portfolio assets (shares and bonds) held by UK residents was £304 billion, as against foreign portfolio holdings in the UK of £181 billion. The overseas assets of UK banks in 1992 were £566 billion, compared with total overseas liabilities of £672 billion.

Transnational firms play an unusually significant role in the UK economy, which has expanded enormously since the Second World War. The UK is both a major source and a major recipient of foreign direct investment. In the 1980s, flows of outward direct investment (overseas investment by firms based in the UK) regularly exceeded those of inward direct investment (investment in the UK by firms based overseas), reflecting the 'hollowing-out' process outlined in Chapter 6. Since 1990, however, there has been substantial net inward foreign investment in the UK. At the end of 1992, the stock of direct investment by UK firms overseas was valued at £163 billion, compared with a £132 billion valuation of foreign assets in the UK.

The impact of inward direct investment on the UK economy

Recent increases in inward direct investment have been welcomed by the government for helping to offset the current account deficit, and for creating jobs. In addition, it is often claimed that inward direct investment, particularly by Japanese firms, has a positive impact on British management practices, particularly in the fields of industrial relations and relationships with suppliers.

Careful study of the behaviour of Japanese transplants in Britain suggests, however, that their overall impact on British industrial performance may be less dramatic. According to the Census of Production, Japanese manufacturing transplants in the UK employed only 41 000 workers in 1991, less than 1% of total UK manufacturing employment. Williams *et al*. (1991) found that many of the plants were more warehouses with final assembly lines than factories in the traditional sense.

Around half of Japanese transplants in the UK did not make a profit, their net productivity (value added per worker) was little higher than in British-owned firms, and their stock turnover was no different to that of British-owned firms. Williams *et al.* suggest that Japanese manufacturing transplants are characterized by 'no profits, low productivity, high stocks and low wages. From this point of view it is hard to distinguish [them] from the rest of British manufacturing.'

It seems that many Japanese transplants in the UK are 'screwdriver' operations which have been set up to ensure market growth by avoiding tariff and other barriers on direct imports of finished products. Because so many of the high value added components are shipped in from Japan, the impact of these transplants on the UK economy is not a straightforward one. In terms of the balance of payments, the initial investment is a positive item on the capital account, but subsequent imports of components from parent plants in Japan often outweigh export earnings by the UK plant, creating deficits on the current account. Job creation, too, is limited by the high import content. In industries like consumer electronics where there are no significant UK competitors, there will be net job gains. In other industries like cars, however, where sales from Japanese transplants displace domestic production, the result is often a net loss of jobs.

European Union

In 1991, EC governments negotiated the Maastricht Treaty on European Union. This Treaty set out a series of further steps to be taken towards full economic, social, and, eventually, political union. We have already, in Chapter 6, considered the 'Social Chapter' of Maastricht, and confine our attention here to the proposed programme for European Monetary Union.

Under the Maastricht Treaty, realignments within the Exchange Rate Mechanism are to be avoided by cooperation between central banks to co-ordinate monetary policy, the aim being to achieve convergence of inflation rates, government borrowing rates and interest rates. Monetary convergence, it is proposed, will lead, by the end of the century, to the establishment of a European Central Bank and the creation of a single European currency.

The current UK government has considerable misgivings about monetary union, and at Maastricht it reserved the right to opt out of the arrangements for a European Central Bank and a common currency. With or without UK participation, however, there are considerable problems in achieving full monetary union by the end of the century. It was always envisaged that a common currency would be based on a strong D-mark, but this cannot be relied upon in the aftermath of German reunification. It is also seen to depend on monetary convergence, yet on present indications this could be achieved only at the expense of considerable divergence in output and jobs between different regions. If, as seems likely, the price of monetary union is high unemployment in the peripheral regions, then political demands may make achievement of a single currency conditional on more effective measures being adopted to promote output and job growth in the periphery, which could encounter German resistance. These issues are explored more fully in Chapter 10.

Conclusion

In an open economy, foreign trade is a crucial determinant of domestic economic activity. Where, as in Japan and West Germany, a country's firms are successful in foreign markets, export earnings can significantly boost domestic output and employment. Where, on the other hand, a country's firms are less successful internationally, domestic output and jobs are threatened, and the government may take measures which intensify the decline in order to restore balance of payments 'equilibrium'.

UK manufacturing firms have suffered an enormous decline in international competitiveness in recent years. The effects of this decline on the current account of the balance of payments were masked, up to the mid-1980s, by growth in exports of oil and financial services. We have already experienced a number of problems associated with this shift in the composition of UK trade, particularly in respect of unemployment. It is quite possible that the negative consequences of UK manufacturing decline will intensify in the late 1990s, as North Sea oil runs out, and as the UK becomes fully integrated into the European internal market.

Further reading

The standard textbook on international trade and the international monetary system is *International Economics*, by L. Alan Winters (Routledge, fourth edition, 1991). For an approach which is more critical of the world trading system's capacity to generate prosperity for all, try Michael Barrett Brown's *Fair Trade* (Zed, 1993).

For detailed information on de-industrialization and the changing structure of UK trade, *Balance of Payments Theory and the UK Experience*, by A.P. Thirlwall and Heather Gibson (Macmillan, fourth edition, 1992), is invaluable.

Peter Dicken's *Global Shift* (Paul Chapman, second edition, 1992) is a mine of useful information on the global production systems which have been evolved by many transnational firms in recent years.

Exercises

1 Using current issues of *International Financial Statistics* and *Economic Trends*, update Figures 8.1 and 8.2 and comment on the trends.

2 Assess the arguments for and against the view that there is nothing wrong with a deficit on manufacturing trade so long as it corresponds to surpluses on non-manufacturing trade.

3 Discuss the main changes in the role of the IMF since it was founded. How would you evaluate its handling of the Third World debt crisis?

4 Assess the effects on the UK balance of payments of the abolition of exchange controls.

5 Choose a transnational corporation, and assess why it has evolved its particular global distribution of production.

6 In many markets, non-price factors have become more significant than price as determinants of consumer demand. What are the implications for

(a) Firms seeking to expand export sales?
(b) Government trade and exchange rate policy?

7 Choose a UK industry, and assess the likely impact of European Monetary Union on:

(a) Company profits in that industry.
(b) Imports and exports by that industry.
(c) UK employment in that industry.

References

Brech, M. and Stout, D. (1981) The rate of exchange and Non-Price Competitiveness: a provisional study within UK manufacturing exports, *Oxford Economic Papers*, July.

Cecchini, P. (1988) *The European Challenge 1992: the Benefits of a Single Market*, Gower Press, Aldershot.

Cutler, T., Haslam, C., Williams, J. and Williams, K. (1989) *1992: the Struggle for Europe*, Berg, Leamington Spa.

Dicken, P. (1992) *Global Shift*, 2nd edn, Paul Chapman, London.

Doyle, P., Saunders, J. and Wong, V. (1986) Japanese marketing strategies in the UK. *Journal of International Business Studies*, Spring.

Dunning, J.H. (1979) Explaining changing patterns of international production. *Oxford Bulletin of Economics and Statistics*, Nov.

George, S. (1988) *A Fate Worse than Debt*, Penguin, Harmondsworth.

Griffiths-Jones, S. (1987) Learning to live with crisis. *The Banker*, Sept.

Henderson, J. (1989) *The Globalisation of High Technology Production*, Routledge, London.

Mitter, S. (1986) *Common Fate Common Bond: Women in the Global Economy*, Pluto, London.

UNCTC (1988) *Transnational Corporations in World Development: Trends and Prospects*, UN, New York.

Williams, K. *et al.* (1987) *The Breakdown of Austin Rover*, Berg, Leamington Spa.

Williams, K., Haslam, C., Williams, J., Adcroft, A. and Johal, S. (1991) Factories or Warehouses: Japanese foreign manufacturing direct investment in the UK and US, *University of East London Occasional Papers on Business, Economy and Society*, no. 6, December.

9 The natural environment

This chapter focusses on global environmental problems, and on the different policies – legal regulations and economic instruments – which have been proposed to resolve them. Environmental policies pose opportunities as well as threats for business, but whether or not firms respond positively to these challenges depends crucially on their willingness and ability to invest in the new products and processes which are required.

Introduction

One aspect of the environmental context of business which is often neglected is the natural environment. This neglect is unfortunate, because services which are made available to us by nature, such as raw materials (including air and water) and waste disposal facilities, are essential to economic activity, and to life itself. Because these services are provided 'free of charge', business calculations have not paid much attention to them, focussing as they do on the flows of production and consumption which result from the transformation of raw materials, not on how these flows affect stocks of natural resources. Stocks and flows are, however, interconnected, and business calculations which divert attention away from problems of resource depletion and pollution can stimulate forms of economic activity which degrade and ultimately destroy the natural systems on which they depend. Case Study 9.1 illustrates this in relation to the problems which arise from intensified consumption of fossil fuels.

Since Rachel Carson's classic denunciation of the destructive effects of the toxic chemicals used by the agricultural industry for pest control

(Carson, 1962), public awareness of the dangers of environmental degradation has been increasing, and few people now doubt the need for some form of environmental controls. There is considerable dispute, however, over how much control is needed, and over what form it should take. We explore in this chapter two specifically economic contributions to this debate, that of neo-classical theory, and that of 'steady state economics', before going on to examine environmental controls in practice, and how business responds to them.

The neo-classical approach to the natural environment

Neo-classical theory suggests that market forces can be relied upon to solve problems of depletion of exhaustible resources, but that they need to be modified in order to counter the harmful effects of pollution and of over-harvesting of renewable resources.

Natural resources are endowments of nature which can be used by humans as food, raw materials, or energy. They fall into three distinct types.

Exhaustible resources are mineral deposits (like copper) and fossil fuels (like oil) which take millions of years to form, so that from a human time-scale they can be regarded as fixed in supply. Some minerals can be recycled, but this is an energy-intensive activity, and there are physical limits (based on 'entropy', or loss of quality) to the number of times the same material can be reused. At the end of the day, exhaustible resources are finite, and consumption inevitably leads to a depletion of stocks.

Renewable resources are derived from living matter which regenerates naturally (like trees or fish). It is possible for humans to 'harvest' a flow of services from these resources, without necessarily diminishing the stock. Over-harvesting, however, will result in resource degradation.

Continuing resources (like solar energy or wind power) are inexhaustible, so that humans can benefit from their services without running down stocks. Such resources are sometimes confusingly termed 'renewable'.

KEY CONCEPT 9.1
Exhaustible, renewable, and continuing resources

Exhaustible resources

Resource conservation, the neo-classical argument runs, is a form of investment, in that costs (in the form of forgone consumption) are incurred in the present to obtain benefits (in the form of extended consumption for future generations) in the future. This investment needs to be evaluated according to the same rules, and using the same discount rate, as any other investment. As a result of the procedure whereby future costs and benefits are discounted back to present values (Chapter 3), there is no point in worrying about the rate at which a resource is depleted until shortly before its known reserves are exhausted. At this point, its price will increase, and this will simultaneously have five effects.

- Stimulate new exploration, and the discovery of new reserves.
- Stimulate technological advances which increase the recoverability of existing reserves.
- Stimulate an increase in the efficiency of resource use.
- Encourage producers to substitute abundant resources for the scarce resource (the substitution effect).
- Reduce real incomes and thus consumption (the income effect).

Elegant though this 'solution' is theoretically, it is extremely doubtful whether the price mechanism could be relied upon in practice to solve all the problems of exhaustion of a key non-renewable resource. Total stocks of most minerals in the earth's crust are still large in relation to current rates of use, and a high proportion of the minerals which are consumed in the production process could, in principle, be recycled. The technological and financial constraints on recovering low concentrations of minerals are considerable, however, and there is no guarantee that these constraints could be overcome. Substitution of abundant for scarce resources would avoid the problem, but such substitution is not always technologically feasible, and we cannot assume that abundant substitutes for scarce resources will always exist. In a situation where a number of key resources faced exhaustion simultaneously, price changes would result in generalized inflation, not substitution.

An additional complication is that when firms discount future costs and revenues at a high rate, they may delay embarking on the necessary technological research until it is too late. As Hans Aage has emphasized, widespread increases in rates of resource recovery and recycling would require abundant, non-polluting sources of energy, and these we do not have. As a result

> Prices . . . cannot be expected to fulfil automatically the functions allotted to them in neoclassical analysis, and they cannot be relied upon in themselves to ensure continuous sufficiency of resources. Proposals for economizing on resources are not inconsequential, their main justification being to gain time in the race between depletion and technical advance.
>
> *Aage, 1984*

Renewable resources

In the case of renewable resources (see Key Concept 9.1), it is possible for users to 'harvest' crops without diminishing the stock, but in practice over-harvesting often occurs, threatening the resource base. This problem is particularly acute where common property rights are involved (water extraction from lakes and rivers, or sea fishing, for example). Tribal cultures often impose effective controls on the rate at which commons are used, to ensure that degradation does not occur. In a free market situation, however, existing users and new entrants alike can use resources at whatever rate they choose. The competitive process tempts them to increase their harvesting activities, at the expense of the stock on which they all depend. In extreme situations (some forms of whaling or logging, for example) species extinction may be the end result.

The free access problem can be seen as an example of an 'externality' (see Key Concept 6.4). Where a renewable resource is freely available to all, it would be socially beneficial for everyone to manage its use so as to ensure its conservation, but in the short run there may be private benefits to be gained by over-exploitation.

It has become fashionable for neo-classical economists to argue that the problem of free access to common property can be resolved by privatization (or enclosure, as it used to be called). If, it is argued, individual property rights for the exploitation of a particular resource could be established, then non-owners would be denied access, users would bear the costs of depletion themselves (internalizing the externality), and over-harvesting would be discouraged.

There are enormous ethical and practical problems associated with the privatization of commons, and there is no guarantee that it would be effective in eliminating over-harvesting, depending as it does on short-term commercial calculations by property owners. In practice, it is perhaps not surprising that most governments have preferred to attempt to manage the exploitation of commons through legal regulation, and, in the case of open seas, by international agreement.

Pollution

Since Pigou's *Economics of Welfare* (1920), neo-classical economists have recognized pollution as an 'externality' – a cost imposed by the polluter on others, for which no compensation is paid. The solution to this problem most favoured by neo-classical economists is to internalize the externality by imposing a tax on polluters, equal to the damage caused to other parties. This, it is suggested, would cause polluters to cut back on the pollutants they produce (by restricting output, and/or introducing pollution control equipment), and a social 'optimum' would be reached where the marginal social cost of production was equal to the marginal social benefit (in terms of consumers' willingness to pay) of the output.

This is illustrated diagrammatically in Figure 9.1. The horizontal line MPC(1) represents the marginal private cost of a production process to a firm, while MSC represents the marginal social cost, including the external cost of the pollution associated with the process. If D is the consmer demand curve, representing the marginal benefits of the product to consumers, then the competitive market equilibrium is at price P_1 and output Q_1. This is inefficient, however, because there is an excess of social costs over social benefits, represented by the shaded area in the diagram.

Now suppose the government imposes a tax, which adds T to the cost of the product. The marginal private cost schedule of the firm moves up from MPC(1) to MPC(2), and there is a new equilibrium at price P_2 and output Q_2. This is socially efficient because now the marginal social costs are equal to the marginal benefits. Note that the

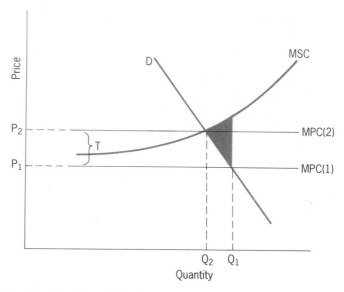

Figure 9.1   The effect of a pollution tax.

price to consumers is higher, and the output lower, than in the original situation. The extent of the price rise and of the reduction in output both depend on the slope of the demand curve – the higher the price elasticity of demand, the smaller the proportion of the tax which is paid by consumers in higher prices, and the greater the reduction in output. If the firm introduces pollution control equipment, because its cost is less than that of the tax, the effects on price and output will be correspondingly less. In terms of the diagram, the MPC schedule will move up by less than T, the MSC schedule will move close to the new MPC schedule, and the new equilibrium price will be somewhere between P_1 and P_2, with output somewhere between Q_1 and Q_2.

The practical problems of devising an appropriate pollution tax are immense. When Pigou discussed externalities, he used as an example the emission of smoke from factory chimneys, and identified social costs such as extra laundry expenses, which were readily quantifiable. Recent experience points, however, to atmospheric pollution having an environmental impact which is both more extensive and less amenable to precise costing than Pigou's illustrations would suggest. Changes such as the acidification of lakes and forests, or the build up of carbon dioxide in the atmosphere (Case Study 9.1) have profound and often irreversible effects, but scientists are seldom able to make an exact estimate of the amount of damage caused by a particular amount of a particular pollutant. Precise identification of marginal social costs is, therefore, rarely possible.

CASE STUDY 9.1
Global warming

Global warming refers to the rise in global temperatures which scientists predict will occur as a result of continued emission of 'greenhouse gases' which trap heat in the atmosphere, such as carbon dioxide (CO_2), methane (CH_4), nitrous oxide (N_2O) and chlorofluorocarbons (CFCs). The predicted rise in global temperatures would bring about massive climatic disruption, causing worldwide changes in vegetation and agriculture. Eventually, sea levels would rise as a result of thermal expansion of oceans and melting of land ice sheets; catastrophic coastal flooding would result.

Global warming can be understood economically as a particularly serious example of a negative externality (see Key Concept 6.4). Free access by firms and individuals to the use of the atmosphere as a dump for greenhouse gases results in excessive emissions, with potentially disastrous consequences for the planet. The social benefits of a more responsible attitude to greenhouse emissions would be enormous, yet there is little incentive for firms and individuals to act responsibly, because of the balance of private costs and benefits. Effective action to combat global warming would need not only to be collective, but international – if a country acted in isolation it would not have a significant impact on global emissions, but its balance of trade would suffer from rising domestic costs.

The general circulation models on which predictions of climate change are based are in their infancy, so there is considerable scientific uncertainty about the extent of global warming, and therefore about the seriousness of the problem. Some politicians argue that further research is needed before any costly action is taken to curb greenhouse gases, in case it transpires that the action is not needed. Others favour taking action now, based on the 'precautionary principle' that if we do nothing until there is more conclusive evidence of the damage caused by global warming, then it may be too late to avert disaster.

CFC production is currently being phased out (largely because of concern about the ozone layer), and it was agreed at the 1992 Earth Summit that all developed countries would stabilize emissions of the other greenhouse gases by the end of the century.

Many economists argue that economic incentives would be the most effective way of implementing reduced production targets for greenhouse gases. One widely discussed possibility is a tax on fuels, graduated according to their carbon content, to encourage greater energy efficiency and a switch to less-polluting fuel sources (see Case Study 9.3).

Further reading
Leggett (1990), Chapters 1–7;
Jacobs (1991), Chapter 10;
Pearce (1993), Chapter 20.

Steady state economics

The origins of steady state economics can be traced back to the chapter 'Of the Stationary State' which John Stuart Mill wrote, with Harriet Taylor, for his *Principles of Political Economy* in 1848. Mill and Taylor agreed with the classical political economists that the end point of industrial progress was a state where growth in population and capital would cease. Far from being dismayed by this prospect, however, they felt that a stationary state would be an improvement on existing conditions of industrial growth.

> I am not charmed [Mill wrote] with the ideal of life held out by those who think that the normal state of human beings is that of struggling to get on; that the trampling, crushing, elbowing, and treading on each others' heels, which form the existing type of social life, are the most desirable lot of human kind, or anything but the disagreeable symptoms of one of the phases of industrial progress.
>
> *Mill, 1965*

He went on to suggest that 'It is only in the backward countries of the world that increased production is still an important object: in those more advanced, what is economically needed is a better distribution, of which one indispensable means is restraint on population', and that 'a stationary condition of capital and population implies no stationary state of human improvement.'

A leading contemporary advocate of a stationary economy is Herman Daly. In his book *Steady-State Economics* (1992), Daly emphasizes that economic growth involves both benefits (in the form of satisfactions from the consumption of products) and costs (in the form of depletion and pollution of natural resources). While growth is desirable when its marginal benefits exceed its marginal costs, environmental costs increase as growth proceeds, until at some point the marginal costs of growth outweigh the marginal benefits. We do not have the information to determine 'optimum' stocks of population and products, where marginal benefits equal marginal costs, but we do know that industrial growth over the past two centuries has been based on running down 'geological capital' – non-renewable stocks of minerals and fossil fuels. This type of growth cannot be sustained in the long term, making the pursuit of ever-increasing levels of consumption an impossible dream. The policy implications, Daly suggests, are clear. Instead of making economic growth the principal objective of economic activity, we need to do two things.

● To limit our use of natural resources to the minimum which is necessary to secure constant stocks of population and products.
● To limit national and global inequalities in income and wealth, so as to secure a sufficient standard of living for everyone.

To minimize environmental degradation, Daly argues that it is more effective to control resource depletion than to tax pollution. This is because depletion is easier to monitor and control, and because depletion controls would in themselves limit aggregate pollution. Governments, he suggests, should set quotas determining the amount of each resource which can be depleted each year, which they then auction to the highest bidders, using the revenues so gained to fund income redistribution. Once the political authorities have placed physical limits on resource throughput, the price mechanism can be relied upon to ensure that the scarce resources are used with maximum efficiency.

Daly's work is a stimulating antidote to those economists who skate over environmental problems, but there are important limitations to his analysis. Some environmentally-concerned economists, for example, would favour a more pragmatic approach, focussing attention on those forms of pollution that cause the most environmental damage, and exploring patterns of growth which could be sustained ecologically. At a practical level, too, few would share Daly's optimism about the feasibility, within the current international political environment, of limiting and auctioning resource-depletion rights.

Sustainability

One of the merits of Daly's work has been to draw attention to potential conflicts between the short-term satisfactions which people obtain from consuming material goods and the capacity of the natural environment to sustain those satisfactions in the long term. Growing awareness of the life-threatening nature of environmental problems such as global warming and the destruction of the ozone layer has led to demands that these conflicts are resolved by policies which ensure that economic development is 'sustainable' (see Key Concept 9.2).

Economists have long been aware that there is a difference between rates of economic growth which can take place in the short term and those which can be sustained over a longer period. In the recovery phase of the business cycle, for example, rapid growth can be achieved as labour and capital resources which had been unemployed are brought back into use. When existing resources are fully employed, however, growth is limited by the rate of new capital investment and by trend productivity growth.

The term 'sustainable development' refers to environmental resource constraints, rather than capital and labour constraints, and sustainability is assessed over a longer time period than the business cycle. The term was popularized by the World Commission on Environment and Development in its 1987 report *Our Common Future* (sometimes called the Brundtland Report). This report sought to reconcile the needs of the world's poor for development with the common need to preserve the environmental resources on which future generations will depend. It defined sustainable development as 'development that meets the needs of the present without compromising the ability of future generations to meet their own needs', thus focussing on the needs of the poor (who are under-represented in market calculations) and of future generations (who are excluded from them). Sustainability, Brundtland proposed, should become a central goal of national and international economic policy.

The Brundtland report has been criticized for ignoring political conflicts over environmental management and development, and for failing to draw a clear enough distinction between resources which must be preserved at any cost and those which can be exploited for human development without significant adverse impacts for coming generations. The report has ensured that the inter-generational distribution of environmental costs and benefits is now discussed in the policy documents of national governments and international agencies like the World Bank. As yet, however, little progress has been made by these official bodies in implementing new policies which

KEY CONCEPT 9.2
Sustainable development

significantly address the needs, identified by Brundtland, for improved environmental protection and for Third World development.

Further reading
World Commission on Environment and Development (1987), Chapter 2;
Pearce *et al.* (1989), Chapters 1–2;
Rees (1990), Chapter 11;
Daly (1992), Chapter 13;
Graf (1992).

It is important to note that sustainable development does not necessarily imply zero economic growth. As Jacobs (1991) has noted, 'To economists, and in most political discussion, economic growth refers to annual increases in Gross National Product (GNP). To environmentalists and Greens, it often means an increasing consumption of environmental resources. These are not the same.' The difference arises because not all economic activities have the same negative impact on the environment. What is required is not so much zero economic growth, as changes in economic structure to encourage activities and processes which economize on use of environmental resources, and discourage activities and processes which degrade them. The basic requirement is that there is systematic assessment of the environmental impacts of different business activities, backed up by policies to ensure that sustainability constraints are respected.

Types of environmental control

Political debate over sustainable development and pollution control has tended to focus more on what targets should be set than on how those targets might be achieved. It is, however, becoming increasingly recognized that if firms are to take more account of the environmental consequences of their activities, then closer attention needs to be paid to the method of implementation. Here, discussion has centred on the choice between legal regulation and economic instruments.

Legal regulation

Governments have tended to rely on legal regulation to minimize adverse environmental impacts, particularly in the case of air pollution. In Britain, the most serious emissions of air pollutants are regulated by government inspectors, who, for more than a century, have required industrial plants to be equipped with the 'best practicable means' of preventing the discharge of 'noxious and offensive gases'. The 'best practicable means' is determined on a case-by-case basis, taking into account factors such as the state of technical knowledge, the financial cost to the firm of installing control devices, and local environmental conditions. Standards determined in this way are known only to the control agency and the regulated firm, and although legal sanctions can be used in the event of infringement, the inspectors prefer not to prosecute, relying instead on co-operation and persuasion. The 'best practicable means' concept was refined by the 1990 Environmental Protection Act into 'best available techniques not entailing excessive costs' (BATNEEC), but little change was made to the basic regulatory framework.

Supporters of the British approach to regulation claim that its flexibility ensures that the right balance between economic and ecological considerations is struck. Critics, however, claim that inspectors give undue weight in their deliberations to the negative implications of controls for firms' balance sheets, and not enough to positive impacts on environmental quality. Certainly there is evidence in Britain that many infringements of consent standards remain undiscovered, that standards are slow to change in response to new evidence of environmental damage, and that when new standards are introduced they apply to new but not to existing plants, slowing down the impact of improved abatement technologies.

Outside Britain, environmental regulation often takes the form of single uniform standards which are determined by a political bargaining process which is open to public scrutiny. Critics of this approach argue that uniform standards ignore the situation-specific nature of many environmental problems, and that the process by which they are determined is unduly influenced by political 'fashion'. Supporters claim, however, that the relative 'openness' of the standards approach ensures consistency, and avoids suspicions that firms may have 'bribed' inspectors into setting lenient standards. In practice, uniform standards are often more lenient than would be required to ensure adequate environmental protection, but there is evidence that countries such as the USA which adopt a standards approach are quicker to respond to new concerns, like the destruction of the atmosphere's ozone layer by chlorofluorocarbons, than countries like Britain which rely more on a consensus approach.

Traditionally, environmental protection has taken different forms in different countries, and different types of pollution have been regulated according to different criteria, even within the same country. Recently, however, governments have come under pressure to adopt a more consistent approach. In Britain, air pollution, water pollution, radioactivity, and the disposal of wastes on land have been controlled by different authorities. One result of this has been that some firms have been able to get out of a need to clean up their waste by choosing as their medium of waste disposal the one which is least effectively controlled. It was partly in response to this that a unified Inspectorate of Pollution was set up in 1987, and encouraged to explore with operators the 'best practicable environmental option' for disposing their wastes. Within the EC, too, member governments are being urged to adopt uniform standards in relation to certain emissions. This reflects concern about phenomena such as acid rain which do not respect national boundaries, and a desire to ensure that countries do not gain an unfair trading advantage over their competitors by adopting lenient control standards. Recently, in addition, some firms have demanded consistency in environmental standards to protect themselves against unfair competition from products whose environmental performance is poor, and to encourage their export sales (see, for example, Case Study 9.2 on the car industry).

CASE STUDY 9.2 *Car exhaust emission* *control*	Internal combustion engines burn fossil fuels, and thus emit carbon dioxide; they are the main source of increased concentrations of greenhouse gases in the global atmosphere. They also emit a number of toxic air pollutants, including nitrogen oxides (which combine with sulphur dioxide in the atmosphere to produce acid rain), lead (which can cause brain damage, particularly in young children), benzene hydrocarbons (which are carcinogenic), and carbon monoxide (which can cause heart and respiratory problems). Increased car use and the development of high-compression engines which needed leaded petrol combined in the post-war period to intensify environmental degradation and ill-health.

Photochemical smogs, triggered by nitrogen oxide and hydrocarbon emissions, became a pervasive feature of city life in the USA and Japan, and in the early 1970s both countries introduced legislation to control car exhausts. This required new cars to be fitted with catalytic converters (add-on devices which clean the exhaust after it leaves the engine), and filling stations to provide unleaded petrol. These measures reduced toxic exhaust emissions per mile, though air quality remained poor as a result of increased car use. The measures also had the effect of restraining car imports, as the modifications needed to make European cars conform to the new standards added significantly to their dollar and yen prices.

The EC country affected most acutely by atmospheric pollution was West Germany, where in the early 1980s a third of all trees were damaged by acid rain. Environmental consciousness was higher here than elsewhere in Europe, producing significant electoral gains for the Greens, a political party which placed environmental concerns high on its agenda. The West German government responded to these pressures by pushing for stricter EC controls over car exhausts. West German car firms, initially resistant to environmentalism, soon welcomed the rewards which pollution control measures would bring them, not least in the lucrative US market. If emission controls were as tight in Europe as in the US, they argued, then they could design all their cars to the same standard, and reap economies of scale in emission-control technology.

Environmental awareness in Britain was less well developed – perhaps because most of the acid rain produced there was blown across the North Sea. The Rover Group, the main domestic car producer, was committed to lean burn technology (which burns fuel inside the engine more completely, to lower fuel consumption). The lean burn approach is cheaper than using a catalyst, and it reduces carbon dioxide emissions, but it increases nitrogen oxide pollution. The UK government, eager to protect Rover's position in the domestic small car market against competitors who were more experienced in catalyst technology, fought within the EC to oppose exhaust controls which could not be met by lean burn methods alone.

In the mid-1980s, the EC legislated to phase out leaded petrol. It also negotiated an agreement for other toxic emissions which was considerably more lenient than US standards for small and medium-sized cars. It was widely believed at the time that the agreement represented a compromise between the needs of German large car producers to promote their US exports and the needs of British, French and Italian small car producers to protect their investments in lean burn technology.

By the late 1980s EC legislation had been tightened up, and since 1993 all new European cars have had to be supplied with catalysts, to meet standards for toxic emissions which are close to those in the US. Meanwhile, still tougher emission controls in the US are raising the stakes for car makers yet again. In California, state legislation requires manufacturers to market zero-emission vehicles by 1998. As a result, any car manufacturer hoping to maintain US sales will need to fund massive investment in the development of alternative fuel sources, such as electricity or hydrogen.

Although technological improvements reduce local pollution from cars, they have, as yet, done little to reduce emissions of greenhouse gases. Electric cars, for example, merely displace carbon dioxide emissions from road to power station, while most current catalysts increase carbon dioxide and nitrous oxide emissions. Although the EC has discussed possible controls over carbon dioxide emissions from cars, negotiations in 1992 were deadlocked, with the Germans favouring different emission limits for different engine sizes (to protect their large car producers), and the Italians favouring a tax on actual carbon dioxide emissions (to benefit their small car producers). Most independent research suggests that much tougher measures to restrain traffic demand would be the only effective way to limit the impact of cars on global warming.

Further reading
Longhurst (1989);
Leggett (1990), Chapter 12;
Whitelegg (1993).

Legal regulation is most effective when there is widespread agreement that a substance is so hazardous that it should be banned altogether. A good example of this is CFCs – chemical compounds which have been widely used as aerosol propellants, coolants, and insulation materials, but which, when released into the atmosphere, destroy the ozone layer. Following widespread concern in the 1980s about the effect of ozone layer depletion on ultra-violet radiation levels (resulting in increased incidence of skin cancers and cataracts), an international agreement was signed by almost all producing countries to phase out production by the year 2000.

Economic instruments

From the standpoint of neo-classical economic theory, and of the present UK government, charges have a significant advantage over legal regulation where anything less than an outright ban is proposed. This is because they provide a continuing incentive for firms to develop new and more economic methods of reducing pollution or conserving resources, rather than just meet what the regulations require. A carbon and energy tax, for example (see Case Study 9.3), would act as a continuing stimulus for producers to search out ways of economizing on energy use and/or switching to non-carbon energy sources.

Imposition of a particular technological solution, in contrast, would only create a one-off improvement, and might be less cost-effective.

Economists have developed elaborate techniques to estimate monetary valuations of environmental quality where direct pricing does not exist. House price variations near airports have been analysed, for example, to determine the 'hedonic price' of aircraft noise. Where people value something even though they do not benefit directly from it (the survival of pandas, for example), 'contingent valuation' questionnaires have been administered to determine how much people would be prepared to pay for their continued existence. The object of these measurements is to establish the 'total economic value' of an environmental feature, based on willingness and ability to pay, as a guide to determining what taxes or subsidies are needed.

CASE STUDY 9.3
Control of carbon dioxide emissions

Since international agreement was reached in 1992 on the stabilization by developed countries of greenhouse gas emissions, attention has focussed on how effective control might be achieved.

The European Commission has proposed an EU-wide energy tax, weighted according to the carbon content of the fuel, to be introduced at the equivalent of $3 per barrel of oil, rising to $10 per barrel by the year 2000. To avoid damaging trade effects, energy-intensive industries like chemicals might be exempted until other OECD countries introduced a similar tax.

From the standpoint of neo-classical economic theory, the advantage of the proposed tax is that it would provide a direct stimulus to producers and consumers alike to cut down on their use of fossil fuels (the main source of carbon dioxide emissions), by switching to less polluting fuel sources or by conserving energy. The disadvantage is rising costs, which would result in some loss of jobs and negative trade effects, and which would have a regressive effect on the living standards of the poor.

The balance of advantage and disadvantage from a carbon and energy tax would vary from country to country, depending on how individuals and firms respond to changed price structures, and on patterns of trade. In Britain's case, a predominance of short-term financial calculations, as identified in Chapter 7, would discourage firms from making the necessary investments, while further shifts from coal to gas would bring about negative trade effects when North Sea reserves run out.

Uncertainty about the extent to which a carbon and energy tax would affect quantities of carbon dioxide emissions has led some economists to favour tradeable permits as an alternative economic instrument. International regulators would set emission targets, and sell permits to allow firms to emit carbon dioxide, leaving the price to be determined by market forces. Such a scheme, it is suggested, would ensure that quantity targets are met, while using market forces as an allocative mechanism. Many non-economists are sceptical, however, of the feasibility of establishing a tradeable permit scheme on an international scale.

An alternative approach would focus more on tackling the barriers to changed producer and consumer behaviour. A package of regulations and incentives could be devised to encourage investment in energy-saving products and processes, for example – some of the implications of such an approach for domestic electrical appliances are explored in Case Study 9.4. More emphasis could be given, also, to funding research into ways of improving the utilization of Britain's energy reserves –

particularly the development of 'renewable' energy sources such as wind and wave power.

Further reading
Leggett (1990), Chapters 8–14;
Pearce *et al.* (1991), Chapters 2–3;
Helm (ed.) (1991), Chapters 3, 4, 10;
Neale (1994).

Governments have until recently made little use of the fiscal system in environmental protection. Where differential taxation has been used to influence demand patterns (as with unleaded petrol), it has usually been based on rough calculations of demand elasticity, rather than on precise measurements of total economic value. Practical applications of hedonic pricing and contingent valuation techniques have largely been confined to project appraisal (see Key Concept 9.3).

The main problem with relying on fiscal incentives to solve environmental problems is that different firms and consumers will respond in different ways to the changed price signals. For firms, organizational structure and institutional context are key intervening variables. If, in large firms, branch managers have to obtain head office clearance to finance the installation of major pollution control devices or energy-efficient motors, they may prefer instead to pay higher charges and 'hide' them within current cost budgets, particularly if the payback period is more than three years. Similar outcomes may result when small firms are unwilling to seek external funds to finance the necessary capital expenditure, because of high interest rates, for example.

For consumers, too, investment costs are an important consideration. Many householders are reluctant to instal effective insulation or to purchase energy efficient appliances, for example, because they are unwilling to pay the initial cost, even though they would benefit financially in the long run (see Case Study 9.4).

CASE STUDY 9.4
The energy efficiency of domestic electrical appliances

Use of domestic electrical appliances (washing machines, fridges, etc.) accounts for a fifth of total UK electricity sales, and for a fifteenth of UK end-user carbon dioxide emissions. There are enormous differences in energy efficiency between different products – a 1990 government report calculated that 40% energy savings could be achieved if all existing appliances were replaced by the most efficient products currently sold in the UK market, while 60% savings could be achieved after new product development resulting from current research.

Energy-efficient appliances usually cost more to produce than standard appliances, and many (but not all) of them command a premium price. Savings in running costs can be considerable, however, and in most cases payback is achieved within four years.

Why, if consumers would benefit so much from reduced running costs, do so few of them buy energy-efficient appliances? A major reason is lack of information – few British consumers know the running costs of the appliances they purchase, and retailers often gear their promotion to 'bargains' in terms of purchase price. Even where running costs are known, current characteristic-filtering processes (see Key Concept 1.2) usually weight initial cost and other design features above energy efficiency.

British government policies in this field have hitherto focussed on voluntary schemes to encourage improved appliance labelling, and publicity campaigns to exhort consumers to buy energy-efficient products. The effectiveness of these policies has been limited. The proposed carbon and energy tax (see Case Study 9.3) would reduce the payback period, but would not tackle the problem of initial cost differences. Much more significant reductions in electricity consumption have been achieved in countries like the US, which outlaw the most inefficient appliances and subsidize the initial cost of the most efficient, and pressures are mounting for similar policies to be adopted in the EU.

In European markets for domestic electrical appliances, UK products tend to have lower energy efficiency ratings than their German and Scandinavian rivals. Lax standards may at present be protecting UK firms in their home market, but rising standards in the future will leave them increasingly exposed unless they can improve the energy efficiency of their products. The problem, in many cases, is one of market limitation and financial constraint – poor sales performance, low levels of profitability, and fear of takeover, make many UK firms in this sector unwilling to make the investments which are needed to meet new energy conservation standards.

Further reading
Leggett (1990), Chapter 10;
Energy Efficiency Office (1990);
Consumers Association (1991).

Concern that pollution taxes may not in practice bring about the desired quantity changes has led some economists to favour instead a tradeable permit system. Here, a central regulator sets a target for emissions of a key pollutant, and issues permits allowing firms to produce a specified quantity of the pollutant, to a total value not greater than the target. These permits can then be traded, so that new entrants can bid for permits from existing firms, and firms which develop new pollution control technologies are rewarded by being able to sell credits to firms which stick with existing technology. Such a scheme is currently being implemented in the USA for emissions from power stations of sulphur dioxide, the main cause of acid rain. It is, as yet, too early to judge how effective the tradeable permit scheme is in practice, and many observers doubt the feasibility of applying it to pollutants which have many different sources.

Perhaps the main lesson with regard to implementation is that there is no single 'best' solution. As Judith Rees has put it:

No one pollution control strategy can provide a blanket solution to all environmental control problems. The most cost-effective method of achieving particular environmental quality objectives will vary from pollutant to pollutant, and from one receiving medium to another. In addition, the political acceptability of different mechanisms will vary over space and time, reflecting changing notions of distributive equity and the balance of power in the economy.

Rees, 1990

Environmental auditing

For some time now, many firms, particularly in the US, have been conducting internal audits to monitor their compliance with environmental regulations. More recently, it has become fashionable for large British companies to publish glossy reports on recycled paper to explain how environmentally friendly they are. As yet, most such reports have been little more than PR exercises.

Now pressure is growing from environmental groups for firms to periodically assess their environmental performance, to have this assessment checked by independent auditors, and to publish the findings. Just as firms have obligations to shareholders over how they use financial capital, it is suggested, so they should have obligations to the planet and its citizens over how they use environmental capital. The CBI and the UK government have supported the development of environmental auditing as an internal management tool, but are opposed to mandatory external reporting, which they see as unwarranted outside interference.

In 1990, the European Commission announced proposals for annual mandatory environmental audits, externally verified for the most environmentally sensitive operations. Opposition from business interests was intense, and in 1992 the Commissioners published a revised 'eco-management and audit' scheme, to take effect from 1994. Relevant firms will be invited (but not required) to participate in an eco-audit, within which they would report every one to three years on their failings as well as their achievements. The revised scheme is a much diluted version of the original proposal, and without legislative backing it is difficult to see it resulting in much improvement in public accountability.

Project appraisal

As we saw in Chapter 3, it has become increasingly common in recent years for firms to use net present value (NPV) calculations as a basis for their investment decision-making. Such calculations consider only those costs and returns accruing to the firm, and ignore externalities. In the public sector, project appraisal often involves some form of cost benefit analysis (see Key Concept 9.3), which extends the methodology of NPV to incorporate external costs and benefits. In addition, EU legislation now requires an environmental assessment of all major projects, public or private, in environmentally sensitive sectors.

KEY CONCEPT 9.3
Cost benefit analysis

Cost benefit analysis is a form of project appraisal which enumerates and evaluates all relevant costs and benefits – i.e. including externalities as well as private costs and revenues. As far as is possible a monetary value is attached to each cost and benefit – thus if a new underground railway line reduces travel times for road users, saved working time could be valued in terms of average gross hourly earnings, and increased leisure time in relation to net earnings. All costs and benefits are dated, and costs and benefits accruing in the future are discounted back to present values (or values at the start of the project) by use of an appropriate discount rate. The basic decision rule is that a project should go ahead only if total (discounted) benefits exceed total (discounted) costs, though the actual decision will depend on other factors as well (for example, political feasibility or financial constraints).

There are three elements of cost benefit analysis which pose particular problems for decision-makers.

1   *The monetary valuation of non-market exchanges and the treatment of risk and uncertainty.* There is necessarily a subjective element in the monetary valuation of, for example, travel time or noise. This becomes particularly contentious in the case of loss of life or loss of biodiversity. In addition, many outcomes of projects are difficult to predict accurately. Cost benefit analysts need to be aware of these issues, and show how sensitive their results are to alternative evaluations, rather than just present single point estimates of values.

2   *Distribution effects.* Most cost benefit studies merely compare aggregate benefits and costs, and ignore how these benefits and costs are distributed between different sections of the population. For many projects, however, distribution issues may be crucial. A project may, for example, have positive net discounted benefits, but worsen the position of people who are already disadvantaged. It would be preferable if analysts gave some indication of the incidence of costs and benefits, as well as the aggregate picture.

3   *Choice of discount rate.* In Britain, government agencies using cost benefit analysis have to use a 'test discount rate', set at the average rate of return on private sector investment. This has the virtue of ensuring some consistency between private and public sector projects, but it means that benefits or costs occurring far in the future are given low weighting. For certain projects, long-term environmental impacts may be irreversible, reducing the options for future generations. If we place a positive value on the welfare of those generations, then this implies that a lower discount rate should be considered.

Further reading
Pearce (1983);
Colvin (1985);
Levacic (1987), Chapter 10;
Jacobs (1991), Chapters 16–17;
Swift (1992).

Cost benefit analysis (CBA)

Cost benefit analysis originated with the evaluation of water projects in the USA in the 1930s. The outputs of these projects (irrigation, flood control, etc.) could readily be quantified in terms of money, and CBA was a useful way of taking into account wider benefits which were not reflected in the revenues of the water authorities.

By the late 1960s, CBA was widely used by UK government departments to review public expenditure plans, but there was some reluctance to incorporate environmental variables. The Department of Transport, for example, developed a standard computer package (COBA) to evaluate new trunk roads. Using this package, monetary values are assigned to user benefits (mainly savings in travel time, but also reductions in vehicle operating costs and accidents). These are then discounted back to present values, and related to construction costs. For many years, the Department preferred to treat environmental impacts in a separate, physically based, assessment. In 1992, however, its advisors recommended that money valuations should where possible be assigned to environmental impacts, to facilitate comparison with the financial appraisal produced by COBA.

Perhaps the most contentious issues in applying CBA to environmental problems involve risk assessment and inter-generational equity. When we interfere with natural ecology, there is often a risk of severe environmental damage. The threshold between 'acceptable' and 'unacceptable' risk is a matter of value judgement, and the human costs are often paid by generations as yet unborn, whose interests are literally 'discounted' in conventional CBA (see Case Study 9.5).

Many electricity suppliers, worried about the cost of cleaning up emissions from coal-fired power stations have embarked on a policy of meeting increases in demand from nuclear fission reactors. Compared with coal-fired power stations, nuclear plants have low operating costs, but high initial construction costs, and high decommissioning costs at the end of their useful life. Environmentally, nuclear power poses special dangers. Uranium mines and nuclear plants emit low-level radiation on a regular basis, while at the end of the nuclear fuel cycle radioactive wastes have to be stored securely for hundreds of thousands of years. In addition, there are the risks of high-level accidental discharge (as at Chernobyl in 1986), and of encouraging the proliferation of nuclear weapons.

In England and Wales, electricity in the 1980s was supplied by a single nationalized industry, the Central Electricity Generating Board (CEGB), which was committed to the expansion of nuclear power. The CEGB, in calculating the costs of new plant, estimated for the expected lifetime of the plant capital charges (excluding research costs borne by the Atomic Energy Authority), fuel costs, and other operating costs (including, for a nuclear plant, reprocessing costs and those decommissioning costs incurred soon after the end of its life). These costs were discounted to present values at the government's test discount rate (currently 5%), and compared with any savings which the new plant would bring to overall system costs (by allowing older, less efficient plant to be retired early, for example). This produced a 'net effective cost', expressed in £ per kW per year.

CASE STUDY 9.5
Costing nuclear power

Critics of the CEGB's costings claimed that they were systematically biased to present nuclear power in a favourable light. In particular, many observers considered that CEGB figures underestimated the actual construction costs of nuclear plant, overestimated likely future coal costs, and failed to include the costs of actually dismantling the reactor (which are considerable, but which need not be incurred until several decades after it is shut down).

Health and environmental risks did not feature directly in the CEGB's cost analysis, but were covered by the safety standards it works to. Critics claimed that these standards were not sufficiently stringent for nuclear plant, citing the following examples.

1   The policy of setting radiation standards 'as low as reasonably achievable', where recent findings on the health hazards of low-level radiation would suggest a more stringent absolute safety requirement.
2   The policy of the Nuclear Installations Inspectorate to recommend improvements only when they cost less than £150 000 per expected life saved. (This contrasts with survey results based on people's willingness to pay for improvements in safety while travelling, which imply a value of around £2 million per life saved.)
3   The lack of allowance for human error in the CEGB's low assessment of the risks of nuclear accidents, despite the significant role this factor has played in most major nuclear accidents.

In the light of these deficiencies, some economists have suggested that the advantages and disadvantages of nuclear power could be adequately assessed only by a full cost benefit analysis. Because of the significance of uncertain, long-term effects, however, assumptions about risks and the appropriate discount rate would be critical. As one cost benefit analyst has noted, if an accident involving nuclear waste takes place in 500 years time, at a cost of £10 billion in today's prices, and this is discounted at 5%, the present value of the accident works out at only 26 pence (Pearce, 1983).

An additional complication occurs in countries, where nuclear power generation is privately funded. As we saw in Chapter 6, private capital markets often take a short-term view of investment opportunities. Where initial costs are high, and the investment is perceived to be risky, as is the case with nuclear power generation, potential shareholders will require an above-average return on their capital, which will have the effect of pushing up the cost of electricity generated by nuclear power.

This was an important issue in the UK government's 1988 decision to privatize electricity supply, and to create duopolistic competition by splitting the CEGB's assets between two private companies, National Power and PowerGen. Under the government's original proposals, PowerGen, the smaller company, would be nuclear-free, but National Power would have taken over the CEGB's nuclear plants. As City analysts became aware of the potential costs of plant decommission and of insuring against nuclear accident, however, it became clear that potential National Power shareholders would be unwilling to take on the risks.

In 1989 the government announced that the nuclear plants would not be privatized, but transferred to a new public sector enterprise, Nuclear Electric. Although the main objective of the government's change of heart was to save the rest of the privatization programme, it had the effect of halting the expansion of nuclear power in Britain. A 'nuclear levy' was imposed on the electricity suppliers to help fund 'unavoidable' costs of decommissioning plant, waste disposal, and reprocessing, but, even taking this into account, Nuclear Electric's liabilities far outweighed its assets.

Further reading
Jeffery (1987);
Marin (1988);
Pearce (1988);
Yarrow (1988);
Burton and Haslam (1989);
Bailey (1991).

The discounting issue has become particularly significant when agencies attempt to integrate sustainability considerations into the appraisal of development projects. Some writers argue that agencies should retain conventional discount rates, but impose sustainability constraints at the programme level to ensure that there is no net destruction of environmental capital (so that development programmes which involve deforestation, for example, would be required to include the planting of an equivalent area of new forest elsewhere). Others suggest that it is unethical to discount the wellbeing of future generations, and that zero discount rates should be applied to irreversible environmental changes like global warming (Pearce, 1989; Broome, 1992).

Environmental Assessment (EA)

Environmental Assessment (sometimes called Environmental Impact Assessment) is a newer technique for evaluating the likely environmental impacts of developments. EA doesn't attempt to reduce all environmental impacts to a single monetary measure, but leaves the work of comparison to the decision-maker. Under an EC directive which came into effect in 1988, EA is required for certain categories of major development, such as motorways, power stations, and oil refineries. It is the developer's responsibility to commission an assessment of likely environmental impacts, and this is submitted alongside the planning application (if required), to be taken into account in deciding whether or not the development should be allowed to go ahead.

EA has the potential to improve the quality of decision-making in relation to development projects, but early experience in the UK has been disappointing. Many EA statements are of low quality, and as yet few planning authorities have the expertise to effectively supervise the procedure. There is concern, too, that in sectors like transport, piecemeal assessments of individual motorway projects take no account of the cumulative environmental impact of the motorway programme as a whole.

Business responses

Business managers often perceive demands for better environmental performance as a threat to be resisted. This is because environmental improvements often require new investment, the finance of which has a depressing effect on short-term profits. In the long term, however, many firms are beginning to recognize that environmentalism can create opportunities as well as threats, and that meeting higher environmental standards might improve their market as well as their environmental performance.

The opportunities which greater environmental awareness can bring for business take three main forms: better resource management, gains from product redesign, and expanded markets for clean technologies.

- *Better resource management*. When there is a significant increase in the price of a natural resource, or when pollution control standards rise, businesses have to re-examine the ways they use natural resources, and this can often result in significant improvements in the efficiency of resource use. An early example of this is provided by the alkali (sodium carbonate) works of nineteenth century Britain, which used a process which released huge quantities of hydrochloric acid into the atmosphere. Such were the destructive effects of this pollution, particularly for agriculture, that as early as 1863 an Alkali Act was passed, requiring manufacturers to condense 95% of their emissions. What the manufacturers then discovered was that the hydrochloric acid which they had been disposing as a noxious pollutant could be used to make bleach – a product whose commercial potential was even greater than alkali itself! More recently, many businesses have been forced by the oil price rises of the 1970s to reassess their fuel requirements, and have found considerable scope for reducing resource use through energy conservation and heat recovery systems. Increased raw material prices, too, have encouraged producers to recycle a higher proportion of waste products.

  The Pollution Prevention Pays programme adopted by 3M (see Case Study 9.6) is a good recent example of a firm consciously seeking financial rewards from the better management of environmental resources.

CASE STUDY 9.6
3M

3M, best known in the UK as the manufacturers of Scotch tape, has been widely admired for its record in product innovation. It was also the first transnational corporation to set waste reduction targets for its operations throughout the world.

Instead of relying exclusively on end-of-pipe control equipment, in the 1970s 3M adopted a Pollution Prevention Pays (3P) programme to cut pollution at source. This focussed attention on product reformulation, equipment redesign, process modification, and recovery of waste products for reuse. Such innovations, 3M stressed, would not only reduce environmental damage but save the company money through reduction of waste.

As a result of the 3P programme, waste per unit of output from 3M's plants fell, but high output growth meant that absolute amounts of waste continued to increase. In 1989 the company, threatened by tighter environmental regulations in the USA, moved beyond the cost-saving emphasis of 3P to adopt a wider-ranging Pollution

Prevention Plus (3P+) programme. Under 3P+, 3M committed itself to a 90% cut in hazardous air emissions by 2000, and to increased R. & D. expenditure to help meet this goal.

In 1992, 3M (UK) published a report to monitor its environmental performance. The record was not particularly encouraging – waste production per unit of output at 3M's UK plants fell by 1% in 1991 (against a target cut of 7%), while energy consumption at most sites increased (instead of a target reduction of 3%). The company's willingness to expose its failures to meet targets does, however, indicate a seriousness about improving environmental performance which contrasts with that of most manufacturing companies.

Further reading
Elkington and Burke (1987), Chapter 9;
ENDS reports nos 174 (July 1989) and 215 (December 1992).

- *Product redesign*. Significant gains can be made by businesses who redesign their products to meet the raised environmental concerns of consumers. In 1983, for example, the Kenyan Renewable Energy Development Project designed a clay-lined stove which could be made by local workers using local materials, and which burned a third less charcoal than traditional stoves made from scrap metal. This increased fuel efficiency brought running costs down to such an extent that the purchase cost of the new stoves could be recovered in two months, and total sales of the new stoves reached 180 000 within two years (Harrison, 1987; Opole, 1988). In developed countries, micro-electronic control devices are being introduced which can have equally dramatic effects on the fuel-efficiency, and thus running costs, of cars and central heating systems. New houses, too, are being designed to reduce energy consumption by incorporating low-conductivity insulation and utilizing passive solar heat.

Consumers are not just interested in resource-saving when it reduces their bills, and some businesses have discovered that there are considerable profits to be made from appealing to the environmental awareness of their customers. Perhaps the most dramatic example of this in Britain is The Body Shop, a cosmetics retailer which grew in its first decade from one small shop in Brighton to 230 shops (two thirds of them overseas), doubling its turnover each year. Financially, The Body Shop is one of the most successful businesses in Britain, but from the start it emphasized environmental values, concentrating on vegetable products, tested without cruelty to animals and sold in refillable containers.

In the long term, the biggest gains are likely to involve firms which can successfully innovate new mass market products which reduce fossil fuel consumption and therefore help contribute to carbon dioxide reduction targets. As more stringent controls are adopted, firms which have effectively targeted R. & D. in this direction will reap financial benefits (see, for example, Case Studies 9.2 on cars, and 9.4 on domestic appliances).

- *Expanded markets for clean technologies.* In an era when popular demands for a better environment are being translated into tougher emission standards, there are big market opportunities for businesses which can provide cleaner products and processes – businesses like Johnson Matthey Chemicals (who make catalytic converters for car exhausts), Davy McKee (who make flue gas desulphurization equipment for reducing sulphur dioxide emissions from power stations), Bio-Technica (who have developed a method of using microbes to biodegrade toxic chemicals on contaminated land), and Vertical Axis Wind Turbines (who have pioneered wind generators with inclined blades to control the power output). British firms such as these have, however, found that their capacity to compete effectively in export markets has been hampered by a lack of domestic demand for their products. Firms based in countries where pollution controls are tight, on the other hand, have been encouraged to develop more advanced techniques, placing them at a competitive advantage in export markets.

Although there are, in general, opportunities as well as threats for business in a more environmentally conscious world, there is a danger that UK firms, because of the problems we have identified in earlier chapters, may not be able to take advantage of them. We have seen in Chapter 7, for example, how the pervasive influence of short-term financial calculations in the UK makes managers prefer short-term profits to long-term development. This can create an unwillingness to invest in the new products and new processes which are the preconditions for constructive business responses to environmental challenges.

Conclusion

In an unregulated market, there is little incentive for firms to consider the negative impact of their activities on the natural environment, and the resulting pattern of development is often not ecologically sustainable. One suggestion which is frequently made by economists is that governments should make firms consider their environmental impact by modifying prices so that they reflect externalities as well as private costs and benefits. This solution is not always practical, however, and political demands for better environmental quality have usually resulted in a framework of controls within which business has to operate. These demands have intensified in recent years as a result of increased awareness of world environmental problems such as global warming.

Environmental controls are often resisted by firms which adopt a short-term approach. Recent experience suggests, however, that some firms which have a longer time horizon can come to perceive environmental controls more as an opportunity than as a threat, and that countries which operate lax controls may suffer in terms of trade as well as environmentally.

Further reading

Environmental Economics: an Elementary Introduction, by Kerry Turner, David Pearce, and Ian Bateman (Harvester Wheatsheaf, 1994) provides a good textbook introduction to neo-classical environmental economics. For a multi-disciplinary view, try the second edition of Judith Rees's *Natural Resources: Allocation, Economics and Policy* (Methuen, 1990).

Michael Jacobs's *The Green Economy* (Pluto, 1991) and Hazel Henderson's *Paradigms in Progress: Life beyond Economics* (Adamantine, 1993) are more critical of the neo-classical approach, from explicitly 'green' perspectives.

Environmental Management and Business Strategy, by Richard Welford and Andrew Gouldson (Pitman, 1993) focusses on the relationship between environmental legislation and business strategy.

ENDS, the monthly report from Environmental Data Services, is an invaluable monitor of those environmental issues which are most relevant to business.

Exercises

1 If governments were to auction resource depletion rights, as Daly suggests, what would be the effects on

   (a) Resource prices?
   (b) Resource conservation and recycling?
   (c) Consumer prices?
   (d) The pattern of aggregate output of goods and services?

2 Assess the advantages and disadvantages of taxes and emission standards as methods of controlling pollution.

3 Why do you think some European car manufacturers are arguing that lenient emission control standards in the EC are hampering their efforts to expand export sales in the USA and Japan?

4 You represent a Central American government which has been approached by a US-based firm for permission to chop down some of your tropical rainforest in order to ranch cattle. You know that the prospects for earning dollars from exporting beef to hamburger chains are good, but you are worried about the effects on forest dwellers, and about possible climatic changes which will reduce water supplies for local agriculture.

   How might economic analysis help in coming to a decision as to whether or not to grant permission?

5 Only two thirds of owners of central heating systems have space temperature controls, even though installing a suitable device can often pay for itself in reduced fuel bills within a couple of years.

   (a) Why do you think this might be the case?
   (b) What alternatives might a government concerned to improve energy conservation consider to remedy this situation?

6   To what extent do the marketing, production, and financial calculations of UK firms hamper their ability to respond constructively to environmental challenges?

References

Aage, H. (1984) Economic arguments on the sufficiency of natural resources. *Cambridge Journal of Economics*, March.

Bailey, R. (1991) Energy policy in confusion, *National Westminster Bank Quarterly Review*, Feb.

Beckerman, W. (1974) *In Defence of Economic Growth*, Jonathan Cape, London.

Burton, W.R. and Haslam, C. (1989) *Power, Pollution and Politics*, Croom Helm, London.

Carson, R. (1962) *Silent Spring*, Houghton Mifflin, Boston, Mass.

Colvin, P. (1985) *The Economic Ideal in British Government*, Manchester University Press, Manchester.

Consumers Association (1991) Appliance energy use, *Which?*, March.

Daly, H. (1992) *Steady-State Economics*, 2nd edn, Earthscan, London.

Elkington, J. and Burke, T. (1987) *The Green Capitalists*, Gollancz, London.

Energy Efficiency Office (1990) *Energy efficiency of domestic electrical appliances*, HMSO, London.

Graf, W. (1992) Sustainable ideologies and interests. *Third World Quarterly*, **13**, no. 3.

Harrison, P. (1987) *The Greening of Africa*, Paladin, London (also extracted in *New Scientist*, 28 May, 1987).

Helm, D. (ed.) (1991) *Economic Policy towards the Environment*, Blackwell, Oxford.

Jacobs, M. (1991) *The Green Economy*, Pluto, London.

Jeffery, J.W. (1987) The Sizewell Report: a foregone conclusion. *Ecologist*, **17** (2).

Kay, J. and Mirrlees, J. (1975) The desirability of natural resource depletion. In *The Economics of Natural Resource Depletion* Pearce D.W. and Rose J. (eds.), Macmillan, London.

Levacic, R. (1987) *Economic Policy Making*, Wheatsheaf Books, Brighton.

Leggett, J. (ed.) (1990) *Global Warming: the Greenpeace Report*, OUP, Oxford.

Longhurst, J. (1989) Auto catalysts and motor vehicle emission control, *Clean Air*, vol. 19, no. 1.

Marin, A. (1988) The cost of avoiding death: nuclear power, regulation and spending on safety. *Royal Bank of Scotland Review*, March.

Mill, J.S. (1965) *Collected Works*, vol. 3, University of Toronto Press, Toronto.

Neale, A. (1994) Climate stability and behavioural change, *Journal of Environmental Management and Planning*, forthcoming.

Opole, M. (1988) The introduction of the Kenyan jiko stove. In Carr M. (ed.) *Sustainable Industrial Development*, Intermediate Technology Publications, London.

Pearce, D. (1983) *Cost Benefit Analysis*, 2nd edn, Macmillan, London.

Pearce, D. (1988) The social appraisal of nuclear power. *Economic Review*, March.

Pearce, D. *et al.* (1989) *Blueprint for a Green Economy*, Earthscan, London.

Pearce, D. *et al.* (1991) *Blueprint 2*, Earthscan, London.

Pearce, D. (1993) *Blueprint 3*, Earthscan, London.

Pigou, A.C. (1920) *Economics of Welfare*, Macmillan, London.

Rees, J. (1990) *Natural Resources: Allocation, Economics and Policy*, 2nd edn, Methuen, London.

Swift, S. (1992) The SACTRA Report: assessing the environmental impacts of road schemes, *British Economic Survey*, vol. 22, no. 2, Autumn.

Whitelegg, J. (1993) *Transport for a Sustainable Future: the Case for Europe*, Belhaven, London.

World Commission on Environment and Development (1987) *Our Common Future* (the Brundtland report), Oxford University Press, Oxford.

Yarrow, G. (1988) The price of nuclear power. *Economic Policy*, April.

Government economic policies   10

This chapter contrasts Keynesian approaches to macro-economic policy (emphasizing demand management to achieve full employment) with monetarist ones (emphasizing monetary controls to achieve price stability). The limitations of each approach are illustrated in relation to post-war UK experience. Government industrial policy has been a crucial ingredient of economic success in some other countries, but the effectiveness of its adoption by the UK would be limited by the 'hollowing-out' process which has taken place in recent years.

Introduction

One of the most important agents in the environmental context of business is the state, and in this final chapter we look at the influence of government economic policies on business. We start with macro-economic policies, which attempt to influence the overall levels of output, employment, and inflation in the economy. We record the shifts which have occurred over the years from Keynesian policies, emphasizing demand management to bring about full employment, to monetarist policies, emphasizing monetary controls to curb inflation. The chapter ends with a look at industrial policy, contrasting the *ad hoc* approaches which have been adopted in the UK with the more strategic approaches which have been developed in countries like France and Japan. What is stressed is the limited effectiveness of macro-economic policy (Keynesian or monetarist) and of conventional industrial policies in improving economic performance in an economy characterized by massive trade deficits and 'hollowing out'.

Keynesian theory

Before Keynes, neo-classical economists assumed that market forces would guarantee the full employment of all resources, including labour. They argued that if there were more people looking for jobs than there were jobs available, wages would fall, raising profits and encouraging employers to take on more labour. In the long run, wage flexibility would have the effect of eliminating involuntary unemployment. Within this perspective, if unemployment persisted, it could only be as a result of the actions of trade unions in resisting wage cuts.

In his *General Theory of Employment, Interest and Money*, written at the end of the great slump (1936), Keynes rejected the neo-classical assumption that market forces would ensure full employment (Key Concept 6.1). He was mindful of the political infeasibility of massive wage cuts at a time of mass unemployment, but he pointed out that even if wages did fall, full employment could not be guaranteed. Prices, for example, might fall in line with money wages, leaving real wages at their previous level. In this case, there would be no reason for employers to take on more labour.

In addition, even if real wages did fall, employment would rise only if the positive effects for firms on labour costs outweighed the negative effects on product demand. An inverse relationship between wages and jobs might apply at the level of individual firms. Such a relationship would depend on product demand being unaffected by a change in wages – a legitimate assumption at the micro-economic level, where employees of a firm account for only a minute proportion of demand for its products. At the macro-economic level, however (the level of the economy as a whole), a fall in wages would result in a decline in consumption expenditure, and thus a decline in aggregate demand (Key Concept 10.1) for output and labour. Wage cuts, which might create jobs at the micro level, could destroy them at the macro level.

In place of the neo-classical emphasis on self-clearing markets, Keynes argued that output, and thus jobs, were determined by the level of effective demand (Key Concept 10.1). The main components of effective demand behaved independently of each other, and there was no reason to suppose that they would interact in such a way as to guarantee full employment. To understand what, in Keynes's theory, determines the level of employment, we need to examine the two main components of effective demand, consumption expenditure by households and investment expenditure by firms.

KEY CONCEPT 10.1
Aggregate and effective demand

Aggregate demand (sometimes called aggregate expenditure) is a schedule which shows how the volume of expenditure in an economy varies with the level of income. Effective demand is a point on this schedule which represents the actual value at a particular time of the sales which firms anticipate.

There are four components of aggregate demand – consumption expenditure on domestic products by households (C), investment expenditure by firms (I), government expenditure (G), and net exports, or exports minus imports (X − M). In the diagrams below, we assume that I, G, and X are autonomous (i.e. they are determined independently of current domestic income), but that C and M increase as domestic income increases.

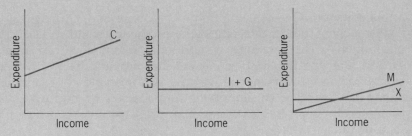

Figure 10.1   Components of aggregate demand.

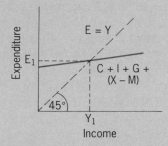

Figure 10.2   A simplified aggregate demand schedule.

A simplified aggregate demand schedule, made up from these components, is shown in Figure 10.2. Adding I and G to C shifts the aggregate demand schedule upwards, while adding net exports changes its slope as well. Expenditure on imports increases with domestic income, so the slope of the open economy aggregate demand schedule (AD) is flatter than that of the domestic consumption schedule (C).

The 45° line E = Y shows the amount of expenditure which is needed to sustain a given level of income, so the point where AD intersects this line, at an effective demand of E_1, represents an 'equilibrium' national income of Y_1. As Keynes emphasized, there is no guarantee that this 'equilibrium' will be sufficient to guarantee full employment.

Consumption expenditure

For most of the General Theory, Keynes assumed a closed economy, ignoring the distinction between consumption of domestic products and expenditure on imports. He suggested that current income is the main determinant of consumption, and postulated a 'fundamental psychological law' that as incomes rise, consumption rises, but by less than the rise in income. Post-war experience in the UK, at least up to the early 1980s, confirmed that the average propensity to consume (Key Concept 10.2) tended to decline as incomes rose over time.

Algebraically, the consumption function can be represented as an equation of the form

$$C = a + bY_D$$

In this equation, C is consumption expenditure and Y_D personal disposable income (personal incomes less income taxes and social security contributions). The parameter a represents autonomous consumption demand (demand unrelated to current income), and its positive value reflects the fact the many individuals will respond to a decline in income by financing consumption from savings or borrowing. The parameter b represents the marginal propensity to consume (Key Concept 10.2).

KEY CONCEPT 10.2
Average and marginal propensity to consume

Average propensity to consume (apc) is total consumption expenditure as a proportion of total personal disposable income (C/Y_D), while marginal propensity to consume (mpc) is the proportion of a change in income which is consumed ($\Delta C/\Delta Y_D$ – the slope of the consumption function depicted in the first diagram in Figure 10.1).

In the 1950s, 1960s, and 1970s, mpc varied considerably from year to year, but the long-run average value was fairly stable, at 0.78 in constant prices (revaluing the expenditure and income figures by an index of consumer prices to remove the effects of inflation, as described in Key Concept 10.5). As real incomes rose over this period, apc fell, reaching a low point of 0.87 in 1980.

In the 1980s, there was a significant change in this pattern. From 1980 to 1982, real consumers' expenditure continued to rise, even though real personal disposable income was falling in the recession. Then from 1984 to 1988, as personal disposable incomes recovered, consumers' expenditure rose at a much faster rate, with real values of mpc consistently greater than unity. By 1988, apc, at 0.94, was higher than it had been for almost three decades. Only after 1988 was the long-term falling tendency of apc re-established.

Average and marginal propensities to consume in selected post-war years (£ billion, 1985 prices)

Year	C	Y_D	ΔC	ΔY_D	apc (C/Y)	mpc ($\Delta C/\Delta Y$)
1954	103.5	107.2	4.1	3.4	0.97	1.22
1960	123.3	133.0	4.6	8.2	0.93	0.56
1968	151.2	164.1	4.1	2.8	0.92	1.45
1972	171.7	190.0	10.1	14.7	0.91	0.69
1980	195.8	225.9	0.2	3.6	0.87	0.05
1988	264.1	279.7	18.3	15.9	0.94	1.15
1992	269.3	304.4	0.1	6.9	0.88	0.02

Source: Economic Trends.
Note: Personal income in the UK national income accounts includes the incomes of unincorporated businesses, charities, and life assurance and pension funds. For the household sector alone, government estimates suggest that apc exceeded unity in 1986–87.

The marginal propensity to consume tends in practice to be positive and less than one, but on a year-by-year basis it is far less stable in value than Keynes had assumed. In attempting to explain observed fluctuations in marginal propensity to consume, some economists in the 1950s suggested that people attempt to even out fluctuations in their consumption by relating this not to their current income but to their average income in the long run (the permanent income hypothesis). This has the effect of raising marginal propensity to consume when people suffer an unexpected drop in income, and reducing it when people receive an unexpected increase.

More recent experience suggests that other factors, such as changes in asset values and in the availability of credit, may be significant. In times of high inflation, such as 1974–5 and 1979–80, for example, the real value of liquid assets falls, and individuals may try to compensate for this by increasing savings (and thus reducing spending) from current income (Cuthbertson, 1982).

Two inter-related developments in the 1980s, financial deregulation and a house price boom (see Case Study 10.1), significantly affected the consumption behaviour of that period. Financial institutions were eager to lend, while a belief that house prices would continue rising indefinitely encouraged many owner-occupiers to take on extra debts. The result was a credit explosion, and a significant rise in the propensity to consume. Conversely, when house prices crashed, in the early 1990s, many home-owners had to make dramatic cuts in consumption spending to finance their debt repayments.

Home ownership, financed by mortgage lending and encouraged by tax relief, is more common in Britain than in other industrial countries, and house price movements can have profound implications for consumer spending, trade, inflation, and labour mobility.

As the table below shows, UK house prices rose dramatically in the period 1982–89, both in their own right and in relation to consumer prices and earnings, but fell almost as dramatically from 1989 until the end of 1992.

CASE STUDY 10.1
The housing market and the UK macro-economy

Indices of house prices, retail prices, and average earnings in selected quarters (UK, 1st quarter of 1983 = 100)

Quarter	House price index	Retail price index	Av. earnings index	House price/ earnings ratio
1982 Q1	92	95	92	3.2
1983 Q2	100	100	100	3.2
1989 Q3	239	140	166	4.6
1992 Q4	191	168	212	2.9
1993 Q4	196	171	217	2.9

Source: Nationwide Building Society Quarterly House Price Bulletin.

A number of factors came together in the 1980s to create the house price boom, including faster growth of disposable income in the higher income groups and faster population growth in the main house-buying age groups. The key factor, however, was financial deregulation – greater competition between banks and building societies and a relaxation of controls over mortgage lending meant that owner-occupiers could borrow a much greater multiple of their incomes than hitherto. This, coupled with slow rates of house building, caused house prices to rise, and many home-owners were encouraged to 'trade up', and take out a bigger mortgage, enabling them to realize part of their higher asset values. 'Housing equity withdrawal', as this process is technically called, resulted in a massive increase in consumption expenditure, much of which leaked out of the domestic economy in the form of imports. It also stimulated inflationary wage demands in south-east England, while discouraging workers from other regions with lower house prices from moving in to take jobs there.

When, inevitably, the speculative bubble burst in 1989–92, a number of home-owners were faced with a 'negative equity' problem (in that the market price of their property fell below the size of their mortgage) and they had to make drastic cuts in consumption spending to protect their mortgage repayments. This was a major contributory factor in prolonging the 1989–92 recession.

Further reading
Carruth and Henley (1990);
Muellbauer (1992).

Investment expenditure

As we saw in Chapter 7, Keynes followed neo-classical economists in positing an inverse relationship between investment spending by firms and interest rates. Unlike the neo-classicals, however, Keynes was acutely aware of the unstable nature of this relationship. The rates of return businesses expect from their investments are based on their expectations of an uncertain future. These expectations fluctuate, Keynes argued, in response to shifts in the 'animal spirits' of entrepreneurs, which affect their confidence in the future. Investment expenditure by firms thus varies with current interest rates and with future expected demand, but not with current income.

The subjective element which Keynes identified in business predictions has profound consequences for the level of economic activity. Business confidence may remain stable over long periods, but then be shaken by a surprise event such as a collapse in share values brought about by speculative activity. If a decline in confidence depresses investment spending, this will depress aggregate demand and thus output (and profit) levels in the future. Swings in business confidence can thus be self-fulfilling – a decline in business expectations of future profits resulting in a drop in effective demand and thus an actual decline in future profits.

We have seen in Chapter 7 the unusual extent to which UK firms depend on retained profits to finance new investment. This can make slumps in investment spending last longer in the UK than elsewhere. Whereas in countries like Japan and Germany firms have been able to

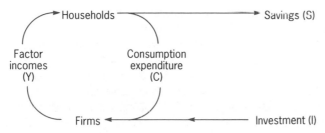

Figure 10.3 The circular flow of income in a closed economy with no government.

rely on a supportive banking system to continue to finance investment through a recession, UK firms often feel they have little alternative but to sit back and wait for demand to recover before they can start investing again.

The circular flow of income

The impact of a change in effective demand on the level of economic activity can be illustrated by a simple model of the macro-economy which focusses on the circular flows of income between firms and households (Figure 10.3).

Imagine a closed economy (where there is no foreign trade) with no government expenditure and no taxes. Households receive incomes from firms (wages and salaries, profits, and rents) in return for the factor services they provide (labour, capital, and land). Some of this income is saved, but most is passed back to firms in the form of consumption expenditure, in return for products. Household savings represent a leakage from the circular flow of income, as they reduce the consumption expenditure which is passed on to firms, and thus the amount of income which can be passed back to households. Firms' receipts are, however, boosted by the investment expenditure of other firms, which constitute an injection into the circular flow.

Before Keynes, neo-classical economists assumed that interest rates would fluctuate to equate savings with investment expenditure, so that income flows could be maintained at a level which corresponded to full employment. Keynes rejected the idea that interest rate changes could be relied upon to perform this market-clearing function, for three main reasons.

Any change in expenditure has a direct effect on income and employment. It also has secondary effects, resulting from the changes in consumption expenditure induced by the change in income. Different multipliers can be calculated for different purposes – the one which is most commonly used in practice is the ratio of total change in national income to the change in expenditure which brought it about.

The size of the multiplier is limited by the extent of leakages from the circular flow of income. For most of his General Theory, Keynes ignored leakages other than savings. In reality, however, part of any increase in expenditure will go on undistributed profits,

KEY CONCEPT 10.3
The multiplier

income and expenditure taxes, and spending on imports, all of which represent significant additional leakages from the circular flow.

If we want to estimate the effect of an increase in expenditure on income and thus jobs within a domestic economy, the key variable is the marginal propensity to purchase new domestic output – the proportion of an increase in expenditure which results in increase in consumption expenditure on domestic products. If there is an initial increase in domestic expenditure of £100 million, and the marginal propensity to purchase new domestic output is 0.25, then the 1st round increase in income is £100 million. Of this £100 million, £25 million (25%) is passed back to domestic firms as increased consumption expenditure. The process continues in successive rounds, as shown below, until a total increase in income of £133.3 million is achieved. The multiplier in this case is 1.33.

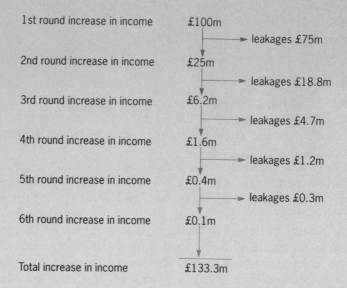

1st round increase in income	£100m
	leakages £75m
2nd round increase in income	£25m
	leakages £18.8m
3rd round increase in income	£6.2m
	leakages £4.7m
4th round increase in income	£1.6m
	leakages £1.2m
5th round increase in income	£0.4m
	leakages £0.3m
6th round increase in income	£0.1m
Total increase in income	£133.3m

A short cut way to calculate the multiplier is to use the formula:

$$\frac{1}{1 - \text{marginal propensity to purchase new domestic output}}$$

Multiplier calculations have to assume stability in the marginal propensities to consume and import. They ignore changing stock levels, and give no indication of the time lags between an injection of expenditure and the ultimate increase in income. They can, therefore, only roughly predict the effect of a change in expenditure on national income.

- Speculative activity in financial markets was an important independent influence on short-run interest rates.
- The general level of interest rates had little influence on the savings decisions of households, which were chiefly income determined.
- Firms' investment decisions were influenced as much by subjectively based predictions of future returns as by current interest rates.

In Keynes's theory, changes in effective demand have a multiplied impact on income, and thus on output and jobs (Key Concept 10.3). In this analysis, it is changes in income, not changes in interest rates, which bring about equilibrium between savings and investment. Suppose an economy is at full employment with a national income (Y) of £1 million, and that the consumption function takes the form C = £100 000 + 0.75Y. Consumption expenditure is £850 000 per year, and savings £150 000. Investment spending (I) then has to be kept at £150 000 per year to maintain national income at the full employment level.

If businesses become pessimistic about future returns, and investment spending falls to £100 000 per year, then firms' receipts will fall by £50 000, and household incomes will fall initially by the same amount. This is not the end of the matter, however, for any reduction in income will induce further reductions in consumption and savings. National income will in fact continue to contract until it reaches a new equilibrium level at £800 000, where savings are again equal to investment at £100 000 per year. Note that in this example a fall in investment spending of £50 000 brings about an eventual fall in national income of £200 000, suggesting a multiplier of four (£200 000 ÷ £50 000).

To make the simplified model of Figure 10.3 more appropriate to the real world, we have to allow for the effects of foreign trade and government, as in Figure 10.4. Receipts from exports and government expenditure count as injections into the circular flow, while expenditures on imports and tax payments constitute leakages.

The additional leakages which result from taking account of the government and foreign trade sectors have the effect of reducing the size of the multiplier. As we have seen in Chapter 1, many UK manufacturing firms have failed in recent years to provide the range of product characteristics that modern consumers demand, and one result of this has been an increased propensity of UK consumers to buy

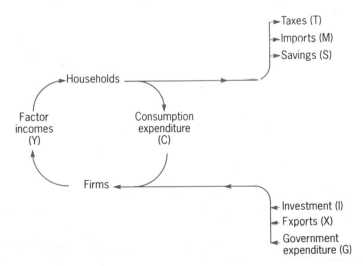

Figure 10.4 The circular flow of income in an open economy with a government.

imported goods. This has played a significant role in reducing the size of the domestic multiplier in the UK, to current levels which are typically below 1.5.

Demand management policies

Keynes's chief aim in the General Theory was to develop a theoretical understanding of why market forces do not guarantee full employment. He did, however, draw clear policy implications from his analysis. His main political conclusion was that if capitalism was to be preserved, governments should make the achievement of full employment a priority policy objective. The most effective instruments of achieving this objective, Keynes argued, would be low interest rates and government controls over investment, to ensure a stable level of investment spending which would be sufficient, together with consumption spending, to guarantee full employment (Keynes, 1936, 1943).

Post-war UK governments followed Keynes in giving priority to the achievement of full employment. They rejected, however, Keynes's suggestions that they should assume greater control over investment spending, preferring instead to use fiscal policy (the relationship between government spending and tax revenues) to influence the level of effective demand.

Consider the circular flow diagram in Figure 10.4. If there is a shortfall in private sector investment spending, so that the economy is working at less than full employment, the government can increase its spending or reduce its taxes. This has the result of boosting effective demand, and returning the economy closer to the full employment level. Initially, as government spending exceeds tax revenues, the government will have to borrow to finance its deficit, but eventually incomes and consumption expenditure will rise, increasing tax revenues again.

The effect of an increase in government expenditure on effective demand and therefore on national income can be analysed with the help of a device we introduced in Key Concept 10.1, the income-expenditure diagram. Figure 10.5, which is based on this diagram, shows an Aggregate Demand schedule AD_1, with an effective demand of E_1 resulting in a national income of Y_1. An increase in government expenditure by ΔG shifts the Aggregate Demand Schedule up from AD_1 to AD_2, which, after the multiplier effect has worked through the economy, increases effective demand from E_1 to E_2 and national income from Y_1 to Y_2.

For two decades after the war, the UK economy, in common with other industrial economies, experienced an economic boom of unprecedented duration. During this period, real GDP grew by about 2.5% per year, and the number of registered unemployed hardly ever exceeded 2% of the labour force. This long boom coincided with the adoption by government of 'Keynesian' demand management policies (involving changes in taxes, public spending, interest rates or credit availability), and it is tempting to see the two phenomena as causally

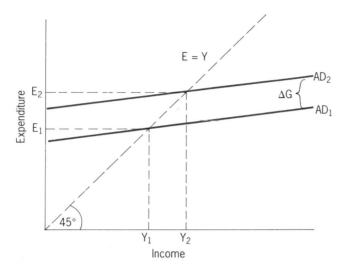

Figure 10.5 The effect of an increase in government expenditure on national income.

related. 'Fine tuning' the economy was an inexact science, however. The economic models used by the Treasury often failed to make adequate allowance for fluctuations in the marginal propensity to consume, for the time needed for multiplier effects to work through the economy, or for the trade effects of boosting aggregate demand. As a result, policy modifications designed to solve one economic problem (increasing unemployment, for example) would create another one (a trade deficit, for example). Governments, too, were tempted to use demand management policies to boost their chances of staying in power – engineering a boom in the run up to an election, for example, and then dealing with adverse balance of payments effects afterwards (or bequeathing them to their successors).

R.C.O. Matthews, in a detailed study of the post-war period (1968), suggested that the long boom was due more to sustained investment in the private sector than to government policy, and that in most years fiscal policy had been used to damp down aggregate demand rather than boost it. It may be, of course, that government commitment to full employment as a policy priority helped to boost business confidence and thus to sustain the boom. Some businesses, however, faced considerable instability in demand for their products as a result of shifts in government policy. Sales of consumer durables like cars, for example, fluctuated considerably with changes in purchase tax or hire purchase regulations. At the level of macro-economic performance too, one study concluded that, far from evening out economic cycles, Treasury policies had exaggerated them, largely because they had underestimated the time lags between changes in policy and their effect on output (Dow, 1964).

The balance of payments constraint and inflation

In the 1950s and 1960s, UK governments were committed to maintain significant exports of capital, which had to be financed by surpluses on the current account of the balance of payments. This was a period of booming international trade, but when internal demand in the UK expanded rapidly, so did imports, shifting the current account from a surplus to a deficit. Governments were also committed to free trade and to a fixed exchange rate, so they were unable to use import controls or devaluation to restore balance of payments equilibrium. In this situation, the only way they could maintain a surplus on the current account after aggregate demand had risen was to use fiscal and monetary policy to deflate aggregate demand (and thus demand for imports) again. One result of this policy stance was a 'stop-go' cycle of economic activity, which, over time, depressed the rate of growth of the UK relative to other industrial economies. As we saw in Chapter 8, import penetration into the UK economy has intensified in recent years, which would make pursuit of Keynesian demand management policies even more problematic. We shall explore this issue further later on in the chapter.

A new problem which emerged in the post-war period was that of permanent inflation (Key Concept 10.4). Before the war, prices would rise in some periods, but fall in others. After the war, there was a continuous rise in the general price level, though this was moderate at first. It seemed to some economists that there was a direct relationship between high levels of effective demand and inflation. A.W. Phillips (1958), for example, studied the historical relationship in Britain between the percentage rate of change in money wages (a measure of wage inflation) and the percentage rate of unemployment (which, in Keynesian theory, is determined primarily by the level of effective demand). The relationship he found (relating to the period 1862–1958) is shown in Figure 10.6.

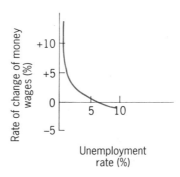

Figure 10.6   The Phillips curve.

KEY CONCEPT 10.4
Inflation and the retail price index

Inflation is a rise in the general level of prices. To measure inflation, we need an index of prices. The index most commonly used in the UK is the Retail Price Index. Each month the Department of Employment notes the prices charged on 600 separate items, chosen to represent the expenditure patterns of most households (excluding older people mainly dependent on state benefits, and households with very high incomes). Each price change is weighted according to the importance of the item in a typical household expenditure budget, and then converted into an index which relates the general price level in the month to a reference date at which the value of the index has been set at 100 (January 1987, for example). Thus if the Retail Price Index in June 1993 is 141.0, this means that retail prices have, on average, risen by 41% since the base month (January 1987).

Annual inflation rates are calculated by working out the percentage change in RPI over the past 12 months. If the RPI went up from 137.2 to 141.0 between June 1992 and June 1993, for example, the annual inflation rate was 1.2%:

$$\frac{141.0 - 137.2}{137.2} \times 100 = 1.2\%$$

Annual inflation rates can be influenced quite significantly by changes in mortgage interest rates, and it has become common for analysts to distinguish between a 'headline' inflation rate, which includes mortgage interest payments, and an 'underlying' rate, which excludes them.

We have already seen, in Key Concept 4.1, how the Retail Price Index can be used as a deflator to convert a nominal series of data into real figures, in order to strip out the effect of inflation. You are recommended to read Chapter 5 of *Quantitative Techniques in a Business Context*, by R. Slater and P. Ascroft (Chapman & Hall, 1990), for more information on the calculation and use of index numbers.

There has, over the post-war period, been little consensus among economists as to either the effects or the causes of inflation. In the 1950s and 1960s, modest inflation tended to be accepted as a lesser evil than that of unemployment, and most worries about inflation centred on its impact on income distribution, and particularly on the living standards of people dependent on fixed incomes. Some economists argued, on the basis of the Phillips curve, that governments could moderate inflation by deflating aggregate demand, and accepting increased unemployment as a consequence. (This is shown in Figure 10.7a by a move from P_1,U_1 to P_2,U_2.) Most 'Keynesian' economists, however, saw inflation as being caused by collective bargaining procedures which encouraged money wages to rise faster than labour productivity, pushing up labour costs. As a result, regulation of growth in money wages would be the most effective counter-inflation policy. A successful incomes policy, they argued, would shift the Phillips curve to the left, enabling inflation to be reduced (from P_1 to P_2 in Figure 10.7b) without any rise in unemployment.

UK experience with incomes policies in the 1960s and 1970s was not very satisfactory. Most incomes policies established a 'norm' for pay

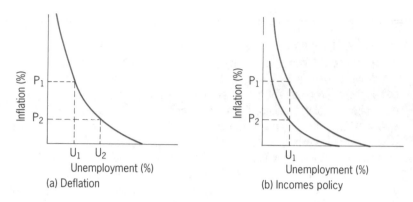

Figure 10.7 Alternative counter-inflation policies.

increases, with some allowance for exceptional increases above the norm in special cases. There was often little consensus on what constituted a special case, however, and incomes policies often broke down because particular groups felt they had been unfairly treated by them. Although the first stages in an incomes policy were often accompanied by a reduction in money wage increases, when the policy broke down a 'catching-up' process often ensued. The end result was that incomes policies had more influence over the timing of pay increases (and thus of inflation) than over their long-term magnitude.

Even more serious for the operation of counter-inflation policy was the breakdown of the Phillips curve relationship in the 1970s. The stable inverse relationship between inflation and unemployment continued until the late 1960s, but then it broke down, with UK retail price increases averaging 13% per year in the 1970s, despite generally rising levels of unemployment.

Keynesian economists continued to focus on factors pushing up production costs as the main source of increased inflation, although they widened their analysis to include changes in world commodity markets, such as the impact of OPEC on oil prices (Kaldor, 1976). This focus on world commodity prices having a major effect on inflation is one for which there is considerable empirical support (Beckerman and Jenkinson, 1986). The policy that was most influential with governments from the late 1970s on was, however, the monetary policy associated with the work of Milton Friedman, and it is to this that we now turn.

Monetarist theory

There are many varieties of monetarist theory in existence. We concentrate here on the version presented by Milton Friedman, because this has been the most influential in terms of UK government policy (though, as we shall see in the next section, Friedman's prescriptions have been considerably modified by the UK government in recent years). Friedman provides a distinctly non-Keynesian perspective on the relationship between inflation and unemployment, based on viewing inflation as an exclusively monetary phenomenon, caused by governments allowing the supply of money to grow faster than output.

Friedman's monetary approach to inflation is an updated version of the eighteenth century Quantity Theory of Money, according to which changes in the stock of money are directly related to changes in the general level of prices. Friedman's approach can be illustrated by the identity:

$$MV \equiv PT$$

(Money supply times the velocity at which it circulates is identical to the price level times the number of transactions. The 3-bar sign $\equiv$ indicates that MV and PT are identical *by definition*, in much the same way as 1000cc $\equiv$ 1 litre.)

Friedman's argument, based on a rather idiosyncratic interpretation of historical data (Friedman and Schwartz, 1963 and 1982), is that the velocity of circulation (V) is constant over time. Because, historically, changes in money supply (M) precede changes in the value of transactions (PT), Friedman suggests that changes in the value of transactions (PT) are caused by changes in money supply (M).

An increase in the value of transactions (PT) can take the form of an increase in the volume of transactions (T), an increase in the price level (P), or a combination of the two. To analyse how an increase in the value of transactions is broken down between price increases and increases in real output, Friedman (1977) re-interprets the Phillips curve relationship between inflation and unemployment, to distinguish between unanticipated and anticipated inflation.

Assume that the economy starts at position A in Figure 10.8, with actual price inflation equal to expected price inflation at zero. For the actual inflation rate to equal the expected rate, Friedman argues, unemployment must be at what he calls its 'natural' rate (U_N). This 'natural' rate (sometimes called NAIRU, or the non-accelerating inflation rate of unemployment) is determined by competitive forces in the labour market (which require, for example, some workers to be frictionally unemployed as they switch jobs). Now suppose a government wishes to use Keynesian policies to bring unemployment down to the full employment level (U_F). Any attempt to boost aggregate demand will require an expansion in money supply, which will create an actual

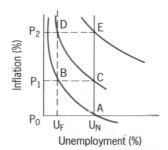

Figure 10.8 Expectations-augmented Phillips curve.

inflation rate of P_1. Inflation will increase (from P_0 to P_1), but in the short term inflationary expectations will remain at zero (P_0), so the economy will move along the Phillips curve from point A to point B.

Any reduction in unemployment below the 'natural' rate, Friedman argues, can only be sustained in the short term, when increased inflation is not anticipated. Eventually, people will come to expect an inflation rate of P_1, and the Phillips curve will shift outwards. The economy will move from point B to point C, where actual and expected inflation are again equal at U_N, but this time with a positive inflation rate P_1. If the government continues to try to achieve full employment, it will move along the new Phillips curve from C to D. This will increase the actual inflation rate to P_2, shifting the curve outwards again, and taking the economy from point D to point E, as people come to expect the new inflation rate P_2.

In Friedman's analysis, the long-term Phillips curve is vertical at the 'natural' rate of unemployment. It follows that monetary expansion can increase real output only in the short term, and that in the long term its sole effect is on inflation. Once inflation takes hold, people build expectations of inflation into their behaviour, causing the rate of inflation to accelerate. Any sustained attempt by a government to reduce unemployment below its 'natural' rate, Friedman argues, is doomed to failure, and can only result in accelerating inflation, the end point of which is a collapse in people's confidence in money.

Friedman goes on to suggest that although, in the long term, unemployment should fluctuate around its 'natural' rate, in the medium term accelerating inflation will bring about increased business uncertainty, causing unemployment to rise above its 'natural' rate.

Theoretically, many economists dispute whether money supply can be measured as precisely, or controlled as rigidly, as monetarist theory would suggest. As Kaldor (1980) pointed out, in a modern economy most 'money' consists of bank deposits created by commercial banks, whose supply is determined largely by private demand for loans. Part of this money supply consists of interest-bearing deposits, making a clear distinction between monetary and non-monetary financial assets difficult to make. This ensures that money supply is inherently difficult for any government to control – as soon as the government attempts to control a monetary aggregate, unsatisfied demand for money spills over into financial assets not included in the official definition. Another implication of Kaldor's analysis is that far from increases in money bringing about increases in expenditure, it is increases in expenditure which bring about increases in money.

There are considerable doubts, too, about the quality of the empirical evidence which has been put forward to support Friedman's theory. Desai, surveying the econometric literature in 1981, found little support for the monetarist propositions that the velocity of circulation of money is stable over time, or that real output in the long term is unaffected by monetary growth. Higham and Tomlinson (1982) found that Friedman's (1977) evidence on the positive links between inflation and unemployment was based on a selective interpretation of the available data. Even more seriously, the historical correlation between growth in money supply and inflation in the UK, supposedly 'established' by Friedman and Schwartz in 1982, has been shown to depend on a crude manipulation of the basic data to fit the hypothesis. This, and the use of dubious statistical techniques, leave Friedman and Schwartz' conclusions 'stranded as assertions devoid of empirical support' (Hendry and Ericsson, 1983).

In the 1970s, many economists were convinced by the superficial plausibility of Friedman's monetary theory, and dissenting views were thin on the ground. Successive UK governments, from 1976 on, were influenced by this theory, and adopted more-or-less strict monetary controls to cure inflation. It is to these monetarist policies, and their effects on the economic environment of business, that we now turn.

Monetarist policies

In the mid-1970s, monetarist ideas became increasingly influential in the UK. The annual inflation rate peaked at 25% in 1975, and many economic journalists (like Peter Jay of *The Times*) felt that this was due more to high rates of monetary expansion and public borrowing than to the OPEC-induced oil price rises of 1974. Public expenditure had risen dramatically in the early 1970s, and successive governments had felt unable to finance the increase with higher taxes. This excess of public spending over taxation, though largely unplanned, was not unwelcome to Keynesians, who appreciated the boost it gave to effective demand, and thus jobs, in a period when unemployment was higher than it had been for three decades. Monetarists were concerned about how the deficit was financed, and they feared that the issue of new short-dated government securities would involve inflationary increases in money supply (Key Concept 10.5). This, they suggested, could not be tolerated.

The Public Sector Borrowing Requirement (PSBR) is the annual excess of spending over income for the public sector as a whole (i.e. including public corporations as well as central and local government). In the 1950s and 1960s, PSBR averaged about 3% of national income. In the early 1970s, however, it rose steadily, peaking at 11% of national income in 1975. This high figure stimulated efforts by successive governments to bring it down, and by 1987–90 PSBR had become negative, helped partly by receipts from privatization (selling off public sector assets to private shareholders). PSBR increased again in the recession of the early 1990s, and was, at the time of writing, forecast to peak at £50 billion (7% of GDP) in 1993–4.

PSBR is financed largely by selling interest-bearing securities to the general public or to the banks. If a government sells securities redeemable at short notice (e.g. Treasury bills) to the banks, it effectively obtains bank deposits in return for assets which form part of the banks' liquid reserves. As the government spends this money, recipients deposit it with the banks again, increasing bank liquidity. This encourages banks to expand their lending (by the process described in Key Concept 6.2), which in

KEY CONCEPT 10.5
PSBR, government securities and money supply

turn expands the money supply. When a government finances a deficit by printing Treasury Bills, it is in effect printing money.

If a government finances a deficit by selling long-dated gilt edged securities or personal sector assets like National Savings Certificates, the financial consequences are different. In these cases, bank liquidity is not increased, and there is no effect on money supply. For this reason, governments which are influenced by monetarist ideas prefer not just to reduce PSBR, but to fund as much of it as possible from sales of medium and long-term securities to the non-bank public.

The main disadvantage in relying on sales of medium and long-term debt to finance PSBR is that it makes the government very dependent on the goodwill of financial markets. To produce increased sales of long-term debt, it is usually necessary to offer higher yields, which has the effect of raising interest rates generally. In addition, if financial institutions are opposed to the direction of government policy, as in 1976, they can force the government to change its policy, simply by postponing their purchases of government securities.

The turning point came in 1976. International currency operators repeatedly speculated against sterling, driving down its exchange value, and financial institutions embarked on a 'gilt strike', refusing to purchase long-term government debt. The government applied for an IMF loan in an attempt to restore the confidence of the financial markets and, to satisfy the conditions of the loan, it adopted target limits to growth in money supply, and a programme of public expenditure cuts. James Callaghan, the Labour Prime Minister, renounced Keynesian policies in a speech to the Labour Party conference, quoted with approval by Friedman in his Nobel lecture (1977)

> We used to think [Callaghan argued] that you could just spend your way out of recession and increase employment by cutting taxes and boosting Government spending. I tell you, in all candour, that that option no longer exists, and that insofar as it ever did exist, it only worked by injecting bigger doses of inflation into the economy followed by higher levels of unemployment as the next step.

While it was the Callaghan government of 1976–79 (assisted by the IMF) which was responsible for introducing monetarist ideas to government policy-making in the UK, it was the Thatcher government elected in 1979 which adopted the most radical monetarist position. The new government announced that levels of output and employment were outside its control, and concentrated its macro-economic attention on a medium-term financial strategy which targeted reductions in the rate of growth in £M3 (Key Concept 10.6) and in Public Sector Borrowing Requirement (PSBR – Key Concept 10.5). These reductions were projected ahead over a four-year period. The assumption was that if decision-makers (including wage bargainers) believed that the government would not allow money supply to grow faster than the target rate, then they would adjust their behaviour, bringing down the inflation rate without creating too much unemployment.

In a modern economy, bank deposits form the main means of exchange. This makes any precise demarcation of what constitutes money impossible, because an increasing proportion of financial deposits are at the same time interest-earning assets and potential means of exchange.

In practice, the UK monetary authorities employ a number of different measures of money supply. Three of the most widely used are defined and measured below.

KEY CONCEPT 10.6
Monetary aggregates

Monetary aggregate	Definition	Size (£bn, end 1992)
M0	Notes and coin in circulation outside Bank of England *plus* Bankers' operational deposits at Bank of England	21
M2	Notes and coin in circulation with public *plus* Private sector holdings of sterling retail deposits with UK banks and building societies	374
M4	Notes and coin in circulation with public *plus* Private sector holdings of sterling deposits (wholesale as well as retail) with UK banks and building societies	519

In the heyday of strict monetarism, in the early 1980s, the UK government specified medium-term targets for a broad aggregate called Sterling M3 (or £M3, which included bank deposits but excluded building society deposits). This became increasingly unsatisfactory as the distinctions between banks and building societies blurred following financial deregulation. The statistical relationship between £M3 and inflation broke down, and government attempts to control 'broad' money were circumvented as funds shifted between different assets, some regulated and some unregulated (Podolski, 1986).

By the late 1980s, monetary targets were specified only for the narrow M0 target, and the behaviour of broader aggregates such as M4 was monitored on a less formal basis. Following Sterling's departure from the ERM in Autumn 1992, the Government set 'monitoring ranges', of 0–4% per year growth in M0 and 3–9% per year growth in M4, which it believed to be consistent with a target rate of underlying inflation of 1–4%.

The techniques of monetary control are complex, and beyond the scope of this book. Suffice it to say that the Bank of England in the early 1980s rejected direct controls, preferring instead to influence demand for money via interest rates. The calculation here was that if

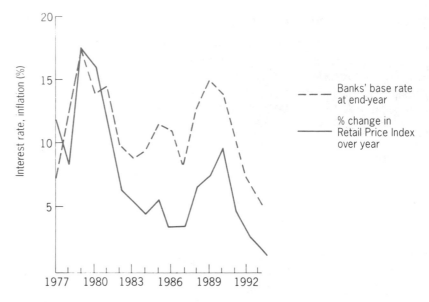

Figure 10.9   Interest rates and inflation, 1977–93.

the authorities charged a higher rate when they lent cash to the banks, bank interest rates would rise, and this would restrain business and consumer borrowing, and hence the ability of the banks to create new deposit money. In practice, the effect of higher interest rates on money supply was difficult to predict. Firms in financial difficulties, for example, had little choice but to increase their bank borrowing to meet higher interest payments on existing loans, so the rise in interest rates could have had the perverse effect of increasing bank lending.

Despite the new policies, and record interest rates, monetary growth continued to exceed the targets, and the government embarked on a process of severe public expenditure cuts, to bring down PSBR (see Key Concept 10.6). As inflation fell (see Figure 10.9), the authorities felt that monetary controls, supplemented by public expenditure cuts, were working, despite the behaviour of £M3. By the mid-1980s, however, evidence was emerging that the most influential factor underlying this fall in inflation was a fall in world commodity prices (Beckerman and Jenkinson, 1986). (For more recent evidence on the contribution of 'world' factors to domestic inflation, see Soteri and Westaway, 1993.) It is not clear whether or not the Treasury accepted this evidence, but it was around this time that the authorities abandoned the £M3 target, and replaced it with a target for a much narrower monetary aggregate, M0. This was more controllable than £M3, but only a tenth of its size, and few people felt that targeting it had any significant effect on economic actitivity.

While the impact of monetarist policies in the early 1980s on the rate of inflation was ambiguous, the outcome for output and jobs, particularly in the manufacturing sector, was not. High interest rates attracted short-term funds into sterling, raising its exchange rate and

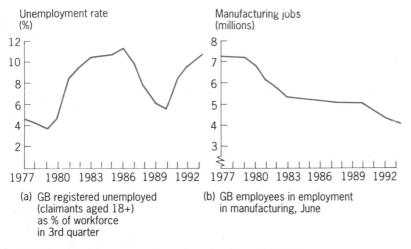

(a) GB registered unemployed
(claimants aged 18+)
as % of workforce
in 3rd quarter

(b) GB employees in employment
in manufacturing, June

Figure 10.10 Unemployment and manufacturing jobs, 1977–93.

making it more difficult for UK businesses to maintain their share of export markets (already depressed as a result of the world recession). Domestic demand was hit by the public spending cuts, and low levels of product demand and high interest rates combined to discourage new investment. Company profitability hit a post-war low, and many firms went into liquidation. Manufacturing output fell by 15% between 1979 and 1982, and almost 1.5 million manufacturing jobs were lost. Registered unemployment rose from 4% to 10% of the working population (Figure 10.10), and in 1983, for the first time in centuries, the UK imported more manufactured goods than she exported.

Exchange rate monetarism

By the mid-1980s, the old-style monetarist emphasis on monetary targets as the main instrument of economic policy had become discredited. The Chancellor of the Exchequer and the Cabinet favoured joining the European Exchange Rate Mechanism (ERM) as an alternative way of restraining inflation, but the Prime Minister was opposed to this, and for a time there was no effective monetary policy. A massive expansion in credit ensued, and this, coupled with tax-cuts for the higher-income groups, fuelled a consumer spending boom in the late 1980s. British industry benefited from the growth in demand, but much of the spending increases (particularly from the higher-income groups) went on imported goods, and the manufacturing trade deficit soared to over £17 billion in 1989 (see Table 8.4).

In 1986–87 inflation had fallen to below 5% per year, but it rose again as the consumer boom took off. The Chancellor of the Exchequer adopted in 1987 a policy of 'shadowing the Deutsche Mark' (intervening on the foreign exchange markets to ensure stability in the £/D-Mark exchange rate) – a policy that was formalized in 1990–92, when Britain finally joined the ERM. It was hoped that this 'exchange rate monetarism' would control UK inflation by keeping down import costs, restraining wage demands, and locking the economy into the lower-inflation conditions prevailing in Germany. In fact, the main effect was to force interest rates up (to secure the capital inflows that were needed to balance the trade deficit at the existing exchange rate) – an important contributory factor to the recession of 1989–92. Inflation rates did come down again in the early 1990s, but more as a result of the recession itself than of the exchange rate policy.

Depreciation of sterling following its departure from the ERM in 1992 led to fears that inflation would take off again. The government reasserted its belief that low inflation was the essential condition for sustained growth, and suggested that this would be achieved by adjusting interest rates to ensure that growth in the key monetary aggregates remained within 'monitoring ranges' judged to be consistent with an underlying inflation rate of 1–4% per year.

The limitations of macro-economic policy

As we have seen in this chapter, Keynesian policies centre around the use of budget deficits to sustain the economy at the full employment level. While this requires the existence of a substantial public sector, and a modest degree of income redistribution, Keynesians see the government's prime role as influencing the overall level of economic activity. Within that level, resources are to be allocated predominantly by market forces.

Monetarists view Keynesian demand management policies as inherently inflationary, and see the removal of inflationary expectations as a prime task for government. The government's role here is limited to controlling the money supply. If price signals are not distorted by inflation, monetarists argue, market forces will guarantee an ideal allocation of resources.

For all their manifest differences, Keynesians and monetarists agree on two fundamental points.

- That government has considerable power to improve (or worsen) the macro-economic environment of business.
- That, if the macro-economic environment is appropriate, market forces will encourage businesses to allocate resources in the most efficient way.

Constraints on macro-economic policy

While not denying the power of government to influence macro-economic variables, we would argue that governments are severely constrained by the environmental conditions we examined in Chapters 6 to 8. Financial institutions, for example, have enormous power to frustrate the ability of governments to finance a large budget deficit or to control the money supply. In the long term, too, ecological considerations place profound constraints on any economic strategy which is based on continued growth of resource-intensive industries.

Perhaps the most significant constraint on UK macro-economic policy in the 1990s is the international one. The UK economy is an unusually open one, and there is a deep-seated weakness in the international competitiveness of many UK businesses, particularly in the manufacturing sector. As Figure 8.2 illustrates, the current account of the balance of payments remained in substantial deficit in 1989–92, despite the restraining effect of the recession on demand for imported goods. In this situation, macro-economic policies designed to improve the domestic economy could easily bring about a balance of payments crisis.

Despite the current problems with ERM, it is clear that monetary policy is increasingly being determined at the level of the European Union as a whole, and that monetary integration will involve significant differences between the different national economies in output, incomes, and employment. Paradoxically, the 'Europeanization' of monetary policy may make it possible for national governments to pursue different fiscal policies, and to give greater priority to national objectives relating to employment and investment (Thompson, 1992). Keynesian reflation in the UK economic context of the mid-1990s, however, would suck in huge quantities of manufacturing imports, and create even larger trade deficits.

Some commentators believe that only coordinated European reflation would offer any hope of returning to full employment. If all European economies expand together, it is argued, then this would get round the trade constraints on national reflation. This argument is correct only up to a point. Because of the structural weaknesses of the UK economy, British firms would not be able to respond as rapidly as their continental rivals to changed market opportunities, and the balance of UK trade with the rest of the EU would deteriorate. Pending full political and economic union, the pressure would still be on the UK government to find some way of bringing import and export earnings into balance.

The efficacy of market forces

The international constraint on macro-economic policy in the UK is at root a constraint which results from UK business failure. This calls into question the assumption, shared by Keynesians and monetarists alike, that, if government macro-economic policies are appropriate, market forces will guarantee business success. As we saw earlier in the book, business calculations cannot be reduced to straightforward responses to changed price stimuli. Business decisions are also influenced by the institutional and organizational context in which they are taken.

One of the key lessons of Chapter 1 was that, in many consumer goods markets nowadays, non-price factors, like quality and reliability, are critical in influencing consumers' choice of products. In these areas, however, the products of many UK businesses are judged unsatisfactory in relation to overseas competition, both in export markets and in the domestic market. To change the poor quality reputation of many British goods would require, in many cases, a complete re-structuring of management attitudes to product design, to production organization and changing technology, and to training and skills. It is difficult to see how 'market forces' could be relied upon to produce such a restructuring, particularly when the financial conditions under which UK businesses operate encourage them to give primacy to short-term calculations.

Government intervention to ease the trade constraint could, in theory, play a positive role, but this would require the presence of domestic substitutes for imported goods, and would have adverse political re-percussions. In the 1970s, the Cambridge Economic Policy Group argued for general import controls to enable the government to expand aggregate demand and reduce unemployment without worsening the balance of payments problem. Critics suggested that general import controls would protect inefficiency, limit consumer choice, and invite retaliation by trade partners. Limited intervention through a policy of selective controls, targeted on key sectors which account for a large proportion of the trade deficit, might have been more effective. Cutler *et al.* (1986), for example, proposed tax incentives to discourage the consumption of motor vehicles and consumer electronics products with a high proportion of value added originating outside the UK. Even such a limited national initiative would, however, now be outlawed by the Single European Act, which came into full effect in 1992.

Whatever form trade policy might take, it would need to be supple-mented by direct encouragement to business to produce the sort of products today's consumers demand. As we shall see later in this chapter, experience elsewhere in Europe and in Japan suggests that this might require active intervention by government in business policy-making to encourage greater international competitiveness. Govern-ments in the UK have, however, been reluctant to intervene too directly in what is seen as the preserve of private business, and industrial policies have tended to be piecemeal in approach.

Industrial policies in the UK

Industrial policies in the UK have taken four main forms – regional policy, competition policy, industrial intervention, and privatization. In this section, we give a brief overview of each of these forms, before going on in the final section to contrast UK experience with that elsewhere in Europe and in Japan.

Regional policy

It has long been accepted in the UK that business location decisions involve significant externalities (Key Concept 6.4), and that government should attempt to reduce the regional inequalities in employment which result from shifts in business location. In the 1950s and 1960s, the main concern was about above-average levels of unemployment in 'peripheral' regions dominated by declining industries – particularly Wales, Scotland, Northern Ireland, and the North of England. More recently, this has been supplemented by concern about the disappearance of manufacturing jobs from inner city areas, in 'peripheral' and 'central' regions alike.

The late 1960s were the high point of regional policy in the UK. A range of incentives was available for all firms locating in regions of high unemployment, including building grants, investment grants, and labour subsidies, while in the more prosperous regions permission for new industrial or office development was made conditional on the government being satisfied that the business could not be relocated in a region of high unemployment.

Regional policies were pursued less energetically in the 1970s, while in the 1980s there was a radical shift in emphasis. The boundaries of assisted areas were redrawn to cover only those areas with very high local unemployment, funding of regional development grants was substantially reduced, and businesses were no longer required to apply to central government for permission to undertake new industrial or office developments. At the same time, the government has made selective assistance available to certain deprived inner city areas and to 'enterprise zones', small districts in older urban areas where firms are freed from certain government regulations, including the requirement to contribute to the financing of industrial training schemes. The main emphasis in the late 1980s has been to channel central government investment, in partnership with the private sector but bypassing local planning controls, into Urban Development Corporations to re-develop areas of urban dereliction, on the model of Docklands (London) and Merseyside (Liverpool).

Regional disparities within Europe are likely to widen as a consequence of the Single European Market and of moves towards full economic and monetary union. It was partly in recognition of the potentially damaging consequences of European integration for the peripheral regions that the EC established the European Regional Development Fund and European Social Fund. These regional policies concentrate on infrastructural improvement and vocational training; critics doubt their effectiveness in countering the tendency of regional inequalities to widen. As Cutler *et al.* (1989) emphasize, better roads to peripheral regions help importers as much as exporters, while improved training does not, in itself, create new skilled jobs. Only policies to influence private sector location decisions would promote effective regional development, but these have been ruled out by the liberal market ideology of the EU.

Competition policy

Competition policy in the UK dates from the establishment of the Monopolies and Restrictive Practices Commission (now called the Monopolies and Mergers Commission) in 1948. The Commission is an independent statutory body which inquires into and reports on matters referred to it by government under the 1973 Fair Trading Act and the 1980 Competition Act.

References mainly relate to monopoly situations (where one firm supplies at least a quarter of a market), and mergers (involving either a potential monopoly or combined assets of over £30 million), but they also include 'anti-competitive practices', and the performance of public sector bodies. There is no assumption in the UK legislation that monopoly situations or mergers are inherently undesirable. Rather, each case is judged on its merits, to determine whether or not it is 'in the public interest'.

The criteria for determining the 'public interest' are vaguely formulated in the legislation, and their interpretation can vary from reference to reference. In practice, the Commission looks, in a monopoly situation inquiry, for evidence of practices like above-average profits, and then assesses whether this is justified on grounds other than abuse of monopoly position. In its 1977 investigation of petfoods, for example, it found Pedigree earning exceptionally high profits, but felt that this was a justifiable reward for their efficient use of new technology. In a merger inquiry, the Commission might attempt to assess whether possible disadvantages from reduced consumer choice might be outweighed by possible advantages from economies of scale.

The Commission's investigations of monopoly situations have generally taken a lenient approach, and where it has recommended remedial action, the government has almost always been satisfied with an informal undertaking by the firm concerned. In no case has the break-up of a monopoly been considered. Some mergers have been stopped as a result of the Commission's recommendations, and some allowed to proceed only after assurances have been given. Only a small proportion of eligible mergers are referred to the Commission, however, despite the research evidence we referred to in Chapter 7 on the generally adverse effects of merger activity on economic efficiency in the UK.

Restrictive trade practices, such as price-fixing agreements and resale price maintenance, are treated differently from monopolies and mergers. The presumption here is that such practices are against 'the public interest'. Restrictive trade practices are therefore illegal, unless the parties can establish a case for exemption before the Restrictive Practices Court, a specially constituted body with the status of a High Court.

Industrial intervention

Industrial intervention policy in the UK is more recent in origin, and has suffered severe discontinuities resulting from changes in the political philosophy of the government in power. Disillusion with the stop-go cycle of economic activity led the Conservative government in the early 1960s to form the National Economic Development Council (NEDC). This brought both sides of industry together, with government, in an attempt to identify obstacles to faster growth, and remove them. The NEDC spawned a number of industrial sub-committees which examined the specific problems for their industries of achieving an overall target of 4% growth in GDP per year, but there was little government commitment to implementing the target.

In 1964, the new Labour government set up a Department of Economic Affairs to demonstrate its commitment to economic growth. This published, in 1965, a National Plan which worked out the detailed implications for each industry and region of a 25% increase in national output over six years. The National Plan was an attempt at 'indicative planning', with the government hoping that businesses would expect targets to be achieved, and so take the actions which would ensure that they were. Because the plan was seen as a self-fulfilling prophecy, little attention was given to implementation. This was an important part of the plan's downfall. To pay for the raw material imports required by the growth targets, the growth rate of exports should have doubled, and this did not happen, The government, hit by waves of speculation against sterling, refused to devalue, and embarked instead on a deflationary package to defend the existing exchange rate. The National Plan was formally abandoned in 1966, less than a year after it was published.

After the abandonment of the National Plan, government attention shifted to the activities of the Industrial Reorganization Corporation (IRC). This body was set up in 1966 to promote industrial change, with the particular aims of improving productivity and the balance of payments. In practice, much of its effort went on promoting mergers like those forming GEC and British Leyland (Case Study 7.1). Mergers such as these, the IRC considered, would enable key British industries to benefit from economies of scale, and thus become more competitive in international markets. There was little analysis of the composition of those markets, or of the importance of non-price factors, however, and there is little evidence to suggest that the IRC's activities did much to improve international competitiveness.

The IRC was disbanded by the Conservative government in 1971, as part of a policy of disengaging from industry, but within a year that policy was reversed, and the same Conservative government introduced selective financial support for weak industrial sectors. The Labour government effectively resurrected the IRC in 1975, renaming it the National Enterprise Board. The NEB was meant to channel finance for industrial investment to promote industrial efficiency, and some of its funds went on establishing new technology enterprises (most notably Inmos). Most of its funds, however, went into the financial rescue of loss-making enterprises like British Leyland. Despite attempts to formulate an Industrial Strategy under the auspices of the NEDC, there was little attempt to relate the *ad hoc* interventions of the NEB either to each other or to an overall strategic perspective.

The election of a new Conservative government in 1979 saw a return to, and intensification of, the 1970–72 philosophy of disengagement. Support for the rescue of 'lame ducks' declined dramatically, and new government financial support for industry in the early 1980s was concentrated on innovation and research and development. By the late 1980s, the main emphasis of government policy towards private industry had shifted to promoting 'enterprise', through measures such as exempting small businesses from 'unnecessary' regulations.

Public ownership and privatization

A number of industries, such as railways, coal, airlines, and energy supply, were nationalized in the 1940s, and the public sector was extended in the 1960s and 1970s by the nationalization of steel, shipbuilding, and aerospace, and by taking some 'lame duck' firms like British Leyland into public ownership. Although public ownership was brought about by Labour governments, there was, in the period from 1951 to 1979, a wide measure of bi-partisan agreement that a few basic industries, where economies of scale or conditions of 'natural monopoly' favoured a high degree of horizontal integration, should be in the public sector, while in most industries competition between private sector firms should be retained.

This agreement was broken with the advent of 'Thatcherism' in 1979. As part of their philosophy of 'disengagement', Conservative governments in the 1980s embarked on a programme of selling off publicly-owned assets (chiefly nationalized industries like British Telecom and British Gas) to the private sector. The privatization programme involves a number of separate objectives, including improved economic efficiency, reductions in PSBR, and wider share ownership.

There is little evidence to support the idea that private sector organizations are inherently more efficient than those in the public sector. Some research that has been done in this area suggests that it is competitive product markets, not private ownership, which promotes greater efficiency (Kay and Thompson, 1986; Yarrow, 1986). This raises interesting questions for the privatization programme, because it implies that the objectives of the programme are in conflict with each other. In practice, the monopolistic market situations of most privatized industries have been retained, reflecting government fears that a more competitive structure would be less attractive to private shareholders and achieve less income from asset sales.

Where public utilities have been privatized with little change to their competitive structure, regulatory authorities (like OFTEL and OFGAS) have been set up to protect consumer interests. The regulatory authorities employ only a small number of staff, and their attention has focussed primarily on setting pricing formulae which avoid excessive monopoly profits. They have done little to protect employment (in the electricity supply industries' negotiations with British Coal, for example), or to protect the environment (by requiring energy suppliers to promote energy efficiency, for example).

Industrial policies in other countries

Negative attitudes to industrial intervention in the UK are linked to negative perceptions of centralized planning in the former USSR and Eastern Europe. What is often not understood in the UK, however, is that competing capitalist economies in Western Europe and in Japan make extensive use of economic planning and industrial intervention to promote national economic objectives. We concentrate here on experience in France and Japan.

France

In France, post-war reconstruction was planned by a small group of government officials in the Planning Commission, who gave priority in spending Marshall Plan aid to the modernization of transport, energy, and iron and steel. When Marshall Aid came to an end, the Commission supervised a series of plans, drawn up after consultation with a wide range of business opinion, to restructure the French economy in the direction of greater productivity and higher growth. The basic approach adopted was for the planners to extrapolate recent trends over the planning period, identifying possible sectoral imbalances. Alternative assumptions about government policies to resolve the inconsistencies were then fed into the projections, and the results shown to a range of business, trade union, and government representatives, in order to identify points of agreement. Resulting from this consultation, detailed projections were then made for each sector, to guide individual businesses in their investment planning.

This sort of approach to indicative planning was what the UK government had in mind when it decided in the mid-1960s to publish a National Plan. Unlike the UK government, however, the French planners paid great attention to the relationship between domestic growth and the balance of payments (even if at times they miscalculated the extent of the trade constraint), and they were not averse to controlling imports in support of their domestic strategy. The French plans were also used as a basis for extensive state intervention in industry. Successive French governments used their power as shareholders in business, as purchasers of equipment, and as owners of financial institutions, to further the priorities identified in the plans. The government used its influence with financial institutions, for example, to guide investment in a coordinated way and make funds available at concessionary rates for selected key investments.

French experience in the 1980s suggests that effective industrial policies can only be pursued in a favourable macro-economic environment. The 1981 Mitterand government gave greater priority than other Western governments to reducing unemployment, and for this they required not just the coordination of investment but its expansion. They felt that they could bypass lack of business confidence in the private sector by making public finance available to nationalized firms. Reliance on increased public sector borrowing, however, led to an export of private capital, and there was little general increase in investment.

Japan

Japan is, of course, the success story of the post-war capitalist world, yet the role of industrial intervention in that story is often inadequately recognized. The key institution here is MITI, the Ministry of International Trade and Industry. Back in 1949, when MITI was first established, the Bank of Japan expressed the view that it would be pointless for Japan to develop a car industry, because the comparative advantage lay with North American and West European firms. The MITI view, however, was that car industry development should be given high priority, and that the infant car industry should be protected from foreign investment and car imports. With these policies, they argued, the Japanese car industry could develop a competitive advantage in the long term, with positive knock-on effects for the capital equipment industry. The MITI view prevailed, with consequences that are familiar to us all.

MITI has continued over the years to identify development priorities in terms of long-term market (and value added) possibilities rather than short-term financial costs. The following quotation from Y. Ojima, a MITI vice-minister, is illuminating:

> MITI decided to establish in Japan industries which require intensive employment of capital and technology, industries that in consideration of comparative costs of production should be the most inappropriate for Japan, industries such as steel, oil refining, petrochemicals, automobiles, aircraft, industrial machinery of all sorts, and electronics, including electronic computers. From a short-run, static viewpoint, encouragement of such industries would seem to conflict with economic rationalism. But from a long-range viewpoint, these are precisely the industries where income elasticity of demand is high, technological progress is rapid, and labour productivity rises fast.
>
> *OECD, 1972*

MITI has been able, not only to determine priority sectors for long-term development, but also to co-ordinate private businesses towards these ends effectively. Its success in implementation has come largely from selective use of its powers to control imports and foreign investment, and to influence the allocation of bank loans. While there are many factors underlying Japanese business success, effective interventionist policy by MITI to promote long-term competitiveness is certainly a positive influence.

Lessons for the UK

Government economic policy in the UK has traditionally given greater emphasis to macro management than micro intervention. Now that both Keynesian and monetarist versions of macro-economic policy have been discredited, it is tempting to see the adoption by government of more effective industrial policies, modelled on those of France or Japan, as the key to solving Britain's economic problems (see, for example, Cowling and Sugden, 1993).

Advocates of industrial policy point, rightly, to the general failure of markets to allocate investment resources optimally, and to the advantages of co-ordination. Copying policies which have been successful in other countries is a dangerous exercise, however, because policies which are appropriate in one environmental and institutional context may not be appropriate in another. The 'hollowing out' of British manufacturing, analysed in Chapter 7, is particularly significant here. In a situation where management is oriented more to financial than productive engineering, the creation of new institutions to coordinate investment is unlikely to have much effect on output or jobs. Instead, as Williams *et al.* have argued (1993), fiscal reforms such as value added promotion (tax rebates for firms which succeed in raising output faster than a given norm) and dividend restraint are needed, to encourage managers to achieve profits by organic growth rather than by overseas acquisition. Such growth would, to a certain extent, be self-sustaining, as output growth would ease the cost recovery problems which, as we have seen in Chapter 4, have bedevilled the recent financial performance of UK firms.

Conclusion

Macro-economics has been dominated in recent years by the debate between Keynesians and monetarists. Each side of the debate has exaggerated the ability of governments to control macro-economic variables, by underestimating both the power of financial institutions and the constraining effects of the UK's trade situation. Experience in other capitalist economies suggests that government industrial policies have a significant role to play in improving business performance. Such policies in the UK have, however, been characterized by inconsistency, discontinuity, and a failure to address the real problems. European integration, far from solving these problems, is likely, in the short term at least, to exacerbate them. The greatest need, in the current UK environment, is for national policies which tackle the issue of 'hollowing out'.

Further reading

Andrew Dunnett's *Understanding the Economy* (Longman, fourth edition, 1992) is a good basic macro-economics textbook, while *The Macroeconomy: a Guide for Business* by Keith Cuthbertson and Peter Gripaios (Routledge, second edition, 1993) takes a specifically business perspective.

British Economic Policy: a modern introduction, edited by Paul Hare and Leslie Simpson (Harvester Wheatsheaf, 1993), gives a comprehensive overview of recent developments in both macro-economic and micro-economic policy.

Exercises

(For exercises 1–6 you should refer to the most recent annual supplement of *Economic Trends*.)

1 Plot the relationship between real personal disposable income (on the vertical axis) and real consumers' expenditure (on the horizontal axis) in the UK at five-year intervals from 1950 to 1980. (This can be done on graph paper, or using a suitable computer package.)

2 (a) Find the straight line which best fits the above points. (This is best done by using linear regression analysis – see our companion volume, *Quantitative Methods in a Business Context*.)
  (b) What are the values of a and b in the equation C = a + bY?

3 What is the correlation coefficient for these data?

4 Using the equation from your answer to 2(b), what would you have predicted real consumers' expenditure to be in 1988, given a real personal disposable income in that year of £279.7 billion?

5 Compare your predicted value with the actual value in 1988. How would you explain the difference?

6 Plot the results for 1988, and for each subsequent year, on you graph. How does recent experience compare with previous periods?

7 What are the effects of a rise in UK interest rates on:
  (a) Business investment?
  (b) The exchange value of sterling?
  (c) Money supply?
  (d) The current account of the balance of payments?
  (e) Capital flows between the UK and other countries?
  (f) The retail price index?

8 In what ways might business in the UK benefit from a more interventionist industrial policy on the part of government?

9 Obtain the latest quarterly house price bulletin from your local branch of the Nationwide Building Society, and use it to update the figures in Case Study 10.1.
  Using the Retail Price Index as a deflator, as explained in Key Concept 4.1, work out the quarterly changes since 1989 in real house prices and in real earnings.
  How might these changes have affected activity in the economy generally?

References

Beckerman, W. and Jenkinson, T. (1986) What stopped the inflation? *Economic Journal*, March.

Beveridge, Lord (1944) *Full Employment in a Free Society*, Allen and Unwin, London.

Carruth, A. and Henley, A. (1990) Spending, saving and the housing market, *Economic Review*, September.

Cowling, K. and Sugden, R. (1993) Industrial strategy: a missing link in British economic policy, *Oxford Review of Economic Policy*, vol. 9, no. 3, Autumn.

Cuthbertson, K. (1982) The measurement and behaviour of the UK saving ratio in the 1970s. *National Institute Economic Review*, Feb.

Cutler, T. *et al.* (1986) *Keynes, Beveridge and Beyond*, Routledge, London.

Cutler, T., Haslam, C., Williams, J. and Williams, K. (1989) *1992: the Struggle for Europe*, Berg, Oxford.

Desai, M. (1981) *Testing Monetarism*, Frances Pinter, London.

Dow, J.C.R. (1964) *The Management of the British Economy 1945–60*, Cambridge University Press, Cambridge.

Friedman, M. (1977) Inflation and unemployment. *Journal of Political Economy*, 83 (3) (also Institute of Economic Affairs Occasional Paper, no. 51, 1977).

Friedman, M. and Schwartz, A. (1963) *A Monetary History of the United States 1867–1960*, Princeton University Press, Princeton.

Friedman, M. and Schwartz, A. (1982) *Monetary Trends in the United States and the United Kingdom 1867–1975*, Chicago University Press, Chicago.

Hendry, D. and Ericsson, N. (1983) *Assertion without Empirical Basis: an econometric appraisal of 'Monetary trends in . . . the UK'*, Bank of England panel paper no. 22, Oct.

Higham, D. and Tomlinson, J. (1982) Why do governments worry about inflation? *National Westminster Quarterly Review*, May.

Kaldor, N. (1976) Inflation and recession in the world economy. *Economic Journal*, Dec.

Kaldor, N. (1980) Monetarism and UK monetary policy. *Cambridge Journal of Economics*, Dec.

Kay, J.A. and Thompson, D.J. (1986) Privatisation: a policy in search of a rationale. *Economic Journal*, March.

Keynes, J.M. (1936) *The General Theory of Employment Interest and Money*, Macmillan, London.

Keynes, J.M. (1943) The Long Term Problem of Full Employment. (Reprinted in *Collected Writings*, vol. XXVII, Macmillan, 1980.)

Matthews, R.C.O. (1968) Why has Britain had full employment since the war? *Economic Journal*, Sept.

Muellbauer, J. (1992) Housing markets and the British economy, *Economic Review*, November.

OECD (1972) *The Industrial Policy of Japan*, OECD, Paris.

Phillips, A.W. (1958) The relation between unemployment and the rate of change of money wage rates in the UK 1861–1957. *Economica*.

Podolski, T.M. (1986) *Financial Innovations and the Money Supply*, Basil Blackwell, Oxford.

Soteri, S. and Westaway, P. (1993) Explaining price inflation in the UK: 1971–92, *National Institute Economic Review*, May.

Thompson, G. (1992) The evolution of the managed economy in Europe, *Economy and Society*, May.

Williams, K., Haslam, C., Williams, J., Adcroft, A. and Johal, S. (1993) Too much reality, *Renewal*, April.

Yarrow, G. (1986) Privatization in theory and practice, *Economic Policy*, April.

Statistical appendix

In this appendix, we present a range of official statistics to indicate some of the main trends, since the 1970s, in the economic environment of UK business. In selecting the tables, our main criterion has been relevance to the analysis in the text. For a fuller picture, you should explore for yourself official publications such as *Economic Trends* and the *Annual Abstract of Statistics*.

Tables A.1–3 examine various aspects of the economic performance of the manufacturing industry in the UK, while Table A.4 concentrates on the service sector. Tables A.5–10 explore the UK's current account balance with those in other countries. The overall picture is summarized in Table A.5, while the subsequent tables focus in greater detail on aspects of this picture which are particularly significant. Finally, in Tables A.11–13, we present comparative data on trends in key macro-economic variables for the seven major OECD countries, and far the EC as a whole.

A useful exercise for any Business Economics student would be to update at least Tables A.1, A.4, A.5, A.6, and A.7, using the latest issues of the sources cited. In doing this, you will encounter a number of potential pitfalls such as:

- Confusing UK figures with those for Great Britain only.
- Confusing balance of payments figures which are prepared on a 'balance of payments' basis with those prepared on an 'overseas trade statistics' basis. (The main difference is that import figures prepared for trade statistics include the cost of insurance and freight, while in the balance of payments accounts these items are deducted.)
- Confusing monetary values which are quoted in current prices with those in constant prices (i.e. discounting inflation).
- Not making allowance for the changes which statisticians make from time to time in their definitions, or in the base year from which their index numbers are calculated.
- Not incorporating revisions to the figures which statisticians make as new information becomes available (this applies particularly to the most recent balance of payments figures).

The ability to analyse official statistics, identifying and avoiding the pitfalls, but focussing on the most significant trends, is an important part of the skills of a business economist. To develop these skills, we would agree with Dudley Jackson (1982), that 'to find the statistics for yourself and to work with them is absolutely essential'.

Appendix tables

A.1   Capital formation, output, employment and labour productivity in the UK manufacturing industry
A.2   Value added in the UK manufacturing industry
A.3   Rates of return (before interest and tax) on capital employed by UK companies
A.4   Capital formation, output and employment in the UK service sector
A.5   The UK balance of payments current account (balance of payments basis, £m)
A.6   The UK current account transactions with other European Community members (balance of payments basis, £m)
A.7   Import penetration and exports/sales ratios in UK manufacturing
A.8   The UK balance of trade, by industry
A.9   Growth of UK manufacturing imports and exports (Index 1985 = 100)
A.10 Area analysis of the UK trade balance (£ billion)
A.11 Economic growth in the seven major OECD economies and the EC
A.12 Inflation and unemployment in the seven major OECD economies and the EC
A.13 Current account balance and effective exchange rates in the seven major OECD economies

Reference

Jackson, D. (1982) *Introduction to Economics: Theory and Data*, Macmillan, London.

Table A.1 Capital formation, output, employment and labour productivity in the UK manufacturing industry

Year	Gross domestic fixed capital formation		Output at constant factor cost	Employees in employment		Output per person hour
	£m (1980 prices)	Index 1980 = 100	Index 1980 = 100	Thousands	Index 1980 = 100	Index 1980 = 100
1972	6344	97.9	104.5	7778	112.1	89.0
1973	6765	104.4	114.2	7828	112.8	95.2
1974	7397	114.2	112.8	7871	113.5	95.8
1975	6781	104.7	105.0	7488	107.9	94.0
1976	6475	99.9	106.9	7269	104.8	98.9
1977	6774	104.5	109.0	7317	105.4	99.8
1978	7221	111.5	109.7	7281	104.9	101.0
1979	7496	115.7	109.5	7253	104.5	101.5
1980	6478	100.0	100.0	6937	100.0	100.0
1981	4865	75.1	94.0	6222	89.7	104.8
1982	4704	72.6	94.2	5863	84.5	110.4
1983	4779	73.8	96.9	5525	79.6	118.9
1984	5752	88.8	100.8	5409	77.9	124.4
1985	6424	99.2	103.7	5362	77.3	128.1
1986	6329	97.7	104.7	5227	75.3	132.2
1987	6674	103.0	110.7	5152	74.3	141.1
1988	7437	114.8	124.7	5195	74.9	148.6
1989	8234	127.1	127.1	5187	74.8	155.3
1990	7812	120.6	123.5	5144	74.1	159.0
1991	7029	108.5	115.3	4822	69.5	162.8
1992	6536	100.0	109.1	4791	69.1	170.4

Sources: Annual Abstract of Statistics; Monthly Digest of Statistics; Economic Trends.
Note: Manufacturing, in this table and in Tables A.3 and A.7 includes all activities in Divisions 2 to 4 of the 1980 Standard Industrial Classification (SIC 1980); 2. Chemicals, metal manufacture, etc. 3. Engineering, vehicles, and metal goods. 4. Other manufacturing industries. Gross Domestic Fixed Capital Formation is expenditure on fixed capital (including depreciation costs) less expenditure on stocks.

Table A.2 Value added in the UK manufacturing industry

	Gross output (£ million)	Value added (£ million)	Value added as % of gross output	Labour's share of value added
1970	47 359	n/a	n/a	74.0
1971	50 325	n/a	n/a	74.0
1972	53 760	n/a	n/a	73.5
1973	63 340	23 731	37.5	73.1
1974	83 153	29 345	35.3	78.3
1975	93 048	32 390	34.8	81.5
1976	113 170	38 832	34.3	80.1
1977	132 030	43 992	33.3	74.8
1978	142 980	48 640	34.0	74.3
1979	165 386	56 418	34.1	77.6
1980	176 632	59 047	33.4	79.0
1981	178 351	54 826	30.7	81.2
1982	189 524	59 472	31.4	77.5
1983	189 200	62 151	32.9	75.8
1984	209 650	65 975	31.5	76.0
1985	226 636	72 538	32.0	74.4
1986	232 499	77 638	33.4	72.9
1987	254 683	82 868	32.5	72.0
1988	283 434	92 368	32.6	69.1
1989	309 020	99 702	32.3	69.5
1990	319 295	105 808	33.1	72.7

Sources: PA1002 *Census of Production* (first three columns) up to 1980 in which the 1968 Standard Industrial Classification is used. Thereafter the Standard Industrial Classification (1980) is used for manufacturing, namely Divisions 2 to 4. Information on Gross Output is taken from the *Annual Abstract of Statistics*, value added and labour costs are taken from *UK Financial Statistics* (Blue Book, Table 2.1).

Table A.3 Rates of return (before interest and tax) on capital employed by UK companies

	All industrial and commercial companies		Manufacturing sector	
	Gross (%)	Net (%)	Gross (%)	Net (%)
1963	10.3	11.3		
1964	10.8	12.0		
1965	10.4	11.3		
1966	9.5	10.0		

Table A.3 *Continued*

	All industrial and commercial companies		Manufacturing sector	
	Gross (%)	*Net (%)*	*Gross (%)*	*Net (%)*
1967	9.5	10.0		
1968	9.6	10.0		
1969	9.6	10.0		
1970	8.8	8.7	7.0	6.5
1971	9.0	9.0	7.3	6.9
1972	9.2	9.3	7.3	7.1
1973	8.7	8.8	7.1	6.9
1974	6.2	5.0	4.4	2.8
1975	5.6	4.0	3.8	1.9
1976	5.9	4.4	4.1	2.2
1977	8.1	7.5	5.8	4.9
1978	8.6	8.2	6.2	5.4
1979	8.3	7.7	4.8	3.3
1980	7.7	6.7	4.3	2.5
1981	7.4	6.3	3.8	1.5
1982	8.4	7.8	4.9	3.4
1983	9.4	9.3	5.4	4.2
1984	10.1	10.5	5.3	4.0
1985	10.6	11.2	6.1	5.4
1986	9.4	9.2	6.4	5.9
1987	9.6	9.7	6.3	5.7
1988	10.0	10.4	7.2	7.2
1989	9.6	9.7	7.1	7.2
1990	8.8	8.3	7.3	7.3
1991	8.3	7.6	6.8	6.4
1992	8.3	7.6	6.8	6.3

Source: CSO bulletin (profitability of UK companies).

Note: Gross operating surplus on UK operations (i.e. gross trading profits less stock appreciation plus rents received) as % of gross capital stock of fixed assets (excluding land) at current replacement cost plus book value of stock.

Net operating surplus on UK operations (i.e. gross operating surplus less capital consumption at current replacement cost) as % of net capital stock of fixed assets (excluding land) at current replacement cost plus book value of stock.

Table A.4 Capital formation, output and employment in the UK service sector

Year	Gross domestic fixed capital formation		Output at constant factor cost	Employees in employment	
	£m (1980 prices)	Index 1980 = 100	Index 1980 = 100	Thousands	Index 1980 = 100
1972	18 011	101.9	86.4	11 863	86.5
1973	19 852	112.4	90.1	12 299	89.7
1974	18 347	103.8	90.2	12 462	90.9
1975	16 300	92.2	91.2	12 788	93.3
1976	16 284	92.2	93.3	12 917	94.2
1977	16 194	91.7	94.6	12 990	94.7
1978	16 743	94.8	97.5	13 003	94.8
1979	18 002	101.9	100.4	13 581	99.1
1980	17 668	100.0	100.0	13 710	100.0
1981	16 592	93.9	100.3	13 466	98.2
1982	17 832	100.9	101.7	13 448	98.1
1983	18 579	105.2	105.0	13 500	98.5
1984	21 103	119.4	109.2	13 838	100.9
1985	22 942	129.9	113.3	14 108	102.9
1986	22 612	128.0	117.5	14 297	104.3
1987	24 122	136.5	123.3	14 594	106.5
1988	29 364	166.2	129.1	15 218	111.0
1989	35 884	203.1	132.5	15 627	114.0
1990	37 598	212.8	134.0	15 938	116.3
1991	32 899	186.2	131.7	15 754	114.9
1992	32 067	181.5	131.7	15 250	111.2

Sources: Annual Abstract of Statistics; Monthly Digest of Statistics; Economic Trends.

Note: Services are all activities in Divisions 6–9 of SIC 1980. 6. Distribution, hotels, catering, repairs. 7. Transport and communication. 8. Banking, finance, insurance, etc. 9. Other services (mainly government). The increase in employees shown in this table exaggerates the increase in hours worked, as much of the increase has been in part-time employment (see Chapter 6).

Table A.5 The UK balance of payments current account (balance of payments basis, £m)

	1970	1971	1972	1973	1974	1975	1976
Visibles	−14	+210	−742	−2566	−5233	−3257	−3959
Oil	−497	−691	−666	−943	−3361	−3062	−3953
Non-oil	+483	+900	−76	−1623	−1872	−195	−6
Invisibles	+830	+901	+940	+1567	+2034	+1753	+3018
Current A/c	+816	+1111	+198	−999	−3199	−1504	−941

	1977	1978	1979	1980	1981	1982	1983	1984
Visibles	−2324	−1593	−3398	+1353	+3350	+2218	−1076	−5336
Oil	−2775	−1989	−738	+308	+3105	+4639	+6972	+6933
Non-oil	+451	+396	−2660	+1045	+245	−2421	−8048	−12269
Invisibles	+2174	+2557	+2902	+1769	+3586	+2467	+4907	+7134
Current A/c	−150	+964	−496	+3122	+6936	+4685	+3831	+1798

	1985	1986	1987	1988	1989	1990	1991	1992
Visibles	−3345	−9559	−11582	−21480	−24683	−18809	−10284	−13406
Oil	+8101	+4070	+4161	+2750	+1257	+1522	+1040	+1333
Non-oil	−11446	−13629	−15743	−24230	−25940	−20331	−11324	−14739
Invisibles	+6136	+9625	+7099	+5302	+2956	+1778	+2632	+4786
Current A/c	+2791	+66	−4483	−16178	−21727	−17031	−7652	−8620

Sources: UK *Balance of Payments Pink Book*; British Business.

Note: Imports and exports, in this table and in Table A.6, are both calculated 'free on board' (i.e. excluding the cost of insurance and freight).

Table A.6 The UK current account transactions with other European Community members (balance of payments basis, £m)

	1977	1978	1979	1980	1981	1982	1983	1984
Visible balance	−1809	−2486	−2709	+757	+85	−1175	−2460	−3466
Invisibles								
Services	−304	−369	−493	−720	−1113	−1818	−1884	−1717
Interest profits and dividends	+290	+610	+1075	+795	+2410	+3425	+4010	+3729
Transfers	−458	−903	−1057	−697	−409	−586	−614	−733
Current A/c balance	−2281	−3148	−3184	+135	+973	−154	−948	−2187

	1985	1986	1987	1988	1989	1990	1991	1992
Visible balance	−2561	−8859	−9657	−13762	−15397	−9896	−531	−3657
Invisibles								
Services	−1483	−2025	−2027	−2619	−2691	−2247	−2331	−2428
Interest profits and dividends	+3074	+2552	+708	+915	+842	+589	+175	+3125
Transfers	−1888	−541	−1622	−1310	−2197	−2388	−459	−1880
Current A/c balance	−2858	−8873	−12598	−16776	−19443	−13942	−3145	−4841

Source: UK *Balance of Payments Pink Book.*

Table A.7 Import penetration and export/sales ratios in UK manufacturing

Year	Imports as % of home demand	Exports as % of manufacturers' sales
1972	18.2	18.5
1973	21.4	19.6
1974	23.3	21.3
1975	22.0	22.6
1976	24.4	24.7
1977	25.1	25.7
1978	26.0	26.1
1979	26.9	25.1
1980	26.2	26.5
1981	27.8	27.2
1982	29.0	27.2
1983	31.1	26.6
1984	33.4	28.4
1985	34.3	30.2
1986	34.3	29.6
1987	35.2	30.3
1988	35.6	29.2
1989	36.7	30.0

Sources: Annual Abstract of Statistics; Monthly Digest of Statistics.

Note: 1972–74 figures are for orders III to XIX of the 1968 Standard Industrial Classification, while for 1975 and after they are Divisions 2 to 4 of SIC 1980. Imports in this table, and in Tables A.8–A.13 include carriage, insurance and freight (c.i.f.), while exports are free on board (f.o.b.).

298 Statistical appendix

Table A.8 The UK balance of trade, by industry

a) Exports less imports, by SITC division (£bn.)

	SITC division						
	0–9	0+1	2+4	3	5+6	7+8	5–8
1975	−3.3	−2.6	−1.5	−3.1	+0.5	+3.3	+3.7
1976	−4.0	−2.9	−2.3	−4.0	+0.9	+4.0	+4.9
1977	−2.3	−3.2	−2.5	−2.8	+1.5	+4.4	+5.9
1978	−1.6	−2.7	−2.2	−2.1	+1.2	+3.9	+5.1
1979	−3.3	−2.9	−2.4	−1.1	+0.6	+2.1	+2.7
1980	+1.4	−2.3	−2.0	−0.1	+1.3	+4.1	+5.4
1981	+3.3	−2.3	−2.1	+2.7	+1.3	+3.2	+4.5
1982	+1.9	−2.7	−2.1	+4.1	+0.8	+1.3	+2.1
1983	−1.5	−3.0	−2.6	+6.3	−0.1	−2.6	−2.7
1984	−5.3	−3.6	−3.0	+5.4	−0.6	−4.0	−4.5
1985	−3.3	−3.7	−2.8	+6.5	−0.4	−3.3	−3.8
1986	−9.6	−4.0	−2.5	+2.7	−0.9	−5.2	−6.1
1987	−11.6	−4.0	−3.0	+2.9	−2.0	−6.3	−8.3
1988	−21.5	−4.5	−3.3	+1.5	−4.0	−11.3	−15.3
1989	−24.7	−4.3	−3.6	0	−4.3	−12.9	−17.3
1990	−18.8	−4.6	−3.3	+0.4	−2.8	−8.9	−11.6
1991	−10.3	−4.0	−2.6	−0.1	−1.2	−2.4	−3.6
1992	−13.4	−3.9	−2.7	+0.2	−0.8	−6.5	−7.3

b) Exports as a % of imports, by SITC division

	SITC division						
	0–9	0+1	2+4	3	5+6	7+8	5–8
1975	85	34	21	28	109	148	131
1976	86	36	24	27	113	146	131
1977	93	40	43	28	118	139	130
1978	96	51	52	32	112	130	122
1979	92	50	80	36	105	113	110
1980	103	59	98	43	111	124	118
1981	107	61	140	39	111	117	115
1982	104	60	158	40	106	106	106
1983	98	58	193	39	99	90	94

Table A.8 *Continued*

	SITC division						
	0–9	*0+1*	*2+4*	*3*	*5+6*	*7+8*	*5–8*
1984	93	56	154	41	97	88	91
1985	96	57	163	44	98	91	93
1986	88	58	144	46	96	87	90
1987	87	58	150	43	92	86	88
1988	79	55	132	39	86	78	81
1989	79	60	101	39	86	79	81
1990	84	60	105	41	91	86	88
1991	91	66	99	44	96	96	96
1992	89	68	103	42	97	89	92

Source: CSO *Monthly Review of External Trade Statistics* (annual supplement).

Notes: (a) The industrial classification used in this table is the Standard Industrial Trade Classification (SITC). Sections 0,1, food, beverages and tobacco; Sections 2, 4, basic materials; Section 3, fuels; Section 5, chemicals; Section 6, other semi-manufactured goods; Section 7, machinery and transport equipment; Section 8, other finished manufactured goods; Section 9, commodities and transactions not classified by kind. (b) Sections 5 and 6 are semi-manufactures; Sections 7 and 8 are finished manufactures.

Table A.9 Growth of UK manufacturing imports and exports (Index 1985 = 100)

a) *Value of exports and imports (current prices)*

	Exports index	Imports index
1970	20	23
1971	21	24
1972	22	25
1973	24	30
1974	31	38
1975	38	44
1976	46	54
1977	54	63
1978	59	66
1979	64	69
1980	71	71
1981	75	75
1982	81	81
1983	87	88
1984	94	94
1985	100	100
1986	104	103
1987	108	106
1988	112	107
1989	119	114
1990	124	118
1991	125	120
1992	128	121

b) *Volume of exports and imports (constant prices)*

	Volume index exports	Volume index imports
1970	61	29
1971	66	31
1972	65	37
1973	74	45
1974	79	48
1975	77	44
1976	83	48

Table A.9 *Continued*

	Volume index exports	Volume index imports
1977	88	52
1978	90	60
1979	88	69
1980	87	65
1981	85	68
1982	85	76
1983	84	85
1984	93	95
1985	100	100
1986	101	106
1987	109	116
1988	116	136
1989	127	149
1990	137	150
1991	140	144
1992	146	156

Sources: DTI Monthly Review of External Trade Statistics, annual supplement; *Monthly Digest of Statistics*.

Note: The figures exclude erratic items, sometimes called SNAPS (Ships, North sea installations, Aircraft, Precious stones, and Silver).

Table A.10 Area analysis of UK trade balance (£ billion)

	EC (12)	Other West Europe	North America	Other OECD	Rest of world
1975	−2.5	−0.4	−0.6	−0.1	+0.3
1976	−2.2	−0.5	−0.8	0	−0.4
1977	−1.9	−0.5	−0.8	−0.1	+0.9
1978	−2.5	−1.0	−0.7	−0.2	+2.9
1979	−2.7	−1.2	−1.0	−0.4	+2.0
1980	+1.1	−0.4	−1.5	−0.5	+3.0
1981	0	−1.2	+0.2	−0.8	+5.0
1982	−1.4	−1.5	+0.8	−1.2	+5.1
1983	−2.9	−2.4	+1.0	−1.8	+4.6
1984	−3.6	−3.8	−0.9	−2.0	+3.1
1985	−2.7	−4.1	+2.2	−2.2	+3.5
1986	−9.0	−4.3	+2.6	−2.8	+4.0
1987	−9.8	−4.7	+2.6	−3.2	+3.5
1988	−13.8	−6.0	+0.2	−3.8	+1.9
1989	−15.5	−7.1	−0.3	−3.6	+1.8
1990	−10.0	−5.9	−1.4	−3.1	+1.6
1991	−0.9	−5.1	−2.2	−3.6	+1.5
1992	−3.7	−5.4	−1.0	−4.7	+1.3

Source: CSO Monthly Review of External Trade Statistics, annual supplement.

Note: EC refers to the 12 European Community countries throughout.

Table A.11 Economic growth in the seven major OECD economies and the EC

a) Annual % change in real GDP

	Average 1967–76	1977	1978	1979	1980	1981	1982	1983	1984	1985	1986	1987	1988	1989	1990	1991	1992	1993
United States	2.6	4.5	4.8	2.5	-0.5	1.8	-2.2	3.9	6.2	3.2	2.9	3.1	3.9	2.5	1.2	-0.7	2.6	2.8
Japan	7.0	4.7	4.9	5.5	3.6	3.6	3.2	2.7	4.3	5.0	2.6	4.1	6.2	4.7	4.8	4.0	1.3	-0.5
Germany	3.8	2.8	3.0	4.2	1.0	0.1	-0.9	1.8	2.8	2.0	2.3	1.5	3.7	3.6	5.7	4.5	2.1	-1.5
France	4.3	3.2	3.4	3.2	1.6	1.2	2.5	0.7	1.3	1.9	2.5	2.3	4.5	4.3	2.5	0.7	1.4	-0.9
Italy	4.3	3.4	3.6	5.8	4.1	0.6	0.2	1.0	2.7	2.6	2.9	3.1	4.1	2.9	2.1	1.3	0.9	-0.1
United Kingdom	2.3	2.3	3.6	2.8	-1.9	-1.2	1.6	3.6	2.3	3.8	4.1	4.8	4.4	2.1	0.5	-2.2	-0.6	2.0
Canada	5.1	3.6	4.6	3.9	1.5	3.7	-3.2	3.2	6.3	4.7	3.3	4.2	5.0	2.4	-0.2	-1.7	0.7	2.5
Total of above countries (G7)	3.9	4.0	4.3	3.6	0.9	1.7	-0.3	2.9	4.6	3.3	2.9	3.2	4.5	3.2	2.4	0.8	1.8	1.2
EC	4.0	2.9	3.2	3.5	1.4	0.1	0.8	1.6	2.3	2.5	2.8	2.9	4.1	3.5	3.1	1.5	1.1	-0.3

b) Annual % change in gross fixed capital formation

	Average 1967–76	1977	1978	1979	1980	1981	1982	1983	1984	1985	1986	1987	1988	1989	1990	1991	1992	1993	1994	1995
United States	3.0	14.3	10.8	4.6	-8.1	0.6	-8.0	6.6	15.9	5.0	0.4	-0.5	4.2	0.1	-1.8	-7.7	6.2	9.8	9.6	7.9
Japan	8.4	2.8	7.8	6.2	0	2.4	-0.1	-1.0	4.7	5.3	4.8	9.6	11.9	9.3	8.8	3.0	-1.0	-2.3	1.3	2.2
Germany	2.1	3.6	4.1	6.7	2.2	-5.0	-5.4	3.1	0.1	-0.5	3.3	1.8	4.4	6.3	8.5	6.1	4.2	-3.3	2.8	5.4
France	4.4	-1.8	2.1	3.1	2.6	-1.9	-1.4	-3.6	-2.6	3.2	4.5	4.8	9.6	7.9	2.9	-1.5	-2.0	-5.5	0	3.7
Italy	2.5	1.7	0.6	5.4	8.5	-3.1	-4.7	-0.6	3.6	0.6	2.2	5.0	6.9	4.3	3.8	0.6	-1.4	-7.1	2.5	5.6
United Kingdom	1.5	-1.8	3.0	2.8	-5.4	-9.6	5.4	5.0	8.5	4.0	2.4	9.6	14.2	7.2	-3.1	-9.9	-0.5	1.8	3.0	4.3
Canada	5.0	2.1	3.1	8.5	10.1	11.8	-11.0	-0.3	2.0	9.3	6.0	10.8	10.3	6.1	-3.5	-2.0	-1.3	1.1	6.3	7.1
Total of above countries (G7)	3.9	7.2	7.2	5.1	-2.5	-0.3	-4.7	3.1	8.7	4.1	2.3	3.6	7.3	4.1	1.8	-3.1	2.6	2.8	5.5	5.8
EC	2.9	1.2	2.3	3.3	1.7	-5.2	-1.4	0.3	1.1	2.3	4.3	5.5	8.8	7.2	4.0	-0.4	-0.1	-3.8	1.6	4.6

Source: OECD *Economic Outlook*.
Notes: Some of the national data in this and subsequent tables are adjusted by the OECD to make them more comparable (for details see 'Sources and Methods' in OECD *Economic Outlook*).

Table A.12 Inflation and unemployment in the seven major OECD economies and the EC

a) Annual % change in consumer prices

	1977	1978	1979	1980	1981	1982	1983	1984	1985	1986	1987	1988	1989	1990	1991	1992
United States	6.5	7.6	11.3	13.5	10.3	6.1	3.2	4.3	3.5	1.9	3.7	4.1	4.8	5.4	4.2	3.0
Japan	8.2	4.2	3.7	7.8	4.9	2.7	1.9	2.2	2.0	0.6	0.1	0.7	2.3	3.1	3.3	1.7
Germany	3.7	2.7	4.1	5.5	6.3	5.3	3.3	2.4	2.2	-0.1	0.2	1.3	2.8	2.7	3.5	4.0
France	9.4	9.1	10.8	13.6	13.4	11.8	9.6	7.4	5.8	2.7	3.1	2.7	3.6	3.4	3.2	2.4
Italy	18.1	12.4	15.7	21.1	18.7	16.3	15.0	10.6	8.6	6.1	4.6	5.0	6.6	6.1	6.5	5.3
United Kingdom	15.8	8.3	13.4	18.0	11.9	8.6	4.6	5.0	6.1	3.4	4.1	4.9	7.8	9.5	5.9	3.7
Canada	8.0	8.9	9.1	10.2	12.4	10.8	5.8	4.3	4.0	4.2	4.4	4.0	5.0	4.8	5.6	1.5
Total of above countries (G7)	8.4	7.3	9.8	12.7	10.2	7.2	4.7	4.7	4.0	2.1	2.9	3.4	4.5	5.0	4.3	3.0
EC	12.4	9.1	10.8	13.7	12.4	10.9	8.6	7.2	6.1	3.7	3.3	3.6	5.3	5.6	5.1	4.3

b) Standardized unemployment rates (% of total labour force)

	1977	1978	1979	1980	1981	1982	1983	1984	1985	1986	1987	1988	1989	1990	1991	1992
United States	6.9	6.0	5.8	7.0	7.5	9.5	9.5	7.4	7.1	6.9	6.1	5.4	5.2	5.4	6.6	7.3
Japan	2.0	2.2	2.1	2.0	2.2	2.4	2.6	2.7	2.6	2.8	2.8	2.5	2.3	2.1	2.1	2.2
Germany	3.6	3.5	3.2	2.9	4.2	5.9	7.7	7.1	7.1	6.4	6.2	6.2	5.6	4.8	4.2	4.6
France	4.9	5.2	5.8	6.2	7.4	8.1	8.3	9.7	10.2	10.4	10.5	10.0	9.4	8.9	9.4	10.3
Italy	7.0	7.1	7.6	7.5	7.8	8.4	8.8	9.4	9.6	10.5	10.9	11.0	10.9	10.3	9.9	10.5
United Kingdom	6.0	5.9	5.0	6.4	9.8	11.3	12.4	11.7	11.2	11.2	10.3	8.6	7.2	6.8	8.7	9.9
Canada	8.0	8.3	7.4	7.4	7.5	10.9	11.8	11.2	10.4	9.5	8.8	7.7	7.5	8.1	10.2	11.2
Major seven countries (G7)	5.4	5.1	4.9	5.5	6.3	7.7	8.1	7.3	7.2	7.1	6.7	6.1	5.7	5.6	6.3	6.9
EC	5.4	5.6	5.7	6.4	8.1	9.4	10.3	10.7	10.9	10.8	10.6	9.9	9.0	8.4	8.6	9.5

Source: OECD Economic Outlook.

Table A.13 Current account balance and effective exchange rates in the seven major OECD economies

a) Current account balance as % of GDP

	1977	1978	1979	1980	1981	1982	1983	1984	1985	1986	1987	1988	1989	1990	1991	1992	1993
United States	-0.7	-0.7	0.0	0.1	0.2	-0.4	-1.3	-2.6	-3.0	-3.5	-3.7	-2.6	-1.9	-1.7	-0.1	-1.1	-1.7
Japan	1.6	1.7	-0.9	-1.0	0.4	0.6	1.8	2.8	3.6	4.3	3.6	2.7	2.0	1.2	2.2	3.2	3.3
Germany	0.8	1.4	-0.7	-1.7	-0.5	0.8	0.8	1.6	2.6	4.4	4.1	4.2	4.9	3.0	-1.2	-1.3	-1.1
France	-0.1	1.4	0.9	-0.6	-0.8	-2.2	-0.9	-0.2	-0.1	0.3	-0.6	-0.5	-0.6	-1.3	-0.6	0.3	0.8
Italy	1.1	2.1	1.6	-2.2	-2.1	-1.4	0.4	-0.6	-0.9	0.4	-0.2	-0.7	-1.3	-1.4	-1.9	-2.2	0.4
United Kingdom	-0.1	0.7	-0.2	1.2	2.5	1.7	1.2	0.4	0.6	-0.2	-1.2	-3.5	-4.4	-3.4	-1.3	-1.4	-1.8
Canada	-2.0	-2.0	-1.8	-0.4	-1.7	0.8	0.8	0.6	-0.7	-2.3	-2.1	-2.6	-3.6	-3.9	-4.3	-4.0	-3.6
Total of the above countries (G7)	0.0	0.4	-0.1	-0.5	0.0	-0.1	-0.2	-0.7	-0.8	-0.3	-0.5	-0.4	-0.5	-0.7	-0.2	-0.2	-0.1
EC	0.0	0.9	-0.2	-1.3	-0.7	-0.6	0.1	0.4	0.7	1.4	0.8	0.3	0.0	-0.3	-1.0	-0.9	-0.3

b) Effective (trade-weighted) exchange rates (1991 = 100)

	1981	1982	1983	1984	1985	1986	1987	1988	1989	1990	1991	1992	1993[b]
United States	115.2	127.1	133.1	140.4	144.1	121.3	104.7	99.7	103.6	100.6	100.0	97.4	99.6
Japan	62.5	59.2	65.4	67.9	70.0	91.1	97.2	106.6	102.6	95.1	100.0	106.2	127.6
Germany	72.3	76.2	80.3	80.0	81.3	90.1	94.2	94.5	93.3	99.6	100.0	104.1	108.1
France	109.1	100.4	94.1	91.6	93.4	97.7	97.0	96.2	95.5	100.3	100.0	102.8	105.8
Italy	117.1	109.8	106.6	102.4	97.6	100.4	99.1	96.8	97.5	100.9	100.0	97.3	82.3
United Kingdom	123.0	118.2	110.5	105.9	106.3	99.6	95.6	101.7	99.1	98.0	100.0	96.6	88.4
Canada	98.7	98.7	100.6	96.9	92.7	86.7	86.5	92.8	97.9	98.3	100.0	93.2	88.1

Source: OECD Economic Outlook.

Index

Accepted sequence 11
Acid rain 240, 244
Acid test 120
Activity Based Costing (ABC)
    83–4
Advertising 5, 13
Aggregate demand 256–7
Airbus 54
Alkali manufacture 250
Americanization 137–42
Amstrad 5
Andersen, Arthur 144–5
Anglo American Productivity
    Council (AAPC) 74, 137–8,
    145
Animal spirits 260
Austin Rover, see Rover Group
Average Cost 7, 8, 45–8
Average propensity to consume
    258
Average revenue 6, 7

Balance of payments
    accounts 214–15
    UK policy and performance
    216–20, 225–7, 266
Balance sheet 73–4
Banking
    client relationships 186
    fractional reserve 182–3
    lending practices 184–5
    retail 183–4
    wholesale 184
Bank of England 186–9
Bank Rate, see Minimum
    Lending rate
Barriers to entry 9, 10
Behavioural theories
    of consumer behaviour 3–4
    of firm 70–1

Benchmarking 145
Best available technology not
    entailing excessive cost
    (BATNEEC) 238–9
'Big Bang' 185–6, 191–2
Body Shop 5, 251
Braverman, Harry 164–5
Break even analysis 84–8,
    118–19
British Leyland, see Rover
    Group
British Steel 43, 48–9, 51, 55–7,
    94–5, 96–8
Budgeting 74–9
Buffer stocks 56, 81

Capital markets
    company shares, see Shares
    government securities 271–2
    new issue market 191
    secondary market 191–2
    unlisted securities market 200
Carbon and energy tax 242–3
Carbon dioxide emissions 235,
    241, 242, 243
Car industry
    environmental impacts
    240–41
    labour costs 64
    labour process 170
    market composition 20,
    29–30
    production 51–2, 143–4
    trade 217–18
Cash flow 117–18
Catalytic converters 240–41,
    252
Central Electricity Generating
    Board (CEGB) 247–8
Chandler, Alfred 134–5

Characteristic filtering 3, 4, 244
Chlorofluorocarbons (CFCs)
    235, 241
Circular flow (of income) 261–4
COBA 247
Collusion 10
Colonialism 225
Common property 232–3
Comparative advantage 205–6
Competitive advantage 23, 284
Competition policy 279–80
Computer Aided Design (CAD)
    25, 26
Computer Aided Manufacturing
    (CAM) 26, 27
Computer Integrated
    Manufacturing (CIM) 26
Confidence, business 260
Consumer behaviour 2–5
Consumer credit 218, 259
Consumer electronics products
    3, 4–5, 14–18, 154
Consumer sovereignty 11–13
Consumption function 257–8
Contingent valuation 242
Continuing resources 231
Controls
    environmental 238–41
    financial 75–9
    foreign exchange 211
    import 207, 208
Core workers 171
Cost–benefit analysis (CBA) 246–7
Cost accounting, see
    Management and cost
    accounting
Cost control, see Cost
    maintenance
Cost drivers 83
Cost maintenance 75–9

Cost of capital 93
Cost recovery 56–65
Cost reduction 56–65, 77–9
Costing
    activity based 83–4
    standard 74, 75–7
Costs
    average 7, 8, 45–8
    conversion 61–2
    fixed 39–40, 46–8, 71
    holding 79, 80
    hourly labour 64–5, 163–4
    long run 39–40, 47
    marginal 6, 7, 71
    opportunity 90
    ordering 79, 80
    prime 82
    private 233–4
    short run 39–40, 45–6
    social 233–4
    target 77–9
    total 45, 84–7
    unit labour 163–4
    variable 39–40, 45, 71, 81–2
Cost–volume–profit
    relationships 84–7
Cyclicality 16–18

Daly, Herman 235–7
Debentures 191, 192
Debt crisis (international) 184,
    188, 215–16
Dedicated technology 26–7
Demand
    aggregate 256–7
    conditions of 2
    consumer 2–5, 11–13
    effective 256–7
    elasticity 2–3, 213
    for labour 152–3
    for money 270, 273–4
    kinked 11
    replacement 15–18
Design and development 52–4,
    57, 251
    see also Research and
    Development
De-skilling 164–5
Developing economies
    bank lending to 184, 188, 225
    investment in 221–2, 222–5
    as manufacturing exporters
    64–5, 207, 224–5
    marketing in 251
    as primary producers 206
Digital 54
Discounted Cash Flow (DCF)
    89–92, 142
    see also Net Present Value

Discounting 90, 232, 247–9
Distributors, relationship of
    firm to 115
Dividend yield 122–3
Divisionalization 133–6
Divisional structure, *see*
    Divisionalization
Domestic appliance industry
    environmental impacts
    242–3
    labour market issues 173
Drucker, Peter 129
Dual sourcing 223

Earl, Peter 3–4
Eco-management and audit
    scheme 245
Economic order quantity (EOQ)
    79–81
Economies of scale 43–52
Economies of scope 26
Effective demand 256–7
Efficiency
    economic 38–9
    technical 37–8
Elasticity
    cross 2
    income 2, 184
    price 2–3, 213
    supply 2
Employment
    full 156, 256, 264–5
    part time 154–5
Entropy 231
Environmental Assessment
    (EA) 249
Environmental auditing 245
Environmental Impact
    Assessment *see*
    Environmental Assessment
Environmental regulation
    238–41
Equal opportunities policies
    160–61
Equilibrium xv, 8, 9, 12
Eurocurrency markets 187–8,
    191, 225
European Central Bank 227
European Community (EC), *see*
    European Union
European Economic
    Community (EEC), *see*
    European Union
European Monetary Union
    227–8
European Regional
    Development Fund 279
European Social Fund 279

European Union (EU)
    environmental policy 240–41,
    242, 245, 249
    labour market policy 162,
    273–4
    monetary union 227–8
    regional policy 279
    trade policy 208–9·
Eurotunnel 99–101
Exchange rates
    effects on business 31,
    213–14
    floating 211–12
    government policy and 2,
    266, 275–6
    pegged 210–11
    and purchasing power parity
    222
Exchange Rate Mechanism
    (ERM) 212–13, 275–6
Exchange rate monetarism
    275–6
Exhaustible resources 231–2
Expectations 260, 270
Externalities 166–7, 233–4, 278

Financial accounting 72–4
Financial control 75–9
Financial deregulation 185, 219,
    260, 273
Financial engineering 198–9
Financial innovation 185
Financial institutions 121–2,
    192–3
Flexibility
    functional 171
    labour market 256
    marketing 20
    numerical 171
    planning 9
Flexible manufacturing systems
    (FMS) 27–8, 165
Flow manufacture 54–9
Flows 226
Ford
    exports (UK) 107
    financial performance (UK)
    87–8, 117–18, 120–21
    foreign investment 29–30,
    223
    labour productivity (UK)
    112–14
    Model T production
    (Highland Park, USA)
    56–8, 130–31
    sales performance (UK) 109
    stock turnover (UK) 114–15
    value added 110–11, 116
Foreign exchange controls 211

Fragmentation
  of jobs 165
  of markets 19–23
France
  industrial policies 283–4
Free riding 166
Friedman, Milton 268–71
Full employment 156, 256,
  264–5
Full line competition 21, 23
Functional structure 133

Galbraith, John Kenneth 11–12
General Agreement on Tariffs
  and Trade (GATT) 210
General circulation models 235
General Motors 53, 134–6
Generic strategy 140
GEC (and its predecessors)
  197–8
Germany
  bank lending practices 186,
    197
  environmental policies 240
  metal working industry
    167–8
  skill levels 166, 167–8
Global warming 235
Globalization 28–31, 223–5
Going concern 72, 85
Greenhouse effect, *see* Global
  warming
Gross domestic product (GDP)
  217
Gross national product (GNP)
  217
Growth
  inorganic 31–3
  maximization 69–70
  sustainable 237–8

Hanson Trust 32–3, 116,
  117–18, 198–9
Hedonic price 252
Hollowing out 198–9, 285
Hoover 173
Hostile takeovers, *see* Mergers
Housing equity withdrawal 260
Housing market 185, 259–60
Human capital 166

IBM 141–2
ICI 106–7, 199
Import controls 207, 208
Income
  circular flow of 261–4
  as determinant of
    consumption and savings
    257–9
Income effect 231

Incomes policy 267–8
Industrial policy
  in France 283–4
  in Japan 284
  in UK 278–82
Industrial relations 63, 169–71,
  223
Industry structure 138–9
Inflation
  causes and policies 266–76
  deflating for 108–9
  measures of 267
Information xv, 8, 12, 13
Injections 261, 263
Inorganic growth 31–3
Inspectorate of Pollution 238–9
Integrated circuits 224–5
Interest rates
  determinants of 186–9
  effects on exchange rates 211,
    212, 213
  effects on investment 189–90
  effects on money supply 276
  government policies 273–4,
    276
Internal labour markets 152
Internal rate of return 189
  see also Net Present Value
International Monetary Fund
  (IMF) 215–16
Investment
  decision making 88–99
  determinants of 181–2,
    260–61
  in design and development
    52–4
  direct foreign 29–30, 221–5
  and effective demand 256–7,
    260–61
  finance of 179–81
  in human capital 166
  lumpy 50
  portfolio 220–21
  in research and development
    193–4
  and value added 182

Japan
  accounting practices 77–9
  bank lending practices 186
  cost reduction in 53, 77–9
  flexible manufacturing
    systems 27–8
  foreign direct investment
    226–7
  industrial policies 284
  labour policies 169–70
  management practices, *see*
    Japanization

management qualifications
  169
  productivity levels 143–4
  stock management policies
    79–81
Japanization 142–5
Just-in-time (JIT) 81, 169–70

Kaizen 53, 81
Keynes, John Maynard 256–64
Keynesianism
  policy 264–5, 267–8
  theory 256–64, 266–7
Knoeppel, Charles 132–3, 136

Labour
  as human capital 166
  as a factor of production 37
  recomposition of 57, 58–9
Labour costs
  international comparisons
    64–5, 163–4
  in relation to value added
    62–3, 87–8, 115–17, 161,
    162
  unit 163–4
Labour force participation
  153–5
Labour markets
  external 152
  flexibility of 171–3, 256
  internal 152
  neo-classical theory of 151–2,
    161
  segmentation of 152
  stickiness in 161
  structural approaches 152,
    161
Labour process 164–5
Lame ducks 281
Leakages 261–2, 263–4
Lean production 143–4
Limited companies 73–4
Limited liability 68
Liquidation approach (to bank
  lending) 184–5
Liquidity 119–21
Long run 8, 39–40, 47
Low pay 159–62
  see also Wages

Maastricht Treaty 163, 227
Management
  education and training 168–9
  by exception 75
  limits to 145–7
  of labour process 164–5
  practices, international
    differences 129–45

Management and cost
    accounting 72, 82–7, 137–
    8, 142
Managerial theory of the firm
    69–70
Marginal cost 6, 7, 71
Marginal propensity to
    consume 258–9
Marginal propensity to
    purchase new domestic
    output 262
Marginal revenue 6, 7, 71
Marketing mix 1
Markets
    commodity 9, 268
    composition 19–23
    cyclicality 16–18
    Eurocurrency 187–8
    foreign exchange 211–12
    fragmentation of 19–23, 207
    labour 151–2
    mature 15–18
    perfectly competitive 11–12,
        129
    product 24–6
    saturated 13, 15–18, 23
    segmentation of 12, 19–23
Markup pricing 71, 81–2
Medium term financial strategy
    (MTFS) 272
Men in the labour market 154
Mergers 31–2, 194–9
Mill, John Stuart 235–6
Minimum efficient scale (MES)
    47–8, 55
Monetarism
    policy 271–6
    theory 268–71
Money supply
    control of 271–6
    and inflation 268–71
    measures of 273
Monopolies and Mergers
    Commission (MMC)
    279–80
Monopoly 280
Motor cycle industry 22
Multinational firms, see
    Transnational corporations
Multiplier 261–2

National minimum wage
    160–62
National Power 248
Nationalization 282
    see also British Steel; Central
    Electricity Generating
    Board; Privatization.

Neo-classical theory
    of consumer demand 2–3
    of the firm xv–xvi, 5–13
    of labour markets 151–2, 161,
        256
    of natural environment
        231–4
    of production and costs
        36–52
    of product markets 2–13
    of unemployment 256
Negative equity 260
Net Present Value (NPV) 92–9
New international division of
    labour 224–5
Newly Industrializing Countries
    (NICs) 64–5, 207
Nissan 77–9
Non-price factors (in demand)
    xvi, 3, 4, 220
Nominal financial data 108–9
North American Free Trade
    Area (NAFTA) 65, 209–10
Nuclear Electric 248
Nuclear power 98–9, 247–9

Objectives of the firm 8, 67–71
Oligopoly 9–11, 12
Open market operations 188
Opportunity cost 90
Optimization 55
Over-harvesting 231
Overheads, allocation of 82–4
Ownership and control of firms
    67–72
Ozone layer 241

Part-time employment 154–5
Payback financial calculations
    88–9, 243
Pay inequalities 158–61
Perfect competition 11–12, 129
Peripheral regions 157, 227–8
Permanent income hypothesis
    259
Phillips, A.W. 266–8
Pigou, A.C. 233–4
Pollution 233–5
Porter, Michael 138–40
PowerGen 248
Precautionary principle 235
Price earnings ratio 122
Price leadership 10
Price reduction 13
Price rigidity 11
Price wars 10–11
Pricing
    markup 71, 81–2

oligopolistic 9–11
    for profit maximization 6–9
    transfer 223
Privatization 248, 271, 282
Product conversion costs 61–2
Product differentiation 4, 12
Product life cycle 24–6
Product market maturity 14
Product mix flexibility 26–8
Product segments 20–23
Production function 37
Productivity
    of capital equipment 40
    of labour 40, 111–14, 153,
        163–4, 167–8, 198
    in relation to output growth
        153
    total factor 41
Profit
    as a constraint on growth 70
    different concepts of 72–3
    distribution of 179
    earned by UK companies 179
    maximization of 5–11, 71
    monopoly 8, 9, 280
    retention of 179
    and value added 116–19
Protectionism, see Import
    controls
Public Sector Borrowing
    Requirement (PSBR) 271–2
Purchasing power parity 212

Quality 60–62
Quantity theory of money 269

Racism 152
Real financial data 198–9
Regional policy 278–9
Renewable resources 231,
    232–3
Research and Development
    193–4, 198, 199
    see also Design and
    development
Restrictive Practices Court 280
Retail Price Index (RPI) 267
Returns to scale 41–3
Revenue
    average 6, 7
    marginal 6, 7, 71
    total 84–7
Revised sequence 11
Rolls Royce 53
Rover Group (and its
    predecessors) 20–21,
    197–8

Sainsbury's 114–5, 120
Sales maximization 69–70
Saturation 13, 15–18, 23
Scientific management 130–32
'Screwdriver' operations 227
Segmentation
    of labour markets 152
    of product markets 12, 19–23
Sexism 152, 154, 165–6
Shares 68–9, 121–3, 178–9,
    180–81, 191–3
Short run 39–40, 45–6
Short termism 192–4, 198, 242
Sinclair 4–5
Single European Market 208–9
Skills 164–8
Small business 170, 200
Social charges 163
Social Chapter, *see* Social
    Europe
Social Chapter, *see* Social
    Europe
Social costs 233–4
Social Europe 173–4
Social settlements 64
Sony 13, 53
Special Drawing Rights (SDRs)
    215
Speculation
    in foreign currencies 211,
        212, 213
    in the housing market 185
    in shares 193
Standard costing 74, 75–7
Standards, environmental 238–
    41
State finance of business 199–
    200
Statistical quality control (SQC)
    60–61
Steady state economics 235–7
Stock control 79–81
Stock market, *see* Capital
    markets; Shares
Stock reduction 81
Stock turnover 114–15
Stocks and flows 226
'Stop-go' 266

Sub-contracting 170, 172
Substitution effect 232
Sulphur dioxide emissions 244
Supermarkets 18–19
Suppliers, relationship of firms
    to 81, 170
Supply
    elasticity of 2
    of labour 153–5
Surprise 9, 260
Sustainable development 237–8
Sweated labour 162

Takeovers, *see* Mergers
Target cost reduction 77
Taylor, F.W. 130–32
Taylor, Harriet 235–6
Terms of trade 206
Tescoplc 18–19, 116, 117–18,
    118–19, 120
3M 250–51
Time value of money 90
Total economic value 242
Total quality management
    (TQM) 60–61
Toyota 31, 60–61, 120–21, 170
Tradeable permits 242
Trade unions 169–71
Transfer pricing 222, 223
Transnational corporations
    221–5
Transplant production 226–7

Uncertainty 9–11, 70–71
Underutilization 50
Unemployment
    causes of 157, 256
    levels of 156–7, 264–5
    'natural rate' of 269–70
United Kingdom (UK)
    balance of payments
        performance 216–20, 225–
        7
    bank lending practices 184–
        5, 186
    car market 20–21, 217–18
    employment composition
        152–7

environmental policies 238–
    9, 240–41
housing market 185, 259–60
industrial policies 278–82
labour polices 162, 166, 167–
    8, 169, 171–3
macro-economic policies 264–
    5, 271–6
management practices 167–8
marketing strategies 220
metal working industry 167–
    8
United States (USA)
    bank lending practices 185
    management practices 129–
        42
Unit labour costs 163–4
Unpaid work 154
Utility maximization 3

Valuation ratio 195–6
Value added
    definition 14
    and investment 182
    and labour costs 62–3, 87–8,
        115–18, 161, 162
    and work in progress 59
Variance analysis 75–9
Vertical integration/
    disintegration 112
Vocational training 166–9, 193

Wages
    and inflation 267–8
    international comparisons
        64–5
    and unemployment 161–2
    see also Labour costs; National
        Minimum Wage; Pay
        inequalities
Wages Councils 162
Women in the labour market
    153–5
Working hours 64, 154–5
Work-in-progress (WIP) 59, 115

Zeneca 106, 199